Lecture Notes in Computer Science 858

Edited by G. Goos, J. Hartmanis and J. van Leeuwen

Advisory Board: W. Brauer   D. Gries   J. Stoer

Elisa Bertino   Susan Urban (Eds.)

Object-Oriented Methodologies and Systems

International Symposium, ISOOMS '94
Palermo, Italy, September 21-22, 1994
Proceedings

Springer-Verlag

Berlin Heidelberg New York
London Paris Tokyo
Hong Kong Barcelona
Budapest

Series Editors

Gerhard Goos
Universität Karlsruhe
Postfach 69 80, Vincenz-Priessnitz-Straße 1, D-76131 Karlsruhe, Germany

Juris Hartmanis
Department of Computer Science, Cornell University
4130 Upson Hall, Ithaka, NY 14853, USA

Jan van Leeuwen
Department of Computer Science, Utrecht University
Padualaan 14, 3584 CH Utrecht, The Netherlands

Volume Editors

Elisa Bertino
Dipartimento di Scienze dell'Informazione, Università di Milano
Via Comelico, 38, I-20135 Milano, Italy

Susan Urban
Computer Science Department, Arizona State University
Tempe, AZ 85287-5406, USA

CR Subject Classification (1991): H.2, D.1.5, D.2, D.3.2

ISBN 3-540-58451-X Springer-Verlag Berlin Heidelberg New York

CIP data applied for

© Springer-Verlag Berlin Heidelberg 1994
Printed in Germany

Typesetting: Camera-ready by author
SPIN: 10478996   45/3140-543210 - Printed on acid-free paper

Preface

The International Symposium on Object-Oriented Methodologies and Systems is the second of a series of annual symposiums that are held in conjunction with the AICA-Italian National Computer Conference, each year focusing on a different topic. The 1994 Symposium is on the object-oriented paradigm.

In response to the call for papers, 68 papers were received from different countries in Europe, America, and East Asia. All papers were reviewed by at least three members of the program committee. The program committee was selective and only 25 papers were accepted for inclusion in the symposium program. We are very pleased with the overall quality of the program, which includes papers covering both technical areas, such as databases and programming languages, and methodological aspects as well as application areas. We gratefully acknowledge all our colleagues who committed their time by submitting papers. Finally, we are very happy that Simon Gibbs, a well-known expert in this area, has agreed to give the invited talk.

We greatly appreciate the help we received from the members of our cooperative and responsible program committee. Special thanks go to Barbara Catania and Pierangela Samarati, who helped us with the program preparation, and to Maria Grazia Baggi from AICA, who managed the symposium correspondence. Finally, we would like to thank Giancarlo Martella, chairman of AICA, for his constant cooperation and advice during the process of organizing the symposium program.

July 1994

Elisa Bertino
Susan Urban

ISOOMS '94 Organization

General Chair
Ignazio Romano, Università di Palermo, Italy

Program Co-Chairs
Elisa Bertino, Università di Milano, Italy
Susan Urban, Arizona State University, Tempe, Arizona, USA

Program Committee
Egidio Astesiano, Italy
Patrick Bobbie, USA
Stefano Ceri, Italy
Sharma Chakravarty, USA
Partha Dasgupta, USA
Valeria De Antonellis, Italy
Lois Delcambre, USA
Ahmed Elmagarmid, USA
Salvatore Gaglio, Italy

Sushil Jajodia, USA
Gerti Kappel, Austria
Rainer Manthey, Germany
Yoshifumi Masunaga, Japan
Oscar Nierstrasz, Switzerland
Tamer Oszu, Canada
Domenico Saccà, Italy
Pierangela Samarati, Italy
Joachim Schmidt, Germany

Local Arrangements
Filippo Sorbello, Università di Palermo, Italy
Edoardo Ardizzone, Università di Palermo, Italy

Sponsors
Consiglio Nazionale delle Ricerche (CNR)
Bull Italia
Enel
Finsiel
IBM Italia

Cooperating Organizations
Dipartimento di Scienze dell'Informazione, Università di Milano
ESPRIT Network of Excellence Idomeneous

Additional Reviewers

Thomas Bode
Alex Brodsky
Silvana Castano
Barbara Catania
Sunil Choenni
Flavio de Paoli
Chiara Francalanci
Piero Fraternali
Maria Grazia Fugini
Iqbal Goralwalla
Giovanna Guerrini
A. Helal
Thomas Lemke

Eugenio Moggi
Youping Niu
Sylvia Osborn
Luigi Palopoli
Stefano Paraboschi
Randal Peters
Stefan Rausch-Schott
Gianna Reggio
Werner Retschitzegger
Heinz Rottmann
Ingrid Wetzel
Elena Zucca

Table of Contents

Issues in Extending a Relational System with Object–Oriented Features

François EXERTIER, Samer HAJ HOUSSAIN

Bull
2, rue Vignate
38610 Gières – FRANCE –
E–mail: F.Exertier@frgu.bull.fr, S.Haj–Houssain@frgu.bull.fr
Tel.: (33) 76 63 48 52 Fax: (33) 76 54 76 15

Abstract. This document describes an approach towards the integration of relational and object technologies[1]. The relational model is extended with object–oriented concepts which include complex objects, methods, inheritance and *object identity*. An important feature is that a "complete" object model is provided, without compromising the relational aspects. The extended relational model and language are briefly described. The presentation focuses on the implementation, based on a cooperation between a relational system and an object manager. Particular attention is devoted to object storage techniques and to the development of the method programming language.

1 Introduction

The generally agreed advantages of Relational Database Systems are mainly the existence of a well known and formal model, the optimization capabilities, the view concept and the integrity constraints support. A general agreement also exists on the interest of several aspects of object orientation which are essentially rich typing and inheritance, object identity, and integration of data and operations in the database. This particulary increases the modeling power. Applications like CAD, office automation, geographical databases and CASE, characterised by complex data types and operations, require a powerful data model and manipulation facilities. In the past, several extensions of the relational model have been proposed in order to provide rich typing capabilities. These extensions are mainly based on nested relations (NF2 model),

---

(1) This work has been partially funded by the ESPRIT programme through project EDS (EP2025)

the entity–relationship model [17], complex objects [4], and Abstract Data Types [6]. These extensions are very interesting by the fact that they all enrich the typing capabilities, some of them provide an inheritance facility as well as the possibility to define operations, but they all lack of a true support of *object identity*, one of the most important object–oriented feature. That means that they do not allow object sharing between relations or objects. GEM [17], which offers an Entity–Relationship database interface over a relational database system, provides only tuple sharing.

The aim of this paper is to discuss several issues to be considered when designing and implementing an extended relational system. The issues will be illustrated using the prototype that we have developed within the EDS project of the ESPRIT programme. This Extended Relational System supports rich typing via Abstract Data Types (ADT), but also includes object sharing via Object Identity. Our approach does not really extend the relational model which in fact remains value–based; it is rather based on cooperation between the relational world and the object oriented world. In Codd's relational model, the notion of domain is defined as a set of values; no restriction is made on the types of values. Therefore, our data model does not restrict these types to scalar types, they can be ADTs. An attribute whose type is an ADT can evolve in the Object Oriented world, but is viewed as an atomic value from the relational point of view. The implementation is based on a cooperative approach between a relational kernel and an object manager. The design of the object manager is described in details as well as the method compilation and execution management. Most of the object management techniques are inspired of those used in OODBMSs. A method programming language has been defined as an extension of C. Compilation and execution mechanisms have been developed so that methods can be called from the relational execution kernel.

This work has been conducted within the EDS project which aims at developping a parallel machine and a database server. The database system is a major component of the EDS project. Database applications are expected to constitute the main market segment in the exploitation of the EDS technology. It has been designed to support high–end on–line transaction processing, e.g. debit–credit environments, and complex decision support queries as well as combinations of both. To this end, both inter– and intra–query parallelism are exploited. The EDS database system is relational in nature, with extensions to support abstract data types and deduction capabilities. This paper focuses on the ADT extension. It supports a powerful query language, ESQL (Extended Structured Query Language) which is an extension to standard SQL. Two main components compose the system: the Request Manager, which mainly performs query compilation, and the Data Manager, which is in charge of query execution.

After this introduction, section 2 briefly presents the extension of the relational model with examples in ESQL. Section 3 describes the overall system architecture with the main design choices to introduce the object support. Object management is presented in section 4. Section 5 defines the method programming language and develops the techniques to compile, bind and execute user defined methods. The conclusion is in section 6.

2 Introducing the Object Concept into the Relational Model

The proposed extensions to the relational model are based on the following statements:

- the data structuration capabilities provided by the relational model are enhanced by introducing *complex objects*.

- the concept of *sharing* is introduced in the model via *object identity*.
- the concepts of *encapsulation*, *methods*, *inheritance* are provided.

- the system should remain *relational*, i.e. the data model and query language are fully compatible with the relational data model and query language.

The main interest of our approach is that we provide *all* these features, which means a complete object oriented model within the relational model. Other works on the subject only propose a subset of these items. As an example Postgres [20][22] provides the concept of ADT (encapsulation, methods), inheritance (for the relational tables, not for ADTs) but lacks of object identity and of object structuration facilities. GEM [17] is an "Entity–Relationship" layer built on top of a relational system; it offers the "tuple sharing" concept but lacks of concepts like methods and inheritance.

From the language point of view, the result is an extension of SQL called ESQL (see [10], [11] or [21]) described below and a method programming language called MPL (see section 5).

2.1 Abstract Data Type Definition

An ADT is defined in the ESQL language and has the following features:
- a *data structure* specified through a composition of "generic ADTs" (*tuple*, *set*, *bag*, *list* and *array* are provided, they are also called "constructors");

- a set of user defined *methods*;

- eventually a *supertype* (single inheritance is proposed);

- and the characteristic *object/value* which indicates if the instances of this ADT will be sharable (i.e. they are objects and have an object identifier) or not (i.e. they are values).

An ADT also contains some implicitly defined methods: those inherited from its supertypes and those of its "first level" constructor which allow to manipulate its data structure (it is still an open issue to decide whether these constructor's methods should be available in ESQL, thus breaking the encapsulation, or should be only accessible from the method programming language).

Examples of ADT definitions are given below:

```
CREATE TYPE Person AS OBJECT TUPLE OF (name CHAR(80),
    firstname CHAR(25));
CREATE TYPE Actor SUBTYPE OF Person WITH (salary
    NUMERIC(8));
CREATE TYPE Actors AS SET OF (Actor);
```

Instances of the type Person are sharable tuples, those of actor have an additional field salary. Actor inherits the *object* characteristic of Person. The first level constructor of Actor is tuple. Therefore, a set of generic methods such as getfield (to access a tuple's field) are available. The Actors ADT defines a set of Actor objects (it is in fact a set of object identifiers). Some methods on these ADTs are defined below (through ESQL statements):

```
CREATE FUNCTION increase_salary (Actor, NUMERIC(2)) RETURNS
    Actor LANGUAGE C;
CREATE FUNCTION max_salary (Actors) RETURNS NUMERIC(8)
    LANGUAGE C;
```

ADT methods are also called ADT functions. The two methods are defined using the C language (in fact a C based extension, see section 5). The first one increases the salary of an actor by x percent, where x is the second parameter; it returns the modified object. The second one returns the maximum salary of a set of actors. The first parameter of a method always represents the type on behalf of which the method is defined.

It is now possible to define relational tables using these ADTs, figure 1 shows the resulting schema:

```
CREATE TABLE FILM (numf NUMERIC(3), title CHAR(50), actors
    Actors);
CREATE TABLE ACTOR (actor Actor);
```

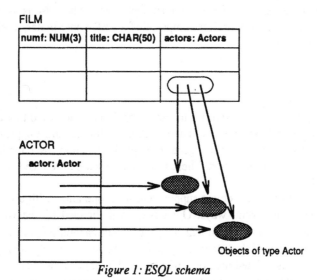

Figure 1: ESQL schema

2.2 Complex Object Manipulation

Complex objects are manipulated through ESQL statements and within the methods. Examples of ESQL statements are given below, object manipulation in methods is presented in section 5. Methods may be called in ESQL statements; of course methods that update objects cannot be used in queries (SELECT) but only in update statements (UPDATE).

```
SELECT max_salary(actors) FROM FILM WHERE numf = 3;
UPDATE ACTOR SET actor = increase_salary(actor,10) WHERE
    name(actor) = 'Depardieu';
SELECT name(actor) FROM FILM, ACTOR
 WHERE title = 'Pretty Woman'
 AND salary(actor) = max_salary(actors)
 AND contains(actors, actor) = 1;
```

The second statement increases the salary of "Gérard Depardieu" by 10 percent. The third query gets the name of the actor who plays in "Pretty Woman" and which is the best payed. `name(actor)` and `salary(actor)` are short notations for `getfield(actor, name)` and `getfield(actor, salary)`. `contains` is a method defined on the constructor SET which returns 1 if an element is contained in the set.

3 General Architecture and Object Support

The architecture of the EDS database server is composed of a Request Manager (RM) and of a Data Manager (DM). The RM compiles ESQL queries into an internal language called LERA that support extended relational algebra expressions. The RM contains an Analyser (which performs syntactic and semantic analysis of ESQL statements and generates LERA) and an Optimizer. The DM is in charge of the execution of LERA programs, it is composed of a LERA Interpreter, a relational engine and an object manager.

3.1 Design Choices

Object support requires facilities to handle ADT definitions and to manipulate ADT instances. This includes on one hand creation, storage and suppression of ADT instances, and on the other hand generic method execution, user methods execution and ADT operation optimization. These functionalities are introduced at different levels of the DBMS.

The introduction of the object support and its cooperation with a relational system can be achieved in several ways. Our design was directed by the wish to keep the system's main orientation relational, i.e., the object capabilities introduced in ESQL appears as extensions of the relational system. We believe that only a limited number of ADT, with their associated methods, will be used in applications. Therefore, relational operations should not be affected, from the performance point of view, by the integration of the object support. This was our main guideline for the following design choices:

i *Cooperative versus integrated storage approach.*

The integrated approach requires merging the object storage and the relational storage facilities in a unique storage subsystem. Integration can be achieved either by decomposing objects in relations (using a relational storage subsystem) or by developing an object storage subsystem to store both objects and relations. The first solution, which consists in building an object layer on top of a relational system results in low performance due to a complex mapping. The second solution implies to modify (at least at a low level) the relational kernel.

In the cooperative approach the relational storage subsystem is not modified and an object storage subsystem is introduced beside the relational system. Relational tuples are stored in an existing relational kernel based on a pure value–based model, with external references to complex objects (i.e. the object identifiers assigned by the object store). Relational operators are separated from ADT methods, which are called as external functions to extract values from ADT instances referred to by object identifiers. Few modifications are necessary to integrate method calls inside the relational operators. The continuity of the cooperative solution with the relational approach allows a low cost implementation. This is the reason why the cooperative approach has been chosen.

ii   *Local versus server based Object Support.*

The server based approach consists in placing the whole or a part of the object support functions in a stand–alone server. This server is called by the relational system for object manipulations. This solution seems attractive for distributing the object management facilities and for increasing the safety of method execution. A physical distribution between the relational system and the object support can provide a better use of the resources. Such a distribution can be easily achieved by means of the RPC mechanism. Safety is an important issue for user methods. In fact, since user method code can misbehave in arbitrary ways, one way to obtain a high degree of safety is to run methods in a separate process, isolated from the database process. However, if the object support software was executed in a separate process, the communication and task switching overhead would substantially interfere with performances. For this reason we discarded the server based approach and chose to integrate the object support with the relational system.

Based on these main design choices, the different components of the object support, their functionalities and their interactions with the relational system are defined in the next section.

3.2 Object Support Components

In order to support the ADT functionalities, the following components are introduced: the Type Manager, the Object Manager and the Method Compiler (see Figure 2). The Type Manager is responsible of handling the definitions of ADT, it is part of the Catalog Manager. The Object Manager provides storage and manipulation of ADT instances, it is part of the Data Manager.

The main functionalities of the Type Manager consist in storing and accessing ADT definitions, handling the inheritance graph and type interdependencies. It is called by the ESQL compiler and the method compilers for type checking purposes. It is implemented as a metabase.

Object management deals with the storage, access and manipulation of ADT instances (complex objects and complex values). These functions are performed by the Object Manager which is part of the DM. The Object Manager interacts with both the Lera Interpreter and the Object Storage Subsystem (GEODE in figure 2). The Lera interpreter calls the Object Manager in order to perform ADT instances manipulation expressed in Lera programs. The Object Manager functions are based on the Object Storage Subsystem services, which provide complex object storage facilities.

Method management consists in compiling, binding and executing methods. The compiler itself is part of the RM and is called by the ESQL Analyser when the "compile method" DDL statement is issued. The binding and execution functions are integrated into the Object Manager module within the DM. The binding function is called by the Lera Interpreter just after method compilation. The method execution mechanism is invoked by the Lera Interpreter when a method call occurs in a query.

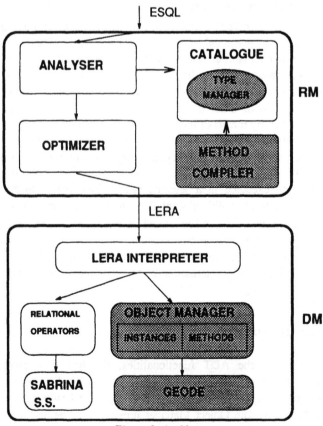

Figure 2: Architecture

The following sections describe the Object Manager built on top of GEODE and the Method Compiler components.

4 Object Management

4.1 Object Storage Subsystem

The Object Manager is built on top of the GEODE Object Storage Subsystem. GEODE stores and retrieves structured values with invariant object identifiers (OID) in a persistent, concurrent and reliable memory. Objects are built by applying basic constructors on atomic or complex objects. GEODE may be split in two distinct layers: the shared virtual memory and the constructor support layers. We briefly introduce this two components below.

The shared virtual memory layer provides the functions for persistent storage, creation and destruction of uninterpreted byte strings in a virtual memory. The virtual memory is divided into pages grouped into segments, which contain collections of objects. Byte strings created in a segment are addressed by the way of logical OIDs managed by the system using reference tables. The virtual memory is mapped onto the physical memory by the OID decoder, a software module that controls the sharing of objects and guarantees the atomicity and reliability of updates.

Built upon the "virtual memory" layer, the constructor support layer implements the data structures and operations for managing collections of objects within segments. The tuple, list, array, bag and set constructors are provided. The tuple constructor is implemented by a C structure. The list is implemented as structures doubly linked by pointers. An array is supported by a heap, which can grow from both sides and which is accessed through indices. Sets and bags are implemented as B-trees. For each constructor, there exists a set of standard operations, which constitutes the basis for implementing those of ESQL described in section 2.

4.2 ADT Instance Storage

As said before, ESQL supports two kinds of ADT instances: objects and values. Conceptually, values are stored inside relations, they cannot be shared and their life time corresponds to the life time of the tuple they belong to. Objects are stored outside relations (in the Object Manager), they are referred to by one or several relations by means of object identifiers. They persist as long as they are referred to either by other objects or by relations.

In the proposed solution, atomic values are stored within tuples while complex values are stored and referred to in the same way as objects. Actually, implementing complex values as a sequence of bytes in a tuple within the relational store presents some drawbacks: (i) all the generic methods should manipulate two storage formats: the Object Manager's one and the relational format (value based); (ii) access to the components of a complex structure is in general inefficient in the case of a value based storage, especially for large objects. That is why both complex values and complex objects are stored in the same way within the Object Manager. However, the semantics of some operations is different when applied to value instances or object instances. For example, the insertion of a new element in a value set will generate a new set while the same insertion in an object set will just modify the set. Moreover this design choice allows storage optimizations based on the mechanism of value–sharing as discussed in section 4.3.

A similar choice is made for implementing ADT instances in the Object Manager. A decomposed structure is used which maps each constructor (generic ADT)'s instance to a structured object referred to by an identifier at the next level. For example, a list of sets is implemented as a list of identifiers referencing the composing sets. In other words, an ADT instance (object or value) is decomposed at constructor boundaries. Each component is stored as an independent object. Object creation, storage and access algorithms are uniform: they process similarly object components (which should be stored by reference for sharing purposes) and value components. Unlike structured values, scalar values (numeric and character strings) are stored directly inside the complex structures, they are not stored as objects in order to increase performance by avoiding dereferencing.

The Object Manager provides a unique way for identifying ADT instances. This ADT instance identifier (AID) contains the location of the instance within GEODE (segment id and Geode object id) and gives information about the nature of the instance (object or value). This information is necessary to determine the behaviour of the generic methods as explained above. Finally, the first level constructor is also indicated in the AID; this avoids to access the catalog at run time.

4.3 Persistence Management

Persistence is defined using the concepts of persistent root and reachability. The persistence rules are the following: every relation is persistent (like in any relational database system); every object which is accessible through a relation (because it is an attribute value or a component of another persistent object) is persistent. Relations are the named persistent roots of our system. Dynamic creation and referencing of objects requires a garbage collection mechanism to maintain persistency. We have chosen a reference count based garbage collector rather than a marking one. Objects appearing in cycles in the objects graph will never be destroyed by such a mechanism; a mark–and–sweep algorithm is still necessary to collect these objects at suitable time intervals.

A reference counter is associated to each object and indicates the number of references to the object. When this counter is null the object can be deleted from the database. When an object is linked to (or disappears from) a relation, its counter is incremented (or decremented); the ESQL compiler generates calls to the Object Manager to update the counter. When an object becomes the component of (or is removed from) another object, its counter is incremented (or decremented).

The advantage of this approach is that these counters (and so the persistence) are managed at the Object Manager level; therefore, the object management is independent of the high level languages being supported (for instance the languages which are used to write methods). A function of the Object Manager which sets an object reference is in charge of updating the reference counter. For instance, the function which inserts an element in a set has to increment the counter of the inserted element.

Temporary objects are created in temporary segments (provided by Geode). Objects in such segments desappear at the end of the session. Promotion of objects from temporary to persistent state requires their migration to a persistent segment: this is achieved by the functions which promote the object, i.e. which assign it to a persistent entity; these are the generic functions of the Object Manager defined on the ESQL constructors.

A specific management scheme is provided for values. Values have a copy semantics although complex values are stored as objects (i.e. they have an identifier): a value cannot be shared, a copy is generated each time a value is accessed or assigned. The major drawback of a direct implementation of this value semantics is that it may generate a large number of useless temporary copies which may saturate the temporary space. In order to avoid such problems, a specific scheme for complex values is implemented, which allows to delay the value copy until update (copy on update). This scheme is based on the idea that a value can be shared temporarily. It is copied only when it is updated (see Figure 3). Thus the user has the illusion that values are never shared. A similar approach is implemented in the O2 system [18]. The reference counter stored in a value is used by generic functions (which modify values) to determine if the value is shared and thus should be copied or not.

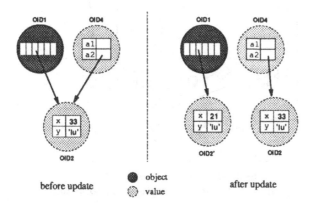

Figure 3: Shared value, copy on write.

The example in figure 3 shows the update of the tuple value OID2 of the third element of the array object OID1 (the field x is set to 21). This value OID2 is shared by the object OID1 and the value OID4, so the update operation generates a copy OID2'.

Note that this mechanism is implementable because values are stored as objects (see section 4.2).

4.4 Clustering

Clustering is an attempt to reduce the I/O overhead by grouping objects frequently accessed together in contiguous storage units. GEODE, our Object Storage Subsystem, provides us with a physical clustering unit: the segment. Our clustering strategy is based on two criteria:

- objects belonging to the same relation are stored in the same segment,
- the components of a complex object (or value) are stored in the same segment.

Objects are accessed through relations by ESQL queries. Such accesses are relation–based: this justifies our first criterion. There is one segment for each relation. When an object belongs to several relations, it is stored in the segment of the relation it was created through. The reason why such a simple solution is used to resolve conflicts is that there is no way to determine the relation through which the object is mostly accessed. A replication based solution is very costly with regard to the benefit in terms of access performance. Our clustering strategy is illustrated in figure 4.

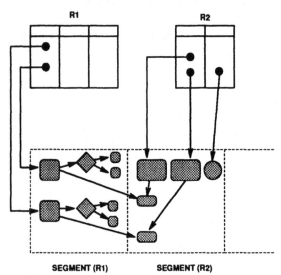

Figure 4: A "relation to segment" clustering strategy

5 The Method Programming Language

This section describes the approach followed to develop a method compilation and execution mechanism. The first step was to define the language to be used for writing methods. It was decided to adopt the C programming language as base language to which extensions were made in order to allow the use of ADTs and the manipulation of ADT instances. The resulting language is called MPL for "Method Programming Language". A precompiler has been developed to translate the methods written in MPL (C plus ADT manipulation) into pure target language (C) modules. Note that the same approach can be followed using another language than C as base language. Also note that in our case the target language of the precompiler is also C, so that the base language and the target language are the same, thus leading to a simpler precompilation process. Methods are compiled into C functions, which are called by the relational engine using a method identification mechanism. The mechanism used to generate calls to methods from ESQL queries relies on the method identifiers. An important choice with regard to the execution mechanism has been to make the methods run directly on the Object Manager by using the generic methods to manipulate the data structures, instead of loading the objects in specific C data structures. Finally, compiled methods are dynamically linked to the system, in order to allow modified or newly defined methods to be readily used without having to disable the system.

5.1 MPL Definition

The Method Programming Language MPL consists of C plus ADT manipulation capacities added to this language. ADT instances are manipulated from MPL by means of variables and methods. We simply added to C the capability to define variables whose type is an ADT, and to apply methods to these variables. This means that methods are the only way to manipulate ADT instances, like in ESQL; therefore, encapsulation as defined in the ESQL abstract data typing scheme is observed. The data structure of an ADT instance is accessible by the programmer through the set of generic methods defined on the ESQL constructors. The programmer has also the possibility to call other user defined methods in the method code. Another approach would consist in representing objects by C data structures. These structures are then manipulated through the operators provided by C. In such an approach the programmer directly accesses the data structure of ADT instances. This has a major drawback: two views of this data structure, the ESQL one, and the C one, and the mapping from one to the other have to be maintained (and known by the programmer). The first approach was chosen for three reasons: (i) it enforces the encapsulation principle, (ii) it keeps the complexity of the system's software low, (iii) generic methods are enough rich to express any data structure manipulation.

The type system of MPL is composed of the ADTs which are new types added to C, and of the basic SQL types which are directly mapped to C types. However, MPL is very close to C. This is in our view a major advantage of our approach. The programmer does not need to learn a new language, but rather uses a well known, familiar language.

In order to illustrate the language, the code of three methods is described below. These methods are defined on two types: the first one, Actor, is a tuple with the fields name, firstname and salary; the second one, Actors, is a set of Actor.

```
int increase_salary (actor, rate)
Actor actor;
int rate;
{
int sal,newsal;
sal = GetField (actor,salary);
newsal = ((sal/100)*rate)+sal; /* New salary */
Assign (actor, salary, newsal);
return newsal;
}


int max_salary (actors)
Actors actors;
{
Actor p;
int sal;
int max = 0;
for (p = First (actors) ; p.tag != null; p = Next (actors))
      {
      sal = GetField (p, salary);
      if (sal > max) max = sal;
      }
return max;
}
```

The method *increase_salary* increases the salary of a given actor by *rate* percent. The ADT *Actor* is used in the method code, among other C types. Generic methods defined on the ADT *tuple* are also used. The method *max_salary* returns the highest salary of a set of actors.

```
Actors inc prolo (actors, rate)
Actors actors;
int rate;
{
Actor p;
int maxsal, sal;
maxsal = max_salary (actors);
for (p = First (actors) ; p.tag != null; p = Next (actors))
      {
      sal = GetField (p, salary);
      if (sal != maxsal) increase_salary (p, rate);
      }
return actors;
}
```

The method *inc_prolo* increases the salary of the actors of the set, except the best payed, by *rate* percent. It uses the two previously defined user methods.

5.2 Access to Objects

The choice has been made to consider system and user methods as routines accessible from C (and from any other language) for simplicity and performance reasons. System defined methods directly call Object Manager routines and use the internal representation of the objects. User written methods are only allowed to call system defined methods or other user defined methods. Therefore, the user does not need to know the internal representation of the objects. The motivation of such an approach is discussed below.

There are two ways for user–defined methods to access objects:

- the first one consists in loading objects into C structures in order to be manipulated.

- the second solution consists in manipulating objects in the storage format used by the Object Manager. In this case, methods are called with object references (Object Identifiers) as parameters.

In the second solution methods access objects in the database itself. This avoids to extract the entire object from within the database and to convert it into C data structures before applying a method (generic or user–defined), and then to convert it back into the database structure for storage. Such a mechanism can be very expensive, especially when dealing with large objects. Furthermore, in the second approach, it is not necessary to provide a different object format for each target language, and consequently there is no need for handling several versions of the system methods (one per target language). The first solution is too expensive both from the performance point of view, as well as from the implementation point of view; it also makes a multi–language approach difficult. Therefore, the second solution has been adopted and has proved to be extremely practical from the implementation point of view.

5.3 MPL Compilation

Method compilation is composed of two phases, precompilation and compilation. The precompilation phase generates a pure target language program. The second phase consists in compiling the result of the precompilation using the target language compiler. Method object modules are then archived. The precompiler deals with ADTs and methods in the MPL in order to generate a pure target language module. ADT manipulation is expressed in terms of the target language, which, in the case described here, is C. The compilation module is called by the Request Manager when a method compilation statement is executed.

The first step deals with the method header. The catalog is accessed to check the validity of the signature and to get the method identifier (meth_id)[2]. This one is used to prefix the method name with *M<meth_id>_*. In fact, *M<meth_id>_<method_name>* is the symbolic name of the C procedure which will be generated for the method. This is necessary to distinguish methods having the same name defined on different types.

A next phase consists in checking that all types which are not C types are ADTs. This is done by accessing catalog information. Each ADT is then replaced by the type REF which is a target language structure corresponding to an ADT reference. Actually, this structure contains the object identifier (AID) as defined by the Object Manager (see section 4.2). Note that, as described above, ADT instances are only manipulated through AID in the Object Manager.

Method calls processing ensures that each called method is defined on the type to which it is applied. The method call is replaced by the corresponding C procedure call according to the inheritance rules. The method identifier (meth_id) is extracted from the catalog and the conformity of the method call with its signature is checked. The C procedure name is obtained by prefixing the method name with *M<meth_id>_*. The precompilation of the method *inc_prolo* defined earlier will generate the following C code, assuming that the identifiers of the three defined methods are respectively 122, 132, and 284:

```
REF M284_inc_prolo (actors, rate)
REF actors;
int rate;
{
REF p;
int maxsal, sal;
maxsal = M132_max_salary (actors);
for (p = First (&actors) ; p.tag != null; p = Next (&actors))
    {
    _sal = NUM_GetField (p, 3);
    if (sal != maxsal)  M122_increase_salary (p, rate);
    }
return actors;
}
```

The precompiler also deals with generic methods. It translates each generic method call into a C procedure call, using the C procedure corresponding to the method working on the right generic parameter type. For instance the procedure which corresponds to the GetField method returning a numeric is *NUM_GetField* (GetField is defined on the ADT *tuple* and returns the value of the field whose name is given as parameter). The precompiler also replaces the tuple field name by its range.

The C procedure generated by the precompiler is now compiled by the standard C compiler and the object module is archived in a library which contains all method object

---

(2) A method identifier is generated when the method is declared (ESQL statement) on an ADT, it is stored in the catalog with ADT definitions.

modules. Methods are identified in the library by their symbolic names
M<id>_<name> generated by the precompiler.

5.4 Method Binding and Execution

The mechanism for method compilation and binding is described in figure 5.

A dynamic linking mechanism is provided in order to allow the definition of a new
method or a change to an existing method to be dynamically captured by the database
system. Dynamic linking of new or modified methods is performed just after
compilation. These methods are statically bound at the next system generation. An
ESQL DDL statement is provided for precompilation, compilation and dynamic linking
purposes. In this way the system provides only one running mode which is convenient
for application development (easy method testing) as well as for exploitation.

Methods are dynamically linked to the Data Manager and archived in the method
library. This library will be linked to the Data Manager at its next generation, so that the
method will be statically linked. When a method is called in the code of another method,
the reference is resolved by the linker using the symbolic name
M<id_meth>_<meth_name> of the method, while in a ESQL statement the method
identifier is enough to generate the call. Method identifiers are generated so that they
contain an entry number in tables of methods managed by the Data Manager (TDM in
figure 5; these tables contains the method code addresses).

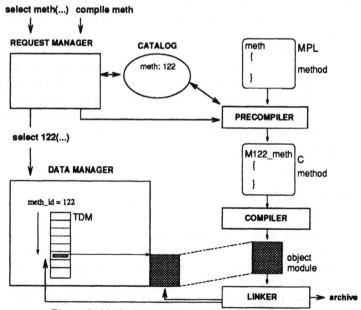

Figure 5: Method compilation and binding procedure

6 Conclusion

A prototype has been implemented and demonstrated within the EDS project. It is based on GEODE as object storage subsystem and on SABRINA as relational engine. A Type Manager has been developed and integrated as part of the relational metabase (catalog) manager. A method compiler has been implemented as a C preprocessor. Finally, an object manager dealing with ADT instance storage and method execution has been developed. This prototype demonstrates the feasability of our approach, based on a cooperation between a relational kernel and an object manager; it also validates the model which adds a complete set of object–oriented features (data abstraction, inheritance, complex objects, object sharing/identity) to the relational model.

The Object Manager includes storage optimisation techniques similar to those offered by object–oriented DBMSs, adapted to our extended relational model (such as value sharing, copy on write, garbage collection mechanisms, object decomposition, etc.).

An important aspect of our solution is that only one object storage and manipulation format is provided. Data structures are only accessible through the set of generic functions defined on the ESQL constructors, which is part of our Object Manager interface.

From the model and language point of view this work represents a significant contribution. To our knowledge, no existing relational extension provides such a complete object paradigm. Both the declarative language (ESQL) and the method programming language (MPL) are defined through a type system extension: ESQL is SQL plus ADT and the initial MPL is C plus ADT. Providing data manipulation capabilities through a procedure interface above the Object Manager avoids the format conversion problem and allows multiple method programming languages to be easily defined.

The main perspectives are to study how the relational query optimiser should be enhanced to take into account the object manipulations, and then to integrate this ADT extension within the parallel database server defined within EDS. Transactional aspects are still to be studied; it could be of interest to define how transactional mechanisms provided by the relational system and those defined on the Object Manager could cooperate. Finally a methodology would be appropriate for the application designer who has to cope with both relational tables and objects.

ACKNOWLEDGEMENTS

The authors wish to thank Mauricio Lopez for his reading and comments; Georges Gardarin for the nice and intensive discussions we had during the specification of the ESQL ADT extensions; Adriana Danes for her contribution to the Object Manager implementation; Christian Lenne for participating to the method compiler implementation; Jean–François Barbé and Béatrice Finance for their contribution to the implementation of the relational kernel extension.

References

1. Jay Banerjee, Won Kim and Kyung–Chang Kim, Queries in Object–Oriented Databases, *IEEE*, 1988.

2. François Bancilhon, Sophie Cluet and Claude Delobel, A Query Language for the O2 Object–Oriented Database System, *Proceedings of the Second Workshop on DataBase Programming Languages, Salishan, Oregon, USA*, June 1989.

3. S. Abiteboul and P. Kanellakis, Object Identity as a Query Language Primitive, *Proceedings of the ACM–SIGMOD Conference on the Management of Data, Portland, Oregon, USA*, June 1989.

4. Patrick Valduriez, Objets complexes dans les systèmes de bases de données relationnels, *Technique et Science Informatiques*, 6(5), pp. 405–418, 1987.

5. Setrag N. Khoshafian and George P. Copeland, Object Identity, *OOPSLA'86 Conference Proceedings*, edited by Sigplan Notice, pp. 406–416, September 1986.

6. P.F. Wilms, P.M. Schwarz, H.J. Schek and L.M. Haas, *Incorporating Data Types in an Extensible DataBase Architecture*, IBM, August 1988.

7. C. Lécluse, P. Richard, The O2 Database Programming Language, *Proceedings of the 15th VLDB Conference*, August 1989.

8. Michael J. Carey, David J. DeWitt and Scott L. Vandenberg, A Data Model and Query Language for EXODUS, *Proceedings of the ACM–SIGMOD Conference, Chicago*, pp. 413–423, 1988.

9. J. Banerjee, H. Chou, J.F. Garza, W. Kim, D. Woelk and N. Ballou, Data Model Issues for Object–Oriented Applications, *ACM Transaction on Office Information Systems*, 5(1), pp. 3–26, January 1987.

10. G. Gardarin, ESQL: An Extended SQL with Object Oriented and Deductive Capabilities, *EDS deliverable EDS.DD.11B.0901*, October 1989.

11. Georges Gardarin and Patrick Valduriez, ESQL: An Extended SQL with Object Oriented and Deductive Capabilities, *1st DEXA Conference*, edited by Springer Verlag, Vienne, August 1990.

12. M. Lopez, Functions and Architecture of the Database System, *EDS deliverable EDS.DD.11B.0801*, November 1989.

13. M. Atkinson, F. Bancilhon, D. DeWitt, K. Dittrich, D. Maier and S. Zdonick, The Object Oriented Database System Manifesto, *Proceedings of the First Conference on Deductive and Object–Oriented Databases, Kyoto, Japan*, December 1989.

14. F. Vélez, G. Bernard and V. Darnis, The O2 object manager: an overview, *Proceedings of the 15th VLDB conference, Amsterdam, the Netherlands.*, August 1989.

15. Georges Gardarin, J.P. Cheiney, Gerald Kiernan, Dominique Pastre and Hervé Stora, Managing Complex Objects in an Extensible Relational DBMS, *Proceedings of the Fifteenth International Conference on Very Large Data Bases*, pp. 55–65, 1989.

16. L. Cardelli, A Semantics of Multiple Inheritance, *Lecture Notes in Computer Science*, 1984.

17. Shalom Tsur and Carlo Zaniolo, An Implementation of GEM – supporting a semantic data model on a relational back–end, *SIGMOD'84*, 14(2), pp. 286–295, June 1984.

18. F. Velez et al, Implementing the O2 Object Manager: Some Lessons, *Proceedings of 4th Int.Workshop on Persistent Object Systems*, September 1990.

19. François Exertier, *Extension orientée objet d'un SGBD relationnel*, Thèse de Doctorat, Université Joseph Fourier Grenoble I, December 1991.

20. Lawrence A. Rowe and Michael R. Stonebraker, The POSTGRES Data Model, *Readings in Object–Oriented Database Systems (edited by S.B. Zdonic and D. Mayer)*, pp. 461–473, 1990.

21. Jean–François Barbé, François Exertier, Georges Gardarin and Samer Haj Houssain, A Cooperative Approach to Extend Relational Technology with Object Oriented Capabilities, *Proceedings of ICSC'92*, pp. 581–587, IEEE Computer Society, ACM Hong Kong Chapter, Hong Kong, December 1992.

22. M. Stonebraker, Inclusion of new types in relational data base systems, *Proceedings of the 2nd Conference on Data Engineering, Los Angeles*, 1986.

A SQL-like Query Calculus for Object-Oriented Database Systems*

Rudolf Herzig and Martin Gogolla

TU Braunschweig, Informatik, Abt. Datenbanken
Postfach 3329, D-38023 Braunschweig, Germany
e-mail: {herzig|gogolla}@idb.cs.tu-bs.de

Abstract. Currently much effort is being spent on providing object-oriented databases with ad hoc query facilities. In this paper we present a SQL-like query calculus whose major contribution lies in its inherent orthogonality and rigorous mathematical foundation. The calculus is essentially a calculus of complex values but it is defined independently of any concrete database model. The calculus can be used to formulate queries in value-based and object-based data models. Moreover it provides a general facility for the manipulation of complex values.

1 Introduction

Object-oriented database systems (OODB) are usually embedded in a programming language environment providing full computational power. Consequently, designers of OODB at first did not feel the need to integrate ad hoc query facilities into their systems. However, it has been recognized that some associative retrieval is of importance even for OODB [8, 12, 13].

A well-tried ad hoc query language is SQL. SQL came up with relational database systems so that many people regard SQL as a typical relational query language. On the other hand SQL has been successfully adapted to semantic data models [32, 30], and there have been many proposals for applying SQL to OODB [8, 16, 19, 22, 34, 14]. A number of these SQL variants have already found their way into commercial products like OSQL [11] in IRIS, Object SQL [26] in ONTOS, RELOOP [16] and its successor O_2Query [9] in O_2, CQL++ [19] in Ode, XSQL [34] in ORION. A derived form of O_2Query is being considered as the query language OQL of the ODMG-93 standards proposal [15, 35].

Unfortunately the syntax of many of these query languages is illustrated by some examples only, and their semantics is mostly described in an informal way. In other cases the semantics is defined by an involved translation into an *algebra-based* framework (e.g., RELOOP [16]) or a *rule-based* (logic programming oriented) formalism (e.g., ESQL2 [22], XSQL [34]). However with regard to SQL *calculus-based* formalisms seem to be more helpful because of their closeness to the basic select-from-where construct found in SQL [42].

* Work reported here has been partially supported by the CEC under Grant No. 6112 (COMPASS) and BMFT under Grant No. 01 IS 203 D (KorSo).

In this paper we present a SQL-like query calculus the aim of which is to provide a general framework for SQL-like query languages. Therefore the calculus is defined independently from any concrete database model. In comparison with other query language proposals we stress the following advantages.

Completely orthogonal SQL: In contrast to many approaches which allow for nested queries only in the *from* and *where* clause of a select term our query calculus allows for arbitrary terms, in particular further select terms, to be used in the *select* clause of a select term.

Abstract syntax: The syntax of the query calculus is precisely defined by mathematical notions being independent from a concrete language and thereby covering both context-free and context-sensitive rules in a formal and compact manner.

Straightforward semantics: Each syntactical category is directly given a rigorous formal semantics based on sets.

The query calculus is essentially a calculus of complex values. With that it stands in the tradition of the query calculi proposed for complex object models [37, 10, 43, 2]. However most of these calculi preserve the traditional hierarchical structure of predicate calculus in that terms are used to build formulas but formulas do not contribute to the construction of terms. These frameworks fail to reflect the fact that SQL queries can be nested. Therefore we propose a query calculus with *non-hierarchical* structure, i.e., terms may be built on the basis of formulas.

A concrete SQL-like language proposal which allows for nested queries in the *select, from,* and *where* clause of a select term is RELOOP (or O_2Query resp.). It is defined in context of an object model with complex values [39]. However we are not aware of a complete formal description of this language.

The paper is organized as follows. In Section 2 we introduce a general model of complex values. In Section 3 we define a calculus for complex values. Applications of this calculus are sketched in Section 4. We give some concluding remarks in Section 5.

2 Complex Values

Notation: Let sets $S, S_1, \ldots, S_n$ be given. Then $\mathcal{F}(S)$ denotes the restriction of the power set of S to finite sets, $\mathbf{S}^*$ the set of finite lists over S, $\mathcal{B}(S)$ the set of finite multi-sets (bags) over S, and $\mathbf{S_1} \times \ldots \times \mathbf{S_n}$ the Cartesian product of the sets $S_1, \ldots, S_n$. Finite sets are written as $\{c_1, \ldots, c_n\}$, lists as $\langle c_1, \ldots, c_n \rangle$, bags as $\{\!\{ c_1, \ldots, c_n \}\!\}$, and elements of the Cartesian product as $(c_1, \ldots, c_n)$.

2.1 Atomic Sorts

We define values as instances of data sorts. Data sorts are usually accompanied by specific operations and predicates. All these are summarized in a data signature.

Definition 1 (data signature). A data signature is given by a triple $\Sigma = (S, \Omega, \Pi)$ in which S denotes a set of sorts, $\Omega = \{\Omega_s\}_{s \in S^* \times S}$ a family of $S^* \times S$-indexed operation symbols and $\Pi = \{\Pi_s\}_{s \in S^*}$ a family of S^*-indexed predicate symbols. □

$\omega_{s_1 \ldots s_n, s} \in \Omega$ is also written as $\omega : s_1 \times \ldots \times s_n \to s$ and $\pi_{s_1 \ldots s_n} \in \Pi$ as $\pi : s_1 \times \ldots \times s_n$.

Examples.

1. The following sorts and associated operations and predicates are standard.

   $S \supseteq \{$ nat, int, real, bool, char, string, $\ldots \}$
   $\Omega \supseteq \{+, -, *, \mathtt{DIV}, \mathtt{MOD} : \text{int} \times \text{int} \to \text{int}, \ldots \}$
   $\Pi \supseteq \{<, \leq, =, \geq, > : \text{int} \times \text{int}, \ldots, \}$

   Data constants are considered as nullary operations symbols, e.g., $42 :\to$ int or true $:\to$ bool.

2. A data signature may also contain *non-standard* data types.

   $S \supseteq \{$ stack, $\ldots \}$
   $\Omega \supseteq \{$ empty $:\to$ stack, push : stack $\times$ int $\to$ stack,
   $\qquad\qquad$ pop : stack $\to$ stack, top : stack $\to$ int, $\ldots \}$

For a data signature Σ we assume an interpretation structure $I(\Sigma)$ to be given.

Definition 2 (interpretation of a data signature). For a given data signature Σ an interpretation structure is defined as a triple $I(\Sigma) = (I(S), I(\Omega), I(\Pi))$.

- $I(S)$ associates each sort $s \in S$ with a set $I(s)$ such that $\perp_s \in I(s)$.
- $I(\Omega)$ associates each operation symbol $\omega : s_1 \times \ldots \times s_n \to s \in \Omega$ with a total function $I(\omega) : I(s_1) \times \ldots \times I(s_n) \to I(s)$.
- $I(\Pi)$ associates each predicate symbol $\pi : s_1 \times \ldots \times s_n \in \Pi$ with a relation $I(\pi) \subseteq I(s_1) \times \ldots \times I(s_n)$. □

An interpretation structure can be viewed as a many-sorted algebra.

Example. The interpretation of standard data sorts may be fixed as follows.

$I(\text{nat}) = \mathbb{N}_0 \cup \{\perp_{\text{nat}}\}$, $I(\text{int}) = \mathbb{Z} \cup \{\perp_{\text{int}}\}$, $I(\text{real}) = \mathbb{Q} \cup \{\perp_{\text{real}}\}$,
$I(\text{bool}) = \{true, false\} \cup \{\perp_{\text{bool}}\}$,
$I(\text{char}) = A \cup \{\perp_{\text{char}}\}$, $I(\text{string}) = A^* \cup \{\perp_{\text{string}}\}$,

in which A denotes a finite set of characters. Standard operations and predicates have the usual meaning.

An element $\underline{s} \in I(s)$ is called a *value*. Values are written *italic*. For example the constant $42 :\to$ int generates the value *42*. For each sort s there is a special *null* (or error) *value* $\perp_s$. For example we have $I(\mathtt{DIV})(1,0) = \perp_{\text{int}}$. Null values are generated by $\mathtt{ERROR}_s :\to s \in \Omega$. For simplicity the index of the null value is dropped in the following.

2.2 Constructed Sorts

Non-standard data types may be specified algebraically [21, 47]. Beside such *abstract* types we also provide *constructed* types by means of predefined sort constructors. Here we propose the constructors *set, list, bag* to describe multi-valued domains, *tuple* to describe composite domains, and *union* to describe alternative domains. Of course, other constructors could be added as well. Sort constructors can be applied iteratively to construct domains of any complexity.

Definition 3 (sort expressions). Let a set of sorts S be given. Then the set *S-Expr(S)* of sort expressions over S is defined as follows.

   i. If $s \in S$, then $s \in$ *S-Expr(S)*.
  ii. If $s \in$ *S-Expr(S)*, then **set(s)**, **list(s)**, **bag(s)** $\in$ *S-Expr(S)*.
 iii. If $s_1, \ldots, s_n \in$ *S-Expr(S)*, then **tuple(s₁,...,sₙ)** $\in$ *S-Expr(S)*.
 iv. If $s_1, \ldots, s_n \in$ *S-Expr(S)*, then **union(s₁,...,sₙ)** $\in$ *S-Expr(S)*.

Let us assume that there is a fixed interpretation I of S according to Definition 2. Then the interpretation of sort expressions is defined as follows.

   i. see Definition 2.
  ii. $I(\text{set}(s)) := \mathcal{F}(I(s)) \cup \{\bot\}$.
     $I(\text{list}(s)) := (I(s))^* \cup \{\bot\}$.
     $I(\text{bag}(s)) := \mathcal{B}(I(s)) \cup \{\bot\}$.
 iii. $I(\text{tuple}(s_1, \ldots, s_n)) := (I(s_1) \times \ldots \times I(s_n)) \cup \{\bot\}$.
 iv. $I(\text{union}(s_1, \ldots, s_n)) := \{1{:}\underline{s}_1 \mid \underline{s}_1 \in I(s_1)\} \cup \ldots \cup \{n{:}\underline{s}_n \mid \underline{s}_n \in I(s_n)\} \cup \{\bot\}$.

$\square$

An element $\underline{s} \in I(s)$ with $s \in$ *S-Expr(S)* is called a *complex value*. As in the case of atomic sorts a special null value belongs to the interpretation of each sort expression.

In tuple or union expressions attributes may be added to underline the meaning of components. For example,

```
tuple(Nodes:set(int),
      Edges:set(tuple(Start:int, End:int)))
```

describes a structure for storing graphs. In union expressions attributes may serve as tags to distinguish several alternatives. For example,

```
union(PrivateAddress: tuple(Num:int,
                            Street:string,
                            City:string),
      BusinessAddress:tuple(Institution:string,
                            Office:string,
                            City:string))
```

describes a structure for storing addresses. Attributes in tuple expressions can be used as projection operators on tuple values. Attributes in union expressions can be used to test for or to select a certain alternative of a union value. In the following we treat attributes in tuple or union expressions as optional items.

As demonstrated by the two examples, sort constructors can be used to define *concrete* non-standard data sorts. Interestingly, sort constructors have been also served as the basis for a wide range of *value-based* data models.

A *schema* of a value-based data model can generally be expressed by a tuple expression $s = \text{tuple}(r_1{:}s_1,\dots,r_m{:}s_m)$. The *state* of a database belonging to this schema is a complex value of sort s. Many variations exist with respect to what is allowed for the sort expressions s_i $(i = 1,\dots,m)$.

- The **relational model** [17] restricts s_i to describe *tables* of the kind $\text{set}(\text{tuple}(a_1{:}d_1,\dots,a_n{:}d_n))$ in which d_j denote atomic sorts.
- The **nested form (NF) models** [41] allow for sort expressions s_i with alternating set and tuple constructors so that *nested tables* can be represented.
- The **complex object (CO) model** [1, 3] does not impose any restriction on the structure of s_i.

2.3 Generic Functions

Sort expressions are usually associated with a large number of *generic* (or overloaded) functions. For instance, there are operations and predicates that

- *generate* complex values from simpler ones. For instance, { } is used as a constructor for set values and ( ) is used as a constructor for tuple values.
- *decompose* complex values. For instance, $\text{SEL}_{\text{list}(s)} : \text{list}(s) \times \text{nat} \to s$ selects an element from a list, $\text{PRJ}^i_{\text{tuple}(s_1,\dots,s_n)} : \text{tuple}(s_1,\dots,s_n) \to s_i$ selects the *i*th component of a tuple, and $\text{PRJ}^i_{\text{union}(s_1,\dots,s_n)} : \text{union}(s_1,\dots,s_n) \to s_i$ selects the *i*th alternative of a union value.
- *convert* complex values. For instance, $\text{BTS}_{\text{bag}(s)} : \text{bag}(s) \to \text{set}(s)$ converts a bag to a set by eliminating duplicates and $\text{LTB}_{\text{list}(s)} : \text{list}(s) \to \text{bag}(s)$ converts a list to a bag.
- *exploit* the distinct properties of certain kinds of sort expressions. For instance, $\text{CNT}_{\text{set}(s)} : \text{set}(s) \to \text{nat}$ counts the elements in a set and $\text{IN}_{\text{set}(s)} : \text{set}(s) \times s$ denotes the membership predicate.

There are many other generic functions (for details see [25, 23, 27]). All operations induced by sort expressions are summarized in the set $\Omega(S\text{-}Expr(S))$. Analogously all predicates induced by sort expressions are combined in $\Pi(S\text{-}Expr(S))$.

From now on let $\Sigma_D = (S_D, \Omega_D, \Pi_D)$ denote a data signature according to Definition 1 so that $\Sigma = (S, \Omega, \Pi)$ denotes an *extended* signature given by $S = S\text{-}Expr(S_D)$, $\Omega = \Omega_D \cup \Omega(S\text{-}Expr(S_D))$, and $\Pi = \Pi_D \cup \Pi(S\text{-}Expr(S_D))$.

3 A Calculus of Complex Values

3.1 Formal Definition

In contrast to the well-known predicate calculus the calculus of complex values (in the following abbreviated as CCV) has a non-hierarchical structure given by

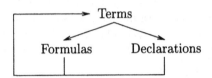

meaning that terms may be used to build formulas and declarations, and both formulas and declarations may appear in the construction of terms. In this respect CCV is derived from a calculus for querying extended Entity-Relationship schemas [25]. CCV is a revision of this query calculus. Firstly the calculus is lifted from a specific data model approach like the ER model to a general model of complex values, secondly we succeeded in drawing the syntactical parts of the calculus (esp. select terms and declarations) in simplified terms.

Terms may consist of variables. For the evaluation of such terms we need a notion of variable assignment.

Definition 4 (variables and variable assignments). Let a family $Var = \{Var_s\}_{s \in S}$ of S-indexed variables be given. The set of variable assignments A is defined by $A := \{\alpha \mid \alpha : Var_s \to I(s) \text{ for all } s \in S\}$. The special assignment $\epsilon : Var \to \{\bot\}$ is called the *empty assignment*. □

Definition 5 (terms). The syntax of terms is given by an S-indexed family $Term = \{Term_s\}_{s \in S}$ and a function free : $Term \to \mathcal{F}(Var)$ defined by the following rules.

i. If $v \in Var_s$, then $v \in Term_s$ with free$(v) := \{v\}$.
ii. If $\omega : s_1 \times \ldots \times s_n \to s \in \Omega$ and $\tau_i \in Term_{s_i}$ $(i = 1 \ldots n)$, then
   $\omega(\tau_1, \ldots, \tau_n) \in Term_s$ with free$(\omega(\tau_1, \ldots, \tau_n)) := $ free$(\tau_1) \cup \ldots \cup$ free(τ_n).
iii. If $\varphi \in Form$ and $\tau_1, \tau_2 \in Term_s$, then $?(\varphi, \tau_1, \tau_2) \in Term_s$ with
   free$(?(\varphi, \tau_1, \tau_2)) := $ free$(\varphi) \cup$ free$(\tau_1) \cup$ free(τ_2).
iv. If $\tau \in Term_s$, $\delta \in Decl$ and $\varphi \in Form$, then $\{\!\!\{\tau \mid \delta, \varphi\}\!\!\} \in Term_{\text{bag}(s)}$ with
   free$(\{\!\!\{\tau \mid \delta, \varphi\}\!\!\}) := ($free$(\tau) \cup$ free$(\delta) \cup$ free$(\varphi)) \setminus$ decl(δ).

For a fixed interpretation I and a variable assignment $\alpha \in A$ the evaluation of terms is defined as follows.

i. $(I, \alpha)[\![v]\!] = \alpha(v)$.
ii. $(I, \alpha)[\![\omega(\tau_1, \ldots, \tau_n)]\!] = I(\omega)((I, \alpha)[\![\tau_1]\!], \ldots, (I, \alpha)[\![\tau_n]\!])$.
iii. $(I, \alpha)[\![?(\varphi, \tau_1, \tau_2)]\!] = \begin{cases} (I, \alpha)[\![\tau_1]\!] & \text{if } (I, \alpha) \models \varphi \\ (I, \alpha)[\![\tau_2]\!] & \text{otherwise} \end{cases}$.

iv. $(I,\alpha)[\![\{\tau \mid \delta,\ \varphi\}]\!] = \{\!\{(I,\alpha')[\![\tau]\!] \mid \alpha' \in A \text{ with } \alpha'(v) = \alpha(v) \text{ for all } v \in \mathit{Var} \setminus \mathrm{decl}(\delta) \text{ and } (I,\alpha') \models \delta \text{ and } (I,\alpha') \models \varphi\}\!\}$. ☐

Variables (i), operation symbols (ii), and if-terms (iii) are standard. Terms (iv) are called *select terms*, because $\{\tau \mid \delta,\ \varphi\}$ is merely a short-hand notation for *select* τ *from* δ *where* φ. As known from SQL select terms are the basic primitive for declarative queries. τ represents the target term fixing the format of the desired result, δ is a declaration binding one or more variables to finite domains (see below), and φ is a qualifying formula.

Example (terms in concrete syntax). 2, 2+3*7 (infix notation of operation symbols is frequently used, operations have the usual bindings), 2+x, {1,4,9} (the curly brackets serve as constructors for set values), IF x<0 THEN -x ELSE x, and SELECT Name(x) FROM x IN PERSON WHERE Age(x)<18 are possible terms.

Terms are evaluated to complex values. With respect to the evaluation of operations and the evaluation of predicates in formulas, term evaluation depends on the interpretation I of the signature Σ. With respect to the evaluation of variables, term evaluation depends on the current variable assignment α. The evaluation of select terms is further discussed in Section 3.2 after having introduced formulas and declarations.

Definition 6 (formulas). The syntax of formulas is defined by a set *Form* and a function free : *Form* → $\mathcal{F}(\mathit{Var})$ defined by the following rules.

i. If $\pi : s_1 \times \ldots \times s_n \in \Pi$ and $\tau_i \in \mathit{Term}_{s_i}$ ($i = 1 \ldots n$), then $\pi(\tau_1, \ldots, \tau_n)$
   $\in \mathit{Form}$ with $\mathrm{free}(\pi(\tau_1, \ldots, \tau_n)) := \mathrm{free}(\tau_1) \cup \ldots \cup \mathrm{free}(\tau_n)$.
ii. If $\tau_1, \tau_2 \in \mathit{Term}_s$, then $\tau_1 = \tau_2 \in \mathit{Form}$ with
   $\mathrm{free}(\tau_1 = \tau_2) := \mathrm{free}(\tau_1) \cup \mathrm{free}(\tau_2)$.
iii. If $\varphi \in \mathit{Form}$, then $\neg(\varphi) \in \mathit{Form}$ with $\mathrm{free}(\neg(\varphi)) := \mathrm{free}(\varphi)$.
iv. If $\varphi_1, \varphi_2 \in \mathit{Form}$, then $(\varphi_1 \vee \varphi_2) \in \mathit{Form}$ with
   $\mathrm{free}((\varphi_1 \vee \varphi_2)) := \mathrm{free}(\varphi_1) \cup \mathrm{free}(\varphi_2)$.
v. If $\delta \in \mathit{Decl}$ and $\varphi \in \mathit{Form}$, then $\exists \delta(\varphi) \in \mathit{Form}$ with
   $\mathrm{free}(\exists \delta(\varphi)) := (\mathrm{free}(\delta) \cup \mathrm{free}(\varphi)) \setminus \mathrm{decl}(\delta)$.

For a fixed interpretation I and a variable assignment $\alpha \in A$ the validity of formulas is defined as follows.

i. $(I,\alpha) \models \pi(\tau_1, \ldots, \tau_n)$ iff $((I,\alpha)[\![\tau_1]\!], \ldots, (I,\alpha)[\![\tau_n]\!]) \in I(\pi)$.
ii. $(I,\alpha) \models \tau_1 = \tau_2$ iff $(I,\alpha)[\![\tau_1]\!] = (I,\alpha)[\![\tau_2]\!]$.
iii. $(I,\alpha) \models \neg(\varphi)$ iff not $(I,\alpha) \models \varphi$.
iv. $(I,\alpha) \models (\varphi_1 \vee \varphi_2)$ iff $(I,\alpha) \models \varphi_1$ or $(I,\alpha) \models \varphi_2$.
v. $(I,\alpha) \models (\exists \delta(\varphi))$ iff there is a variable assignment $\alpha' \in A$ with $\alpha'(v) = \alpha(v)$
   for all $v \in \mathit{Var} \setminus \mathrm{decl}(\delta)$ and $(I,\alpha') \models \varphi$ and $(I,\alpha') \models \delta$. ☐

There is nothing special about formulas. Note that the constant formulas TRUE and FALSE, the other logical connectives $\wedge$, $\Rightarrow$, $\Leftrightarrow$, and the quantifier $\forall$ might be defined by the given material.

With the aggregate functions CNT it is always possible to replace the formula $\exists \delta(\varphi)$ by $\text{CNT}\{c \mid \delta, \varphi\} \geq 1$ (in which c represents an arbitrary constant term). In this respect quantifiers can be regarded as syntactic sugar [23].

Example (formulas in concrete syntax). x<4 (infix notation of predicate symbols is frequently used), x=y, NOT x=y, x=y AND x=z OR y=z (logical connectives have the usual bindings), and EXISTS p IN PERSON Name(p)="Smith" are possible formulas.

Definition 7 (declarations). The syntax of declarations is given by a set *Decl* and the functions free, decl : *Decl* → $\mathcal{F}(\mathit{Var})$ defined by the following rules.

i. If $v \in \mathit{Var}_s$, $\tau \in \mathit{Term}_{\mathrm{set}(s)}$ and $v \notin \mathrm{free}(\tau)$, then $(v : \tau) \in \mathit{Decl}$,
   $\mathrm{free}((v : \tau)) := \mathrm{free}(\tau)$ and $\mathrm{decl}((v : \tau)) := \{v\}$.
ii. If $v \in \mathit{Var}_s$, $\tau \in \mathit{Term}_{\mathrm{set}(s)}$, $\delta \in \mathit{Decl}$ and $v \notin \mathrm{free}(\tau) \cup \mathrm{free}(\delta) \cup \mathrm{decl}(\delta)$,
   then $(v : \tau; \delta) \in \mathit{Decl}$, $\mathrm{free}((v : \tau; \delta)) := (\mathrm{free}(\tau) \setminus \mathrm{decl}(\delta)) \cup \mathrm{free}(\delta)$ and
   $\mathrm{decl}((v : \tau; \delta)) := \{v\} \cup \mathrm{decl}(\delta)$.

For a fixed interpretation I and a variable assignment $\alpha \in A$ the validity of declarations is defined as follows.

i. $(I, \alpha) \models (v : \tau)$ iff $\alpha(v) \in (I, \alpha)[\![\tau]\!]$.
ii. $(I, \alpha) \models (v : \tau; \delta)$ iff $\alpha(v) \in (I, \alpha)[\![\tau]\!]$ and $(I, \alpha) \models \delta$. □

Following the definition declarations are generally given as *declaration sequences* of the kind $(x_1 : \tau_1; (x_2 : \tau_2; \ldots; (x_n : \tau_n)))$. Declarations are used in select terms or in quantified formulas to bind variables to finite sets of values.

Example (declarations in concrete syntax). x IN {1,2,3}, p IN PERSON (in which PERSON denotes a set-valued term), p IN PERSON; c IN CAR, and h IN Hobbies(p); p IN PERSON (in which Hobbies(p) denotes a set-valued attribute of persons) are possible declarations.

Finally we define queries as closed terms, i.e., terms without free variables.

Definition 8 (queries). Every term $\tau \in \mathit{Term}$ with $\mathrm{free}(\tau) = \emptyset$ defines a query. The evaluation of queries is determined by $(I, \epsilon)[\![\tau]\!]$. □

In the following brackets are dropped as far as unambuigity is preserved. Infix notations are used where appropriate. $\{\tau \mid \delta\}$ is used as a short-hand for $\{\tau \mid \delta, \text{TRUE}\}$.

3.2 Evaluation of Select Terms

Terms are evaluated like applicative programs — may be except for select terms. A select term of the general kind

$$\{\ \tau \mid x_1 : \tau_1;\ x_2 : \tau_2;\ \ldots;\ x_n : \tau_n, \varphi\ \}$$

is evaluated by examining all possible assignments of values to the variables $x_1, \ldots, x_n$. Variable assignments have to fulfill the declarations and the qualifying formula φ. Having found a possible assignment this assignment contributes to the query result by evaluating the term τ. Assuming all terms τ_i to be evaluated to finite sets there can only exist a finite number of possible assignments to variables $x_1, \ldots, x_n$. Hence evaluation of select terms always results in finite sets. The query calculus is *safe* [45] (which can be formally proved by induction over term construction [25]). Importantly there is no need to define safe queries in a semantic way as in the case of relational domain calculus.

There is a simple scheme of describing the semantics of a declarative select term by an imperative program. More precisely a select term of the above kind can be evaluated by the following procedure:

```
result := {| |};
for each xₙ ∈ [ τₙ ] do
   ...
      for each x₁ ∈ [ τ₁ ] do
         if |= φ then result := result ∪ [ τ ] fi;
      od;
   ...
od;
```

The order of the for-each statements reflects the scope of variables in declaration sequences extending from the right to the left.

Next we try to explain the semantics of select terms by giving some examples.

Examples.

1. The first example demonstrates the basic *filter* function of select terms.

   $\{$ x | x:{-2,-1,0,1,2}, x>0 $\}$

   The term is evaluated to $\{\!| 1, 2 |\!\}$.

2. In general select terms are evaluated to true bags. For instance, the term

   $\{$ x^2 | x:{-2,-1,0,1,2} $\}$

   results in $\{\!| 0, 1, 1, 4, 4 |\!\}$. The aggregate function BTS can be used to convert bags into sets by eliminating duplicates.

3. Declarations may be given as declaration sequences. This can be used to describe the *cross product*. For example

   $\{$ (x,y) | x:{1,2}; y:{1,2,3} $\}$

   is evaluated to $\{\!| (1,1), (1,2), (1,3), (2,1), (2,2), (2,3) |\!\}$. Together with a qualifying formula φ this allows the formulation of *joins*.

4. In a declaration sequence like $x_1:\tau_1; \ldots; x_n:\tau_n$ the variable x_i is allowed to be free in $\tau_1, \ldots, \tau_{i-1}$. This can be used to express the *union* of sets being demonstrated by

$\{ \text{ x } | \text{ x:y; y:} \{\{1,2\}, \{2,3\}\} \ \}$

which is evaluated to $\{\!\!\{\ 1,2,2,3\ \}\!\!\}$. By applying the function BTS the result can be converted into a proper set.

5. With nested select terms *groupings* can be expressed. This is shown by the next example which groups the flat value $\{(1,2),\ (1,3),\ (2,3)\}$ by the first component resulting in $\{(1,\{2,3\}),\ (2,\{3\})\}$ (x.*i* is used as an abbreviation for $\text{PRJ}^i(\text{x})$).

$\text{BTS}\{ \text{ (x.1,BTS}\{ \text{ y.2 } | \text{ y:} \{(1,2),(1,3),(2,3)\}, \text{ y.1=x.1) } \}) \ | $
$\quad \text{x:} \{(1,2),(1,3),(2,3)\} \ \}$

6. The result of the last select term can be *unnested* again by the select term

$\text{BTS}\{ \text{ (x.1,y) } | \text{ y:x.2; x:} \{(1,\{2,3\}),\ (2,\{3\})\}\}$

yielding the original value.

3.3   Properties

Comparison with Query Algebras. The calculus allows to express all standard operations on complex values. This is shown in Table 1. The first group of operations subsumes the classical operations of relational algebra, showing that CCV is at least *relationally complete*. In the second group ν denotes the *nest* and μ the *unnest* operator of [44]. Specific operations for CO models can be expressed as well. For example, *set construction* ν' and *set collapse* μ' can be derived from the corresponding ν and μ representations by dropping the first tuple component in both cases.

Table 1. Standard operations on complex values[1]

$\cup$	$\text{set}(s) \times \text{set}(s) \to \text{set}(s)$	$\{ \text{ x } | \text{ x:y; y:} \{\tau_1, \tau_2\} \ \}$
$-$	$\text{set}(s) \times \text{set}(s) \to \text{set}(s)$	$\{ \text{ x } | \text{ x:}\tau_1, \neg\text{IN}(\tau_2, \text{x}) \ \}$
$\times$	$\text{set}(s_1) \times \text{set}(s_2) \to \text{set}(\text{tuple}(s_1, s_2))$	$\{ \text{ (x,y) } | \text{ x:}\tau_1; \text{ y:}\tau_2 \ \}$
π_i	$\text{set}(\text{tuple}(s_1, \ldots, s_n)) \to \text{set}(s_i)$	$\{ \text{ x.}i \ | \text{ x:}\tau \ \}$
σ_φ	$\text{set}(s) \to \text{set}(s)$	$\{ \text{ x } | \text{ x:}\tau, \ \varphi \ \}$
ν	$\text{set}(\text{tuple}(s_1, s_2)) \to \text{set}(\text{tuple}(s_1, \text{set}(s_2)))$	$\{ \text{ (x.1, } \{ \text{ y.2 } | \text{ y:}\tau, \text{ y.1} = \text{x.1}\}) \ | \text{ x:}\tau \ \}$
μ	$\text{set}(\text{tuple}(s_1, \text{set}(s_2))) \to \text{set}(\text{tuple}(s_1, s_2))$	$\{ \text{ (x.1,y) } | \text{ y:x.2; x:}\tau \ \}$
ν'	$\text{set}(s) \to \text{set}(\text{set}(s))$	$\{ \ \{ \text{ y } | \text{ y:}\tau, \text{ y} = \text{x} \ \} \ | \text{ x:}\tau \ \}$
μ'	$\text{set}(\text{set}(s)) \to \text{set}(s)$	$\{ \text{ y } | \text{ y:x; x:}\tau \ \}$

It should be noted that all the operators found in Table 1 could also find their entrance into the query calculus as generic functions on complex values. In some cases this may assist the formulation of complex queries.

---

[1] In every calculus expression τ_i stands for the *i*th argument of the corresponding operation. The dot notation is used for projection. To allow comparison, here all select terms are assumed to evaluate to proper sets by implicit duplicate elimination.

Comparison with other Query Calculi. CCV stands in the tradition of query calculi proposed for models of complex values [37, 10, 43, 2] from which the calculus of Abiteboul and Beeri (denoted CALC), which was studied in more detail in [1], can be considered as an archetype. Comparing CCV with CALC we find the following distinguishing features:

1. The consideration of *non-logical components* (data functions, aggregate functions) as important ingredients of concrete query languages.
2. The treatment of *duplicates* in the evaluation of select terms.
3. The *non-hierarchical structure* of the query calculus guided by the idea of fully orthogonal SQL.

We will briefly discuss the three points in more detail.

ad 1. The incorporation of externally defined functions in the query calculus clearly does not contribute to its inherent computational power. This was the main reason why such functions were not considered in [1]. On the other hand the pure calculus, even augmented with an fixpoint operator for expressing recursive queries (see below on expressiveness), still fails in solving such a trivial problem like testing a given finite set for even cardinality (*even problem* [6]). It has been argumented in [7] that the role of a query language should be primarily the selection and combination of data from a database, rather than arithmetic or other general computation on this data. So it should not be considered harmful when a query language does not show full computational power. Lack of expressive power can always be compensated by a careful combination of a query language with a general purpose programming language. Of course, then the main problem still consists in overcoming the well-known *impedance mismatch* between the set-oriented type system of a query language and the record-oriented style of conventional programming languages.

ad 2. In CALC a query is simply given by a formula φ with a single free variable v, for instance $\exists x \; x \in \{-2,-1,0,1,2\} \wedge x^2 = v$ (compare with CCV query 2 above). The answer to such a query is the set of all possible assignments of values to v making the formula φ true (here $\{0, 2, 4\}$). It is clear that in such a way one cannot obtain duplicates in query results.

ad 3. Since queries in CALC are given as usual formulas it is nearly impossible to structure complex queries. The decreased readability of CALC queries in comparison with SQL-like queries has been critized in [12]. It follows from the fact that the only way to deal with subqueries in CALC consists in using *set variables*. For example, the following CALC query with v as single free variable and a as a set variable corresponds to the grouping example (query 5) of the CCV queries given above (let M stand for $\{(1,2),(1,3),(2,3)\}$, duplicate handling neglected).

$$\exists x \; x \in M \wedge \exists a \; ((\forall t \; t \in a \Leftrightarrow \exists y \; y \in M \wedge y.1 = x.1 \wedge t = y.2) \wedge v = (x.1, a))$$

Since in CCV every select term is nothing else than a special kind of term, select terms may appear in any place as subterms of other select terms achieving full orthogonality for composing queries from subqueries.

Expressiveness. There exist two variants of CALC:

1. CALC$^-$ where like in CCV all variables must always be bound to constant, stored or computed sets, and
2. unrestricted CALC where variables may directly range over data domains.

It has been shown in [27] that, when ignoring data functions and duplicate handling, every CCV query can be transformed into a corresponding CALC$^-$ query by making use of set variables for representing results of subqueries.

It is important to note that CALC is more expressive than CALC$^-$. Like the relational calculus and the calculus presented in this paper CALC$^-$ lacks the power of expressing the computation of the transitive closure of a relation. It is shown in [1] that in a query algebra a special power set operator is needed to express transitive closure. Notably, power set of M can be expressed in CALC by $\forall x\ x \in v \Rightarrow x \in M$ where v represents the only free variable. Unfortunately, the so-called *domain-dependent* calculus CALC is not safe (take for example the query $v \neq 42$). Moreover, using power set to compute transitive closure is not very efficient at all.

Transitive closure can be easily described by *recursion* in a rule-based framework. Hence another idea is to include a *fixpoint operator* μ into the calculus (see [36] for a concrete language proposal). One can show that first-order calculus with inflationary fixpoint operator is equivalent to algebra with inflationary *while* and Datalog with negation (see [5, 6] for details).

Here we follow a more pragmatic approach based on an extensible signature Σ. Whenever a special operator like power set $\text{POW}_{\text{set}(s)} : \text{set}(s) \rightarrow \text{set}(\text{set}(s))$ or transitive closure $\text{TC}_{\text{set}(\text{tuple}(s,s))} : \text{set}(\text{tuple}(s,s)) \rightarrow \text{set}(\text{tuple}(s,s))$ is needed this can always be defined *externally* by a corresponding generic function.

4 Applications

The calculus of Section 3 was developed independently of any concrete database model. Queries were formulated over data constants instead. Clearly in real applications we want to apply the calculus to stored values. Therefore in this section we first discuss the application of the calculus to existing database models. Secondly we give some insight into an approach to object-oriented specification where the query calculus is used in the formulation of axioms expressing object properties.

4.1 Queries in Value- and Object-Based Data Models

A database schema generally includes a number of *containers* for storing objects that share common structure and common behavior. In value-based data models these containers are given by *relations* (or *relational schemas*); in object-based data models they are given by *classes*. The fundamental difference between value-based and object-based data models lies in their particular approach to the representation of real-world entities [31]. While in value-based models a real-world entity is represented directly as a tuple of its attribute values (*internal structure*), object-based data models spend a special object identifier (surrogate) for this purpose and attributes are functions on object identifiers (*attribute structure*). The latter approach enables updates on objects.

Referring to stored values in queries is based on references to containers. Hence a simple way of extending the query calculus to database states consists in including containers as set-valued terms into the logic. In addition, in object-based data models attributes must be admitted as functions on object surrogates. This is summarized in Table 2.

Table 2. Including containers into the query calculus

value-based	relation $r(a_1{:}s_1,\ldots,a_n{:}s_n)$	$r \in Term_{set(tuple(s_1,\ldots,s_n))}$
object-based	class c with $osort(c) = o$	$c \in Term_{set(o)}$
	attribute $a : o \to s$	$a \in \Omega$

The first line of the table also holds for the extensions of the relational model mentioned in Section 2.2. In the object-based approach we strictly distinguish between a class c and a sort of object identifiers $osort(c)$ belonging to a class c although in many data model approaches same names are used to denote both classes and corresponding object identifier sorts.

Dependent on the current state of a database, containers are evaluated to the current set of tuple values (or object identifiers respectively). Also in a state-dependent way attribute functions return the current attribute values.

Examples.

1. Let a relational schema PERSON(Name:string, Age:nat) be given. Then the following query returns the names of all stored persons:

   { Name(p) | p:PERSON }

   or in concrete syntax:

   SELECT Name(p) FROM p IN PERSON

   In this query p ist a variable of sort tuple(Name:string, Age:nat) so that Name acts as an projection operator.

2. Let us replace the relational schema by a class `PERSON` with attributes `Name:string` and `Age:nat`. A query returning the names of all stored persons is again given by $\{$ `Name(p)` | `p:PERSON` $\}$. But unlike in the former query here p is a variable of object identifier sort person = osort(`PERSON`) and Name is used as an attribute function. Note that both select terms are of sort bag(string) reflecting the fact that a given name may appear more than once in a query result. Note also that in the object-based database it is even possible that two persons with the same name and the same age exist while this is excluded in the corresponding relational database.

   Next we assume all queries being formulated in context of the object-based database.

3. The following query gives an example of a select term with a nested select in the select-clause (grouping).

   BTS$\{$ (p1, BTS$\{$ p2 | p2:PERSON, Age(p2)>Age(p1) $\}$) | p1:PERSON $\}$

   or in concrete syntax:

   ```
   BTS(SELECT (p1, BTS(SELECT p2
                       FROM   p2 IN PERSON
                       WHERE  Age(p2)>Age(p1)))
         FROM   p1 IN PERSON)
   ```

   The query results in a value of sort set(tuple(person, set(person))). It contains all persons together with the older ones.

4. The next query gives an example of a nested select in the where-clause of a select term.

   BTS$\{$ x | x:PERSON, Age(x)=MAX$\{$ Age(y) | y:PERSON $\}$ $\}$

   or in concrete syntax:

   ```
   BTS(SELECT x
       FROM   x IN PERSON
       WHERE  Age(x)=MAX(SELECT Age(y)
                         FROM   y IN PERSON))
   ```

   The query returns the set of the oldest persons. Note that in concrete syntax we did not write `SELECT MAX(Age(y))` as it would have been done in standard SQL showing some peculiar inconsistency of this standard [20].

   The same query could also be formulated without making use of an aggregate function by:

   BTS$\{$ x | x:PERSON, $\forall$ y:PERSON Age(y)<=Age(x) $\}$

5. Let \<Q4\> denote the query given in item 4. Then the following query returns the names of the oldest persons.

   BTS$\{$ Name(p) | p:\<Q4\> $\}$

This also gives an example for a query with nested select in the from-clause of a select term.

6. Let Hobbies:SET(string) be a further attribute of PERSON. Then the following query which makes use of a declaration sequence returns the set of hobbies of persons with age less than 18.

   BTS{ h | h:Hobbies(p); p:PERSON, Age(p)<18 }

or in concrete syntax:

```
BTS(SELECT h
    FROM   h IN Hobbies(p); p IN PERSON
    WHERE  Age(p)<18)
```

4.2 Axioms in Object-Oriented Specifications

The calculus of complex values was motivated by a concrete language proposal for describing static and dynamic properties of objects called TROLL *light* [18, 24, 28, 27]. For TROLL *light* a sublanguage was needed for the axiomatic part of object descriptions called *templates*. This includes static integrity constraints, rules to describe the effect of events on attributes, derivation rules for attributes, rules for the synchronization of events in different objects, event preconditions, etc.

Example.

```
TEMPLATE Node
    DATA TYPES   String, Nat;
    SUBOBJECTS   Children(Name:string):node;
    ATTRIBUTES   Info:nat;
                 DERIVED Total:nat;
    EVENTS       BIRTH create(nat);
                      updateInfo(nat);
                      createChild(Name:string, Info:nat);
                 DEATH destroy;
    CONSTRAINTS  CNT(Children) < 5;
    VALUATION    [create(I)]     Info = I;
                 [updateInfo(I)] Info = I;
    DERIVATION   Total = Info + SUM(SELECT Total(x)
                                     FROM x IN Children);
    INTERACTION  createChild(N,I) >> Children(N).create(I);
    BEHAVIOR     PROCESS Node =
                   ( create -> Nodelife );
                 PROCESS Nodelife =
                   ( updateInfo -> Nodelife |
                     createChild -> Nodelife |
                     {CNT(Children)=0} destroy );
END TEMPLATE;
```

The template describes nodes (of a tree). Every node is assigned a natural number as node information. Each node may have up to four subnodes being identified by a string. For a given node n the derived attribute Total returns the sum of all node information found in the subtree rooted at n (*bill of material problem*). Besides the birth and death of a node other possible events in a node's lifecycle concern updates of the node information and adding of subnodes. A node may only die when currently there are not any subnodes.

Templates may describe object communities as trees of arbitrary width and depth. In this special case the object community is a homogeneous one with all objects being of the same sort. In general object communities will be composed of rather different kinds of objects.

Let us now pay closer attention to how the query calculus is used in the construction of templates. Here we focus on the description of *derived attributes* which may be considered as predefined queries and the formulation of (static) *integrity constraints* which may be regarded as invariants.

It is a distinctive feature of TROLL *light* object descriptions that they do not presume a certain global schema view as this is usually done in most value- or object-based data models. This follows from the fact that with TROLL *light* descriptions of complex object systems can be iteratively composed from descriptions of subsystems using the subobject concept of templates [28]. This has a certain impact on the manner how queries are formulated against object communities. To summarize the difference: Queries are formulated from the perspective of local objects rather than starting from a fixed schema level.

Table 3, being a continuation of Table 2, shows the technical details to deal with queries in context of TROLL *light*.

Table 3. Support for queries formulated in the context of objects

TROLL *light*	template t with $osort(t) = o$	$self \in Term(t)_o$
	attribute $a : o \rightarrow s$	$a \in \Omega$
	subobject slot $u : o \rightarrow s$	$u \in \Omega$

Instead of referring to (global) containers, every query to be formulated in context of a certain object $\underline{o}$ starts with a self-reference to this object. Depending on the template t of which this object is an instance, the self-term to be evaluated is of object identifier sort $osort(t)^2$ and, as you might already guess, in context of $\underline{o}$ self is evaluated to $\underline{o}$.

In concrete syntax the self-term is often omitted. To show the difference we give the abstract conterpart of the derivation rule.

```
Info(self)+SUM{ Total(PRJ²(x)) | x:Children(self) }
```

---

[2] In TROLL *light* there is the following convention: Names of templates start with an upper case letter while same names but with a lower case letter are used for the corresponding object identifier sorts.

Having the reference to an object one may firstly observe its attribute or subobject slots. Both are considered as functions on object identifier sorts. Attributes are evaluated to the current attribute values. Subobject symbols can be parametrized but they need not. A non-parametrized subobject symbol is evaluated to the object identifier of the corresponding subobject if this does currently exist. Otherwise it is evaluated to the error value $\perp$. Parametrized subobject symbols are treated as map-valued functions. For instance, in the above example Children is treated as a function Children : node $\rightarrow$ map(string, node). Such a function yields the set of object identifiers of all existing subobjects together with their logical names in the superobject.

Now to explain the above query in full detail: Children(self) is a term of map(string,node) being evaluated to the set of current subnodes together with their names. In turn map(string,node) can be regarded as a subsort of set(tuple(string,node)) with a functional dependence of the second component onto the first. Hence x is a variable of sort tuple(string,node) so that Total(PRJ^2(x)) returns the Total value of a subnode (in concrete syntax Total(x) has to be considered as an abbreviation of the full path expression). All Totals of subnodes are summed up and the local Info value is added to give the desired result.

With this information in mind the constraint expressed in the node template should be self-explaining. It is important to note that in the cited form the query calculus can only be used to express static integrity conditions (invariants). Apart from other means for behavior specification transitional integrity conditions could be expressed by adding special *old* and *new* predicates referring to the state before or after the current state. For arbitrary temporal constraints temporal logic may be employed.

5 Conclusions

In this paper we gave a formal definition of a query calculus in the context of complex values. We showed that this calculus can be easily applied to both value-based and object-based database models. Moreover it provides a general facility for the manipulation of complex values. For instance, it can be used for stating axioms in object-oriented specifications.

Regarding general issues of object-oriented query languages [13] we claim that our query calculus fulfills basic requirements. For instance, *navigation* is supported by having surrogate-valued attributes as operations, and *methods* are integrated by user-defined operations and by derived attributes. The calculus is *extensible* by changes to the basic signature. We stress the fact that in contrast to many other query proposals our query calculus is completely *orthogonal*. This can smooth out some need to explicitly store interim query results.

Object-oriented query languages have been classified along the lines of *value-generating*, *object-generating* and *object-preserving*. With respect to this classification the presented calculus may be called value-generating. (However, it is a characteristic feature of values in contrast to objects that their existence is

time-independent. Only objects can be created or deleted [40]. So a better de-
nomination would be *value-resulting*.) When restricting select queries to select
terms of sort set(o) where o represents an object identifier sort the corresponding query calculus could also be called object-preserving. Queries based on the
invention of new object identifiers were not considered in this paper (cf. [4]).

A prototype implementation of the calculus using the facilities of the
OODBMS ObjectStore [38] to store complex values has been finished. The
term & formula evaluation unit is part of a validation tool for object-oriented
specifications [46, 29, 27]. The aim of this tool is to support the animation of
object descriptions according to [18]. At the time being term evaluation is based
on the (naive) evaluation scheme of Section 3.2 which does not take into account
query optimization [33]. Since query evaluation is close to evaluation of applicative programs, optimization strategies developed in this field may be adopted
for our approach.

References

1. S. Abiteboul and C. Beeri, *On the Power of Languages for the Manipulation of Complex Objects*, Research report 846, INRIA France, 1988.
2. S. Abiteboul, C. Beeri, M. Gyssens, and D. Van Gucht, *An Introduction to the Completeness of Languages for Complex Objects and Nested Relations*, In Abite-boul et al. [3], pp. 117–138.
3. S. Abiteboul, P.C. Fischer, and H.J. Schek (eds.), *Nested Relations and Complex Objects in Databases*, Springer, Berlin, LNCS 361, 1989.
4. S. Abiteboul and P. Kanellakis, *Object Identity as a Query Language Primitive*, Proc. ACM Int. Conf. on Management of Data (SIGMOD) (J. Clifford, B. Lindsay, and D. Maier, eds.), ACM SIGMOD Record 18:2, 1989, pp. 159–173.
5. S. Abiteboul and V. Vianu, *Datalog Extensions for Database Updates and Queries*, Research report 715, INRIA France, 1988.
6. _____, *Expressive Power of Query Languages*, Research report 1587, INRIA France, 1992.
7. A.V. Aho and J.D. Ullman, *Universality of Data Retrieval Languages*, Proc. 6th ACM Symp. Principles of Programming Languages (POPL), 1979, pp. 110–120.
8. F. Bancilhon, S. Cluet, and C. Delobel, *A Query Language for the O_2 Object-Oriented Database System*, Proc. 2nd Int. Workshop on Database Programming Languages (R. Hull, R. Morrison, and D. Stemple, eds.), Morgan-Kaufmann, San Mateo (CA), 1989, pp. 122–138.
9. F. Bancilhon, C. Delobel, and P. Kanellakis (eds.), *Building an Object-Oriented Database System - The Story of O_2*, Morgan-Kaufmann, San Mateo (CA), 1992.
10. F. Bancilhon and S. Khoshafian, *A Calculus of Complex Objects*, Proc. 5th ACM Symp. Principles of Database Systems (PODS), 1986, pp. 53–60.
11. D. Beech, *A Foundation for Evolution from Relational to Object Databases*, Ad-vances in Database Technology, Proc. Int. Conf. on Extending Database Tech-nology (EDBT) (J.W. Schmidt, S. Ceri, and M. Missikoff, eds.), Springer, Berlin, LNCS 303, 1988, pp. 256–270.
12. C. Beeri, *A Formal Approach to Object-Oriented Databases*, Data & Knowledge Engineering **5** (1990), no. 4, 353–382.

13. E. Bertino, M. Negri, G. Pelagatti, and L. Sbattella, *Object-Oriented Query Languages: The Notion and the Issues*, IEEE Trans. on Knowledge and Data Engineering **4** (1992), no. 3, 223–237.
14. J. Van den Bussche and A. Heuer, *Using SQL with Object-Oriented Databases*, Information Systems **18** (1993), no. 7, 461–487.
15. R. Cattell, *The Object Database Standard: ODMG-93*, Morgan-Kaufmann, San Mateo (CA), 1994.
16. S. Cluet, C. Delobel, C. Lécluse, and P. Richard, *RELOOP, an Algebra Based Query Language for an Object-Oriented Database System*, Data & Knowledge Engineering **5** (1990), no. 4, 333–352.
17. E.F. Codd, *A Relational Model of Data for Large Shared Data Banks*, Communications of the ACM **13** (1970), no. 6, 377–387.
18. S. Conrad, M. Gogolla, and R. Herzig, *TROLL light: A Core Language for Specifying Objects*, Informatik-Bericht 92–02, Technische Universität Braunschweig, 1992.
19. S. Dar, N.H. Gehani, and H.V. Jagadish, *CQL++: A SQL for the Ode Object-Oriented DBMS*, Advances in Database Technology, Proc. Int. Conf. on Extending Database Technology (EDBT) (A. Pirotte, C. Delobel, and G. Gottlob, eds.), Springer, Berlin, LNCS 580, 1992, pp. 201–216.
20. C. Date, *A Critique of the SQL Database Language*, ACM SIGMOD Record **14** (1984), no. 3, 8–54.
21. H. Ehrig and B. Mahr, *Fundamentals of Algebraic Specification 1: Equations and Initial Semantics*, Springer, Berlin, 1985.
22. G. Gardarin and P. Valduriez, *ESQL2: An Object-Oriented SQL with F-Logic Semantics*, Proc. 8th Int. Conf. on Data Engineering (ICDE), IEEE Computer Society Press, 1992, pp. 320–327.
23. M. Gogolla, *An Extended Entity-Relationship Model — Fundamentals and Pragmatics*, Springer, Berlin, LNCS 767, 1994.
24. M. Gogolla, S. Conrad, and R. Herzig, *Sketching Concepts and Computational Model of TROLL light*, Proc. 3rd Int. Conf. Design and Implementation of Symbolic Computation Systems (DISCO) (A. Miola, ed.), Springer, Berlin, LNCS 722, 1993, pp. 17–32.
25. M. Gogolla and U. Hohenstein, *Towards a Semantic View of an Extended Entity-Relationship Model*, ACM Trans. on Database Systems **16** (1991), no. 3, 369–416.
26. C. Harris and J. Duhl, *Object SQL*, Object-Oriented Databases with Applications to CASE, Networks, and VLSI CAD (R. Gupta and E. Horowitz, eds.), Prentice-Hall, 1991, pp. 199–215.
27. R. Herzig, *Zur Spezifikation von Objektgesellschaften mit TROLL light*, Ph.D. thesis, Technische Universität Braunschweig, 1994.
28. R. Herzig, S. Conrad, and M. Gogolla, *Compositional Description of Object Communities with TROLL light*, Proc. Basque Int. Workshop on Information Technology (BIWIT): Information Systems Design and Hypermedia (C. Chrisment, ed.), Cépaduès-Éditions, Toulouse, 1994, pp. 183–194.
29. R. Herzig and M. Gogolla, *An Animator for the Object Specification Language TROLL light*, Proc. Colloquium on Object Orientation in Databases and Software Engineering (V.S. Alagar and R. Missaoui, eds.), Université du Quebéc à Montréal, 1994, pp. 4–17.
30. U. Hohenstein and G. Engels, *SQL/EER — Syntax and Semantics of an Entity-Relationship-Based Query Language*, Information Systems **17** (1992), no. 3, 209–242.

31. R. Hull, *Four Views of Complex Objects: A Sophisticate's Introduction*, In Abiteboul et al. [3], pp. 87–116.

32. R. Hull and R. King, *Semantic Database Modelling: Survey, Applications, and Research Issues*, ACM Computing Surveys **19** (1987), no. 3, 201–260.

33. M. Jarke and J. Koch, *Query Optimization in Database Systems*, ACM Computing Surveys **16** (1984), no. 2, 111–152.

34. M. Kifer, W. Kim, and Y. Sagiv, *Querying Object-Oriented Databases*, Proc. ACM Int. Conf. on Management of Data (SIGMOD) (M. Stonebreaker, ed.), ACM SIGMOD Record 21:2, 1992.

35. W. Kim, *Observations on the ODMG-93 Proposal for an Object-Oriented Database Language*, ACM SIGMOD Record **23** (1994), no. 1, 4–9.

36. K. Koymen and Q. Cai, *SQL*: A Recursive SQL*, Information Systems **18** (1993), no. 2, 121–128.

37. G.M. Kuper and M.Y. Vardi, *A New Approach to Database Logic*, Proc. 3th ACM Symp. Principles of Database Systems (PODS), 1984, pp. 86–96.

38. C. Lamb, G. Landis, J. Orenstein, and D. Weinreib, *The ObjectStore Database System*, Communications of the ACM **34** (1991), no. 10, 50–63.

39. C. Lécluse and P. Richard, *Modeling Complex Structures in Object-Oriented Databases*, Proc. 8th ACM Symp. Principles of Database Systems (PODS), 1989, pp. 360–368.

40. B.J. MacLennan, *Values and Objects in Programming Languages*, ACM SIGPLAN Notices **17** (1982), no. 12, 70–79.

41. A. Makinouchi, *A Consideration on Normal Form of Not Necessarily Normalized Relation in the Relational Data Model*, Proc. 3rd Int. Conf. on Very Large Data Bases (VLDB), 1977, pp. 447–453.

42. M. Negri, G. Pelagatti, and L. Sbattella, *Formal Semantics of SQL Queries*, ACM Trans. on Database Systems **16** (1991), no. 3, 513–534.

43. M.A. Roth, H.F. Korth, and A. Silberschatz, *Extended Algebra and Calculus for Nested Relational Databases*, ACM Trans. on Database Systems **13** (1988), no. 4, 389–417.

44. H.J. Schek and M.H. Scholl, *The Relational Model with Relation-Valued Attributes*, Information Systems **11** (1986), 137–147.

45. J.D. Ullman, *Principles of Database and Knowledge Base Systems, Vol. I*, Computer Science Press, Rockville (MD), 1988.

46. N. Vlachantonis, R. Herzig, M. Gogolla, G. Denker, S. Conrad, and H.-D. Ehrich, *Towards Reliable Information Systems: The KORSO Approach*, Advanced Information Systems Engineering, Proc. 5th CAiSE'93 (C. Rolland, F. Bodart, and C. Cauvet, eds.), Springer, Berlin, LNCS 685, 1993, pp. 463–482.

47. M. Wirsing, *Algebraic Specification*, Handbook of Theoretical Computer Science, Vol. B (J. Van Leeuwen, ed.), North-Holland, Amsterdam, 1990, pp. 677–788.

Schema Evolution for
Object-Based Accounting Database Systems

Jia-Lin Chen and Dennis McLeod
Department of Computer Science
and
Daniel O'Leary
School of Business

University of Southern California
Los Angeles, CA 90089, USA

Abstract When an (accounting) database schema does not meet the requirements of a firm, the schema must be changed. Such schema evolution can be considered as realizable via a sequence of operators. This research proceeds in the following three steps. First, we define a set of basic evolution schema operators and employ the evolution heuristics to guide the evolution process. Second, we explore how domain-specific knowledge can be used to guide the use of evolution operators to complete the evolution task. A well-known accounting data model is used here to guide the schema evolution process. Third, we discuss a tool built to implement the evolution operators, using the evolution heuristics and domain-specific knowledge.

1. Introduction

1.1 Motivation

The static meta-data view of database management is that the schema of a database is designed before the database is populated and remains relatively fixed over the life cycle of the system. However, the need to support database evolution is clear: a static meta-data view of a database can support neither next generation dynamic database applications such as interactive multi-media information systems [5] nor traditional database applications such as accounting information systems.

There are at least two reasons that a database schema would need to change. First, the current schema may not meet the original requirements. Such a schema may be called a "premature schema," resulting from erroneous schema design or incomplete requirement analysis. Second, the current schema may not meet new requirements. This type of database schema may be termed an "obsolete schema"; such obsolete schema may be caused by changes in the real world and/or changes of users' views or perceptions thereof.

In a traditional setting, a database administrator (DBA) and programmers would spend substantial time to correct a premature schema and update an obsolete schema even after the database has been populated. However, with the proliferation of databases within organizations, end-users today often act as DBAs. For example, often an accounting database may be directly maintained by its users (accounting specialists or clerks). Unfortunately, these users may lack the database knowledge and programming skills required to change the database schema.

1.2 Research Approach

When an accounting database schema does not meet the requirements of a firm, the schema must be changed. One important issue is how the data can be adapted to a new schema. A classical way to deal with this is to write a conversion program to manipulate the data to fit the new schema. An alternative approach is to develop a set of evolution operators to handle the data adaptation. Database schema evolution can be considered as realizable via a sequence of operators. These schema evolution operators manipulate the original schema into a new schema, and the populated database is modified accordingly. We can consider two key questions here:
- Can we find a set of schema evolution operators that can be effectively used by an end user?
- What heuristics are necessary to guide a user in the choice of a sequence of operators to complete a given evolution task?

This research addresses the above two questions in the following three steps. First, we define a set of basic schema evolution operators and employee evolution heuristics to guide evolution process. Second, we explore how domain-specific knowledge can be used to guide the evolution operators to complete tasks. The REA accounting data model [9] is used here to guide the schema evolution process of an object-based accounting database system. Third, we discuss a tool built to implement the evolution operators, using the evolution heuristics and domain-specific knowledge. The tool provides a user-friendly interface to guide a non-expert user to complete evolution tasks.

This paper is organized as follows. Section 2 provides background on related research and introduces an object-based data model and its schema evolution operators. Section 3 introduces an object-based REA accounting model and discusses how the REA model is used to guide schema evolution. Section 4 describes the architecture and implementation of a schema evolution administration tool, REAtool, and shows the look and feel of its prototype. The last section, Section 5, summaries this research, and discusses some future research directions.

2. Background

2.1 Related Research

ORION [2], ENCORE [13], and GemStone [12] use object-oriented data models and support evolution mechanisms; ORION and ENCORE employ a screening approach and Gemstone uses a conversion approach. They define modeling invariants and rules as schema evolution constraints. The semantics of schema evolution operators is used to maintain the evolution constraints. PKM [8] identifies a rich set of evolution patterns that can be used in a conceptual evolution process. OSAM* Schema Tailoring Tool [11] is based on OSAM* data model [14] and allows a non-expert user to redesign an OSAM* schema by tailoring its old schema. The tailoring process is accomplished through evolution operations. These operations maintain the schema constraints. If the modeling constraints are violated, the operations will be aborted.

Thus, several researchers have formulated schema evolution constraints as invariants and rules of object-oriented data models. The semantics of a set of evolution operators are then defined, based on the evolution constraints they proposed. However, their research did not employ heuristics or domain knowledge to guide an end-user in completing evolution tasks. In the research described in this paper, we indeed employ heuristics and domain knowledge to structure the evolution process.

2.2. Object-Based Data Model and Schema Evolution Operators

A basic Object-Based Data Model (OBDM) is used here. Modeling constructs of OBDM such as class, class hierarchy, attribute, inheritance, and their associated constraints can be found in the literature of object-based data models [1, 4, 7].

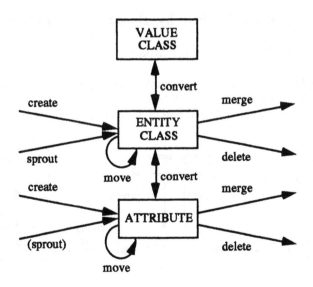

Figure 2.1 Schema Evolution Operators

Based on OBDM, we define four groups of schema evolution operators: 1) Schema Enhancement Operators create and sprout; 2) Schema Reduction Operators merge and delete; 3) Schema Restructure Operator move; and 4) Schema Conversion Operator convert. (See Figure 2.1) The operator create creates a new class or attribute. The new class can be a generalized class of several classes or a specialization of some class. The operator sprout generates a new class with its instances having a one-to-one mapping to its source class. The operator merge merges a class into another class or an attribute into another attribute. The operator **merge** deletes the meta-data such as classes or attributes, but keeps the data unchanged. The operator **delete** will delete data as well as meta-data. The operator **move** changes the structure of class hierarchy by moving classes or by moving attributes. The operator **convert** converts a modeling construct among a value class, an entity class, and an attribute.

These schema evolution operators should obey modeling constraints to keep a schema consistent after they have been applied. This is the consistency principle of schema evolution. For example, the instances of a subclass should be the instances of its superclass. To keep database consistent in schema evolution, evolution operators will be ruled by modeling constraints to propagate the changes to related parts of a schema. This is called a propagation effect. Since a propagation effect could change the data and meta-data of a schema that a user does not intend to change, a propagation effect must be controlled to maintain the losslessness of the data and meta-data. This is called the preservation principle of schema evolution. For example, when a subclass is merged into its superclass, its attributes and the values defined by these attributes could be lost. One way to avoid this kind of loss of meta-data and data is to move these attributes of the subclass to a superclass. The preservation principle is realized by using a set of evolution heuristics to guide an evolution process. The details of these evolution heuristics are described in [3].

3. Schema Evolution Guided by Domain Knowledge

3.1 Object-Based REA Accounting Model

Domain-specific knowledge can be used to guide a non-expert user to conduct schema evolution tasks. In particular, this research explores an well-known accounting model to guide the schema evolution in the context of accounting information systems.

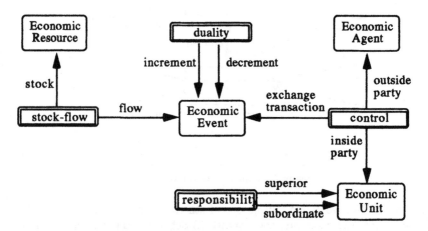

Figure 3.1 The Object-Based REA Accounting Model

The REA accounting model is a generalized accounting framework to capture the interaction of economic resources, economic events and economic agents for accounting systems [9]. Economic resources are scarce assets such as inventory or cash under the control of an enterprise. Economic events are phenomena that reflect changes in economic resources resulting from production, exchange, consumption, and distribution. Purchase and cash disbursement are the examples of economic events. Economic agents are persons and parties who participate in the economic events, e.g. vendor. Economic units are a subset of economic agents and are inside participants, e.g. cashier and buyer. (See Figure 3.1)

Their are four types of relationships between these REA entities:

1) Stock-flow relationship: This relationship is used to connect an economic resource and an economic event. The stock part of the relationship is an economic resource; and the flow part of the relationship is an economic event. For example, the stock-flow relationship between Inventory and Purchase has Inventory as its stock part and Purchase as its flow part.

2) Duality relationship: A duality relationship links two events. One event is an increment part of the relationship and the other corresponding event would be a decrement part of the relationship. For example, Purchase Payment is a duality that links the event, Purchase, as its increment part and the event, Cash Disbursement, as its decrement part.

3) Control relationship: A control relationship is a three-way association among an economic event (as exchange transaction part), an economic agent (as outside party), and an economic unit (as inside party). For example, Purchase Supply is a control relationship that associates Purchase (an event with a role as its exchange transaction part), Vendor (an agent with a role as its outside party), and Buyer (a unit with a role as its inside party).

4) Responsibility relationship: This relationship indicates one economic unit as its superior part and the other economic unit as its subordinate part. For example, the relationship "works for" is a responsibility that has Cashier as its subordinate part and Treasurer Department as its superior part.

REA model was originally described in an entity-relationship representation. Since this paper employs an object-based approach, the REA entities are modeled as classes and their relationships are modeled as associative classes in an object-based model. Since the evolution operators discussed here are based on the object-based data model, the object-based REA model will be used directly to guide the use of these evolution operators.

3.2 REA Guidance and Schema Evolution

The REA accounting model is used to guide schema evolution of an object-based accounting database. From the viewpoint of an accounting database schema, REA classes are meta-classes. A class of an accounting database are an instance of one of classes of the REA model. For example, the class Purchase Payment is an instance of the meta-class Duality. A class in an accounting database is said to be REA-compliant if and only if:

• The class is an instance of one of REA meta-classes;
• It inherits all the attributes from this REA meta-class; and
• The values of these attributes of the class are defined.

For example, Class **Purchase Payment** is defined as an instance of REA meta-class **Duality**. The class inherits the attributes, **increment and decrement**, from the meta-class **Duality**. Furthermore, its increment part is defined as **Purchase** and its decrement part is defined as **Cash Disbursement**. Both of them are events. Hence, Class **Purchase Payment** is REA-compliant. While all classes of an accounting database are REA-compliant, the schema of this accounting database is REA-compliant.

There are two contexts where the REA model is used to guide schema evolution: 1) A schema is not REA-compliant. The schema is required to evolve to be REA-compliant. This case is called non-REA-to-REA evolution. 2) A schema is already REA-compliant. The schema must be maintained to be REA-compliant while schema evolution is required. This case is called REA-to-REA evolution.

Both cases of REA-to-REA and non-REA-to-REA evolution involve the following three tasks:
- REA Description Tasks - Specify an accounting database class as an instance of an REA meta-class. For example, Purchase is described as an economic event or Purchase Payment as a duality relationship.
- Evolution Operation Tasks - Apply evolution operators to manipulate an accounting database schema.
- REA Verification Tasks - Verify if an accounting database schema is REA-compliant.

The following three different methods will use the above tasks to guide evolution process: (The next section, Schema Evolution Scenario, will give an example for each method introduced here.)
1) REA Relationship-Driven Schema Evolution Method: This evolution method starts with an REA relationship description task. While an REA relationship is specified for an accounting database class, the system will evoke the related operators (i.e. an evolution operation task) to complete the schema evolution required by the specification and then evoke the REA verification task to examine if the current schema is REA-compliant.
2) REA Entity-Driven Schema Evolution Method: This evolution method starts with an REA entity description task. While an REA entity is specified for an accounting database class, the system will evoke the related operators (i.e. an evolution operation task) to complete the schema evolution required by the specification and then evoke the REA verification task to examine if the current scheme is REA-compliant.
3) Operation-Driven Schema Evolution Method: This evolution method starts with applying an schema evolution operator. While the accounting database schema is manipulated by evolution operators, the REA verification task is evoked to examine if this evolution operation meet the requirements of REA-compliantness.

3.3 Schema Evolution Scenario

This section describes a schema evolution scenario and demonstrates how three evolution methods can be used in the case of non-REA-to-REA evolution. The example used here is a primitive accounting database for inventory purchases and it is not compliant to the REA model. Its schema is shown in Figure 3.2. The task is to evolve this non-REA-compliant schema into an REA-compliant schema. The scenario of this non-REA-to-REA evolution contains several sessions where each session corresponds to a major schema evolution task. After five sessions, this evolution process reaches its target schema, an REA-compliant schema. The target schema is shown in Figure 3.3.

Each session contains several steps, where each step corresponds to an REA specification task or an evolution operation task. An REA verification task is the final step of each session and will not be shown in the following discussion. To illustrate this evolution process, we rename the classes of the starting schema to meet the class names of its target schema, i.e. "Purchase Record" becomes "Purchase" and "Payment Record" becomes "Cash Disbursement." (See Figure 3.2)

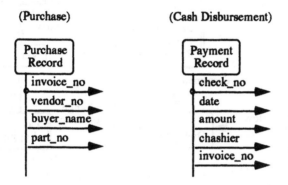

Figure 3.2 Initial Schema of Inventory Purchase

Session I. Evolution Session for Purchase Payment In this session, an REA relationship-driven schema evolution method is used.

Step 1 A user specifies a duality between Class **Purchase** and Class **Cash Disbursement**.

```
[duality instantiate: "Purchase Payment"
increment: "Purchase"
decrement: "Cash Disbursement"]
```

Step 2 The system specifies Class **Purchase** and Class **Cash Disbursement** as events. Then, Classes **Purchase** and **Cash Disbursement** become the instances of events.

```
[Event instantiate: "Purchase"]
[Event instantiate: "Cash Disbursement"]
```

<u>Step 3</u> The domain of Attribute **invoice_no** of Class **Cash Disbursement** will merge with Class **Purchase**. First, the domain of Attribute **invoice_no** will evolve from a class which contains atomic data values (a "value class") to one which contains abstract objects (an "entity class). Then, this entity class will merge with Entity Class **Purchase**. Attribute **Invoice Number** will evolve to Class **Purchase Payment**. Then, Class **Purchase Payment** becomes an instance of Duality.

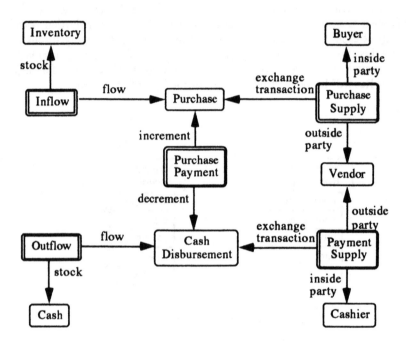

Figure 3.3 Target Schema of Inventory Purchase

<u>Session II</u>. <u>Evolution Session for Purchase Supply</u> In this session, an REA entity-driven schema evolution method is used.

<u>Step 1</u> The user specifies Buyer as a unit and Vendor as an agent.

```
[Unit instantiate: "Buyer"]
[Agent instantiate: "Vendor"]
```

<u>Step 2</u> Since the system already has Classes **Purchase** and **Cash Disbursement** as events and REA control is a three-way relationship connecting an event, a unit and an agent, the system creates a control relationship. Since there are two events in the current schema, the user must decide which one participates in this control relationship and also name the control. Here, Class **Purchase** is chosen by the user.

```
[control instantiate: "Purchase Supply"
exchange_transaction: "Purchase"
inside_party: "Buyer"
outside_party: "Vendor"]
```

Step 3 According to the previous REA description, class **Purchase** will sprout itself and generate a new class "Purchase Supply." Attributes **vendor_no** and **buyer_name** of Class **Purchase** will be moved to Class **Purchase Supply.** The domains of these attributes will be converted to Entity Classes **Vendor** and **Buyer**, respectively.

Session III. Evolution Session for Payment Supply (This session uses the same method as the Session II, and is omitted here.)

Session IV. Evolution Session for Inflow Class In this session, an operation-driven schema evolution method is used.

Step 1 A user applies schema evolution operators to convert the domain of Attribute **part_no** of Class **Purchase** into a class and merges this class with Class **Inventory**. The user also renames Attribute **part_no** as "Inflow." Then, the user converts Attribute **Inflow** to an associative class (viz., a class whose instances model relationships). Class **Inflow** becomes a two-way relationship connecting Class **Purchase** and Class **Inventory**.

Step 2 The user describes Class **Inventory** as a resource and Class **Inflow** as an REA relationship stock-flow. Since Class **Purchase** is an Event, Class **Inflow** generated by schema operators should be an REA-compliant class.

Session V. Evolution Session for Outflow Class (This session uses the same method as the Session IV, and is omitted here.)

4. REAtool: a Schema Evolution Guidance Tool

4.1 The Architecture of REAtool

A Schema Evolution and Administration Tool, SEAtool for short, is an experimental prototype that implements the proposed schema evolution methodology and assists a database user, designer, or administrator with the schema evolution. It also can employ domain-specific knowledge, such as REA accounting model, to guide a user to complete evolution tasks. The version of SEAtool that uses the REA accounting model to guide schema evolution is called REAtool. The architecture of REAtool is shown in Figure 4.1. Three main modules of REAtool are SEAshell, SEAengin and SEAbase.

SEAshell provides necessary context information and guides a user through a dialog to complete an evolution task. It also gives feedback to allow a user to validate evolution operations. SEAshell supports the interaction required by evolution operation tasks. SEAshell (REA Option) also supports the interaction required by REA description tasks.

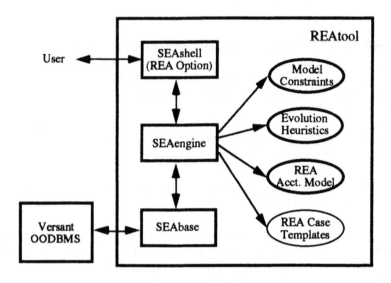

Figure 4.1 The Architecture of SEAtool

The SEAengine module accepts the requests issued by a user from SEAshell and uses two kinds of generic knowledge to guide schema evolution:
- Model Constraints: The constraints required by Object-Based Data Model should be maintained to keep database schema consistent.
- Evolution Heuristics: Schema evolution is guided by Preservation Principle to minimize the loss of the data and meta-data.

The SEAengine module in REAtool uses two additional kinds of domain-specific knowledge to guide schema evolution:
- Domain Knowledge: The REA accounting model is used as a generic model to guide evolution process.
- Templates: Knowledge specific to a sub-domain can be used to guide schema evolution, for example, industry-specific information about REA schema. The current version of SEAtool does not include it.

The SEAbase module defines the internal data structure to store the data and meta-data of a database. SEAbase is built on the top of Versant Object-Oriented DBMS and uses function calls provided by Versant libraries [15]. SEAshell and SEAengine are implemented in Objective-C and SEAbase is implemented in C++. SEAtool prototype is developed under the NeXTSTEP programming environment [10].

4.2 REA Task Guidance

An evolution task is guided by the Task Guidance Panel (TGP), portion of SEAshell. TGP has four components:

1) Schema Browser. There are three kinds of browsers to be used. Network Browser and Hierarchical Browser show the semantic relationship and hierarchical structure of classes. REA Browser shows REA meta-classes and their instances.

2) Context Display illustrates graphic objects involved in an evolution process. Therefore, a user can get a comprehensive and coherent control of the evolution process.

3) Task Catalog. A list of evolution tasks is listed in an organized way to allow a user to choose. Three major kinds of tasks are: REA description, operation specification and REA verification. For example, a user can choose to do the task of duality description.

4) Working Space. Evolution tasks are guided and completed here. Working Space consists of a stack of Dialog Pages. A user is guided by the system to fill Dialog Pages step by step to complete an evolution task.

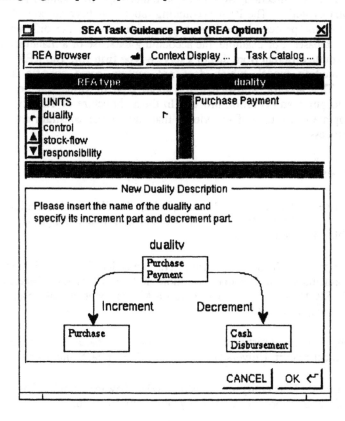

Figure 4.2 Snapshot of REAtool's Task Guidance Panel

A snapshot of Task Guidance Panel is shown in Figure 4.2 to demonstrate the look and feel of SEAtool. Assume a user has chosen the task New Duality Description from Task Catalog. A Dialog Page for describing a new duality is placed in Working Space. The user is first asked to supply the name of the new duality. The user is also asked to specify the Increment and Decrement parts of this duality. After the user clicks the OK button to confirm the REA description, evolution operators will be evoked to complete the evolution task. After that, a newly created duality is shown in the REA Browser.

5. Concluding Remarks

In this research, we have defined a set of basic evolution schema operators, and have employed evolution heuristics to guide the evolution process. We have also explored the use of domain-specific knowledge to guide the use of the evolution operators. The REA accounting model has been used on our research as an example of such domain-specific knowledge. The SEAtool and REAtool experimental prototypes demonstrate our reseults.

As a future research direction, we will explore more specific domain knowledge to guide schema evolution. The REA accounting model has been successfully used to guide an evolution process, but different types of firms may use different types of accounting databases. For example, the accounting database of a manufacturing-type firm may be quite different from that of a service-type firm [6]. The REA model is a general accounting model, which does not capture some specific sub-domain knowledge. This specific knowledge for some type of firms can be used as a "template" to guide an evolution process. In the architecture of REAtool, the sub-domain template is a source of knowledge that can further constrain and guide the evolution process.

References

1. Banerjee, J., Chou, H-T., Garza, J., Kim, W., Woelk, D., Ballou, N., and Kim, H., "Data Model Issues for Object-Oriented Applications," ACM TOOIS, 5:1, January, 1987.

2. Banerjee, J., Kim, W., Kim, H., and Korth, H., Semantics and Implementation of Schema Evolution in Object-Oriented Databases, Proc. ACM/SIGMOD Annual Conference on Management of Data, San Francisco, California, May 1987.

3. Chen, J.-L. "Heuristic-Based Conceptual Database Schema Evolution," Technical Report, University of Southern California, September 1994.

4. Chen, P. P., "The entity-relationship model: Toward a unified View of data.," ACM Transactions on Database Systems, 1:9-36, 1976.

5. Chiristodoulakis, S., Vanderbroek, J., Li, J., Wan, S., Wang, Y., Papa, M., and Bertino, E., "Development of a Multimedia Information System for an Office Environment." In Proc. of the 10th Int'l Conf. on VLDB, 1984, Pp. 261-271.

6. Grabski, S. and Marsh, R., "Integrating Accounting and Advanced Manufacturing Information Systems: An ABC and REA-Based Approach," AIS Research Symposium, 1994, Phoenix, AZ.

7. Hammer, M. and McLeod, D., "Database Description with SDM: A Semantic Database Model", ACM TODS 6, 3, September 1981, 351-387.

8. Li, Q. and McLeod, D., Conceptual Database Evolution Through Learning, Object-Oriented Databases and Applications, Gupta, R. and Horowitz, E. (Editors), Prentice-Hall, 1989.

9. McCarthy, W., "The REA Accounting Model: A Generalized Framework for Accounting Systems in a Shared Environment," Accounting Review, July 1982, pp. 554-578.

10 NeXTSTEP Version 3, NeXT Computer, Inc., 1990. (note: NeXTstep is a registed trademark of NeXT Computer, Inc.)

11. Navathe, S. B., Geum, S., Desci, D. K., and Lam, H., "Conceptual Design for Non-database Experts with an Interactive Schema Tailing Tool", Proc. of the 9th Int'l Conf. on the Entity-Relationship approach, Lausanne, Switzerland, Oct., 1990.

12. Penney, D. J. and Stein, J., Class Modification in the GemStone Object-Oriented DBMS. In Proceedings of the Conference on Object-Oriented Programming Systems, Languages, and Applications, pages 111-117, 1987.

13. Skarra, A. H., and Zdonik, S. B., The Management of Changing Types in an Object-Oriented Database, Proc. ACM Conference on Object-Oriented Programming Systems, Languages, and Applications, Portland, Oregon, September 1986.

14. Su, S., Krishnamurthy, V. and Lam, H., "An Object-Oriented Semantic Association Model (OSAM*)," AI in Industrial Engineering and Manufacturing: Theoretical Issues and Applications, Kumara, S., Kashyap, R., and Soyster, A. (Eds.). American Institue of Industrial Engineering, 1989.

15. Versant ODBMS, "Versant System Manual," Versant Object technology, 1992, Menlo Park, CA. (note: Versant is a trademark of Versant Object Technology Co.)

Designing and Implementing Inter-Client Communication in the O_2 Object-Oriented Database Management System

Antonio Carzaniga, Gian Pietro Picco
and Giovanni Vigna

CEFRIEL
via Emanueli 15, 20126 Milano (Italy)

Abstract. One of the requirements for an object-oriented database to support advanced applications is a communication mechanism. The Inter-Client Communication Mechanism (ICCM) is a set of data structures and functions developed for the O_2 database, which provides this kind of service. Communication is achieved through shared persistent objects, implementing the basic idea of mailbox. One to one connections are established between different processes accessing the database. Methods and data structure defined in the ICCM support connection set-up, disconnection, and all the basic data transfer facilities. In this paper, we describe the concepts of the ICCM and an overview of its implementation.

Keywords and phrases: object oriented database, client/server architecture, communication.

1 Introduction

Object-oriented databases are widely used in many engineering fields requiring a sophisticated data modeling system, like software engineering environments and CAD applications. In such environments complex data are shared by many persons; cooperation among developers and interaction with tools is a critical issue.

Nearly all OODBMSs currently available are based on a client/server architecture. In particular, we are using O_2 [7] which is based on a client-oriented concept that gives computational power to each client. Others (like GemStone [4]) prefer to have methods executed by the server according to a more centralized schema.

Our experience in building a process-centered software engineering environment (PSEE) has pointed out the importance of distribution of data and computations among clients [2]. The management of such a distributed model requires complex data sharing and communication, in order to address both architectural and tool integration issues.

A specific communication system other than the standard UNIX ones is necessary if we want to exchange complex structured data among clients. Thus, we isolated the problem of communication from the context of our application, and developed a stand-alone, general-purpose O_2 module, called ICCM (Inter Client Communication Mechanism), intended to be an extension of the services provided by the OODBMS.

These services do not depend upon the particular application. They may be of any use whenever complex data have to be passed between user applications allocated to different clients.

In this paper we present the idea behind ICCM, together with an overview of the provided services. Since it is based on the O_2 OODBMS, in Section 2 we provide a short description of this system. In Section 3 the underlying ideas and concepts are described, while Section 4 explains the data structures and services provided by the ICCM. Section 5 describes the ICCM communication protocol. Section 6 gives some insights on how ICCM can be used in a real user application and how such an application has to be structured in order to interact with ICCM. Section 7 outlines ICCM evolution. Finally, Section 8 draws some conclusion and highlights some issues about our future work involving the ICCM.

2 The O_2 OODMBS

O_2 [10, 7] is a distributed Object-Oriented Database Management System, based on a client-server architecture.

The logical structure of an O_2 data base is bound to a *schema*, i.e., a collection of names and definitions of classes, types, functions, objects and values. There may exist any number of logically separate schemas at one time.

A *base* is a collection of data whose structure conforms to the structural definition in a schema. Several different bases might be associated with each schema.

Data manipulation is achieved using the O_2C language, an extension of ANSI-standard C, as well as the O_2SQL, an *ad hoc* object-oriented query language, whose syntax is styled on IBM SQL standard, and which is likely to become the SQL standard for OODBMSs. O_2 also provides interfaces towards standard programming languages, namely C and C++.

Data are represented by *values* and *objects*. A value is an instance of a given *type*. A type is a generic description of a data structure in terms of atomic types (integers, characters, and so on) and structured types (tuples, sets, and lists). An object is an instance of a given *class* and encapsulates a value and the behavior of that value. The behavior of an object is fully described by the set of *methods* attached to it.

An object or a value may be given an identifier, i.e., a *name*, by which O_2 commands, methods, and application programs may refer to it quickly and specifically. Such name is global within the schema.

Objects and values in the system can be either *persistent* or not. An object is persistent if it remains in the database after the successful termination of the transaction which created it. Persistence is granted as follows: *Every named object in the database is persistent, and every component of a persistent object is persistent. No other objects are persistent.* The same rule applies to values.

Thus, named objects and named values are the roots of persistence. That is, they are used as handles from which every persistent object or value can be referenced.

Every update to persistent data must be performed within a transaction. If two clients access the same object or value in transaction mode, the locks obtained by the first client force the second to wait. Thus, critical sections corresponding to updates should be limited in time, and should not involve several objects, in order to improve performance and avoid deadlocks[1].

Objects and values not bound to a persistency root are automatically garbage-collected at the end of a transaction.

3   The Underlying Idea

Common UNIX inter-process communication mechanisms, like pipes and sockets, cannot be used for communication among O_2 clients, since these mechanisms are suitable only to transfer non-structured data, like integers or strings.

Our goal, on the contrary, is to exchange true O_2 objects. O_2 objects may have any internal structure, consequently, in order to transfer an object, e.g., via a socket, it would be necessary to transform it in a character stream and then reassemble it again upon receipt. This solution is not feasible since it would be very inefficient and, in any case, it would produce *a copy* of the original object. In addition, it is not possible to simply pass to another client the identifier of an object, because object identifiers exist only in the O_2 engine, and they are not accessible from the user environment.

Intuitively, since we can use neither UNIX mechanisms, nor dedicated O_2 primitives, the only mean currently available to support communication is the *database itself* or, in other words, *persistent objects* which can be accessed by every client, as explained in section 2.

---

[1]In the current implementation of O_2, locks are associated with pages rather than with objects. This may lead to the odd situation in which clients working on completely different objects within the same base can experience deadlocks. O_2Technology is steering towards replacing page locking with object locking.

Figure 1: Using a persistent object to communicate two clients.

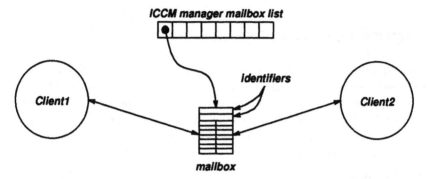

Figure 2: Two clients communicating through the ICCM.

The raw solution using this concept implements the mechanism illustrated in figure 1: the message sender puts an O_2 object into a named (i.e., persistent) variable, whose name is known by both the sender and the recipient. The recipient can read the contents of the persistent named variable and operate on it. This initial solution suffers from some drawbacks, if applied as it is within a concurrent multi-client perspective:

- The shared object name must be hard-wired within clients code.

- No parallelism is allowed. After the message sender begins a communication session by filling the named variable, no other client can update this variable (without causing data loss) until the recipient has actually read the variable.

We could improve parallelism by increasing the number of named variables that support data exchange. Still, the number of common variables, would be statically limited. Furthermore, it would be proportional to the square of the number of communicating clients.

On the contrary, a highly parallel and dynamic mechanism is desirable, in order to limit the overhead imposed at run-time on the environment, and to provide a highly flexible communication mechanism.

Figure 2 shows the Inter-Client Communication Mechanism (ICCM), an enhancement of the basic mechanism described above, that we designed to improve the communication among O_2 clients [9]. Once again, there is an object, called

ICCM manager, that is given a name (i.e., O2ClientMgr) in the clients schema, and it is therefore visible within clients scopes. The ICCM manager is not an information container itself, instead it owns a list of *mailboxes*. The mailbox objects are the communication channels through which information flows from a client to another. The ICCM manager provides services (i.e., methods) to correctly create and manage these mailboxes when establishing a connection between clients.

4   ICCM Features and Services

ICCM is actually an O_2 schema (i.e., class definitions together with persistent objects name definitions) providing communication services. ICCM has to be imported into the user application schema whenever it is necessary to use inter-client communication facilities. In the following subsections we describe the basic components of our mechanism: mailboxes, messages, and the communication service manager.

4.1   Mailboxes

ICCM mailboxes are not just like the well-known mailboxes. Usually mailboxes are associated with recipients. Whenever a message has to be delivered, the message queue, representing the mailbox, is reached using a reference to the recipient. For example, to send a message to A one would use A->mailbox->putmsg(msg).

We could not afford this solution because write operations must be performed during a transaction, in order to make changes in the recipient message queue visible to the recipient itself; hence, accessing the recipient mailbox would lock the recipient object altogether.

We decided to cluster the queues, acting as mailboxes between two objects, in a unique data structure, in order to avoid the recipient object locking. Each communicating client owns a unique identifier, assigned by the ICCM manager at setup time. The mailbox queues are tagged with the identifiers corresponding to the connected clients, so that read/write operations access the proper queue. Adopting this solution, accessing the mailbox queues does not involve any of the communicating objects, allowing a greater level of parallelism and better performance.

By the way, ICCM mailboxes own methods to insert and retrieve messages, and to test emptiness, this way implementing an easy-to-use two-way communication link. ICCM mailboxes allow 1 : 1 connections only, for performance reasons. In fact, since mailboxes are persistent, write operations have to be performed during a transaction; if 1 : n connections were possible, any of the several clients, accessing a queue during a write operation, should synchronize with the others. Implementing n : n connections could only worsen the problem.

4.2 Messages

Mailboxes can contain only ICCM messages, which are O_2 objects. They can be logically divided into two classes:

- *User-defined messages.* They are general-purpose object containers.

- *Built-in messages.* They are used for "system" operations, like setting up or removing a connection.

ICCM messages contain a **name**, which is a string, and a **data** field, which is a list of objects of class **Object**. The **Object** class is the root of the O_2 class hierarchy. Consequently, due to polymorphism and late binding, every O_2 object fits in the **data** field, no matter what its type is. It is up to the receiver to correctly handle (cast) such objects.

Note that the current solution has both advantages and disadvantages: polymorphism allows to pass any kind of object (no matter what is its complexity and structure), but if you need to transmit bare *values*, you need to envelope them into *ad hoc* classes. We are investigating solutions to allow a "smart" inclusion of values into ICCM messages, in order to allow generic data to be exchanged.

4.3 ICCM Manager

The ICCM manager provides all the data structures and services needed to establish and manage communication between clients.

It contains, in its data structure, a list of mailbox objects representing all the communication channels connecting client pairs during ICCM execution. This structure is centralized. It constitutes the only bottleneck to communication management, because access has to be serialized. Anyway, since such access is needed only at connection setup, the additional overhead is little, and generally negligible if compared with the longer time needed for client actual invocation.

The most important services provided by the ICCM manager are:

- *Connection set-up.* The ICCM manager object provides two distinct methods to set up a communication link: **setupO2Client**, which performs both the invocation of the callee O_2 client and its connection to the caller, and **connectToO2Client**, which establishes a connection between the caller and an already running client.

- *Mailbox retrieval.* As soon as the callee is either invoked or requested for a new connection, it has to scan the mailbox list owned by the ICCM manager, in order to retrieve the mailbox created by the caller, and that ought to be used for further communication. The ICCM manager provides the method **seekForMailbox**, which searches the mailbox list for a mailbox matching the caller and callee identifiers. Identifiers management is transparent to the user.

- *Communication shutdown.* The ICCM manager provide means to discard a communication channel between two clients. ICCM clients can remove mailboxes calling the `removeMailbox` method on the ICCM manager. Since *in itinere* data would be lost, the application programmer is responsible for the management of a data-loss free shutdown protocol.

5 Communication

An ICCM session has three phases: i) connection, ii) message exchange, iii) disconnection. We will describe here only the first phase, since it is the most important. A detailed description can be found in [9].

The connection phase follows a defined sequence of steps, which are coded into ICCM manager services. For the caller, the sequence is:

1. Create a new mailbox object.

2. Post a connection message in the newly created mailbox.

3. The connection may involve a client already using the ICCM, or a client that has to be invoked, and then connected.

   (a) In the former case, the caller client searches the ICCM manager mailbox list for an existing mailbox already bound to the callee, and posts a message of connection request, containing its own identifier. In other words, it "hires" a mailbox currently used by the callee to communicate with another client.

   (b) If the connection involves a client that does not yet exist, the O_2 client is invoked. During the client start-up phase, the new client is given its own identifier, and is also informed about the identity of the client that invoked it.

4. Wait for the acknowledgement, which must be sent by the callee through the mailbox created in 1.

If the callee client already exists, it will simply find in one of its mailboxes the connection request message, containing the identifier of the caller.

Otherwise, the newly created client is informed by the invocation mechanism about the identity of its creator. In both cases, the callee will:

1. Search the ICCM manager mailbox list for an existing mailbox whose identifiers match both caller and callee identifiers.

2. Read the message from the mailbox, checking if it is the right connection message.

3. Send an acknowledge message back to the caller, through the same mail-box.

Since mailboxes are attached to the ICCM manager which is a persistent object, every mailbox is persistent too. Nevertheless, after the first scanning of ICCM manager mailbox list, performed at communication set-up time, the callee client creates a local direct reference to the mailbox, thus allowing fast access.

Since every read/write operation on a persistent object has to be performed within a transaction, the situation described above has an important consequence: *once we have retrieved the correct mailbox M from the global mailbox list, we can lock M exclusively without locking the whole persistent structure.*

In other words, we use the ICCM manager mailbox list only to ensure persistency and visibility of mailboxes to all the clients, but we can lock just one mailbox at a time (except for the relatively unfrequent communication set-up phases), thus maximizing parallelism[2].

6 An Example

In this section we describe a "toy" example, whose purpose is to show how mechanisms described in previous sections can be used within actual applications.

Three clients are involved:

- Client1 and Client2 play the role of "master" O_2 clients, e.g., they could be applications performing some kind of independent computation.

- Tool represents a "slave" service provider, receiving both connection and service requests from "master" clients and returning outputs to them. Obviously, it is an O_2 client.

Figure 3 represents the following situation. Client1 calls the setupO2-Client method on the ICCM manager, in order to actually invoke the Tool. Hence, a new mailbox is created and filled with a connection message. As soon as Tool is running, it calls the method seekForMailbox on the ICCM manager. The method retrieves the callee and the caller identifier from the Tool process environment, and it searches the centralized mailbox list for a mailbox carrying the corresponding identifiers pair. When the mailbox is found, a connection acknowledge is sent back to the caller.

After the connection is successfully set up, Client1 posts a service request message to Tool. Tool retrieves the message, performs the service, and sends a reply message. Meanwhile, Client2 requests a connection to client Tool.

---

[2]This will have an even greater impact when O_2 will support object locks, as pointed out in section 2.

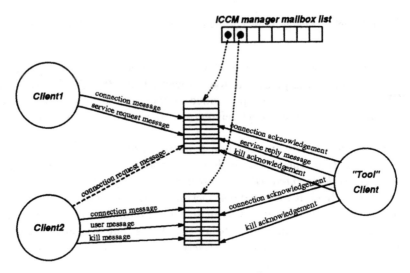

Figure 3: An example.

Since `Tool` is already up[3], `Client2` has to call the method `connectToO2Client` instead of `setupO2Client`. This method performs the following actions:

1. It creates a new mailbox object, tagged with `Client2` and `Tool` identifiers, and filled with a connection message.

2. It searches the ICCM manager mailbox list for a mailbox already connected to `Tool`, and posts a connection request message in it.

After receiving the connection request message, `Tool` calls the method `seekForMailbox` on the ICCM manager. The method retrieves the newly created mailbox and posts an acknowledge message in it, thus establishing a new connection.

At a given time, `Client2` decides that `Tool` is no longer needed, neither by `Client2` nor by other "master" clients. Thus, `Client2` terminates the execution of `Tool` by sending a kill message. `Tool`, upon receiving the message, performs the correct clean-up operations. Then, it broadcasts a message of acknowledgement to all clients connected with it, to warn them that it is going to terminate. Among the clients receiving this message, there is also `Client2`, that is now ready to remove the `Tool` mailbox from the ICCM manager list.

Note that all message processing is made synchronously, by polling the mailboxes connected to clients. In this respect, ICCM resembles somehow programming with plain X, following an event-driven programming paradigm. In fact, the main polling loop has to contain conditional tests in order to recognize the received messages and execute the corresponding "callbacks".

---

[3]We assume that `Client1` and `Client2` are clients of the same application. Thus, they are aware of which clients have already been invoked.

7 Evolution of the ICCM

We designed the ICCM for the purpose of supporting the distributed architecture of SPADE-1 2.0 [3, 1, 6]. The evolution of this architectural schema revealed some issues related to the ICCM. In particular, the ICCM serves the enactment environment of SPADE-1 2.0, supporting computation distribution, and the data integration mechanism, passing O_2 parameters to integrated tools. Performance and small critical sections are requested by the enactment environment. Flexibility and easy connection set-up are the requirements posed by the data integration mechanism.

7.1 A new ICCM

In order to fulfill the needs of performances and flexibility, we re-designed the ICCM. The new ICCM resembles much the concepts of UNIX sockets [5].

It features *port* objects that are the well-known access points for communicating clients. Two straightforward primitives set up the connection, namely, **connect** and **accept**. When an O_2 client issues a **connect** on a port, two connection end-points are created: one is returned to the calling client, the other one is enqueued in a list associated to the port. When another client calls the **accept** method on the same port, it retrieves the enqueued connection end-point, so that the communication link is completely established. Once the connection is available, methods **read**, **write** and **isEmpty** can be used to exchange data.

This mechanism passes object references, one at a time. There is no particular message format. It does not need any identifier. No handshake protocol is defined: it is up to the application programmer to coordinate the communication session. No explicit shutdown procedures are defined: the channels are persistent as long as the two communicating parties keep their references. Furthermore, the schema of the new ICCM comes with no pre-defined persistent objects; again, the application programmer is responsible for defining his/her own ports.

Summing up, the new ICCM is faithful to these principles:

- It is simple and, thus, very efficient.

- It provides low-level primitives. Thus, it is flexible.

Almost any object-oriented communication protocol can be built on top of the new ICCM layer.

8 Conclusions and future work

We presented here an Inter-Client Communication Mechanism for the O_2 OODBMS. The need for such a mechanism stemmed from some issues concerning the architecture of a process-centered software engineering environment.

Nevertheless, the findings and the outcomes of our experience might be generalized to a wider range of applications, which use an object-oriented repository, possibly even different from O_2. We described here the idea underlying the mechanism, an overview of the data structures and a brief description of the services exported. We are currently using ICCM in the development of our PSEE, both testing and enhancing its features.

Future work will include:

- the development of a sound technique to allow generic messages (including any value or object) to be passed between clients;

- the integration of new O_2 features, provided by future releases. In particular, O_2 Technology plans to introduce active database issues, as described in [8]. This feature will be based on the *trigger* concept, which should achieve asynchronous message passing.

Acknowledgments

The authors wish to thank Sergio Bandinelli, Alfonso Fuggetta, and Luigi Lavazza for their comments and insights, which have been helpful both in developing ICCM, and in writing and refining this paper.

References

[1] S. Bandinelli, M. Braga, A. Fuggetta, and L. Lavazza. The Architecture of the SPADE-1 Process-Centered SEE. In *3rd European Workshop on Software Process Technology*, Grenoble (France), February 1994.

[2] Sergio Bandinelli, Luciano Baresi, Alfonso Fuggetta, and Luigi Lavazza. Requirements and Early Experiences in the Implementation of the SPADE Repository using Object-Oriented Technology. In *Proceedings of the International Symposium on Object Technologies for Advanced Software*, Kanazawa, Japan, November 1993.

[3] Sergio Bandinelli, Alfonso Fuggetta, Carlo Ghezzi, and Sergio Grigolli. Process Enactment in SPADE. In *Proceedings of the Second European Workshop on Software Process Technology*, Trondheim (Norway), September 1992. Springer-Verlag.

[4] Paul Butterworth, Allen Otis, and Jacob Stein. The GemStone Object Database Management System. *Communications of the ACM*, 34(10), October 1991.

[5] Antonio Carzaniga. O_2 sockets. Tecnical report, CEFRIEL, Milano (Italy), March 1994.

[6] Antonio Carzaniga and Giovanni Vigna. The Design and Implementation of SPADE-1 2.0. Technical report, CEFRIEL, June 1994.

[7] O. Deux. The O_2 System. *Communications of the ACM*, 34(10), October 1991.

[8] O_2Technology, Inria, CEFRIEL, University of Frankfurt, and University of Grenoble. Architecture and functionalities of the GoodStep repository as implemented in the first prototype. Technical report, O_2Technology, 1993. Esprit Project 6115 (GOODSTEP) deliverable.

[9] Gian Pietro Picco and Giovanni Vigna. The SPADE Way to Inter-Client Communication in O_2. Technical report, CEFRIEL, 1993. Technical Report N.99401.

[10] O_2 Technology. *The O_2 User Manual.* O_2Technology, 1993. Release 4.3.

Rigorous Object-Oriented Analysis

Ana M. D. Moreira and Robert G. Clark

Department of Computing Science and Mathematics
University Of Stirling
STIRLING FK9 4LA, Scotland, UK
amm@cs.stir.ac.uk
rgc@cs.stir.ac.uk

Abstract. The Rigorous Object-Oriented Analysis (ROOA) method provides a systematic development process which takes a set of informal requirements and produces a formal object-oriented analysis model. The model, which is expressed in LOTOS, integrates the static, dynamic and functional aspects of a problem and acts as a requirements specification. As LOTOS specifications can be executed symbolically, rapid prototyping can be used to check the conformance of the specification against the requirements and to detect inconsistencies, omissions or ambiguities so that feedback can be given to the requirements capture process.

1   Introduction

Object-oriented approaches and formal methods have both been proposed as ways of alleviating problems in the development and maintenance of reliable software systems. In the Rigorous Object-Oriented Analysis (ROOA) method [13], they are applied in combination to the requirements analysis phase of the software life cycle.

The starting point in formal software development is a *formal requirements specification* of what the proposed system is to achieve. Once a formal specification has been produced, it is possible, at least in theory, to verify a design and eventual implementation with respect to that specification. Two important questions remain, however. How is the initial formal requirements specification created from a set of informal requirements and how can it be validated with respect to those requirements? It is clear that these cannot be formal processes.

Requirements analysis methods are concerned with structuring and understanding the information collected during requirements capture. They achieve this by building one or more models. The ROOA method provides a systematic development process which takes a set of informal requirements and produces a formal object-oriented analysis model which is expressed in the standard formal description language LOTOS [1, 2]. The aim of the model is to give a complete, unambiguous and accurate description of the problem in terms of entities from the problem domain. It describes both the static and dynamic aspects of a problem and acts as a requirements specification.

Building a model will often expose shortcomings in the captured requirements. This is especially true when the language used has a formally defined semantics and can be executed symbolically, as is the case with LOTOS. Tools are available for checking the model's syntax and static semantics and this, combined with prototyping, allows omissions, contradictions, ambiguities and inconsistencies in the requirements to be detected sufficiently early in the development so that feedback can be given to the requirements capture process.

The LOTOS SMILE simulator [5] supports nondeterminism and value generation. Value generation allows symbolic execution of a specification where sets of possible values are used rather than particular values. Nondeterminism can be used to model behaviour in such a way that premature design decisions are not made.

The resulting specification can be used as the first stage in a software development trajectory where a requirements specification is transformed into a design specification either by using correctness preserving transformations or by using prototyping to ensure that the two specifications conform to one another [3].

2 Object-Oriented Analysis and LOTOS

Object-oriented analysis (OOA) methods, such as [4, 10, 16, 17], create an informal analysis model or set of models. The *object model*, based on an extension to entity-relationship diagrams, describes the static properties of a system while the *dynamic model*, normally expressed in terms of state transition diagrams, describes its behaviour. Some methods, such as [16], also propose a *functional model*, which uses data flow diagrams to describe the meaning of the services in the object model and the actions in the dynamic model. In most methods, the object model is central with the dynamic and functional models being of lesser importance.

The purpose of an analysis model is to describe the problem, not to propose a solution. Entities in the real world exist in parallel. A major advantage of the object-oriented approach is that it supports the direct modelling of real world entities as a set of autonomous objects which communicate with one another by sending messages. An object-oriented analysis model should therefore represent the requirements as a set of communicating concurrent objects even when the eventual implementation is to be sequential. The formal language used to represent the formal model must support this view.

LOTOS has a process part (based on a combination of CSP [8] and CCS [11]) and a data typing part based on abstract data types (ADTs) [6]. Processes communicate by synchronizing on events during which information may be exchanged. As there is a straightforward mapping between concurrent objects and process instances and between message passing and event synchronization, LOTOS is well suited to representing the requirements as a set of communicating concurrent objects. In Section 4, we describe how inheritance can be modelled in LOTOS.

As we believe that a practical method should be based on standard languages, we have not used any of the suggested object-oriented extensions to

LOTOS (e.g. [15]). An important part of the ROOA method is to give a formal interpretation of object-oriented analysis constructs in ISO Standard LOTOS.

Producing an analysis model from a set of informal requirements is not easy. Object-oriented analysis methods propose strategies for the identification of objects and their attributes, services and relationships. The ROOA method gives a set of rules for the systematic creation of a single integrated formal object-oriented analysis model which brings together the static and dynamic aspects of a problem. This is in contrast to other OOA methods which produce separate models that can be difficult to integrate and keep consistent. Most of these other methods are also much better at describing the static aspects of a problem than they are at describing the expected behaviour. The LOTOS model produced by ROOA is primarily a dynamic model and is therefore good at the description of behaviour. Nevertheless, its structure is directly related to the structure of the object model and so it is equally good at describing the static properties.

Other work on integrating LOTOS with object-oriented development methods has been reported by Hedlund [7]. He does not, however, deal with the analysis phase and his study is restricted to one particular method [10]. Our approach has similarities with that of Zave [18], although a major feature of ROOA is its integration with OOA methods. A description of the application of ROOA to a banking problem has been given in [14].

3   Objects, Classes and Class Templates

There are many different definitions of objects and classes in the object-oriented literature. We have adopted the definitions used in the Open Distributed Processing Reference Model [9]:

- A *class template* specifies the common features of a collection of objects.
- A *class* is the set of objects which possess the common features specified by a class template.
- An *object* is a member of a class and is created by instantiating a class template.

Using these definitions, the entities in an object model created by the informal OOA methods correspond to class templates.

4   The ROOA Method

ROOA consists of a preliminary task of building an object model followed by the two main tasks of refining the object model and building a formal LOTOS OOA model. Figure 1 illustrates ROOA in the context of the software development life cycle and shows how it interacts with the requirements capture and the design phases. It is important to note that the steps of ROOA are iterative.

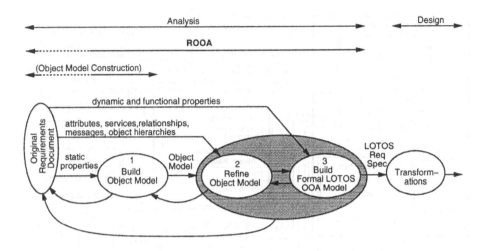

Fig. 1. Context of ROOA in the development life cycle

Task 1: Build an Object Model

The construction of the object model is, of necessity, informal. It is performed by applying any of the existing OOA methods, such as [4, 10, 16, 17], and can be accomplished by a separate team. The advantage of starting with an object model produced by any OOA method is that much of the initial work involved in identifying objects in the informal requirements will have already been done. Application of the next two tasks of ROOA may lead to changes in the object model. If any omissions or inconsistencies are found, the requirements document must be changed.

Task 2: Refine the Object Model

Task 2.1: Complete the Object Model. OOA methods differ in the information they put in the object model during the analysis phase. For example, Coad and Yourdon [4] give attributes, services, static relationships and message connections while Rumbaugh *et al.* [16] give only attributes and static relationships. Also, many OOA methods do not include *interface objects*, i.e. the objects through which the environment communicates with the system. We must ensure that the object model includes attributes, services, static relationships, interface objects and message connections, although the identification of services and message connections may be left to Task 2.2.

A Coad and Yourdon object model for a version of the warehouse management system presented by Jacobson [10] is shown in Figure 2. This model was created using ObjecTool[1]. Each node shows the object name, its attributes and the services offered. Arrows indicate message connections, i.e. calls on an object's services.

---

[1] ObjecTool is a trademark of Object International, Inc.

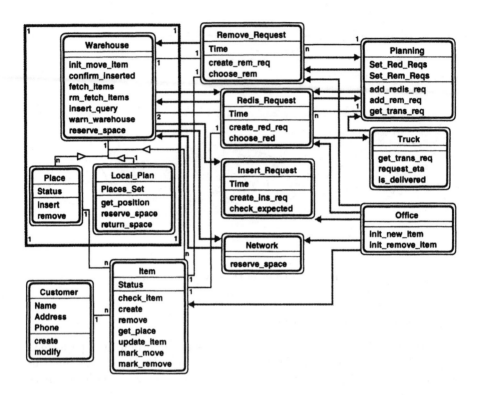

Fig. 2. Coad and Yourdon object model for a warehouse management system

Task 2.2: Initial Identification of Dynamic Behaviour. An object model describes the static properties of a system. To capture and record dynamic behaviour from the information given in the informal requirements, we model the behaviour that the environment requires from the system as a set of *interface scenarios*, called *use cases* by Jacobson [10]. Starting with an interface scenario event, we trace through the object model identifying the object interactions required to satisfy the requested behaviour and record the information in an Event Trace Diagram (ETD) [16]. The information from the different ETDs is then collected in an Object Communication Table (OCT). Eventually, this table will consist of five columns, but here we only build the first four which contain: (i) the objects that form the object model; (ii) the services offered by each object; (iii) the calls of lower level services that a service requires to carry out its function; (iv) the clients of a service.

Table 1 shows the entries in the OCT which correspond to the objects Office and Remove_Request defined in the object model of Figure 2.

The first two columns in the OCT duplicate information given in the object model. Tools such as ObjecTool permit extra information to be recorded about attributes, services, etc. Such information is not presented diagrammatically in the object model, but is available in textual form. Instead of building the OCT

Objects	Services Offered	Services Required	Clients	Gates
Office	init_new_item	Network.reserve_space	Interface	usr3
		Insert_Request.create_ins_req		
	init_remove_item	Item.check_item	Interface	usr3
		Network.reserve_space		
		Redis_Request.create_red_req		
		Item.mark_move		
		Remove_Request.create_rem_req		
		Item.mark_remove		
Remove_Request	create_rem_req	Planning.add_rem_req	Office	req2
	choose_rem	Warehouse.rm_fetch_items	Planning	p1

Table 1. Part of an OCT

by hand, we can record, for each service, its clients and the lower level services it requires. We have constructed a translator which takes the textual output from ObjecTool and creates the corresponding OCT.

Task 2.3: Structure the Object Model. This task is difficult and so we cannot expect to do it completely and correctly in the first iteration. We use *aggregates* and *subsystems* to structure a complex model. Aggregates are complex objects which are defined by combination of simpler objects called *components*. An aggregate is a representation of an entity from the real world. It usually has behaviour of its own which is combined with the behaviour of its components. Aggregation is a strong mechanism for structuring a model and, in its more interesting form, the components are hidden from the rest of the world. Components may, however, be visible so that they can be shared with other objects. In the object model shown in Figure 2, for example, Warehouse is an aggregate with components Place, Local_Plan and Item. The components Place and Local_Plan are hidden, but Item is visible.

The fundamental difference between an aggregate and a subsystem is that, while the components are an intrinsic part of the aggregate, and the aggregate is itself an object from the problem domain, a subsystem is merely a grouping of related objects. Objects within a subsystem should be logically related, highly coupled and the interaction between subsystems should be low. Candidates for grouping are a superclass and its subclasses, a set of clients which use the same servers, and a set of servers which have the same clients. We have found that the low level objects in an object model often remain almost unchanged during the development, but that the high level structure is less stable.

Task 3: Build the LOTOS Formal Model

In the LOTOS formal model, a class template is either specified as a process[2] together with one or more ADTs (the attributes are specified by one or more *sorts* given as parameters of the process) or, if it only plays the role of an attribute, it is specified as an ADT. A LOTOS ADT defines a sort together with a set of operations on that sort. LOTOS processes communicate by synchronizing on events which take place at gates. Communication between client and server is modelled by two processes synchronizing on an event with the structure:

⟨*gate*⟩ ⟨*service name*⟩ ⟨*object identifier of server*⟩ ⟨*optional parameters*⟩

The LOTOS formal analysis model:

- Specifies the object model by giving a mathematical definition for each class template and relationship.
- Adds the dynamic behaviour of each class template.
- Shows the message connections between objects in the system and specifies the information passed when objects communicate.
- Models the whole system as a set of communicating objects which are composed using the LOTOS parallel operators. The operator | | | indicates *interleaving* while | [a, b] | indicates that processes synchronize with one another on gates a and b.

An object model gives a static description of a system and is composed of class templates. The central feature of a LOTOS analysis model is that it is primarily a *dynamic* model, although it contains all the static information given in an object model. The required overall behaviour is described by means of a LOTOS *behaviour expression* which is composed of objects.

A major task in the creation of the formal LOTOS model is the transformation from a static to a dynamic model. The OCT and the Object Communication Diagram, described below, are two intermediate structures created to help in the transformation. As we shall see, the structure of the static object model is preserved in the structure of the behaviour expression in the LOTOS dynamic model. Human beings find static structures much easier to understand than dynamic ones. Hence, the close connection between the dynamic model and the object model is of major help in understanding the specification.

Task 3.1 : Create an Object Communication Diagram (OCD). The OCD is a graphical representation of the eventual LOTOS behaviour expression. In the first iteration, each class template is replaced by an instantiation of the class template (an object) and each message connection is replaced by a named gate. We must first determine the gate names. Where several clients require a common set of services from a server, they do so at a common gate. If there

---

[2] An object corresponds to the instantiation of a LOTOS process. When the distinction is clear from the context, we use the term *process* for both a process definition and a process instantiation.

is no overlap between services, then separate gates are used. This information can be automatically calculated from the information in columns 1 to 4 of the OCT and is entered in column 5, as shown in Table 1. The OCD corresponding to the object model of Figure 2 is given in Figure 3. The only difference is that Insert_Request, Remove_Request and Redis_Request have been grouped to form the subsystem Request. In later iterations, the diagram is generalised to deal with multiple instances of the same class.

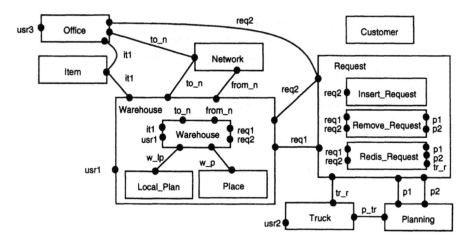

Fig. 3. Initial OCD

In the beginning, some of the objects (e.g. Customer) may not be connected by arcs to the rest of the diagram. As the method is applied, these objects will either disappear from the OCD (i.e. they will be demoted to being only attributes of other objects) or be connected to the others. New groupings may also appear, refining the diagram.

Task 3.2: Specify Class Templates. The simplest object behaviour is specified as a process offering its services as the alternatives of a LOTOS choice expression. Two kinds of service are offered: selectors and modifiers. A selector will return the value of an attribute to a client while a modifier will update an object's attributes. Specifying a class template often shows up inconsistencies or omissions in the object model and in the requirements.

Suppose that we have a class template A which inherits from an abstract superclass template B. Using incremental inheritance, this can be specified by the following LOTOS processes:

```
process B[g](state : State_Sort) : exit(State_Sort) :=
    g !selector_1 !Get_id(state) ... ;
    ...
```

```
    exit(state)
  []
    g !modifier_1 !Get_id(state) ... ;
    ...
    exit(F1(state))
  []
    ...
endproc

process A[c, d](state : State_Sort,
        ext_state : Ext_State_Sort) : noexit :=
  (   B[c](state) >> accept new_state : State_Sort
        in exit(new_state, ext_state)
    []
      c !new_selector_1 !Get_id(state) ... ;
      ...
      exit(state, ext_state)
    []
      c !new_modifier_1 !Get_id(state) ... ;
      ...
      exit(F2(state), F3(ext_state))
    []
      ...
  ) >> accept new_state : State_Sort,
            new_ext_state : Ext_State_Sort
        in A[c, d](new_state, new_ext_state)
endproc
```

The operator [] is the LOTOS nondeterministic choice operator and >> is the enable operator. The behaviour expression Y >> Z means that on successful completion of process Y, we start execution of process Z. The operator accept ... in is used to pass values as we exit from one process and enable another.

The attributes of B are components of sort State_Sort which A extends with components of sort Ext_State_Sort. The operations which actually access or update an object's attributes are defined in ADTs. Examples are F1 and F2 which return a new State_Sort value, F3 which returns a new value of sort Ext_State_Sort and Get_id which returns the object identifier. The object identifier has been assumed to be a component of sort State_Sort. In [12], we describe how incremental inheritance in LOTOS can be restricted so that behavioural inheritance is guaranteed.

A series of events is often required to provide a service. In the warehouse problem, for example, when the interface scenario synchronizes with Warehouse on event insert_query to ask if an item can be entered, Warehouse synchronizes with object Insert_Request on event check_expected to determine if the item is expected and then, in order to provide the result, synchronizes with the interface scenario on event rtn_insert_query.

```
usr1 !insert_query !ware_id ?ins_id:Ins_Req_Id ?t:Time;
req2 !check_expected !ins_id ?ok:Bool !ware_id !t;
usr1 !rtn_insert_query !ware_id !ok !ins_id;
```

The events **insert_query** and **rtn_insert_query** are to be interpreted as a single non-atomic communication between the interface scenario and **Warehouse**, corresponding to a call/return in programming languages.

As we are in the analysis phase, we are interested in the kind of information that is to be transferred between objects rather than in the details of the algorithm by which the information is to be calculated within an object. Hence, only the minimum information is specified in the ADTs which define an object's state. The functionality of all the required operations is given, but the defining equations are given only when they are needed to prototype the system. Further equations will be defined during the design phase.

Task 3.3: Compose the Objects into a Behaviour Expression. Once the class templates have been specified, it is necessary to ensure that they interact correctly with one another. Single instances of each class template are composed in parallel using the OCD as a model to give a LOTOS behaviour expression. We have an algorithm which converts an OCD into a LOTOS behaviour expression; it identifies the few pathological cases where this cannot be done [13]. An important rule is that if a server has several clients at the same gate then the server can either be grouped with all the clients or with none of them.

Task 3.4: Prototype the Specification. LOTOS tools are available to check the syntax and static semantics of the LOTOS specification and a LOTOS simulator can be used to check its dynamic behaviour. In Task 2, interface scenarios were used to define possible service requests from the environment and the expected responses from the system. Interface scenarios encoding this information are now defined and used to drive the simulation and to ensure that the specification has the expected behaviour. If prototyping shows up any omissions or inconsistencies, we must update the requirements and propagate the modifications through the various tasks.

The SMILE simulator [5] allows the use of uninstantiated variables within conditions and uses a *narrowing algorithm* to determine when a combination of conditions can never be true. Many more behaviours can then be examined with each simulation than is possible when all data values have to be instantiated.

In the first iteration, a behaviour expression consisting of single instances of class templates is prototyped as the emphasis is on ensuring that the individual class templates have been correctly specified. In later iterations, a behaviour expression consisting of multiple instances of class templates is prototyped so that we can check that the complete system has been properly specified.

Task 3.5: Refine the Specification

Task 3.5.1: Model Static Relationships. The first task in the second iteration is to model static (conceptual) relationships. A static relationship is modelled as an attribute in one of the objects involved in the relation (or both if the relationship is bidirectional) [13]. Depending on the cardinality of the relationship, the attribute will either be an object identifier or a set of object identifiers.

Task 3.5.2: Introduce Object Generators. Dealing with single instances of a class template simplifies the problem and allows us to prototype with a specific number of objects. However, in general, several instances of the same class may be required. This is achieved by defining an *object generator*. A possible object generator for the class template A shown in Task 3.2 is:

```
process Object_Generator_A[a, b](ids: Id_Set) : noexit :=
  a !create ?id: Id_Sort
             ?init_val1: Value_Sort1 ... [id notin ids];
  ( A[a, b](Make_State(id, init_val1, ...), Make_Ext_State(...))
    |||
    Object_Generator_A[a, b](Insert(id, ids))
  )
endproc
```

When a new instance of A is required, a **create** message such as:

```
a !create ?id:Id_Sort !val1 ... ;
```

is sent to the object generator. Note that while values such as **val1** are passed into **Object_Generator_A**, the object identifier **id** uses LOTOS value generation, i.e. the variable remains uninstantiated. The object generator holds the set of identifiers already allocated and the *selection predicate* [id notin ids] imposes the condition that the new object identifier is different from all existing ones.

The OCD must now be modified to incorporate multiple instances. In the first version of the OCD, the nodes had the same name as the class templates in the object model. When a node refers to multiple instances, it is named with the template's name in the plural.

Task 3.5.3: Identify Subsystems. In the warehouse example, **Planning** and **Requests** can be grouped to form the subsystem **Plan_Requests**. This requires changes in the OCT and OCD. A modified OCD which includes multiple instances, is shown in Figure 4. The corresponding LOTOS behaviour expression is:

```
( (Office[usr3, req2, it1, to_n]
   ||| Warehouses[usr1, req1, req2, it1, to_n, from_n]
```

```
)
|[it1, to_n, from_n]|
  (Items[it1] ||| Network[to_n, from_n])
)
|[req1, req2]|
(Plan_Requests[req1, req2, tr_pr] |tr_pr]| Trucks[usr2, tr_pr])
```

For simplicity, we have not shown the state parameters of the LOTOS processes.

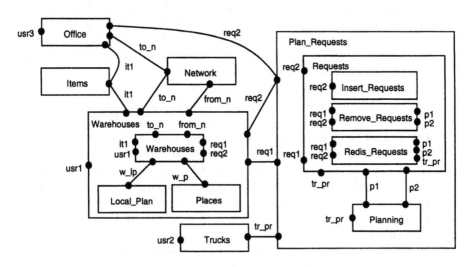

Fig. 4. Final OCD

Tasks 3.5.4 and 3.5.5: Demote or Promote Objects. If an object plays a secondary role in the system, i.e. it only acts as an attribute of other objects, it is specified as a single ADT. In such a case, we delete that object from the OCD. An example is **Customer** which occurs in Figure 3, but not in Figure 4. The decision as to whether an object should be specified as an ADT or as a process plus ADTs may change as we add more detail to the system.

Task 3.5.6: Refine Processes and ADTs. The definition of a process and an ADT is incremental. When more information is added to the formal model, more static relationships, attributes, services, and message connections can be identified.

There is not a clear boundary between analysis and design, there never was. Therefore the old question "when does analysis finish and design start?" is still an open question. Before we move to the design, we have to ensure that the requirements specification is internally consistent and deals with all the essential objects identified from the original requirements. For a specification to be internally consistent, we have to guarantee that: (i) for every message connection there are appropriate events in the calling and the called objects; (ii) for every static relationship there are all the objects involved in the relationship; (iii) a complete trace through the system can be made for every interface scenario.

5 Conclusions

The ROOA (Rigorous Object-Oriented Analysis) method enables a formal object-oriented analysis model to be produced systematically from a set of informal requirements. Having an executable formal specification means that prototyping can be used to identify omissions and inconsistencies in the original requirements and to give feedback to the process of requirements capture.

Two drawbacks of most OOA methods are that they are informal and that they produce separate models which can be difficult to visualise as a whole, to integrate and to keep consistent as the development proceeds. The advantage of ROOA is that, although it is used in conjunction with these other OOA methods, it leads to a single model which integrates the static, dynamic and functional aspects of the problem, which has a formal semantics and which can be executed symbolically. The model acts as a formal requirements specification. Although this model is primarily dynamic, its structure is directly related to the structure of the static object model. This is of great help in the understanding of a specification.

In ROOA, a problem is modelled as a set of communicating concurrent objects. Much of the concurrency may be removed in an implementation, but we are performing analysis and therefore our goal is to understand the problem, not to propose a solution.

6 Acknowledgments

We would like to thank Peter Ladkin, Charles Rattray and Ken Turner for their helpful comments on the paper.

This work was supported by the Junta Nacional de Investigação Científica e Tecnológica (JNICT), Portugal.

References

1. T. Bolognesi and E. Brinksma. Introduction to the ISO Specification Language LOTOS. *Computer Networks and ISDN Systems*, 14(1):25–59, 1987.
2. E. Brinksma (ed). *Information Processing Systems — Open Systems Interconnection — LOTOS — A Formal Description Technique Based on the Temporal Ordering of Observation Behaviour, ISO 8807*, 1988.
3. R.G. Clark and V.M. Jones. Use of LOTOS in the Formal Development of an OSI Protocol. *Computer Communications*, 15(2):86–92, 1992.

4. P. Coad and E. Yourdon. *Object Oriented Analysis*. Yourdon Press, Prentice-Hall, 2nd edition, 1991.

5. H. Eertink and D. Wolz. Symbolic Execution of LOTOS Specifications. In M. Diaz and R. Groz, editors, *Formal Description Techniques V*, pages 295–310, North-Holland, 1993.

6. H. Ehrig and B. Mahr. *Fundamentals of Algebraic Specifications*, volume 1. Springer-Verlag, 1985.

7. M. Hedlund. The Integration of LOTOS with an Object Oriented Development Method. In J.C.P. Woodcock and P.G. Larsen, editors, *FME '93: Industrial-Strength Formal Methods*, Lecture Notes in Computer Science, 670, pages 73–82. Springer-Verlag, 1993.

8. C.A.R. Hoare. *Communicating Sequential Processes*. Prentice Hall, 1985.

9. ISO/IEC JTC1/SC21/WG7. Basic Reference Model of Open Distributed Processing. Technical report, 1994.

10. I. Jacobson. *Object-Oriented Software Engineering*. Addison-Wesley, 1992.

11. R. Milner. *A Calculus of Communicating Systems*. Lecture Notes in Computer Science, 92. Springer-Verlag, 1980.

12. A.M.D. Moreira and R.G. Clark. LOTOS in the Object-Oriented Analysis Process. In *BCS-FACS Workshop on Formal Aspects of Object Oriented Systems*. London, December 1993.

13. A.M.D. Moreira and R.G. Clark. Rigorous Object-Oriented Analysis. Technical Report CSM-109, Computing Science Department, University of Stirling, Scotland, 1993.

14. A.M.D. Moreira and R.G. Clark. Combining Object-Oriented Analysis and Formal Description Techniques. In *ECOOP '94*, Lecture Notes in Computer Science. Springer-Verlag, 1994, to appear.

15. S. Rudkin. Inheritance in LOTOS. In K.R. Parker and G.A. Rose, editors, *Formal Description Techniques IV*, pages 409–423, North-Holland, 1992.

16. J. Rumbaugh, M. Blaha, W. Premerlani, F. Eddy, and W. Lorensen. *Object-Oriented Modelling and Design*. Prentice-Hall, 1991.

17. S. Shlaer and S.J. Mellor. *Object Lifecycles — Modeling the World in States*. Prentice-Hall, 1992.

18. P. Zave. An Insider's Evaluation of PAISLey. *IEEE Transactions on Software Engineering*, 17(3):212–225, March 1991.

Object Oriented Methodologies
for Large Scale Projects:
does it work?

Christophe ROUXEL (1, 2)

Jean-Pierre VELU (3)

Michel TEXIER (1, 4)

Didier LEROY (1)

(1) DGA/DEI

Centre de Maquettage de Systèmes d'Information et de Communication [1]

18 rue du docteur Zamenhof

92131 Issy-Les-Moulineaux, France

email : texier@etca.fr

telephone : (33.1) 40.95.36.81

(2) GENICORP	(3) SAGEM	(4) CR2A
Paris, France	Eragny-sur-Oise, France	Courbevoie, France

Abstract. As for most other complex software systems, Military Communication and Information Systems (CIS or C3I Systems) raise numerous software engineering problems such as design, development, requirements compliance, evolution and maintenance. To these problems, object oriented methods and tools claim to bring a solution. But beyond the current fashion of the object oriented technology in the software industry, is this new approach mature enough for developing large and industrial strength applications such as CIS? This article presents the preliminary results from a pilot project undertaken by the "Centre de Maquettage des SIC" of the French Ministry of Defense, aiming at assessing the promises of object orientation. A both theorical and pratical object oriented technologies state of the art is first presented, followed by the findings of our experiment, still under progress, in which an object oriented methodology based on prototyping and various object oriented tools have been applied together on the development of a real CIS. Those findings deal with methods and tools as well as methodology and people.

1   INTRODUCTION

System designers are becoming more and more interested in object technologies, not only because of the recent explosion of methods and tools and the hype about them, but also because of the technological revolution they seem to imply. These potential users see in

---

[1] The Centre de Maquettage de Systèmes d'Information et de Communication (CMS) is the CIS specification and rapid prototyping center of the General Armament Purchasing Body (DGA) of the French Ministry of Defense.

them a paradigm closer to the real world, an abstraction capability higher than traditional approaches, and above all, the long dreamed of benefits of reusing components and of a modularity allowing an easy evolution of systems.

But what are the real consequences, advantages and drawbacks of those technologies on large scale systems (equivalent to hundred of thousands of traditional lines of code)? Is it possible to evaluate the actual impact of OOAD methods and tools, OOL, OODBMS, and OO User Interface Development Environments (OO UIDE), on the design, development, quality control and maintenance of CIS?

In this context, the French Ministry of Defense has decided to take a fully object oriented approach on a pilot project typical of the CIS regularly developed. A theoretical study together with a product state of the art has been completed and an application has been specified. Then an OOAD method, an OODBMS, an OOL and an OO UIDE have been chosen to develop this application while analysing simultaneously the findings.

This article presents the major findings made so far with this practical experience. They focus on an OO project life cycle, prototyping in this context, the software architecture, the C++ language, and reuse, from a design and development as well as from a project management point of view.

2   CONTEXT OF THE PROJECT

2.1   The organization and its systems

2.1.1   Délégation Générale pour l'Armement (DGA)

Depending directly from the French Ministry of Defense, DGA's role is to manage all the armament projects on behalf of the Armies. To answer their needs, it has to evaluate technological evolution capable of bringing new functionalities into their systems or of improving their quality and modernization process.

As the architect of military CIS, it is interested specifically in improving the efficiency of the overall system development. Practically, it is looking for solutions to reduce the cost of its systems, which today means a 70% maintenance cost in the overall ownership cost, in which 40% is due to an evolution of user needs [Nato 91].

2.1.2   SIC or CIS

We call "Système d'Information et de Communication (SIC)" or Communication and Information System (CIS), a set of software and hardware tools allowing to collect, send, process, present and store information. CIS allows the forces to master information and to plan, manage, coordinate and control military operations. A CIS is therefore not designed to be a loose aggregate of software tools but rather a cohesive system including people, various types of hardware, an organization, a set of missions, potentially geographically distributed on fixed or mobile sites.

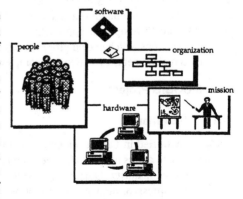

These tools and services, although they can be found in other Information Systems (IS) - such as banking systems, enterprise or office information systems, network administration, decision support systems, etc - are nevertheless unique because they encompass most design and development problems/issues that might be found in any IS, ie:

- Complexity, evolutivity, interactivity, interoperability and security, which are CIS main constraints,
- All hope for a good and definitive specification at the first stage of the project is doomed due to endless needs evolution,
- Improving the quality of systems while reducing their ownership costs, due to military budget cuts.

Thus CIS are complex at all levels, and often based on contradictory technical or organizational requirements. This is why it is necessary to find techniques and tools to improve the management of CIS development complexity.

2.1.3 Development Strategy

According to the general framework of managing armament programs [IM 1514], CIS life cycle includes three stages: Design, Production and Use. In order to comply with this decree, the development methodology [GamT17] details, for the complete life cycle, the activities that are linked to each phase of each stage, as well as expected "deliveries", plus provides project management and quality control. But its traditional "V" life cycle has shown a number of shortcomings, such as the need to stabilize operational requirements in the early phases of the project whereas they evolve in time by nature. It was thus necessary to improve and make more flexible this life cycle.

Traditional Defense Program Life Cycle

In order to reach this goal, DGA introduced the "Programme d'Armement à Logiciel Prépondérant (PALP)" or "Software Intensive Armament Project" concept for those systems where software plays a major role and has the biggest share of the project cost. By adopting an incremental development approach, this methodology should allow the delivery of successive versions which extend progressively the operational functionalities of CIS. Thus, the systems requirements evolution and complexity are better mastered.

2.2 MOOSIC Project

2.2.1 Motivation

Problems identified in CIS development and until now without any satisfactory solution lead naturally to assess new technologies that bring new concepts and seem to have reached some degree of maturity. Object oriented technologies enjoy since the beginning of the nineties an impressive amount of promotion and an explosion of products, but wisdom reminds us that technologies mature slowly. For instance, Relational Database Management

Systems took 10 years to reach adulthood, and expert systems generators, on which big hopes have been raised for over 10 years only now find a respected niche in operational systems [Leroy 92].

However, the object oriented approach, first restricted to programming languages - Smalltalk [Goldberg 83], Eiffel [Meyer 88], C++ [Stroustrup 91] – then to MMI development (or UIDE) tools for which it is naturally suited [Texier 92], quickly reached DBMS tools [Bancilhon 90] and analysis and design tools [Arnold 91], and seem now to spread into all software engineering fields. Furthermore, various market studies, such as [Ovum 91], lead to think that object oriented technologies will play a major role in all software areas and predict an industrial take off towards 1995-96. For instance, the total revenue of OODBMS products could be in 96 equivalent to the RDBMS one of 91-92, and they should be used by then mostly for Management Information Systems instead of today's naturally fitted scientific applications. It is of course always hard to predict precisely when a market will reach the mature stage, but other signals, such as OMG and ISO standardisation efforts strengthen the idea of a significant OO market before the turn of the millennium.

That is why DGA has launched at the end of 1991 the MOOSIC ("Méthodologie Orientée Objet pour les SIC" or Object Oriented Methodology for CIS) exploratory development to evaluate the effectiveness of OO methodologies, methods an tools for the design, development, quality control and maintenance of CIS systems.

2.2.2 Approach

To reach the evaluation goals of the MOOSIC project, we have decided to develop the prototype of a CIS corresponding to real user operational requirements and representing around 50000 of traditional code. To achieve that, we are managing this project like a regular DGA armament program, with a first stage of requirement analysis and specification based on our methodology evolving around rapid prototyping [Fonteneau 93] that led to a requirement specification. It was used as the base for the request for proposals sent to DGA regular big CIS subcontractors that had to commit to deadlines and deliveries, like in any other DGA project, for the production stage.

However, we are not trying to develop all of this CIS functionalities, since it would be too costly for a system that is not committed to be put into real use, due to the results of the experiment being unknown at the beginning of the project. But this project covers the full development life cycle: analysis, design, programming, tests, and maintenance.

The criteria we want to evaluate being numerous and of different levels, we have organized the production stage in two steps of about one year each. First, we try to assess if object technology can be used to develop a full scale CIS by developing the system specified in the requirement specification. But more traditional methods and tools might have been enough to develop the CIS. Because of that, we'll shake up the object technology in a second step to check if all the hopes put on it are justified. For instance, we'll modify a few but major elements of the requirements to check if it really allows evolutivity, we'll try to encapsulate existing applications relying on a RDBMS and we'll modify some data types and analyse the consequences on existing classes and instances. Those modification scenarii will be given at the last minute to the development team in order not to bias the experiment.

Before all the steps described here, we started with a preliminary study on the object technology in order to define the criteria to be evaluated in the project. To achieve that, we studied the theoretical concepts of object orientation with the help of some researchers from INRIA (French national research institute in computer science) and we conducted a state of the art study of the tools available on the market.

3. STATE OF THE ART

The goal of the preliminary study was to prepare the exploratory development with a both theoretical and practical state of the art of the object world. The practical study unearthes valuable industrial criteria but with only a short term validity whereas the theoretical study brings more general and long term criteria. Due to time constraints, we focused on these so-called object oriented technologies that seemed to us capable of having the strongest impact on the design and development of CIS, while relying on independent and sometimes differing approaches (and even terminologies), ie OOL, OODBMS and OOAD.

Object Oriented Languages introduced the object technology with encapsulation, inheritance and the separation between the object interface and its implementation. Today, even if languages such as Smalltalk, Eiffel, ObjectiveC or CLOS have their strengths, it is difficult to go around C++. It is well known that ObjectiveC was overtaken by C++, that Smalltalk and CLOS are not used beyond the research world and rapid prototyping, and that Eiffel, although widely appreciated didn't make it in the industrial world. C++ has become the defacto OOL standard in the industry, as studies such as [Ovum 91] show that C++ had more than half of the market as early as 91, also confirmed by the fact that basically all the industrial OO tools developed today rely on C++ and in the rare cases when they don't, have to support an interface to C++. However, although it verifies the basic OOL criteria, C++ remains a very complex and low level language which needs very high programming expertise, mastering of OO concepts and discipline as it encourages everything but clean programming.

Concerning design methods, classical approaches, that separate data from processing, without any reuse goal and with a poor support of dynamic components, are not compatible with the object approach. Since 1991 we have seen a flood of so called object oriented methods (30 to 40) that claim to help cope with programming those now trendy object oriented languages. A lot of these methods are still at the paper stage, many are poorly tooled, others are targeting a specific domain such as knowledge based systems or a specific programming language. We have thus decided to concentrate on well documented and reasonably well known methods : OOA from S. Shlaer and S. Mellor, OOAD from G. Booch, OMT from J. Rumbaugh, OOA/OOD from P. Coad and E. Yourdon, and Class-Relationship from P. Desfray. We chose OOAD because it differentiates on the one hand classes and instances and on the other hand static and dynamic modeling, in both logical and physical levels. Furthermore, Booch is the only one who tackled the incremental and iterative approach centered on the almost permanent availability of demonstrable prototypes, which should allow to master the complexity of systems developed in large scale projects.

Object Oriented databases bring persistency, facilitate storage, management and access to large volumes of data, and focus on object identity in contrast to the equality of values in relational databases. As far as OODBMS are concerned, the number of products offered on the market is more reasonable although more important than RDBMS. We studied all of them, ie Ontos from Ontologic Inc, Gemstone from Servio Corporation, Itasca from Itasca Systems Inc, Objectivity/DB from Objectivity Inc, Versant from Versant Object

Technology, Objectstore from Object Design Inc, O2 from O2Technology and Matisse from Intellitic International. We chose the O2 system because it offers a real database approach, a clean object model independent from the C++ language while being reasonably compatible with it, which offers the most advanced query language and verifies most of the Manifesto criteria [Atkinson 90].

4 OUR OBJECT-ORIENTED METHODOLOGY

4.1 Goals and Target Application

As an exploratory development, the MOOSIC project puts us in the context of developing a real and industrial CIS, in which the object concept is integrated at all the life cycle phases in order to evaluate its advantages and drawbacks. In the first step, which is under progress, it is tackling two main goals:

- the production of a CIS prototype,
- the foundation of an object oriented development methodology.

The target application is a multimedia document management system for intelligence, corresponding to the potential new version of an existing system which cannot evolve. An interesting (and difficult) side to this application is that in the intelligence domain information types cannot usually be predefined!

Organized in a client/server architecture, this application includes four main modules which are clients of an OODB managing forms, pictures, blueprints and sound :

- a hardware form manager,
- a document handler,
- a photo library,
- a hardware blueprint manager.

Some of these modules have to be completely developed whereas others, such as the document handler, rely completely on an off the shelf software product, or are built from a generic structured graphics editor, like the blueprint manager.

The second goal pursued at the same time as the prototype production is to lay down the basic concepts of an object oriented methodology for building CIS. This project is thus unusual in this respect that an application is being developed at the same time as a study is being led on the methodology to be used for this development.

4.2 Development Process

The core idea that we have focused on when making the first design of the methodology presented hereunder is a permanent validation throughout the production. Thus the validation procedure is always available and can be replayed at any time in order to check that:

- the specifications match the customer's requirements,
- the implementation matches the specifications.

To reach this goal, several approaches were possible. The first one was to use formal solutions. Since there is no formal theory defining the object concept and because of the difficulty of implementing formal methods, we have preferred to differ this solution... Another way is to use simulation. This technique, which is proposed by some software engineering methods, although seductive, has a number of drawbacks such as a validation procedure conducted outside the real context, which raises doubts about its reliability.

The object technology allows to go further. More specifically, it allows to build very early and rapidly executable prototypes. Thus we have chosen for the MOOSIC project a methodology - inspired from the OOAD method [Booch 91] - based on building real prototypes, each of them representing an agreed on step toward the final prototype. The title of prototype, and not of rapid prototype (which is throwaway by definition), gives to these steps the main property of being an evolution, ie a permanent convergence toward the final product. Therefore, all along the MOOSIC project, a prototype is being built and is converging toward the expected result while showing continuously that it is matching the customer's requirements.

Unlike the Booch proposal, we have identified two types of prototypes : Booch Prototypes (BP) and Functional Prototypes (FP). The first ones implement one or several mechanisms that are essential for the project and difficult to implement. The second ones allow to reach convergence as described above. The BP only concern the development team while the FP are shown to the customer during the production stage. He can evaluate these since they are described in his vocabulary.

All along the continuous development of the product through all these prototypes, we don't only plan for the refinement of code itself but also for:

- a refinement of user requirements. In fact, each prototype will be defined according to a specific user requirement that we call prototype requirement. The converging evolution of the prototype requirement should lead to the sum of the originally specified user requirement and of its evolutions.
- a refinement of specifications matching the prototype requirement.
- a refinement of tests in two directions: unitary tests and integration tests.

The production of each FP is composed of two generic and tightly coupled actions: "building/checking". These actions instantiation depends on the step we are at in the project cycle. Therefore, in this approach, a software life cycle is a kind of convergent stacking up of identical <building/checking> cycles. The result is a convergent "V" life cycle model in order to evoke convergence. A prototype is developed by following generalization life cycles. When these cycles stop, we obtain for the current step a stable state which is the targeted prototype.

The life cycle defined in MOOSIC includes four phases: the global analysis, the refinement loop, the global validation and maintenance.

- The global analysis is a building/checking plan instantiated in <preliminary analysis/validation>. More specifically, it is a phase in which we have initialized the system architecture and the validation. The result is a set of documents plus a prototype: the architecture prototype. Let's note that this prototype, defined by Booch, was hard to understand and fit in our methodology and was more or less reduced to the initial BP.

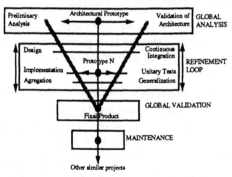

- The refinement loop is a set of generalization loops or spirals made of the following plans: <detailed design/integration>, <coding/unitary tests> and <aggregation/generalization>. Its stability points, as Booch calls them, are intermediate functional prototypes which are successive refinements of the architecture prototype.
- The global validation phase is at the bottom of the "V" and is similar to the classic contract acceptance procedure.
- The maintenance phase, which usually is not a phase in the software development life cycle becomes here more important. In an object oriented approach, it is necessary to finalize the project, ie prepare for future evolutions of the system and following projects. Indeed, software reuse is essential when following an object oriented approach. This phase thus has two goals: preparing reuse, and preparing an effective maintenance.

The documentation associated with this life cycle is a line of documents produced for each functional prototype : definition dossier, design dossier, validation dossier. During the maintenance phase, all these documents are synthetized in order to create a documentation well suited, ie sufficient but not overwhelming, for the final product.

4.3 Project Organization

The MOOSIC development team is composed of two developers and one project manager. Because of the particular goal of the project where the design then the critique of the methodology used in it are as important as the production of the final prototype, we had to adopt an unusual project management approach. It is based on four guidelines, the first one being obvious for such a project:

- technical problems are to be solved by following an object oriented approach even if other approaches seem at first more naturally fitted,
- every developer has to fill out and maintain up to date the Object Technology Validation Manual (OTVM),
- all technical problems encountered by the team on technical and methodological issues have to be systematically analysed,
- the methodology is to be constantly criticized. The team must not hesitate to modify its methodological approach for one that seems better adapted.

As far as configuration management is concerned, we have built a common referencing system submitted to configuration management. This reference or common project directory contains all the documentation and all the source code that have been stabilized at a given time of the project development, as well as an integration space of the prototype being currently built. The transfer between the private developers' development spaces and the reference is called a delivery procedure and is under the librarian direct responsibility. One of the librarian main roles is to check that deliveries are correct. That means that every source code has to come with its documentation and more specifically, that every class has to be associated with at least a manual precisely describing how it should be used and test programs. Thus the basic (common to all prototypes) classes used by developers have to compulsorily come from the reference.

4.4 Design Method

One of the main difficulties is to converge toward the final product. Indeed, focusing too much on the BPs development can easily make the project diverge if one is not careful. Functional prototypes allow to avoid this deviation. Therefore, the method we use, even if it based on the Booch method, deviates from it since we had to reintroduce some features typical of more classic approaches. The preliminary analysis that was led first by the rapid prototyping team for the requirements then by the exploratory development team for the domain analysis is however the one recommended by Booch, ie : requirements analysis and domain analysis (which means finding the classes which are specific to the application). All along this analysis we constantly asked ourselves the same important question : in what respect the class we are currently defining is specific? This allowed us to position the project in relation to similar ones and allowed us to identify external classes (from other projects or on the shelf) that we could reuse. After this analysis, we defined a number of Booch prototypes as well as the initial architecture prototype (still following the Booch method and wondering about the difference between those two types of prototypes). In retrospect the preliminary analysis allowed the development team to identify a number of basic classes, common to a number of Booch prototypes that make a FP. And more specifically, an in depth analysis of the user requirements coming from the requirements analysis allowed the development team to define the intermediate FPs, the BPs needed for the first FP and a first planning.

Actually, the process of building a FP is always the same :

1) basic classes development,
2) Booch prototypes (BP) development,
3) integration of BPs into the current functional prototype (FP) and loop back to step 1) if stabilization is not reached,
4) MMI development for the FP.

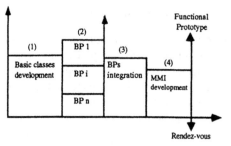

For steps 1), 2) and 4), the approach is fully object oriented but it is rather classic for step 3).

The global project planning is based on these four FP steps. To design it, the following information is necessary :

- customer delivery constraints (obviously),
- the result of a detailed analysis of user requirements, which is based on i) listing all the functionalities in the user requirements document, ii) for each one, identifying as many basic classes as possible, iii) defining the mechanisms that will implement these classes,
- an as precise as possible definition of BPs for all FPs after the previous task,
- then an initial MMI specification of FPs from the original user requirements document.

4.5   Customer Deliveries

A project based on the object technology is no longer seen in terms of functionalities but through the objects that make the application. This approach seems less natural and usually puzzles the customer and the user who don't find anymore what they specified in the customer requirements. Two major obstacles perturb them: the vocabulary (objects, classes and so on) is the developer's one, and the lack of focus on functionalities.

The customer/user is thus unable to assess the work that has been done and the developer has many difficulties to assemble a functional presentation. There is another problem : with the functional approach, it was possible to set a number of rendez-vous where some functionalities could be demonstrated. With the object approach, this is less easy and in fact it is only possible to show mechanisms, ie a localized dynamic behaviour involving a few objects only. For the customer, these mechanisms look like very low level application layers which are not his problem. Therefore we can guess (and we have experienced) that he won't easily accept such demonstrations and that he will have a hard time understanding the agenda of the various object approach rendez-vous.

Functional prototypes allow to solve this problem because, by definition, they cover functionalities coming from the customer requirements. Thus we have associated customer rendez-vous to FPs (but at least showing some of the difficult BPs can be useful still, as we experienced). During these rendez-vous, the prototype is validated by the customer and may be delivered upon request. The validation is based on the prototype requirement, ie the requirement specific to this prototype. The following documents are delivered :

- the definition dossier of the prototype, which contains among other things an up to date class hierarchy,
- the design dossier, itself made of the architecture dossier which describes all the mechanisms involved by the prototype and of the class manual for the classes involved in the prototype,
- the validation dossier of the prototype.

5   FINDINGS

5.1   Implementation

The C++ standard seemed stabilized enough to us but we had a number of problems with templates of the SparcC++ 3.0.1 compiler. Particularly they increase link edition a lot. We also felt a strong need for a C++ garbage collector, to the point of thinking of developing one ourselves but we quickly realized that its use would have been very complex with the graphic object library which behaviour is difficult to master.

Unitary tests that need the database are difficult to implement. Indeed, by definition, each developer is independent from the other ones for this type of tests. This means that each needs his own database within his own context. In practice, this is difficult to do because we would need as many licences for the product as developers. There were not too many problems for the MOOSIC application but we tried to put ourselves in the (realistic) context of a big project (with several developers) which only has one server licence. Its uniqueness necessitates a rigorous testing discipline which was hard to implement.

The continuous integration of the prototype being built is very interesting because it allows a continuous tuning which limitates long term bad surprises. However, it requires a careful configuration management and a precise planning from the prototype manager in order to avoid undoing what already works!

5.2   Methodology

In practice, our approach is a rather good guideline to design the planning. However, class generalization might distort it. For instance, a generalization that became necessary made us locally modify our planning several times by lengthening step 1) but also by shortening step 3). Experience showed that the planning can be disrupted by the introduction of new basic classes that were not identified at the time of domain analysis.

As far as the global approach is concerned, classes defined at the time of domain analysis are progressively specialized with the refinement of intermediate FPs. More specifically, specialization is always linked to a given prototype: a given class may be used globally for the first prototypes then specialized for the following ones. We thus have the following cycle for classes:

- from the concrete (study of user requirements) to the abstract: definition and creation of general classes for the abstract (first) functional prototypes,
- from the abstract to the concrete: specialization of previous classes for the following intermediate prototypes.

5.3 Interaction with the Customer

Experience showed us that the presentation of all Functional Prototypes to the customer/user is useful for the following reasons :

- checking that the development team has taken into account all the details of the user requirements is made possible by focusing on a subset of functionalities only,
- correcting problems is reasonably easy since the code has a reasonable size, which is never the case when problems raise at the end of the project.

5.4 Project Management

Submitted to strict industrial deadlines, the development team, when dealing with a problem which actual cause might be methodological, is thus often forced to find a compromise between an extended study of the issue that might feed the OTVM and going on with coding. But the biggest problem we had was to properly estimate schedules. Indeed, contrary to the traditional approach, where software layers are piled up, the object approach looks more like a puzzle to be put together. The consequence is that the building of prototypes implies a precise and very early study of the "pieces" that compose it. In order to solve that problem, an object-oriented methodology requires from the project leader an estimate of the work to come more precise and therefore more complex than for more traditional projects.

We realized that the librarian position is essential in object oriented projects. At least five librarian roles seem essential to us in addition to the obvious task of class library management:

- maintain a class diagram up to date (it contains the class hierarchy only, the other relationships make the diagram impossible to read, and are not so difficult to manage),
- help the project leader for the planning,
- class library management : obvious but major role
- configuration management
- put together the documentation and maintain an on line help (like a unix man) for the class manual.

Maintaining a class hierarchy up to date has been an effective way to avoid rewriting code. Furthermore, this project cartography has allowed new developers to get started more easily. The general knowledge of classes acquired by the librarian facilitates long term estimates and thus the planning design.

In practice, beside the essential role of the librarian, the MOOSIC experience has showed us that for large scale projects, it is necessary to create the position of (functional) prototype manager whose main tasks are:

- to supervise the development of the current prototype,
- to manage cycles and in particular supervise generalisations,

- to maintain the prototype evolution history up to date,
- to test the prototype,
- to manage and control the continuous integration.

Of course, not every project requires all those roles. For our MOOSIC project, librarian and prototype manager responsabilities are held by the project manager.

5.5   Productivity of the Object Approach

The object oriented approach productivity is roughly proportional to the heritage we own, ie to the number of class libraries accumulated in previous projects that can be reused in the current project. The management and upgrading of this heritage, which is the organization know how in a way, has to be handled by an inter-project librarian. The productivity is linked to the quality of his management.

MOOSIC started with an almost non existing heritage, beside the graphic objects library, therefore the only productivity component that we have been able to analyse in this project is the own internal productivity of the object oriented approach. We realized that the generalization process, when justified, allowed to save a lot of development time. For instance, the generalization of a class dedicated to the implementation of dynamic visualisation screens allowed us to develop quickly, by internal reuse, the print features which are well known for being a time consuming coding effort. Therefore we have been able to increase our productivity by favouring this internal reuse, by reusing and specializing the classes on which the implementation of the first prototypes was based, these classes being by nature more abstract. As far as development is concerned, this approach means that a first and long phase of design and implementation of the basic classes is followed by rapid phases of actually building FPs. We aren't advanced in the project enough yet, obviously, to compare the global internal productivity of the object approach with the traditional one.

Another key criteria to evaluate productivity is the late assignment of properties to objects. The classic approach doesn't generally allow to give to components of the system properties that they hadn't been planned to have. When such a "situation" occurs, it is a very bad experience for project leaders and customers as well : it looks like someone is guilty of having forgotten something. The object technique has mechanisms allowing to solve this major problem. It is possible, late in the project, to give to some objects properties that had not been though of at the beginning of development. For instance, in MOOSIC, the "printable" property is easy to attribute "at the last minute". Thus productivity is improved indirectly because oversights (at least, some of them) don't provoke crisises.

In the object oriented approach therefore, looping back seems natural and even saves time each time it is due to justified generalizations. However, experience showed us that such a move had to be carefully monitored. Indeed, one can be tempted to generalize too much and generalizations may break older prototypes and thus provoke worrying setbacks.

Using BPs and FPs proved to be quite effective. Being generally small (although some grow with the project progress), it is easier to find mistakes in them and solve them. They also are guarantees against bad interpretations of user requirements or of specifications because they can be shown to the customer/user. For instance, when the architecture prototype (or initial BP) was shown (ie very early in the project), a concurrent access need to the database was identified but not planned for before. If this need had been discovered later, it would have been more difficult to identify in the middle of all the functionalities shown and much more difficult to accommodate!

In conclusion, we think, so far, that it is possible to have a good (if not better, especially when the final vs initial user need and partial deliveries are taken into account) software development productivity with the object oriented approach. However, this is possible only with :

- a more rigorous and complex project management than for classic developments,
- a specific organization of the development team(s) in the organization (heritage management, librarian duties, etc),
- very high quality developers, with a strong abstraction and design ability (which confirms what other studies have already underlined).

5.6   Of Tools, Methods and Men

Using the object technology requires sophisticated tools because the concepts that have to be handled are complex and numerous. Furthermore, the abstraction level that is necessary is high and as a consequence requires giving up old and well mastered habits. Thus, to handle this complexity, the developer, however bright he may be, needs appropriate tools.

In our view, there are two approaches that tools can offer :

a) tools try to reduce complexity by controling it,

b) tools try to reduce complexity by limiting the number of available concepts.

The first solution is by far the most common : it is based on the management of analysis and design components (through databases) and of a given and permanent consistency between them. The basic idea is: if there is an inconsistency, then the designer introduced at least one mistake. Most of the modern tools on the market are well suited to this approach but they are too incomplete. For instance, those tools don't handle the global object model: they only check local relationships, which is useful, but doesn't help to design a globally consistent model.

The other solution (b) is more ambitious since the tool should suggest generic and tried concepts taken from an heritage that it could manage, and help to properly handle these concepts by showing how to use them in an optimal way. This solution is based on the property concept and is close, in some ways, to the formal approach.

Today no tool fully covers one of these solutions. Most of the time, they are just sophisticated graphic editors, often very constraining and cumbersome. In our project, the tool we used (Rose from Rational) was of little help. Furthermore, it was not compatible with the configuration management we chose and which is based on a common reference.

Object oriented methods are plentiful as we discovered in the MOOSIC preliminary study. However the development experience brought us the following findings :

- the project leader expects from a method that it helps him to find the structuring elements of the project, ie those which are going to become increasingly important as the development goes forward. We lived indeed difficult times due to the unexpected evolution of some classes.
- it is naive to believe that any method can solve the fundamental problems encountered in such projects (particularly, looking for classes). Like there is no general method for solving a math problem, there is no general method to build, for instance, the architecture of an object system. The human brain has to be put to work with its reasoning strength, its experience and maybe talent!

- there must be a strong integration between the tool and the method, the first one completely implementing the second one. Lacks in tools can make the method difficult to use if not useless.

- finally, and obviously, there must be a strong continuity between all the method phases. Unfortunately, they all lack continuity between analysis and design, and design and coding. The issue is indeed still a research issue but it is especially acute in the object oriented approach, where back loops are frequent.

Still the Booch method that we use for MOOSIC helped us a lot, among other things, thanks to the self correcting process that it offers. Thus looking for classes is not a once for all effort but on the contrary constantly going on as long as the model is not stabilized. During an iteration, entities may naturally disappear because they are not classes. As a consequence, there is a sort of natural adjustment of class diagrams during the refinement process. However the first class diagram must be complete because successive iterations do not guarantee that what was forgotten can be added. The other advantage of the method is prototyping. In fact, it was the base for our methodology.

By opposition to Ada where development is done in an integrated environment, C++ suffers from a lack of positive software engineering platforms (ie not constraining but helping the developer). In Ada, the concept of compilation unit is the basis for an efficient integrated management, but all this is lacking in C++ and is very costly : a lot of things have to be done "by hand", including the class library management and especially the templates management. Furthermore, contrary to Ada, where a design method is suggested by the language itself, C++ suffers from still being seen as a continuation of C. Which means that in the mind of a lot of developers, writing C++ code is often equal to "practising" the object oriented approach and MOOSIC taught us that it is quite different.

Finally, and hopefully temporarily but still quite annoyingly, there doesn't seem to be yet an identical implementation of the C++ standard.. Most of the development environment/compilers we tried on our Sun workstations either worked with the DBMS but not the UIDE, or conversely, not only making us waste valuable time (the problem was not always identified right away) but also forcing us to settle for a basic, featureless compiler.

6   CONCLUSION

Beyond the practical, serious and well known but hopefully temporary problems we met because of the lack of maturity of the object oriented tools available on the market, that either made us waste a lot of time or proved to be of very little help, like the tool supporting the Booch method, we had to deal with a more fundamental issue. Since MOOSIC is a two year long industrial project, with a customer requiring deadlines and deliveries, since there is a 3 people development team, a methodology was needed, and it was one of the project goals to use an object oriented method. But we couldn't find any on the shelf. So we tried a careful blend of the Booch approach [Booch 91], which at least introduces the concept of permanently demonstrable prototypes, and of the French Ministry of Defense methodology [GAM-T17], which is quite traditional, but addresses the reality of industrial projects and of customer deliveries. The result, presented at length in chapter 4 of this article, is far from simple, but it works and in our view better than before. Moreover, it is interesting to note that the last OOAD release [Booch 93] draws similar conclusions. It distinguishes, in its incremental and iterative development life cycle, the macro-process and micro-process in order to allow a just balance between the intuitive approach of object orientation and the more formal approach of traditional and reasonably well-ordered processes.

The MOOSIC methodology adds to the "Booch prototypes" the functional prototypes to be validated by the customer and user and kind of gets rid of the architecture prototypes concept of the Booch approach (it is ambiguous) to limit it to the number 1 Booch prototype, which is longer and more difficult to develop than the following ones. The life cycle is a spiral of spirals (ie functional prototype developments), creates many positions to be filled by members of the development team (and the librarian or prototype manager ones are not easy ones), requires a lot of documentation work, and customer rendez-vous may have to be done beyond the easy functional prototypes ones, thus involving difficult communication issues. Furthermore, we confirm that the development team needs to master the object oriented approach very well, which is a rare skill, since on its talent rests the discovery of the project objects!

However, our experience showed that, even if the development of the first Booch prototype (and therefore of the first functional prototype) takes time and care, and even if the generalization of classes takes time (and might sometimes be overdone), we can deliver something to the customer quickly and periodically enhance it: instead of waiting two years for a complete (and maybe obsolete) system, he can get a first partial version after 6 or 8 months, and the following ones at a high rate. This is because the methodology reduces the time spent on the initial analysis and design (the benefits of the OO approach) and allows to successively deliver to the customer the functional prototypes. Furthermore, at any time, and starting very early in the development process, it is possible to identify issues (technical ones, within the development team, or architecture, functional or performance ones when meeting with the customer) and solve them rather easily by simply adding properties to objects, by specializing or (carefully) generalizing classes, or in most of cases, by rebuilding a few classes.

In the second part of the exploratory development side of the MOOSIC project, we'll still have to check if a major shake up of the requirements specification doesn't impose on it serious modifications. We wish to assess if object technologies allow to evolve smoothly from the current careful blend, which considers the initial and final phases special and doesn't really consider yet each functional prototype as a product, with serious specification, validation and delivery procedures, toward a completely incremental and iterative industrial object oriented methodology, with a perfect spiral of spirals form.

Lastly, it seems our work in object oriented methodology for large scale project arouses a great interest. Some of entities in industry and foreign Defense Departments over the world such as Swedish, German, British and some American who don't have, as far as we know, similar experiment, would to set up a partnership to share those findings. Moreover, in 1993, our results have been adopted by the "mock-up and prototype in software engineering" committee [Afnor 93] of the French Association of Standardization and as a work basis by the JTC1/WG7 "Software life cycle model tailored for mock-up and prototype" group [ISO 93] of the International Standard Organization. This future work should provide a clear definition of terms and conditions covered by different kinds of prototypes, and clarify the connection between software project life cycle stages which can use prototyping, in order to define a complete methodology covering all facets of managing software project life cycle.

7 REFERENCES

[Arnold 91] "An evaluation of five object-oriented development methods", P. Arnold, S. Bodoff, D. Coleman, H. Gilchrist and F. Hayes, Software Engineering Department, HP Laboratories Bristol, June 1991.

[Afnor 93] "Mock-up and Prototype in Software Engineering", Z67-111, Afnor/CNTI/CN7, 1993.

[Atkinson 90] "The object-oriented database system manisfesto", M. Atkinson, F. Bancilhon, D. DeWitt, K. Dittrich, D. Maier, S. Zdonik, 1990.

[Bancilhon 90] "Object-Oriented Database Systems", F.Bancilhon, Altaïr 1990.

[Boehm 88] "A spiral model of software development and enhancement", BW. Boehm, May 1988.

[Booch 91] "Object-oriented Design with applications", G. Booch, Benjamin / Cummings, 1991.

[Booch 93] "Object-oriented Analysis and Design with applications", G. Booch, Benjamin / Cummings, 1993.

[Coad & Yourdon 91] "Object-Oriented Analysis" 2nd edition, P. Coad and E. Yourdon, Yourdon Press 1991.

[Colin de Verdière 92] "Méthodes, techniques et outils pour les logiciels des programmes d'armement: Une question d'équilibre", IPA Antoine Colin de Verdière, DGA/DEI/CMS, Défense & Technologie International, June 1992.

[Davis 90] "Software Requirements Analysis and Specification", AM. Davis, Prentice Hall, 1990.

[Desfray 90] "A method for object-oriented programming: the Class-Relationship method", Tools'90, June 1990.

[Fonteneau 93] "Rapid Prototyping to assist requirement specification", J.Fonteneau, C.Rouxel, D.Leroy, DGA/CMS, November 93.

[GamT17 89] "Gam-T17 v2 : Development methodology for embedded software in defense systems", Ministry of Defense, July 1989.

[Goldberg 83] "Smalltalk-80 : The language and its implementation", A. Goldberg, D. Robson, Addison-Wesley, 1983.

[IM 1514] "Instruction Générale sur le Déroulement des Programmes d'Armement", Ministère de la Défense, N° 1514, 7 May 1988, edition 2 : 17 January 1992.

[ISO 93] "Project of international standard information processing — Software life cycle model tailored for mock-up and prototype", ISO/JTC1/WG7, July 93.

[Jacobson 92] "Object-Oriented Software Engineering : A Use-Case Approach", I. Jacobson, Addison-Wesley/ACM Press, 1992.

[Leroy 92] "CORSAIRE : Planificateur Temps Réel", 12th International Conference on Expert Systems and Applications, D. Leroy, P. Théret, Avignon, June 1992.

[Meyer 88] "Object-oriented software construction", B. Meyer, Prentice Hall, 1988.

[Nato 91] "Software Methods & Tools : Technical Aspects of Lifecycle Methodologies", Nato Information Systems Working Group, June 1991.

[Ovum 91] "Object Technology Sourcebook", J. Jeffcoate & C. Guilfoyle, Ovum Ltd, 1991.

[PALP 92] "Conduite des Programmes d'Armement à Logiciel Prépondérant", Groupe de Travail DGA, February 1992.

[Rumbaugh 91] "Object-Oriented Modeling and Design", J. Rumbaugh, M. Blaha, W. Premerlani, F. Eddy, W. Lorensen, Prentice-Hall International Editions, 1991.

[Shlaer & Mellor 91] "Object Lyfecycles : Modeling the World in States", S. Shlaer & S. Mellor, Yourdon Press 1991.

[Stroustrup 91] "The C++ Programming Language", B. Stroustrup, Addison-Wesley 1992.

[Texier 92] "Evaluation et comparaison d'outils de développement d'intefaces homme machine", M. Texier, Convention Unix, March 1992

Quantitative and Qualitative Aspects of Object-Oriented Software Development

Gustav Pomberger, Wolfgang Pree

C. Doppler Laboratory for Software Engineering
Johannes Kepler University Linz, A-4040 Linz, Austria
Voice: ++43 70-2468-9431; Fax: ++43 70-2468-9430
E-mail: {pomberger,pree}@swe.uni-linz.ac.at

Abstract. Although object-oriented programming techniques have evolved into an accepted technology with recognized benefits for software development, profound investigations of qualitative and quantitative aspects about its pros and cons are missing.

This paper tries to answer crucial questions based on the experience gained by the authors and their partners in several projects where object-oriented technology was applied. These projects cover different areas like prototyping tools, information systems, real-time process control components, and development environments for object-oriented programming languages.

A case study comparing the object-oriented (C++) and module-oriented (Modula-2) implementation of a user interface prototyping tool concludes this paper.

Keywords. Design patterns, object-oriented design, object-oriented software development, application frameworks, class libraries, reusability

1   Introduction

Since the software industry can hardly efford to implement large-scale software systems twice most comparisons of conventional and object-oriented programming techniques are based on small projects. This situation served as an incentive for us to compare representative software systems.

But even reimplementations have to be considered carefully. For instance, a system should not be implemented twice by the same project team. Experience gained in the first implementation will help in the reimplementation whether or not the team starts with the conventional or object-oriented solution. Thus a system has to be implemented by two different project teams which have about the same knowledge in the beginning.

The type of a system to be built also has an undeniable influence on the comparison. Strongly algorithm-oriented systems won't benefit as much from object-orientation as systems that have to deal with various different and complex data structures.

This paper starts with a presentation of results based on several systems which have been developed in various object-oriented programming languages (C++, Smalltalk, Object Pascal, Eiffel and Oberon) and compared to conventionally implemented systems over the past five years. The overall size of these projects is about 500,000 lines of code. The projects were carried out together with partners from industry, for example, the Union Bank of Switzerland (UBS), Siemens AG Munich, and the Austrian Industries Corporation.

After discussing qualitative and quantitative aspects derived from several case studies, we present one specific case study that demonstrates how our results were obtained.

We presuppose that the reader is familiar with the object-oriented concepts of inheritance, polymorphism and dynamic binding, as well as with principles of application frameworks (like ET++ [12] and UniDraw [10]).

2 Condensed Results

The quantitative and qualitative evaluations of various projects presented in this section were compiled by our department. The projects taken into consideration include, for example, a user interface prototyping tool (see Section 2 for details), a real-time process control system [5, 13] and software development environments such as the module-oriented SCT [1] and the object-oriented Omega [2].

In the following two subsections positive aspects of object-oriented software development are marked with a "+", negative ones with a "-". If there is no significant difference as compared to conventional software development, an "o" sign is used.

2.1 Quantitative Aspects

The numbers given for various quantitative aspects express the impact of object-orientation compared to conventional approaches. These numbers have to be seen as a percentage with reference to the conventional solution. A value of 120%, for instance, means that the quantitative measure increases by a fifth if the object-oriented paradigm is used instead of a conventional paradigm.

Impact on Source Code Size. In the case of object-oriented programs, we have to discern between the newly written source code and the reused source code:

+ *Newly Written Code: 25-50%* The reduction of source code that has to be written is often considered to be a very important achievement of object-oriented programming. In fact, this number directly influences the duration of a software project and its maintenance costs. Since many standard problems of a specific domain have already been solved by classes of an application framework, usage of an appropriate framework can even reduce the size of newly written source code up to 90%. Such extreme reductions are typical for small projects (about 5,000 to 15,000 lines of code) where an existing application framework has to be adjusted to specific needs. Code reductions are less in case of systems that contain many algorithm-oriented parts.

Even if there is no class library at hand reductions of the size of newly written code can be observed. These reductions are proportional to the project size. The larger the project the less code has to be written. The reason for this lies in the internal reuse of components within a project. A careful design (especially factoring out commonalities into superclasses) implies that more components can be reused as compared to conventional (e.g., module-oriented) software development.

- *Overall Source Code Size: 120-300%* Although less code has to be written, the overall size of the source code increases. This is caused by inherited code and indirectly used classes. The given number may vary extremly depending on the size and cohesion of the used class library. Using classes only for data structures, for example, results in a minimal increase of the overall source code size and almost neglectible savings in code that has to be written newly. On the other hand, using an application framework implies importing numerous classes that do not contribute directly to the solution of a particular problem. But these additional classes also provide functionality for free which could only be achieved with enormous effort if no application framework is used. The generality of directly and indirectly used classes constitutes another factor that influences the size of imported code. In order to increase the generality of a class additional methods have to be provided that enlarge the code size even if they are not used.

Impact on Run-Time. More precise numbers can be given about the impact of object-oriented programming on run-time issues than can be given about the overall code size. The time elapsed during a procedure call and method call can be measured resulting in a factor. The same is true for accessing object components. Of course, garbage collection effects a program's run-time too, since searching for unreferenced objects consumes time. Implications on the overall run-time are more difficult to determine, since it depends on the quality of the underlying class library and the programming style.

- Method Call: 105-120% Due to dynamic binding, method calls are more expensive than procedure calls. But it has to be taken into consideration that the overhead for passing parameters and the stack-like management of procedure call chains remains the same in both cases. Thus the given numbers describe calls without parameters based on method search with indexing. So-called dynamic method searching approaches used in some pure object-oriented languages cause significantly more overhead.

- Accessing Object Components: 100-?% We assume that pointers to dynamically allocated memory are also used in the conventionally implemented system. The required machine code does not differ in either case (conventional and object-oriented) if the object-oriented language allows access to object components from outside. This kind of component access also occurs when object components are accessed within an object's method.

Accessing object components becomes much more expensive if method calls have to be used. In that case this operation can cost up to ten times more than a direct access. But this increase also occurs in conventional programs that are based on encapsulation and abstract data types.

- Automatic Garbage Collection: 105-150% Several factors determine the costs of automatic garbage collection: number and size of objects, available memory, frequency of object generation and, obviously, the method of garbage collection. Normally automatic garbage collection does not cost more than 5% of the overall run-time. This minimal overhead is made possible by sophisticated garbage collection methods that take into account that object-oriented programs generate numerous objects with short life times. Unfortunately, since many objects are generated during calculation intensive periods most garbage collection methods become active then. Thus slow downs may occur that cannot be tolerated in real-time applications. Incremental methods avoid this disadvantage. They search for unreferenced objects and dispose them quasi parallel to the actual program. This parallel garbage collection effort avoids abrupt slow downs but also retards normal execution.

o Overall Run-Time: 80-120% Though some factors cause a negative impact on a program's run-time, we could not observe a significant increase of the overall run-time. We believe that there are three reasons for this:

- Systems written in hybrid languages do not only use objects. Methods contain not only method calls but also "regular" statements. Many local variables and basic data types are used in hybrid languages. This means that no dynamic binding and access of object components occurs.

- Class libraries use highly efficient implementation techniques. For example, sets of objects are implemented by means of hash tables resulting in a constant factor required for searching an element. Usage of such classes means an increase of several magnitudes in run-time efficiency.

- Dynamic binding is less expensive than a sequence of selection statements. Conventional programs are cluttered with case statements that can be avoided in object-oriented systems.

- Memory Requirements: 120-200% Memory requirements of object-oriented systems depend not only on the source code size but also on method tables and dynamically allocated objects. The latter two aspects are discussed below.

The used class library exerts a strong influence on the memory requirements caused by source code. As already mentioned above the overall source code size increases due to direct and indirect reuse of classes. Finally, the compiler and linker determine the overall memory requirements. Some linkers are smart enough to identify classes and methods that are not used so that this overhead can be avoided.

o Method Tables: 101-110% The ratio of method table size and source code size depends on the number of methods provided by objects of a particular class as well as on the method size. If a class implements 20 methods, for example, all subclasses will cause at least 20 entries in the method table even though the methods are not overridden in subclasses. Thus many small methods lead to huge method tables. Nevertheless, the memory requirements of method tables are almost neglectable compared to the overall memory requirements.

- Dynamically Allocated Objects: 100-120% Usage of dynamically allocated objects means increased memory requirements to manage the objects. This is especially true for automatic garbage collection which requires additional information about an object's structure. If there also exists a method table that stores references to all objects, memory requirements can increase up to 20%. In case of simple memory management without garbage collection, objects are not more expensive than other dynamically allocated data.

2.2 Qualitative Aspects

This section presents qualitative aspects focused on project management and the final software product. The presented results are also corroborated by other authors, e.g., [4].

Impact on Project Management. The positive effects of object-oriented programming on several phases of the software life cycle result from the reduction of the semantic gap (developers can think in terms of real world objects), increased improvements result from the reuse of already tested components. Subsequently, implications of object-oriented software development on crucial software quality criterions are presented.

+ *Correctness and Reliability.* Since the correctness of a software system depends on the correctness of its components, the probability of producing a correct system is the higher when more matured software components can be reused. Components of a class library usually have been reused a number of times so that their correctness can be regarded as high (ideally 100%).

Furthermore, the usage of an application framework has a positive effect on the correctness of a software system, since cookbook recipes describe of how to combine framework components in order to achieve a certain goal. Adhering to these guidelines means avoiding typical errors.

The reliability of a software system is also tightly coupled with its correctness. So reusable object-oriented components exert a positive effect on this quality aspect.

Experience has proven that the time consumed for stabilizing a software system can be reduced to a third of the time required for conventional systems.

+ *User Friendliness.* The ease of use is especially improved if a system is based on a GUI application framework. GUI application frameworks anticipate much communication between application and user. This provides functionality that would not have been implemented in conventional applications since many features that make GUIs easier to use are hard to implement. Most GUI application frameworks, for example, support undoing/redoing of commands. Furthermore, several different look and feel standards are supported by some GUI frameworks so that applications based on such a framework can easily be ported to other look and feel standards.

Offering too much functionality could also be a disadvantage. Since it is very simple to provide certain features just by reusing components, many details could detract users from what they really want to do.

+ *Maintenability.* Due to the modularity of object-oriented programs, errors can easier be detected and localized: operations associated with objects are gathered in one class. Thus testing of object-oriented programs becomes easier, too.

Since frameworks define already much of a system's design, they cause a uniformity of all systems built on top of them. Thus learning details about an object-oriented system often means less effort compared to conventional ones.

Finally, polymorphism and dynamic binding promote extensibility as they can help to avoid case statements spread over a software system.

- *Efficiency.* Object-oriented software development might have a negative influence on a program's run-time and memory requirements (see the section about quantitative aspects for details). Taking the advances in hardware into consideration, these costs can almost be neglected.

- *Portability.* Porting object-oriented systems based on class libraries that depend on a specific hardware and operating system can be considered as hard as porting such conventionally implemented systems.

Furthermore, porting an object-oriented system from one language to another is anything but trivial: a C++ program, for example, cannot be transformed into a Smalltalk program or vice versa simply by syntactical changes. The different ways of thinking in both language worlds have to be matched.

reusability and thus the fact that less new code has to be written. It is no surprise that most disadvantages are related to the management of class libraries.

+ *Planning.* It can easier be determined in the planning phase of a project which subprojects/tasks will require most efforts. The reason for this lies in the reduced semantic gap and the better reusability of object-oriented building blocks. Because of the almost schematic way in which object-oriented systems are designed (especially if application frameworks are used), more time remains for planning.

+ *Organizational Effort.* Due to the reduced design and implementation efforts, smaller project teams are sufficient. Smaller teams ease the communication among the people and the coordination of subtasks.

+ *Design and Development.* Frameworks already anticipate much of a system's design. Thus elbowroom diminish which could else lead to bad design is diminished. Object-oriented programming supports a more homogeneous style so that programmers who are not involved in design decisions will be able to understand a systems's design more quickly.

Furthermore, design and implementation are more intertwined so that intermediate results will be produced within a shorter time frame. Thus project team members will experience a sense of achievement which can strongly motivate them.

+ *Division of Labor.* Object-oriented analysis and design produce class definitions which create a modularization of the system under development. The classes can be refined (i.e., implemented) almost independently by different teams or members of a team. Another kind of division of labor can be observed in larger organizations where a dedicated group is responsible for providing elementary classes and concepts.

+ *Prototyping.* Due to a reduced implementation effort, extensible prototypes (in the sense of evolutionary prototyping) for some system components can be developed within a short time. Application frameworks for graphic user interface programming also help to come up with user interface prototypes within a reasonable time if user interface prototyping tools are missing.

- *Settling-In Period.* Programmers with experience in conventional programming often have a hard time getting used to the new way of thinking which object-oriented software development requires. A couple of months are ususaly required to accomplish this migration from conventional paradigms to the object-oriented paradigm.

- *Management of a Class Library.* In order to benefit from a class library it has to be kept up-to-date. The required effort directly depends on the number of users of a particular class library, its size (i.e., number of classes) and the number of projects that are based on it.

- *Project Cost Calculations.* Due to reuse of software components it becomes unclear how to split the costs among several projects. A class developed in a project causes costs which are higher if the class is designed to be reusable in other projects. But other projects benefit from this additional effort. The costs of class library management have to be treated in a similar way: they have to be shared among several projects.

Implications on the Quality of the Final Product. Object-oriented software development improves the overall quality of the produced software. Quality

3 A Representative Case Study

We pick out the case study where a conventionally implemented user interface prototyping tool is compared to its object-oriented solution. This case study is representative since the two software systems have the "critical mass" as far as complexity is concerned. Furthermore, the software systems have been implemented by different teams—one at the University of Zurich and the other at the University of Linz. The case study mirrors the results presented in the previous section.

The conventionally implemented User Interface Construction Tool (UICT [1], implemented in Modula-2) and the object-oriented Dynamic Interface Construction Environment (DICE [6, 7], implemented in C++ with the application framework ET++ [3, 11, 12]) form the basis of one such large-scale case study used to evaluate the promises of object-oriented programming as well as its pros and cons compared to module-oriented software system development. (Both projects have been supported by Siemens AG Munich.) UICT and DICE serve for the prototyping-oriented development of graphic user interfaces under UNIX and the X11 window system.

The comparison of UICT's and DICE's development is based on concepts which the tools have in common. Table 1 shows these concepts and their realization in UICT and DICE.

Concepts	Realization in UICT	Realization in DICE
Prototype Specification	User Interface Description Language (Text-Oriented)	Graphic-Oriented Specification Formalism
Prototype Representation (Data Structures)	Intermediate Language Based on Arrays	(Sub)classes of an Application Framework
Prototype Simulation	Interpreter	Simulation Framework
Code Generation	Conventional Generator	Code Generation Framework

Table 1 Common UICT and DICE concepts together with their realization

We pick out the prototype representation component as typical example that corroborates the results presented above.

Prototype Representation—Employed Data Structures. The qualitative and quantitative comparison of UICT's and DICE's internal prototype representation considers the following aspects:

- We compare employed data structures as well as their management and investigate the influence of different ways of thinking (due to the module-oriented and object-oriented paradigm) on the internal prototype representation.

- The internal prototype representation plays an important role in each user interface prototyping tool. Effects of extensions/modifications of the internal representation are contrasted.

- The particular software components that implement the internal prototype representation are compared (using lines of code as a metric for a quantitative comparison). This comparison particularly considers the degree of software reuse.

Data Structures and Their Management. UICT and DICE have to store a prototype specification in an appropriate format. This is the precondition of a later simulation and code generation. We induce the following general statements from the comparison of employed data structures:

Data structures employed in the module-oriented implementation are not *active*. This means that modules dedicated to internal prototype representation store only *descriptions* of user interface objects, but not objects in an object-oriented sense. This causes other modules to implement routines that are based on these descriptions— descriptions (= data) and operations (= routines that manipulate and interpret these descriptions) are *separated*. This decreases the extensibility of the data structures.

A typical object-oriented implementation unifies data and operations and makes data structures active. This means that the description of an object's behavior forms a unit (the attributes of an object that constitute its state and all methods that determine its functionality). Furthermore, common behavior is factored out into an abstract class so that other components can be based on that class. Therefore modifications of common behavior are easier to accomplish.

Implication: The employed data structures and module/class architecture primarily result from different ways of thinking in the design of module-oriented and object-oriented software systems.

These general statements are drawn from UICT's and DICE's internal prototype representation:

Data Structures and Their Management in UICT: We first try to explain the main reason for UICT's overall module structure in order to outline the influence of such a modularization on the internal prototype representation: If a system is modularized, only the system's functionality is taken into account in most cases. UICT is a typical example. It consists of modules that *parse* a prototype specification, modules that *handle* tables (=the internal prototype representation), modules that *simulate* a prototype, and modules that *generate* code. Modules that handle an intermediate language stored in arrays (called UI Tables) realize UICT's internal prototype representation. All other modules are built around the table handler modules. (E.g., prototype specifications in UISL are parsed by Translator modules and then transformed and stored in UI Tables.)

A UI Table logically consists of two parts: an *object list* and a *symbol list*. The object list is a set of descriptions of user interface building blocks that are specified for a particular prototype. Thus an object list contains descriptions of user interface elements supported by UICT (e.g., menus, buttons, windows). The symbol list stores all names used in the prototype specification and for each name a reference to its description in the object list. Two modules, called *Table Handler* and *Symbol Table Handler*, manage UICT's prototype representation. This fine-grained modularization is based on the two logical parts of a UI Table.

Data Structures and Their Management in DICE: One design goal of DICE's internal prototype representation was that classes representing user interface elements should not only consist of their attributes described in instance variables but also of methods that determine their functionality, so that data and operations are really unified.

Another important design goal of DICE's internal prototype representation was to define an abstract class that factors out common behavior of user interface elements. Thus classes implementing graphic editor components as well as classes which initiate attribute definition (see below) of a user interface element, simulation of the particular prototype, and code generation can be based on such an abstract class. This is a precondition of a satisfying extensibility of the overall system.

We designed an abstract class called DICEItem for the reasons stated above. Subclasses of this abstract class represent specific user interface elements. Data management (i.e., management of several DICEItem instances) is accomplished by means of already existing ET++ classes for managing object collections.

Extensions of the Prototype Representation. By "extensions of the prototype representation" we mean adding new interface elements that are to be represented (this is the most important extension in connection with user interface prototyping tools). In this section we discuss the impact of such extensions on other components of the particular user interface prototyping tool.

In UICT's implementation object descriptions can be accessed from any other module in the system that imports the proper routines and data types from the modules that handle these descriptions. Changes (i.e., new kinds of object descriptions) to modules that handle these descriptions affect the whole software system. (Only changes to data structures that are internally employed by the table handler modules in order to store object descriptions do not affect the overall system.)

In DICE's implementation abstract classes define the common behavior of objects realizing the prototype representation. Other components of a system can be based on these abstract classes. Subclasses of the abstract classes describe specific object behavior. The software system is so flexible because new kinds of user interface elements can be added as subclasses to abstract classes without affecting the other components of the system.

Implications: The concepts inheritance, polymorphism and dynamic binding as offered by object-oriented programming languages are the preconditions for building extensible and reusable software systems: Inheritance opens the possibility of incrementally extending and adapting object descriptions of abstract classes that factor out common behavior. This is done in subclasses without changing the code of the abstract class. Polymorphism and dynamic binding allow the implementation of software components that are based on abstract classes. Thus these components are independent of specific object types.

Extensibility Aspects of DICE's Internal Prototype Representation: We illustrate the extensibility of DICE's components that are based on DICE's internal prototype representation (class DICEItem). We choose the attribute definition of user interface elements, which is part of DICE's specification component, as our example.

Attributes that describe a user interface element's behavior are defined in appropriate dialog boxes. Let us sketch the attribute definition of user interface elements from the user's point of view as a precondition of understanding its object-oriented implementation described below: In order to set attributes of user interface elements, one selects the particular user interface element and chooses the menu item "Item Attributes..." from a DICE-specific menu. A dialog box is opened where element-specific attributes are manipulated.

The implementation of attribute definition is based on the abstract class DICEItem: The crucial point is that classes comprising DICE's specification component should only implement a *framework* for attribute definition, i.e., handle mouse events, menu selections and the opening/closing of a dialog box in which attributes are manipulated. Only the window contents (i.e., the specific attributes) of the dialog box must be provided by the particular user interface element. The update of specific attributes which may be changed in the dialog box has to be accomplished by the particular user interface element, too, since attributes are instance variables of each user interface element. So the abstract class DICEItem defines two (abstract) methods for attribute definition called GetAttributesDialog and UpdateAttributes.

Arbitrary new interface elements can be added as subclasses of DICEItem. They just have to override the element-specific methods for attribute definition GetAttributesDialog and UpdateAttributes. Furthermore, instance variables representing their attributes must be added. Algorithms for attribute definition as implemented in the specification component still work since they are based on the abstract class DICEItem.

Thus typical object-oriented programming techniques (inheritance, dynamic binding, and polymorphism) are the precondition for the implementation of a framework for attribute definition.

Methods of DICEItem for simulation and code generation are designed in an analogous way. So simulation and code generation frameworks can be implemented based on DICEItem. They need not be changed if new user interface elements are added as subclasses of DICEItem.

Software Reuse. The comparison between UICT and DICE components that realize the particular internal prototype representation points out significant differences between module-oriented and object-oriented systems regarding reuse of already existing software components (see the discussion of the "Impact on Source Code Size" in Section 2.1).

We use the written lines of code and the average number of lines of code per routine/method to directly compare UICT's and DICE's components (see Table 2).

The amount of code that has to be written in UICT's Table Handler Module is about seven times as much as in DICE's component for internal prototype representation. The complexity of routines can be cut back to about one third in the object-oriented implementation. The main reason for such code and complexity reductions is the high reusability of application framework components.

The module-oriented user interface prototyping tool does not even reuse existing modules for managing data structures like lists, etc. Everything is implemented from scratch. This is done in such a way that modules implemented for that purpose in UICT are again very specific.

The object-oriented realization of the internal prototype representation reuses as much code as possible from the application framework it is based on. In case of DICE's prototype representation component, we can also calculate the ratio of reused and newly written code (see Table 3).

This ratio (newly written lines of code : reused lines of code = 1052 : 1307 = 1 : 1,24) strongly depends on the application framework that is used and the originality of the problem at hand.

	UICT's Prototype Representation Component	DICE's Prototype Representation Component
written lines of code	7600	1052
routines/methods	159	62
lines per routine/method	47,8	17,0

Table 2 Comparison of UICT's and DICE's prototype representation components based on common metrics

	DICE's Prototype Representation Component
newly written lines of code	1052
reused from ET++ classes	1307

Table 3 Ratio of reused and newly written code

4 Conclusion

The comparison of module-oriented and object-oriented system development demonstrates that object-oriented programming techniques are important techniques to produce software components that are open for extensions and thus reusable. Thus software quality can be raised and the amount of code to be written can be reduced.

However, the object-oriented programming paradigm is not sufficient for the achievement of systems that are extensible/reusable without problems (see, for instance, [8, 9]). Extensibility/reusability still has limits that cannot satisfy a system developer.

5 References

1. Bischofberger W., Pomberger G.: Prototyping-Oriented Software Development—Concepts and Tools; Springer Verlag, 1992.

2. Blaschek G.: Object-Oriented Programming with Prototypes; Springer Verlag, 1994.

3. Gamma E., Helm R., Johnson R., and Vlissides J.: Design Patterns—Microarchitecturs for Reusable Object-Oriented Software; Addison-Wesley, 1994.

4. Loves T.: Object Lessons; SIGS Publications, 1993.

5. Plösch R., Weinreich R.: An Extensible Communication Class Library for Hybrid Distributed Systems; Proceedings of TOOLS Pacific '92 conference, Sydney, 1992.

6. Pomberger G., Bischofberger W., Kolb D., Pree W., Schlemm H.: Prototyping-Oriented Software Development, Concepts and Tools; in Structured Programming Vol.12, No.1, Springer 1991.

7. Pree W.: Object-Oriented Versus Conventional Construction of User Interface Prototyping Tools; doctoral thesis, University of Linz, 1992.

8. Pree W.: Reusability Problems of Object-Oriented Software Building Blocks; EastEurOOPe'91, Bratislava, Czecho-Slovakia, September 15-19, 1991.

9. Taenzer D., Ganti M., Podar S.: Problems in Object-Oriented Software Reuse, Proceedings of the 1989 ECOOP, July 1989.

10. Vlissides J.M.: Generalized Graphical Object Editing; PhD Thesis, Stanford University, 1990.

11. Weinand A., Gamma E., Marty R.: ET++ - An Object-Oriented Application Framework in C++; OOPSLA'88, Special Issue of SIGPLAN Notices, Vol. 23, No. 11, 1988.

12. Weinand A., Gamma E.: The GUI Application Framework ET++; in Object-Oriented Software Frameworks (ed. Ted Lewis), Prentice Hall, 1994.

13. Weinreich R.: Concepts and Techniques for Object-Oriented Software Development—Illustrated by an Application Framework for Process Automation; doctoral thesis, University of Linz, 1993.

Towards a General Purpose Approach
to Object-Oriented Analysis

Flavio Bonfatti and Paola Daniela Monari

Dipartimento di Scienze dell'Ingegneria
Universita' di Modena

Abstract: *It is the aim of this paper to present an approach to object-oriented analysis that tends to be general purpose, in that it represents entities and events of the application domain without being affected by implementative issues. Thus, we wish to overcome major limitations of current object-oriented analysis methodologies: they produce schemas that are actually usable only in object-oriented development environments, and still express dynamic knowledge in natural language or in procedural form. Our approach is based on a object-oriented model that replaces the method, or routine, primitive with the law primitive and establishes a strict dependency between object structural and behavioural representations. In particular, the dynamics is described by constraining variations of object states by means of invariants expressed in the form of predicate calculus formulas.*

Keywords: *object-oriented analysis, object-oriented model, constraint representation.*

Introduction

A number of Object-Oriented Analysis (OOA) techniques has been developed as a consequence of the introduction of object-oriented programming languages and database systems. Such techniques are aimed at expressing the aspects of reality perceived by the observer by means of constructs that are derived from the basic concepts of the object-oriented paradigm. An analysis technique adopts a knowledge representation model and defines criteria (the methodology) for its correct application. Every model is characterized by a specific ontology that distinguishes it from the others. Analysis is applied in the early stage of the process that leads to design and implement data structures and software, with the purpose of filtering, organizing and relating the information available on the application domain. The analysis activity results in a schema that captures the knowledge considered necessary for the application development.

The current OOA models adopt, though in a rough version, the typical object-oriented programming means, that is, cross references between objects, methods, service requests and so on. The resulting schemas tend to anticipate the application organization in that they can be translated directly into data structures and routines. In other terms, the OOA techniques are strongly affected by implementative issues [15] and are conditioned by the underlying development environments. The consequence of this situation is that application design and development are better supported, but only in object-oriented environments.

This determines an objective limitation of OOA applicability. Thanks to its basic natural capability of capturing static and dynamic aspects of reality, the object-oriented paradigm could be conveniently employed as a general purpose analysis approach. In fact, at present, only a small number of applications makes use of object-oriented environments, while most are still developed by means of structured languages and relational database systems. Unfortunately, the analysis techniques available for these traditional environments are based on models, such as Entity/Relationship [9] and Data Flow Diagrams [10], that present low levels of formalization and mantain a cumbersome separation between data and process representations.

Further reasons in favour of a general purpose analysis approach are: (i) independence between analysis and next phases, that is, possibility of carrying out analysis before choosing the software development environment; (ii) independence from the computer system, that is, possibility of using analysis results as a basis for application developments in different environments; (iii) independence from evolution of technology, that is, opportunity of keeping the same schema valid even when the software environment is upgraded or replaced. In general, we can extend what is said in [16] by asserting that, in the long run, the reuse of analysis results is probably more important than the reuse of code.

In addition to the previous requirements, the analysis approach should guarantee a higher and more uniform level of formalization in representing static and dynamic aspects of the application context. Both traditional and object-oriented models are informal or semi-formal, since they leave most knowledge expressed in natural language or in procedural form. They pursue ease of use, through adoption of graphical primitives, rather than completeness and verifiability of results, thus being suitable and satisfactory only in the very early stage of domain representation. Several object-oriented models [8, 13] offer primitives for describing object structural properties, a few [11] allow a formalization of conditions and invariants, but none assures a homogeneous and complete representation of real world dynamics.

It is the aim of this paper to present an approach to OOA that tends to overcome the above problems. The approach adopts an object-oriented model whose primitives are based on Bunge's ontology [7] as proposed in [15]. The model sets strict dependence between structural and dynamic aspects through the introduction of the concepts of complex object and law. The method, or routine primitive is abandoned. The dynamics is described by constraining object state variations by means of invariants expressed in the form of predicate calculus formulas [1].

The paper consists of four sections. Section 1 introduces the basic features of our approach, in comparison with major current OOA approaches. Section 2 shows how the ontological concepts of entity and event are modelled in terms of the complex object and law model primitives. In Section 3, the case of related events is discussed and our idea of bedded encapsulation, aimed at increasing object independence, is explained. Finally, in Section 4 we show other types of constraints including context-free laws, class-object laws and state diagram laws.

1.   A General Purpose Approach

In order to show the main features of our approach, it is useful to refer to other OOA techniques in the literature. In particular, we consider four different approaches: the first, proposed by Coad e Yourdon [8], is generally known as a data-driven approach; the second, more recent, by Wirfs-Brock [16], is known as the responsibility-driven approach; the third, a very practical object modelling technique (OMT) is presented in [13]; the fourth is the approach implied by the Eiffel model, developed by Meyer and described in [11].

With the data-driven approach, every object represents a real world entity and is characterized step by step: first in terms of attributes, then through its positioning within the classification structure, furtherly by specifying possible composition relations, and finally by modelling its behaviour as the set of services it can perform. Three graphical primitives represent, respectively, specialization relations (isa), composition relations (part-of) and other kinds. Relation attributes must be expressed as attributes of the objects participating in it. Relations involving three or more entities should be split into a number of binary relations. A similar point of view is adopted in [13] in defining the object model and the dynamic model of the OMT technique: even though a relation may have its own attributes, its behaviour must be modelled as the behaviour of the participating objects. All these choices confirm the strong dependence of current approaches on implementative issues: the analysis method mirrors capabilities and limitations of the classical object-oriented paradigm.

The responsibility-driven approach [16] sets as main analysis objective the identification of services exchanged between objects in terms of collaborations and contracts. In order to obtain a high degree of encapsulation, objects are described just through the services they can perform on request, and the services themselves are given simply an external representation. Thus, the application domain is perceived through the information processes that objects perform when required by other objects. Since relations are expressed by a net of cross references, mutual influences among three or more objects must be coded by a number of methods, each related to a single object. Even this approach looks heavily influenced by implementative questions, the processes being conceived for a straightforward translation into software routines.

Both in [8] and in [13] state diagrams are proposed as a means for representing single object dynamics. In addition to a very low level of formalization, this solution is not exhaustive since mutual influences among objects are left out, in particular the possibility that state variations of an object induce state variations on related objects. A more formal approach is proposed by Meyer [11] through the Eiffel model, where object dynamics is partially expressed in assertional form. More precisely, Meyer distinguishes between an invariant associated to the object definition and pre- and post-conditions associated to the object routines. The former represents the legal condition of the object state, while the latter express requirements that clients must satisfy whenever they call a routine and conditions that the supplier (the routine itself) guarantees on return. Unfortunately, Eiffel mantains splitting and hiding a significant part of object dynamics into routines, following once more an implementative viewpoint.

The approach we propose in this paper is based on two phases: the *requirement specification* phase and the *modelling* phase. The former is aimed at informally expressing the perception the observer has of static and dynamic aspects of the application domain in particular entities and events that involve them. The latter is aimed at formally describing the application domain with the Multidata model primitives [2, 4], that represent entities as objects, relations as complex objects and behaviours in the form of laws and actions. The Multidata model has been developed within the homonymous project of the Italian National Research Council (CNR), with the purpose of studying a unified representation paradigm suitable for applications characterized by great complexity and a wide variety of informational aspects (descriptive, geographic, textual).

The requirements specification phase follows an itinerary proposed first in [15], and ispired to the formal ontology of M. Bunge [7]. In the following, the basic informal principles derived from Bunge's ontology are briefly presented:

--   Real world *entities* are modelled as objects. Properties by means of which entities are perceived are expressed as attribute values. The object states are given by the sets of their attribute values. In general, an object is characterized by a structure and a behaviour: isomorphic objects, that is, objects sharing the same structure and behaviour, are grouped as belonging to the same class. The analysis of the application domain is aimed at identifying and modelling the structure and behaviour of the observed classes. The state of the whole application domain is given by the states of all the objects that realize its representation.

--   *Events* occurring in the real world modify its state, the state of the representation must change accordingly. State changes are the means the observer has available to perceive entity dynamics. When the states of some objects change contextually, a relationship exists among them. In other words, objects are related when changes in the state of one or more of them depend on the states of the others. In this way the observer identifies the existence of relationships: the behaviour of an entity being determined by the combined states of other n-1 entities, an n-ary relationship is recognized.

--   An event is characterized by the conditions of its occurrence (time, place, and so on), the entities it involves and the effects it produces. Effects concern state changes, creation or deletion of entities. Events present regularities that can be expressed in the form of laws, that is, invariants among the states of the involved entities. Laws act as constraints on domain representation, since they force the representation to behave like the real world.

--   The effects of an event include the possibility of triggering other events. The variations introduced in the system state can determine the conditions that force other events to take place. A necessary condition to have events induced by others is sharing one or more involved entities. Dependences among events are modelled as further relationships and propagation regularities can be expressed by laws.

These considerations highlight the role the analysis of events plays in the design of an information system. In the requirements specification phase the observer has to identify, besides the entities of interest for the application, all the events that can influence the system state. In the modelling phase he/she has to define by abstraction the event types, describe each type in terms of involved objects and characteristic attributes and express possible laws determining their effects. The dynamics is then modelled by laws capturing all the observable regularities about object states and transformations and, as we shall see, by actions representing how the system must react in order to restore the correct relations among the object states. This idea of dynamics differs substantially from that of the classical object-oriented paradigm, and leads to a unified representation of states and state transformations, thus overcoming the burdensome separation between object structure and object methods (or routines).

The emphasis this methodology puts on recognizing and characterizing dynamics in terms of relations and invariants is particularly suitable to face the analysis of complex applications. We consider an application complex where a large variety of events must be taken into account, each entity participates in many events under different conditions, and events are related with each other by the entities they share. The methodology is presently employed in the areas of Computer Integrated Manufacturing and Engineering, Software Engineering and Geographical Information Systems.

2. Entities and Events

The concept of *object* we adopt is similar to that of the classical object-oriented paradigm, with the exceptions of methods. Real world entities are modelled as objects. A class of objects is constituted by the objects of a certain type that are present, at a certain time, in the real world. From a structural point of view, an object type is characterized by a name and a list of attributes. An attribute is declared by a pair (Attribute: domain) that gives the set of values it can take. These are two examples:

```
object Product
Name: string
MinQty,QtyOnHand: integer
AvgValue,ValOnHand: real
Availability: (Full,Critical,None);

object Supplier
Name,Address: string
Credit,MaxCredit: real;
```

The *complex object* primitive is introduced, in its turn, to represent the existence of relationships among entities. The complex object structure is also described through a type declaration. It includes, besides the attribute declarations, the component declarations, that is, the objects that participate in the relationship. A component is declared by a pair (Role: Object) defining the type of object that can play the given role, as in the following examples:

```
object Offer
Suppl: Supplier
Prod: Product
Price: real
FromDate,ToDate: date;

object Delivery
Date: date
Suppl: Supplier
Prod: Product
Qty: integer
Price: real;
```

Both these complex objects express relationships between suppliers and products. The former relates suppliers to the products they sell, while price and relative validity period are attributes of the relationship. The latter refers to the relationship that is established between a supplier and a product as a consequence of a delivery event. As we shall see, consistency constraints can be defined between offer and delivery.

Laws are introduced to constraint the behaviour of objects to which they are applied. Conceptual representation of dynamics implies that the space of states of an object type is partitioned into the space of legal states and the space of illegal states. The space of legal states is a subset of all possible combinations of values that can be taken by the attributes of that type of object (and by the attributes of its components). Partition is obtained by a set of laws. Moreover, a state transformation may be considered illegal even though it maps from a legal state to another legal state: other laws are required to delimit the space of legal trasformations. If taken in conjunction, all the laws defined for an object type constitute the invariant that expresses the dynamics of the object with respect to its attributes and components.

Laws are written as expressions of the predicate calculus, applied to the current and previous states of the object and its components [1]. Thus, the invariant establishes a bridge between the state of the object and the states of its components. In order to clearly separate the object laws from those associated to the single components alone, we assume that they cannot refer directly to the states of components of these components. The implications of this assumption will be examined later.

```
laws on Product
L1: QtyOnHand ge 0
L2: MinQty le 500
L3: Availability eq Full <=> QtyOnHand gt MinQty
L4: Availability eq Critical <=>
      QtyOnHand lt MinQty and QtyOnHand gt 0
L5: Availability eq None <=> QtyOnHand eq 0
L6: ValueOnHand eq QtyOnHand * AvgValue;
```

In this example we can see some typical constraints: restrictions of the definition domains of attributes (L1, L2), functional dependences between attributes (L6), and equivalences between predicates and attributes values that are introduced to characterize significant situations (L3, L4, L5).

In complex objects, laws are used to relate the spaces of legal states and transformations of the object itself to those of its components. For instance, the following laws:

```
laws on Delivery
L1: Prod.QtyOnHand eq old Prod.QtyOnHand + Qty
L2: Suppl.Credit eq old Suppl.Credit + Qty * Price;
```

show how the current (modified) states of product and supplier depend on the previous (old) states, through the attributes Qty and Price of Delivery. Note that the *old* notation behaves, mutatis mutandis, like the homologous notation used in Eiffel [11]. In addition, particular constraints based on presence or absence of components can be of interest, as in laws L2 and L3 below:

```
laws on Offer
L1: FromDate lt ToDate
L2: Supplier ne nil
L3: Product ne nil;
```

As in the classic object-oriented approach, an object type can be defined as a specialization of another type of upper level. The specialized type inherits the properties of the object it descends from, apart from those added or redefined. Redefining a component means mapping the role into a subtype. The object definition by specialization is obtained relating it to the supertype by the keyword *isa*, and possibly adding new attributes and components or restricting their definition domains, as in the following example:

```
object Pump isa Product
Displacement: real;

laws on Pump
L1: Displacement in [25 to 100]
L2: MinQty eq 100;
```

where the restriction predicates are expressed in form of laws.

Observe that all laws can be viewed as post-conditions, in that they apply to the effects of events in order to check whether they satisfy the object invariant. In the application that will be derived from the domain schema, errors may be made in notifying event occurrences and effects, and this could result in wrong or incomplete updates of the system state. Each error violates one or more laws: in order to code the reaction the application should have to keep the representation legal, we associate *actions* to laws.

Consider, for example, law L1 on Delivery and suppose that a delivery instance has been created without modifying the QtyOnHand attribute of the Product component. The action to undertake should be:

```
L1: Prod.QtyOnHand eq old Prod.QtyOnHand + Qty
    {action:Prod.QtyOnHand:=old Prod.QtyOnHand+Qty}
```

while in other cases a diagnostic message can be issued or the update operation can be aborted. In general, actions take the aspect of informal comments or algorithms written in a procedural language. They represent the residual part of the schema that eludes consistency and correctness controls. Nevertheless, we invite the analyst to code them, no matter in which form, since they integrate objects and laws definitions in specifying the functions that the application will perform.

The association of restoring actions to laws must satisfy serializability criteria. In general, a state variation may imply violations of a number of laws and, hence, execution of the corresponding actions. It is necessary that the result of these actions is independent of their execution order. If the restoring actions associated to two or more laws are not serializable, such laws are dependent from each other. This calls for a schema revision involving, for instance, conjunction of the laws into a unique predicate with a compound action. The trivial solution of expressing the whole object invariant as a single law and a single restoring algorithm is always correct. However, splitting the invariant into the largest possible number of independent laws provides much more information to the development phase, particularly towards software modularity. In the following examples, actions are not specified as they often derive strightforwardly from the relative laws or their definition would require burdensome considerations.

With this approach, laws and the related actions replace methods and message connections of the classical OOA techniques. A first advantage arises from expressing a significant part of dynamic knowledge in declarative form, available to validation and suitable for consistency checking. Furtherly, the resulting schema is no more finalized to use in object-oriented environments, since laws and actions can be mapped indifferently into methods or structured routines. Observe that this solution differs substantially from that proposed in [12], where Minsky and Rozenshtein propose laws as meta-knowledge to regulate message passing and methods execution.

Modelling relationships among entities as complex objects originates a composition graph where every object is a node, and the composition relation is expressed as an oriented arc connecting the components to the complex object. The existence of cycles is allowed in most current object models, in particular in [13]. Our modelling strategy tends to remove cycles in order to obtain a composition direct acyclic graph, with evident semantic advantages. For instance, consider the following cyclic definition:

```
object Agent isa Supplier
Firm: Supplier;
```

Even though this recursion looks effective, its interpretation on the basis of the ontology we have adopted becomes difficult: an agent is seen as an event concerning the represented firm. Instead, a clearer semantics results from the following acyclic definitions:

```
object Agent isa Supplier;
```

```
object Agency
Responsible: Agent
Firm: Supplier;
```

Finally, material composition is considered nothing but a particular case of relationship, and it is modelled as well in form of complex object. As an example, we can detail the above definition of pump:

```
object Pump isa Product
Displacement: real
Bdy: Body
Rtr: Rotor;
```

so that a pump is seen as a relationship between a body and a rotor. However, if the objects Body and Rotor are considered themselves specializations of Product, a cyclic definition is obtained. As we have seen, the cycle can be removed by going back to the first definition of pump and introducing the following relationship:

```
object Assembly
Compound: Pump
FirstComponent: Body
SecondComponent: Rotor;
```

An alternative solution is based on the following definitions:

```
object PumpBody              object PumpRotor
Compound: Pump               Compound: Pump
Component: Body;             Component: Rotor;
```

The former is chosen if laws exist that consider together properties of pump, body and rotor while the latter is preferred if pump is related separately to body and rotor.

3.   Complex Events

Entity and event representation, in the form that has been proposed in the previous section, becomes more and more complex if the situations to model include related events or events that induce other events. With our approach, every complex object is introduced with the main purpose of creating the seat for laws that express event dynamics. As further relations are identified by going deeper into the application domain analysis, the schema is modified, previous complex objects are revised and new complex objects are introduced. Our model supports this refinement process, as it is shown in the following examples. We introduce first the concept of purchase order:

```
object Order
Prod: Product
Suppl: Supplier
IssueDate,DueDate: date
RequestedQty,DeliveredQty: integer
Price: real
Status: (issued,inProgress,closed,cancelled);
```

```
laws on Order
L1: RequestedQty gt 0
L2: DeliveredQty ge 0
L3: DeliveredQty le RequestedQty
L4: IssueDate lt DueDate
L5: Prod.QtyOnHand eq old Prod.QtyOnHand +
            DeliveredQty - old DeliveredQty
L6: Suppl.Credit = old Suppl.Credit +
            (DeliveredQty - old DeliveredQty) * Price;
L7: old Suppl.Credit + RequestedQty * Price
            le Suppl.MaxCredit
```

where, in particular, laws L5 and L6 relate product quantity on hand and supplier credit to the order information, while law L7 constitutes a sort of order acceptance constraint in that it fixes an upper limit for the credit the supplier can have (clearly, payment events decrease the credit values). Now we introduce the event DeliveryOnOrder:

```
object DeliveryOnOrder
Date: date
Order: Order
Qty: integer
Price: real
InTime: boolean;

laws on DeliveryOnOrder
L1: Date ge IssueDate
L2: InTime <=> Date le DueDate
L3: Price eq Order.Price
L4: DeliveredQty eq old DeliveredQty + Qty;
```

where the association between supplier and delivery is no more direct, but it passes through order. If we compare this definition with that of delivery given in the previous section, we observe the following differencies: (i) in place of law L1 of Delivery, stating that the delivered quantity increases the product quantity on hand, we have law L4 of DeliveryOnOrder to be combined with law L5 of Order; and (ii) in place of law L2 of Delivery, stating that the supplier credit is increased of the value of the delivered goods, we have laws L3 and L4 of DeliveryOnOrder to be combined with law L6 of Order.

A further difference appears if we imagine that DeliveryOnOrder has an attribute that says whether the product quality is controlled by the supplier, and this information is also associated to Product:

```
object DeliveryOnOrder          object Product
Controlled: boolean             Controlled: boolean
... ... ...                     ... ... ...
```

A law should establish that the two values must be equal for every delivery event, but Product is not a component of DeliveryOnOrder, since the Order definition is put in between, and hence a law directly involving DeliveryOnOrder and Product cannot be written. The solution consists in providing Order with an homologous attribute:

```
object Order
Controlled: boolean
... ... ...
laws on Order
L8: Controlled eq Prod.Controlled
```

and issuing the following law on DeliveryOnOrder:

```
L5: Controlled eq Order.Controlled
```

In conclusion, whenever it is required to define constraints between the state of an object X and that of a sub-component A1 of a component A of X, the solution consists in splitting the law into two parts: the one, associated to A, introduces (imports) A attributes that mirror the A1 attributes of interest; the other, associated to X, expresses the constraints with respect to the imported attributes. At a first sight, this gives rise to redundancies in the schema definitions, but the degree of independency between definitions, as well as that of reusability and replaceability, is substantially increased.

Following this approach, every object in the schema is characterized by two kinds of laws: internal (context-free) laws, that represent its intrinsic constraints possibly related to the component states, and external (context-dependent) laws, associated to the complex objects where it participates as component, that express its behaviours in the corresponding contexts. This realizes a neat partition of laws, since some of them can be changed without affecting those belonging to other contexts, thus obtaining a sort of additional bedded encapsulation. On the other hand, context-free and context-dependent laws must be consistent, in that the latter should result more restrictive than the former. The logical form that has been adopted for laws makes consistency controls easier and creates the conditions for realizing coherent and reliable schemas of the application domain.

4. Further Constraints

While modelling complex events, some situations occur that are of noticeable interest for their frequency and for being associated to special kinds of constraints. In this section we examine three of them involving, respectively, context-free constraints defined on two or more objects, constraints defined on classes of objects, constraints describing state diagrams.

If two or more objects participate together in different relationships, the corresponding complex objects have associated constraints depending on the relative contexts. It may occur that these laws share a common part: if existing, it represents the constraints that such objects must satisfy in any context, that is, their context-free constraints. These rules can be removed from the single relationships and associated to a virtual object, introduced to this purpose, where the involved objects play the role of main components.

As an example, suppose that in all the events where a product is associated to the relative supplier (offers, orders, deliveries) the Controlled attribute of Product may depend on the Certified attribute of Supplier. More precisely, if supplier is certified to sell controlled products, the quality of all its products is assured. This constraint can be expressed once for all within the following virtual object:

```
object SupplierProduct as S: Supplier, P: Product;

laws on SupplierProduct
L1: S.Certified => P.Controlled;
```

Law L1 is considered applied to all the complex objects that include Supplier and Product as components, in conjunction with the other laws of those objects. In other words, the virtual object plays the role of virtual component.

So far we have dealt with constraints that are considered applied to single instances of simple or complex objects, but sometimes constraints relating the state of an istance to the states of the other instances of the same class are required. These typically involve conditions on class cardinality or synthesis (average, maximum, sum) values. From the modelling point of view, a class is represented as any other object, with the addition of an implicit component (*Instances*) constituted by the set of all the instances. For example, we can avoid overlapping offers with the following constraint:

```
object Offers as class of Offer;

laws on Offers
let LastOffer = difference(Instances,old Instances)
L1: LastOffer ne nil =>
        not exists O in Instances suchthat
        LastOffer.Prod eq O.Prod and
        LastOffer.Suppl eq O.Suppl and
        LastOffer.FromDate lt O.ToDate
        {action: msg "pricelist overlapping",
            LastOffer.FromDate := O.ToDate};
```

where the *let* pseudo-instruction introduces a temporary variable representing the last instance added to the offer class, obtained as difference between the successive states of the Instances implicit component: if the last state variation of object Offers was not the creation of a new instance, LastOffer results nil.

A combined use of virtual object and class object is shown in the following example:

```
object DeliveryOffers as D: Delivery, Os: Offers;

laws on DeliveryOffers
L1: exists O in Os.Instances suchthat
D.Suppl eq O.Suppl and
D.Prod eq O.Prod and
D.Date ge O.FromDate and D.Date le O.ToDate =>
        D.Price eq O.Price;
```

where it is imposed that, for each delivery, an instance must exist in the class of offers that fixes the product price.

Finally, among all the possible states an object is allowed to take, the analyst can choose some that are particularly suitable to express an automaton-like evolution of the object itself. The idea that the behaviour of an object could be described by state diagrams is widely accepted: in [8] it is proposed as a strategy for identifying object methods, in [13] it is considered fundamental to define the dynamic model.

In order to represent the object as a finite-state automaton, we introduce an attribute with as many values as the automaton states, and express transitions as changes of its value. With our approach, transitions are triggered by events that modify the state of the object or those of its components. As an example, consider the evolution of Order in terms of the attribute Phase with the following significant values:

```
Phase: (issued,inProgress,closed,cancelled)
```

Firstly, we associate the issued phase to the initial condition of an order, by the following class law:

```
object Orders = class of Orders;

laws on Orders
let LastOrder = difference(Instances,old Instances)
L1: LastOrder ne nil => LastOrder.Phase eq issued;
```

Then, we represent the following transitions: issued -> inProgress, inProgress -> closed; issued -> closed, issued -> cancelled. The triggers of the first three transitions are identified by internal modifications of the object Order:

```
let Partial = old DeliveredQty eq 0 and
 DeliveredQty gt 0 and DeliveredQty le RequestedQty
let Total = old DeliveredQty lt RequestedQty and
 DeliveredQty eq RequestedQty
```

and the corresponding transitions, expressed as laws of Orders, become:

```
L9:  old Phase eq issued and Partial =>
 Phase eq inProgress
L10: old Phase eq inProgress and Total =>
 Phase eq closed
L11: old Phase eq issued and Total =>
 Phase eq closed
```

The last transition, moving from the issued phase to the cancelled phase, is directly triggered within an event represented by:

```
object OrderVerification
Date: date
Order: Order
... ... ...

laws on OrderVerification
L1: Date ge Order.IssueDate
let Expired = Date gt Order.DueDate + 90
L2: old Order.Phase eq issued and Expired =>
 Phase eq cancelled;
```

Observe that, in order to group within Order all the laws referring to state transitions, we can add the new attribute `Cancel:boolean` to Order, modify law L2 of OrderVerification:

```
L2: old Order.Phase eq issued and Expired => Cancel
```

and issue the following law on Order:

```
L12: old Phase eq issued and Cancel
     => Phase eq cancelled;
```

Conclusions

An approach to object-oriented analysis that tends to be general purpose has been presented. It is based on a model that replaces the method, or routine primitive, with the law primitive and establishes strict dependence between structural and behavioural representations. Major advantages of this approach are explicit representation of relationships, expression in declarative form of a significant part of dynamic knowledge, realization of schemas available for validation and suitable for consistency checking.

The approach is presently being experimented. In the area of Computer Integrated Manufacturing and Engineering it is employed to represent products and production processes for design and planning purposes; this problem constitutes the core of project 8224 of the ESPRIT programme named RUMS = a Rule-based Manufacturing Modelling System [6]. In the area of Software Engineering it is under study as a means for specifying software requirements for programmable logic controllers; this activity is carried out within project 10542 of the ESSI initiative named EASIER = Enhancing Application Software Implementation for programmable logic controllERs. Finally, it is tested in the conceptual design of the Geographical Information Systems of the National Geological Survey of Italy [3, 5].

A computer-aided support, based on the approach proposed in this paper, is under development to help the observer realize a rich, reliable conceptual schema of the application domain. The observer enters definitions of objects and laws and the system provides a number of correctness and consistency controls. In particular, two kinds of controls are identified: consistency along the classification hierarchy to ensure that specialized objects do not contradict the definitions of the upper objects, and consistency along the composition graph to ensure the compatibility of internal and external laws of all objects. The resulting schema can be navigated in order to verify and validate the depth and quality of the representation, or it can be used as a sound basis for the design of database structures and application software.

Further developments of the proposed approach include:
--   Introduction of a graphical notation to help the analyst focus the main aspects of the application domain. Consider, however, that such notation will remain limited to the static (structural) component of the schema and to particular dynamic constructs (e.g. automata).

-- Definition of mapping functions from the conceptual schema to both relational and object-oriented data structure, in order to provide effective design strategies.

-- Definition of mapping functions from schema laws and actions to structured and object-oriented routines, with the final aim of studying possible automatic code generation procedures.

References

[1] Bertino E. et al.: Object-oriented query languages: the notion and the issues, IEEE Trans. on Knowledge and Data Engineering, 4, 3, 1992.

[2] Bonfatti F., Pazzi L.: Modeling object complexity and behaviour: towards an ontological paradigm, COMPEURO 91 International Conf., Bologna, 1991.

[3] Bonfatti F.: Intensional design of geographical information systems, EGIS 93 International Conf., Genova, 1993.

[4] Bonfatti F., Pazzi L.: An ontology-driven approach to knowledge representation, International workshop on Formal Ontology in Conceptual Analysis and Knowledge Representation, Padova, 1993.

[5] Bonfatti F., Monari P. D.: Spatio-temporal modeling of complex geographic structures, CSEIA 93, IFIP WG5.11 Working Conference, Como, 1993.

[6] Bonfatti F., Monari P. D., Paganelli P.: Towards a rule-based unified product modelling, DKSME94 (Data and Knowledge System for Manufacturing and Engineering) International Conf., Hong Kong, 1994.

[7] Bunge M.: Treatise on Basic Philosophy, vols. 3 and 4, Ontology, Reider Publisher, 1979.

[8] Coad P., Yourdon E.: Object Oriented Analysis, Yourdon Press, 1990.

[9] Chen P. P. S.: The entity-relationship model - toward a unified view of data, ACM Trans. on Database System, 1, 1, 1976.

[10] De Marco T.: Structured Analysis and System Specification, Yourdon Press, 1978

[11] Meyer B.: Object Oriented Software Construction, Prentice Hall, 1988.

[12] Minsky N. H., Rozenshtein D.: A law-based approach to object-oriented programming, Proc. of the OOPSLA 87 Conf., Orlando Fla, 1987.

[13] Rumbaugh J. et al.: Object-Oriented Modeling and Design, Prentice Hall, 1991.

[14] Spivey J. M.: The Z-notation, Prentice Hall, 1989.

[15] Wand Y.: A proposal for a formal model of objects, in Object-Oriented Concepts, Databases and Applications, W. Kim F. Lochowsky eds., Addison Wesley, 1989.

[16] Wirfs-Brock R. J., Johnson R. E.: Current research in object-oriented design, Communications of the ACM, 33, 9, 1990.

A Seamless Model for
Object-Oriented Systems Development

Stephen W. Liddle
David W. Embley
Scott N. Woodfield
{liddle,embley,woodfiel}@cs.byu.edu

Department of Computer Science
Brigham Young University
Provo, UT 84602 USA

Abstract. Existing approaches to object-oriented system development are poorly integrated in several ways. This inadequate integration is ubiquitous and causes numerous inefficiencies in the object-oriented development process. These problems can be addressed by abandoning typical object-oriented models in favor of a single, seamless system model. By using a seamless model, such as the one we propose, not only do we overcome the integration inefficiences to which we allude, but we also raise the level of abstraction for object-oriented system implementation and enable same-paradigm system evolution.

1 Introduction

Object-oriented development systems are poorly integrated across several spectrums. These include:

(1) the software development lifecycle and the models, languages, and tools used to develop software;

(2) the impedance mismatch between the semantics of persistent objects and the behavioral protocols for objects, between declarative and imperative programming paradigms, and between visual and textual styles of programming; and

(3) the reification of abstract objects — particularly, meta-information and high-level abstractions of low-level modeling components.

Poor integration over the software development spectrum causes unnecessary difficulties in making transitions from one phase of development to another, from one model to another, from one language to another, and from one tool to another. Impedance mismatches cause users to devise interoperability interfaces among mismatched views or to suffer difficulties that arise such as switching from associative to record-based access, implementing naturally declarative subapplications imperatively and vice versa, and converting diagrammatic specifications into linear code and, sometimes, vice versa, such as for user interfaces. Lack of reification prevents natural access to meta-information and thus makes applications that involve evolution, reflection, and megaprogramming more difficult. Lack of reification also prevents natural abstraction scalability and leads to awkward and unusable abstractions.

In this paper, we propose an approach for object-oriented systems that tightly integrates lifecycle, model, language, tool, persistence, behavior, programming paradigm and style, information and meta-information, and high- and low-level abstraction. The foundation for our approach is a formally defined logical model that is seamless in three ways.

(1) It maintains a single software development paradigm across analysis, design, and implementation, and consequently also provides for software evolution in the same paradigm.

(2) It resolves the impedance mismatch between structural and behavioral components of the language, between imperative and declarative programming paradigms, and between visual and textual representation.

(3) It addresses reification by making meta-level information fully accessible and modifiable and by making all high-level abstractions first-class components.

Section 2 of the paper discusses the principles involved in integrating across all the spectrums of interest.

In addition to discussing underlying principles, we also demonstrate our approach by describing our state-of-the-art model and programming language for active object database systems that is seamless in all three ways. In Section 3 we provide an overview of our logical system model and explain how it addresses the problems we have identified. In Section 4, we briefly describe our implementation language, and explain how it is tightly woven together with our logical model to implement our software development principles. We also give a brief general description of our language to indicate why it is indeed sufficient for implementation of active object database systems, and we report on our implementation status.

Although this is a framework paper and therefore written at a high, summary level, we emphasize that considerable detailed work has been accomplished. The references to our own work throughout this paper provide much of the detail. Technical reports and pre-alpha versions of much of this material is available through anonymous ftp at osm7.cs.byu.edu and through the World Wide Web, also at osm7.cs.byu.edu (URL http://osm7.cs.byu.edu/HomePage.html).

2 Integration Problems and Principles

In this section, we further motivate our system development approach by illustrating problems that arise because of lack of integration in various areas. We discuss the principles behind our approach and describe how these principles can help alleviate the problems we have identified.

2.1 Object-Oriented Software Development Approaches

The typical object-oriented software development lifecycle has several phases: analysis, specification, design, implementation, and evolution. Usually, these phases feed back into one another. For example, the output of design may be the input for analysis as another round of development occurs; or a problem may be discovered during implementation that requires changes to the specification.

Often, the object-oriented model changes as the development proceeds from one phase to another. For example, a general logical model such as OMT [27] may be used for analysis, while a specific language model, such as Smalltalk or C++, is used for implementation. This happens because during analysis, we do not want to consider the details of computer-based implementation, but during implementation we must make the model executable and efficient.

As a system moves through the development lifecycle, transformations between different models are frequently difficult to make and may involve loss of information. Approaches that try to alleviate this problem, such as CASE tools, usually are applicable only to a narrow problem domain, such as accounting or manufacturing process control. Other approaches encourage analysis and design to be done with specific target language concepts. For example, Booch's method pushes C++ language concepts (e.g., public, protected, and private class interfaces) into the analysis and design model [3]. This can be a problem if general concepts are missing in the target-language model. For instance, C++ does not have persistence or concurrency control. Thus, an analysis model based strictly on C++ or targeted specifically to C++ would be inappropriate for data modeling problems that require database facilities, such as a general ledger system or a point-of-sale/inventory-control application.

Systems that splice data models and programming languages together are likely to have the integration problems we are talking about (e.g., [1,27]). It is typical to do analysis and design using ER models, data-flow diagrams, and Harel statecharts, and then have the development tool generate class templates for the system in, say, C++. However, at this point we lose important features from our analysis/design model such as persistence and concurrency.

Another problem is the difficulty of maintaining traceability. This is because changes to the implementation may not have a direct correspondence to concepts in the analysis/design model and vice versa. Unless a development tool is strict about controlling changes to the implementation and analysis/design, evolution of the system on either the implementation or analysis/design side will cause a loss of traceability between the two.

2.2 Development Lifecycle Unification

The software development lifecycle should have a unified paradigm. That is, a single model should be used for analysis, specification, design, implementation, and evolution. A single model can guarantee information-preserving transitions from one phase of development to another. Furthermore, a single model creates a greater likelihood that supporting computer-based tools will be cogent and cohesive, especially since tool-driven transformations can be closed under the single model. The components of a system implemented using such a model are fully traceable from specification to implementation, making system verification and maintenance more manageable.

The greatest objection to a unified paradigm may be the question of whether a single model is appropriate for all phases of software development. Our answer is a qualified, "yes." A single logical model can address the needs of analysis, specification, design, and high-level implementation. However, low-level implementation is problematic. To achieve required efficiency, we must often resort to fine-tuning at a lower level. For example, we may program in a language such as Smalltalk, but use a library of methods that has been hand-optimized in the assembly language of our target machine. As our languages become more abstract, the need for fine tuning will only increase. However, as shown by the database industry, we can focus our optimization efforts on the most critical parts of a system to achieve acceptable performance while still implementing our system at a higher level of abstraction. This is our strategy: create a single model that is appropriate for system modeling and high-level implementation, then concentrate on optimization research so that system performance becomes acceptable.

Making this work for production systems will require extensive optimization research. However, we gain crucial benefits of integration, including:

- the ability to move freely between various phases of development without changing system models,
- traceability of all components between various phases,
- a more powerful and complete implementation language,
- evolution in the same modeling and implementation paradigm, and
- relative simplicity since analysts and programmers alike only need to learn one comprehensive model.

This leads to better communication between different groups working on a system, and hence greater productivity. This also leads to increased opportunity for formal verification of various aspects of the system.

A driving principle of our research is that we consider the underlying model to be more important than the process by which a software system is constructed. It is the model that should drive the language (and the other parts of system development), and not vice versa. We have already mentioned problems that occur when a system model and a language implement different concepts (e.g., if the system model has persistence, then the language should support persistence as well). A programming language should implement all the features of the chosen logical system model. Thus, we advocate a *model-driven approach* to the development of implementation languages and other software development tools.

We also recognize that, under this unified development paradigm, there are many opportunities for parts of the software creation process to be automated, but we are nowhere near being able to completely automate system generation. We advocate the use of synergistic tools (others call them intelligent tools) that do low-level, tedious work that is best suited to automation (e.g., automatic schema normalization [14]). These tools should give the developer an opportunity to review and modify automatic changes to the system (e.g., resolve conflicts between theory and practice when the weak-instance assumption is not satisfied [14]). Tools should free the human programmer to concentrate on the creative parts of software construction, and yet still be able to control all aspects of system development.

2.3 Languages and Impedance Mismatch

Database programming language research has identified a so-called "impedance mismatch" between database systems and programming languages [30]. The problem is that database structures do not match well with structures found in traditional programming languages. More expressive data models have come under the umbrella of database research, while more expressive behavioral models have been explored under the guise of programming language research. The research community recognizes the need to combine the results of these traditionally separate areas, and hence the past decade has seen a wide variety of database programming language research.

We can observe other, similar impedance mismatches. For example, language technology has explored a number of different programming paradigms, including functional, logic-based, and procedural programming. Declarative languages provide more opportunity for optimization because they present more order independence. But general logic languages such as Datalog present formidable optimization challenges. Procedural languages are much easier to optimize, perhaps because the paradigm more closely matches traditional computer hardware architecture. At any rate, a general software development model should be able to support multiple programming-language paradigms.

To accomplish this goal, we propose that implementation be done using a higher level language whose model for persistent objects and behavior protocols is precisely the same model used for analysis, specification, and design. Such an implementation language is a level of abstraction above current programming languages and paradigms, and hence is more inclusive. Thus, we resolve the programming-paradigm mismatch and the database-programming language impedance mismatch simultaneously.

Another kind of impedance mismatch involves program representation paradigms. Traditionally, we have programmed by specifying a sequence of statements, usually as text. However, object-oriented analysis and design models are increasingly using graphical specification and presentation techniques, since graphical models form an excellent basis for information organization and communication. There is some pressure to represent programs graphically as well. Recently there has been a considerable amount of research into graphical and visual programming [2,12,13,17]. However, there are a number of objections to pure visual programming, including the need to learn a new alphabet of icons, the relatively large amount of space required to represent a visual program, and the difficulty of actually writing visual program descriptions. Therefore, we specify as a design goal that we should support multiple levels of system representation along the spectrum from fully graphical to fully textual.

2.4 Reification of Abstract Objects

The third area of integration we seek is between various levels of abstraction supported by the system model. We can achieve this integration by reifying abstract objects in the model. We consider two kinds of abstract objects: first, meta-level information, and second, high-level abstractions of low-level model components.

A system model can represent three major levels of information. At the lowest level is a data instance, which includes the objects in a system, together with their relationships and state. A data instance must conform to a scheme, which we call a model instance; this scheme should include object classes, relationship sets, potential state transitions, and potential object interactions. Finally, the model instance must conform to a model, which we call the meta-model. The meta-model contains rules describing what constitutes a valid model instance.

The meta-model can be captured using the model itself. Thus, the meta-model should be a self-describing model instance. Object classes and relationship sets in the meta-model (top layer) contain object classes and relationship sets in the model instance (middle layer). Model-instance object classes and relationship sets contain objects and relationships in the data instance (bottom layer). The meta-model is to the model instance as the model instance is to the data instance. That is, the meta-model is the scheme for a model instance, just as the model instance is the scheme for a data instance. The consequence of this organization is that we can use the same mechanism for accessing and modifying both the data instance and the model instance. In other words, elements of the meta-model are also first-class elements in the model instance, and thus fully reified.

The second category of abstract objects we want to reify is high-level abstractions of low-level constructs. There are several high-level abstractions we can consider. For example, an object could be high level, in the sense that it contains objects and relationships, but is, itself, considered as a single object. The high-level object abstraction conceals lower level detail, but also lets us treat the high-level object just as if it were an atomic object. By reifying high-level abstractions in this way, we introduce a powerful concept of scalability and abstraction into the system model. A high-level object could represent something as simple as a database record, or something as complex as the global climate system. In either case, we can treat these high-level objects as first-class objects in the system.

The reification we encourage yields significant benefits. First, we have full access within our model both to meta-information and data, allowing for model-instance evolution and reflection, in addition to more traditional data access. Second, high-level abstractions are first class and highly scalable. These benefits are of particular importance when the problem being modeled falls in the domain of megaprogramming [28].

3 The OSM Model

In this section, we introduce *Object-oriented System Modeling* (OSM), a logical system model that provides a solid foundation for the system development approach we are proposing.

3.1 Overview

OSM is an object-oriented model for systems analysis, specification, design, implementation, and evolution. The OSM model includes an object-relationship model, an object-behavior model, and an object-interaction model [15].

The structural components of OSM are object classes and relationship sets. *Object classes* support abstraction in two forms: classification and generalization/specialization. *Objects* can be members of object classes. An object has unique identity, may be lexical or non-lexical, is active concurrently with other objects, and may simultaneously have several active threads of behavior. OSM supports the modeling of relationships among object classes using relationship sets. *Relationship sets* support abstraction in several forms: general *n*-ary relationships among objects, whole/part aggregations, and set/member associations. A *relationship* is a member of a relationship set. Relationship sets may be treated as object classes in OSM, giving all the properties of objects to relationships.

Intra-object behavior in OSM is defined using a *state net* for an object class. A state net is a template for the behavior of objects in an object class. A state net consists of *states* that may be on or off, and *transitions* from one set of states to another. A transition has a *trigger* and an *action*, and is associated with one or more prior states and one or more subsequent states. A transition is enabled when various combinations of its prior states are on and fires if enabled and its trigger is true. A state net can model multiple threads of control, and hence objects in OSM may exhibit intra-object concurrency as well as inter-object concurrency.

OSM supports inter-object behavior through *object interactions*. An object may synchronize and interact with other objects via interactions. An interaction may be directed to a specific object, or it may be broadcast to a set of objects. Interacting objects may also exchange information in the form of sets of objects. OSM can be characterized as an active object model with non-uniform service availability [25]. That is, an interaction only occurs when objects are in specific states.

OSM supports encapsulation at several levels. First, state is fully protected within the boundary of an object. That is, no other object can change an object's current state (this includes states that are on and transitions that are firing). Second, OSM allows all state and structural information to be visible to all objects in a system. However, the system modeler may choose to restrict visibility of various portions of the model through views. Third, a view may contain object classes and relationship sets that are encapsulated as read-only components. Read-only components may be observed, but not modified.

Encapsulation in OSM can be seen along another dimension as well. OSM has a property we call *implementation independence*, meaning that a state net may have several corresponding low-level, physical implementations. As long as the logical properties defined by the state net are preserved, the particular low-level implementation is unimportant. This low-level implementation is always hidden from OSM model instances. Access to low-level implementations is through an interface specification, defined by the interactions in which an object may participate. The accessible portion of an object's interface may be modified in different views, as discussed above.

OSM supports several kinds of high-level components, including high-level object classes, relationship sets, states, transitions, and interactions. These high-level components give OSM powerful and scalable abstraction capabilities. A high-level object class, for example, may contain other object classes and relationship sets, but can also be treated in exactly the same way as a non-high-level object class and thus is fully reified. Furthermore, since high-level object classes can be nested to any depth, a complex subsystem can be abstracted as a single object class. High-level component boundaries can also give clues to the compiler about how to optimize a particular system's implementation.

OSM also supports a rich set of constraints, including various cardinality constraints [19], general constraints, and real-time constraints. Real-time constraints can apply to various kinds of behavior in OSM, including interactions, interaction sequences, states, and transitions. If an activity violates a real-time constraint, the system generates an exception event that can be detected and processed. Cardinality and general constraints, however, are continually enforced; a transaction cannot commit if its effects would violate such a constraint.

3.2 Formal Foundation

An important aspect of OSM is that it has been formally defined using a first-order, temporal logic language called *OSM-Logic* [6,7]. Every OSM model instance can be converted to a set of OSM-Logic formulas. We then formally interpret these formulas by mapping the language's symbols to objects, points in time, functions, and relations in a mathematical structure. An interpretation for a set of formulas is valid if and only if the formulas are true in the mathematical structure. Given an OSM model instance, we formally define its semantics as the set of all valid interpretations for the set of formulas resulting from the conversion of the model instance to OSM-Logic.

An important benefit of this formal foundation is that we have a formally defined execution model for OSM. An execution model is a mechanism for generating valid interpretations of a model instance, or in other words, for specifying the precise temporal evolution (behavior) of a model instance. With a formal execution model, we have a mechanism for simulating, prototyping, and executing OSM model instances directly. One consequence of this formal foundation is that we immediately resolve the lifecycle integration problem because analysis, specification, and design models are all executable. This lets us move to implementation without changing models, and thus also lets us evolve the system without changing models.

Another way that OSM supports the shift in focus from analysis to design and implementation activities is through a concept called *tunable formalism* [8]. Portions of OSM model instances need not be fully formal. For example, a general constraint could be written in a natural language (e.g., English). Such a general constraint is not enforceable in the mathematical interpretation. To make the general constraint formal, we need to rewrite it either in OSM-Logic, or some other language that maps to OSM-Logic. By allowing various levels of formal completion in an OSM model instance, OSM becomes appropriate for all levels of users, from theoreticians to practitioners, and from analysts to programmers.

3.3 OSM Meta-Model

An OSM model instance has three layers: a meta-model, a model instance, and a data instance. We have constructed our meta-model for OSM, using OSM to model itself. The OSM meta-model thus has object classes such as Object Class, Relationship Set, State, and Transition. When we create an OSM model instance, we populate the OSM meta-model with object classes, relationship sets, states, transitions, and so forth, from the model instance. In turn, these object classes, relationship sets, and so forth, constitute an OSM model instance. All three layers are stored together in an OSM storage facility.

Figure 1 shows a tiny portion of a model instance. Rectangles enclosing names represent object classes. Triangles represent generalization/specialization, black dots represent objects, and a half-dot on an object class provides both object-class-as-object and object-class-as-container points of view. Thus, from Figure 1 we have object class `Person` (as an object) is a member of `Object Class`, and objects `Mary`, `Joe`, and `Sally` are members of `Person`. The full meta-model is far more complex than what we have shown, and it is impractical to try to write down the full set of relationships between the meta-model and a model instance. These are implicitly provided for free, however, when a model instance is created.

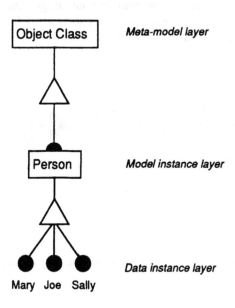

Figure1. Portion of seamless OSM model instance.

Access to meta-information provides an opportunity for both structural and behavioral reflection. Furthermore, objects in a model instance can modify object classes and relationship sets in the system. Thus, OSM provides a mechanism for evolution of the model instance as well as the data instance.

4 OSM-L

This section describes OSM-L, a language created to implement OSM models [20]. In describing OSM-L, we leave out most of the detail and concentrate on design principles and unique features, but also add some discussion to show that OSM-L is suitable for general object-oriented database and programming needs.

4.1 Design Principles

In designing OSM-L we have followed several usual design principles, which we do not mention explicitly, but we have also followed several unusual design principles, which are important to our integration approach. These unusual design principles include a model-driven implementation language, accommodation of both graphical and textual representation, and incorporation of both declarative and procedural programming paradigms.

Model-Driven Implementation Language

The structural and behavioral models for OSM-L come directly from OSM. Because of this, we call OSM-L a model-driven implementation language. In contrast, most programming languages stand alone, defining their own data model and execution semantics. We do not take this approach for reasons discussed in Section 2.

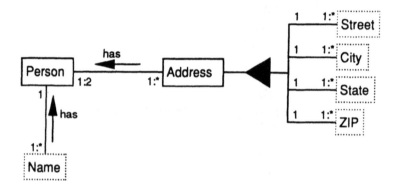

Figure 2(a). Simple OSM model instance — graphical version.

```
Person[1:2] has Address[1:*];
Person[1] has Name:STRING[1:*];

Address INCLUDES
        [1] Street:STRING [1:*],
        [1] City:STRING  [1:*],
        [1] State:STRING [1:*],
        [1] ZIP:STRING  [1:*];
```

Figure 2(b). Simple OSM model instance — textual version.

Graphical and Textual Representation

In support of our system-representation design goal, OSM-L supports various representation modes. An OSM model instance can be written using OSM's graphical notation, as Figure 2(a) shows, or it can be written entirely in text, as Figure 2(b) shows. In both figures, the model instance is the same. Here, Address is an aggregation of a Street, City, State, and ZIP, which are all lexical (STRING). Person is associated with a single Name and one or two Address objects through the relationship sets Person has Name and Person has Address. The numbers near the relationship-set connections in Figure 2(a) and in square brackets in Figure 2(b) are participation constraints.

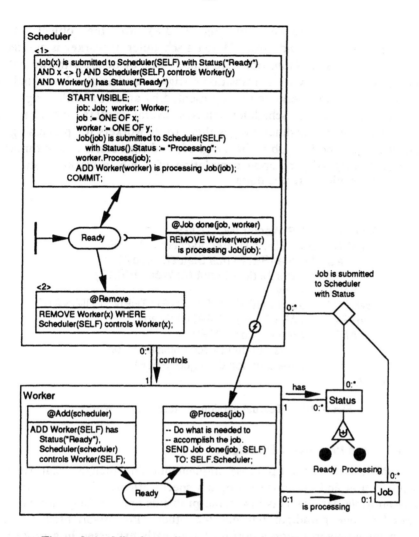

Figure 3(a). Mixed-paradigm concurrent behavior specification.

Figure 2 shows two ends of the graphical/textual spectrum, which is all we have for objects and relationships. For behavior, however, there is a smooth transition from one end of the spectrum to the other. Figure 3(a) shows how we may describe the high-level aspects of a work-scheduling system using a graphical notation to represent the structure and high-level concurrent behavioral specification, but textual statements to describe procedural steps in finer detail. Figure 3(b) shows a textual version of the Worker state net from Figure 3(a). State nets can either be written graphically, textually, or in a mixture.

The main components of Figure 3(a) are the object classes Scheduler, Worker, and Job. When a scheduler or worker is created, it enters a Ready state. Transitions are represented by boxes with two halves; in the upper half we write a transition's trigger, and in the lower half we write the action. An interaction is represented by an arrow with a zig-zag in a circle in the center. A scheduler controls several workers, and when jobs become available, a scheduler assigns them to its workers for processing. A worker waits for another job to be assigned, and then starts a new thread to process each assigned job; upon completion of a job, a worker notifies its controlling scheduler that it is done.

```
STATE NET FOR Worker INCLUDES
    WHEN CREATED AND @Add(scheduler) THEN
        ADD Worker(SELF) has Status("Ready"),
        Scheduler(scheduler) controls Worker(SELF);
    ENTER Ready;
    WHEN IN Ready AND IF DESTROYED THEN TERMINATE;
    WHEN IN START THREAD FROM Ready
    AND IF @Process(job) THEN
        -- Do what is needed to accomplish the job.
        SELF.Scheduler.Job done(job, SELF);
END;
```

Figure 3(b). Textual version of state net for Worker.

Declarative and Procedural Paradigms

OSM-L is a general-purpose implementation language that supports both procedural and declarative program specifications. The reason for supporting multiple paradigms is that some problems are concisely and naturally expressed in one paradigm but not the other. Process-oriented problems (e.g., an image compression algorithm) are neatly expressed in a procedural language, but order-independent problems (e.g., a transitive database query) are better written declaratively.

OSM-L provides first-order logic rules that can be unified and resolved in a traditional logic-programming fashion [4]. Predicates in these rules represent object classes and relationship sets. We explain this more below, when we discuss queries. Here, we point out that declarative specifications can be written in OSM-L. In Figure 3, the trigger of transition <1> is a Boolean expression written declaratively; also, the action of transition <2> is declarative.

OSM-L also provides procedural statements such as would be found in Ada, C++, or Smalltalk. For example, OSM-L has traditional control statements like IF ... THEN and WHILE ... DO. If such statements are written in the action of a transition, the statements are executed sequentially when the transition fires. In Figure 3, the action for transition <1> is a sequence of statements to start a transaction, extract elements from two sets, update a relationship, send an interaction, create a new relationship, and commit the transaction.

4.2 Active Database Programming Language Features

In support of its design goals, OSM-L incorporates a number of advanced features, including a uniform model of persistence, multiple database query capabilities, an interesting model for concurrency control, and active object behavior [21]. In this section we highlight these features.

Persistence

Objects, relationships, and system state are persistent in OSM-L. This persistence is transparent to the programmer, because it is automatic. As long as an object (relationship) is a member of an object class (relationship set), it exists in the system. Object destruction is handled automatically when an object (relationship) is removed from all classes (relationship sets).

Queries

For queries, OSM-L provides a predicate for each object class and relationship set in the model instance. For example, the following predicates are immediately and automatically available in OSM-L for the model instance from Figure 2:

```
Person(), Name(), Address(),
Street(), City(), State(), ZIP(),
Person() has Name(),
Person() has Address(),
Street() is subpart of Address(),
City() is subpart of Address(),
State() is subpart of Address(),
ZIP() is subpart of Address()
```

The first seven predicates are object-class predicates; all object-class predicates have one place. Relationship-set predicates are n-ary, where n is the arity of the corresponding relationship set. As can be seen, we use an infix notation for our predicates.

Using these predicates and a logic style of programming, we can specify queries over the model instance. For example, if we want to find all people named "Mary" we could write the query Person(x) has Name("Mary"), which binds to x all objects representing someone whose name is "Mary." If we want to find all the ZIP codes of addresses in Kansas, we could write

```
ZIP(x) is subpart of Address(y),
State("Kansas") is subpart of Address(y).
```

The desired result is again bound to x.

For convenience in constructing complex queries, we also provide a path traversal mechanism called the *dot operator*. The dot operator represents traversal over a unique path in the object-relationship graph of a model instance. For example, we could have written our first query as `x := Name("Mary").Person;`, and our second as `x := State("Kansas").ZIP;`. The dot operator requires that there be a unique path from its left-hand side to its right-hand side, but the traversal can cover arbitrarily many relationship sets. This operator constitutes a form of adaptive software [22].

It is also interesting to observe that since an OSM model instance includes its meta-model, meta-model predicates are available for query. For instance, we can retrieve all states named *Idle* across all state nets in the system with the query `State Name("Idle") names State(x)`.

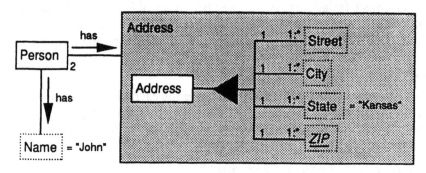

Figure 4. OSM-QL graphical query.

We also have a graphical query facility [9,29]. The graphical query language, called OSM-QL, is a calculus-based query language specified by creating views. Figure 4 shows an OSM-QL query that lists all the ZIP codes of people named "John" who have exactly two addresses in "Kansas." An underscore on ZIP indicates that its contents (after execution) constitute the output; the 2 participation constraint on *Person* in the *Person has Address* relationship set ensures that any data instance that satisfies the query will have exactly two addresses, and the high-level *Address* object-class acts like a parentheses to ensure that addresses are limited to those in "Kansas" before the number of connections to persons named "John" are counted.

Transaction Processing

In OSM there is a high degree of concurrency, both inter-object and intra-object. Many objects may be active simultaneously, and active objects may have several concurrent threads of control. The OSM model provides a single synchronization construct: the object interaction link. Two objects are synchronized when they interact.

This simple model of concurrency control is inadequate for general implementation needs. While the simple model is extremely flexible, it is also cumbersome to use, because it relies on a single, low-level synchronization primitive. So, OSM-L provides additional, higher level concurrency-control constructs. We call the OSM-L transaction model an *adjustable transaction* model. The main points of this model are that (1) it combines features of the nested [24] and split-transaction [26] models, (2) it allows visibility of a transaction's effects to be controlled on a per-transaction basis, and (3) it is up to the programmer to decide whether serializability will be enforced.

Active Behavior

Object behavior, as modeled by state nets, corresponds to rule systems defined in active database systems. We can consider others' rules to be roughly equivalent to triggers in our transitions. A trigger (rule) within a transition can be enabled or disabled (by turning prior states on and off). A trigger (involving either events or conditions or both events and conditions) allows an enabled transition to fire, which in turn executes the action associated with the transition.

Our model is most closely related to HiPAC [10,11,5], though there are many similarities with other systems [16,23] as well. HiPAC uses event-condition-action (ECA) rules to support active database features. In HiPAC an event can be a database operation, a temporal event, or a signal from a process. Since OSM events are any detectable changes in the system, they include all HiPAC events. Similarly, since OSM conditions are arbitrary Boolean expressions, they include HiPAC conditions, which are limited to database queries. As in OSM, HiPAC actions can be any program. It is interesting to note that both HiPAC and OSM use similar terminology with similar semantics, even though they were developed independently.

5 Conclusions

Object orientation is becoming increasingly widespread in both academia and industry. There is a clear need to provide better models, methods, tools, and languages to support the paradigm. To this end, many researchers are pushing object orientation in various directions. As research progresses, we need to integrate separate pieces carefully. We have identified three ways in which integration can be improved:

- A single development model and paradigm can be applied to all phases of the software lifecycle.

- The implementation language can resolve various kinds of impedance mismatches, merging ideas from traditionally separate disciplines.

- The development model can reify both meta-level information and high-level abstractions, and thus can provide first-class access to all model components.

Within relatively narrow problem domains, some or all these concerns have already been addressed. The contribution of this paper is that we have outlined a general-purpose object-oriented model, OSM, and a novel active-object database programming language, OSM-L, that together address these problems simultaneously and over a broader application domain.

We are trying to produce a revolutionary advance in systems development by combining the evolutionary advances of different disciplines. As our research with OSM continues, and our implementation of OSM is gaining momentum. Using C++ on HP 700 series workstations running under HP-UX 9.01, we have written an OSM model instance diagram editor, which lets us create OSM model and meta-model instances. We have also implemented a storage facility that not only stores OSM model instances, data instances, and meta-model instances, but also checks all model-specified constraints over these instances. The graphical query language OSM-QL, which we described above, has been implemented. We have also created a rapid prototyping tool, which executes model instances with both formal and informal triggers, actions, constraints, and interactions [18]. This prototyping tool also fully executes a subset of OSM-L. The subset includes the basic features described above such as persistence and active behavior; however, it only allows a limited logic language to be embedded in state nets; it does not support any transaction processing or crash recovery; it executes only one thread of control at a time; and it has no optimization features. We are currently enhancing our tools and working on a more complete implementation of OSM-L.

References

1. C. Batini, S. Ceri, and S. Navathe, *Conceptual Database Design: An Entity-Relationship Approach,* Benjamin/Cummings, Redwood City, California, 1992.

2. B. Bell, J. Rieman, and C. Lewis, "Usability Testing of a Graphical Programming System: Things We Missed in a Programming Walkthrough," *CHI '91 Conference Proceedings—Reaching Through Technology,* pp. 7-12, New Orleans, Louisiana, May 1991.

3. G. Booch, *Object-Oriented Analysis and Design with Applications,* Benjamin/Cummings, Redwood City, California, 1994.

4. S. Ceri, G. Gottlob, and L. Tanca, *Logic Programming and Databases,* Springer-Verlag, New York, 1990.

5. S. Chakravarthy and et al., "HiPAC: A Research Project in Active, Time-Constrained Database Management," *Final Technical Report, XAIT-89-02,* Xerox Advanced Information Technology, August 1989.

6. S.W. Clyde, D.W. Embley, and S.N. Woodfield, "The Complete Formal Definition for the Syntax and Semantics of OSA," Technical Report BYU-CS-92-2, Computer Science Department, Brigham Young University, 1992.

7.   S.W. Clyde, "An Initial Theoretical Foundation for Object-Oriented Systems Analysis and Design," Ph.D. Dissertation, Computer Science Department, Brigham Young University, 1993.

8.   S.W. Clyde, D.W. Embley, and S.N. Woodfield, "Tunable Formalism in Object-oriented Systems Analysis: Meeting the Needs of Both Theoreticians and Practitioners," *OOPSLA '92 Conference Proceedings*, pp. 452-465, Vancouver, British Columbia, Canada, October 1992.

9.   B.D. Czejdo, R.P. Tucci, D.W. Embley, and S.W. Liddle, "Graphical Query Specification with Cardinality Constraints," *Proceedings of the Fifth International Conference on Computing and Information*, pp. 433-437, Sudbury, Ontario, May 1993.

10. U. Dayal, "Active Database Management Systems," *Proceedings of the Third International Conference on Data and Knowledge Bases: Improving Usability and Responsiveness*, pp. 150-169, Jerusalem, Israel, June 1988.

11. U. Dayal and et al., "The HiPAC Project: Combining Active Databases and Timing Constraints," *SIGMOD Record*, vol. 17, no. 1, pp. 51-70, March 1988.

12. S.-K. Chang (ed.), *Principles of Visual Programming Systems*, Prentice Hall, Englewood Cliffs, New Jersey, 1990.

13. S.-K. Chang (ed.), *Visual Languages and Visual Programming*, Plenum Press, New York, New York, 1990.

14. D.W. Embley and T.W. Ling, "Synergistic Database Design with an Extended Entity-Relationship Model," *Proceedings of the Eighth International Conference on Entity-Relationship App roach*, pp. 118-135, Toronto, Canada, October 1989.

15. D.W. Embley, B.D. Kurtz, and S.N. Woodfield, *Object-Oriented Systems Analysis: A Model-Driven Approach*, Yourdon Press Series, Prentice-Hall, Englewood Cliffs, New Jersey, 1992.

16. N.H. Gehani, H.V. Jagadish, and O. Shmueli, "Event Specification in an Active Object-Oriented Database," *Proceedings of the 1992 ACM SIGMOD International Conference on Management of Data*, pp. 81-90, San Diego, California, June 1992.

17. T. Ichikawa, E. Jungert, and R. Korfhage (eds.), *Visual Languages and Applications*, Plenum Press, New York, New York, 1990.

18. R.B. Jackson, D.W. Embley, and S.N. Woodfield, "Automated Support for the Development of Formal Object-Oriented Requirements Specifications," *Proceedings of the 6th International Conference on Advanced Information Systems Engineering, in Lecture Notes in Computer Science*, vol. 811, Springer-Verlag, Berlin, June 1994.

19. S.W. Liddle, D.W. Embley, and S.N. Woodfield, "Cardinality Constraints in Semantic Data Models," *Data and Knowledge Engineering*,

vol. 11, no. 3, pp. 235-270, North-Holland, Amsterdam, December 1993.

20. S.W. Liddle, "Melody Language Specification," Technical Report, available via anonymous ftp at osm7.cs.byu.edu, Computer Science Department, Brigham Young University, 1994.

21. S.W. Liddle, D.W. Embley, S.N. Woodfield, and B.D. Czejdo, "Analysis and Design for Active Object Bases," *Proceedings of the Sixth International Conference on Computing and Information*, Sudbury, Ontario, 1994. (in press)

22. K.J. Lieberherr and C. Xiao, "Customizing Adaptive Software to Object-Oriented Software," *to be published*, February 1993.

23. G.M. Lohman, B. Lindsay, H. Pirahesh, and K.B. Schiefer, "Extensions to Starburst: Objects, Types, Functions, and Rules," *Communications of the ACM*, vol. 34, no. 10, pp. 94-109, October 1991.

24. J.E.B. Moss, in *Nested Transactions: An Approach to Reliable Distributed Computing*, MIT Press, Cambridge, Massachusetts, 1985.

25. O. Nierstrasz, "Regular Types for Active Objects," *OOPSLA '93 Conference Proceedings*, pp. 1-15, Washington, D.C., October 1993.

26. C. Pu, G.E. Kaiser, and N. Hutchinson, "Split-Transactions for Open-Ended Activities," *Proceedings of the Fourteenth International Conference on Very Large Data Bases*, pp. 26-37, Los Angeles, California, August 1988.

27. J. Rumbaugh, M. Blaha, W. Premerlani, F. Eddy, and W. Lorensen, *Object-Oriented Modeling and Design*, Prentice Hall, Englewood Cliffs, New Jersey, 1991.

28. G. Wiederhold, P. Wegner, and S. Ceri, "Toward Megaprogramming," *Communications of the ACM*, vol. 35, no. 11, pp. 89-99, November 1992.

29. Hoaran Andy Wu, "OSM-QL: A Calculus-Based Graphical Query Language for Object-Oriented Systems Modeling," Master's Thesis, Computer Science Department, Brigham Young University, 1993.

30. S.B. Zdonik and D. Maier, "Fundamentals of Object-Oriented Databases," in *Readings in Object-Oriented Database Systems*, ed. S.B. Zdonik and D. Maier, pp. 1-32, Morgan Kaufmann, San Mateo, California, 1990.

Structural and Behavioural Views on OMT-Classes

Jürgen Ebert
Koblenz University
Dept. of Computer Science
ebert@informatik.uni-koblenz.de

Gregor Engels
Leiden University
Dept. of Computer Science
engels@wi.leidenuniv.nl

Abstract

Object-oriented specification languages provide means to specify the static structure, as well as the allowed dynamic behaviour of objects. Here, the dynamic behaviour is usually described by giving the methods and a state transition diagram which defines the allowed sequences of methods on objects of a certain class.

Specialized classes are defined using the inheritance relationship. In order to enable reusability while guaranteeing type substitutability, subclass specifications have to be compatible with respect to static and dynamic aspects with their corresponding superclass specifications.

Classes have to provide a large shopping list of operations to satisfy the needs of all possible users. The interests of specific users are often restricted to a subset of operations and thus to a restricted behaviour.

This paper describes a formalization of class descriptions given by attributes, operations, as well as state transition diagrams. It defines compatibility between sub- and superclasses and introduces the notion of views in the sense of hiding parts of a class description. It turns out that a view has the same properties as a (virtual) superclass.

1   Introduction

Today, *object-orientation* is the state-of-the-art paradigm for software development. Terms like object-oriented analysis, object-oriented design, and object-oriented programming are used for describing this approach in different phases of the software life cycle ([RuBlPr 91], [Booch 91], [Jaco 92]).

In object-oriented approaches the entities of the system are grouped into *classes*. Class definitions contain detailed descriptions of

▷ its static structure,
▷ its operations,
▷ restrictions on the execution order of these operations, and
▷ the semantics (realization) of these operations.

Descriptions of software systems usually consist of a set of different *documents*, each of which describes another aspect of the system to be built. Depending on their purpose, different design language paradigms are used to describe the different aspects. Among these are the entity relationship approach, the data flow approach, the control flow approach, and the state transition approach ([EbeEng 93]).

To describe the different aspects of classes in object-oriented systems, documents of all design language paradigms are used in integrated approaches to software specification. Besides control flow and data flow descriptions for defining the semantics of operations, the OMT (object modeling technique) approach ([RuBlPr 91]), for instance, uses an *extended entity relationship language* to describe the static structure and the operations (the "object model") and a *state transition language* to describe the restrictions on the execution order of operations (the "dynamic model"). Thus, they define the set of all observable orders of calls to the operations (the "object life cycles").

Since both languages have their own approaches to semantics and hierarchy, they are not compatible in the first place. This deficiency has been detected and mentioned in the literature on object-oriented analysis and design methods ([RuBlPr 91], [ShlMel 92]). Especially, the interrelation between dynamic behaviour descriptions in subclasses and their corresponding superclasses has to be clarified in order to be able to speak about reusability and type substitutability. In this paper, we show how to integrate object models (given by entity relationship descriptions) with dynamic models (given by state transition descriptions) with respect to specialization in the context of the *object modeling technique (OMT)* of [RuBlPr 91]. To achieve this, a simple mathematical model is defined, which allows reasoning about compatibility in a formal way. The model is abstracted as far as possible to only those descriptional aspects which are relevant for discussing integration.

In database modelling it is a well known technique to derive new models from existing ones by defining *views*, which are restricted or even slightly modified variants of the given model. A view of an object is a (usually simpler) object which has only some of the features of the former and a reduced functionality. Advantages for introducing views to databases are ([Date 90])

 ▷ (partial) immunity of the users to growth and restructuring of the database schema,
 ▷ simplification of the user's perception,
 ▷ automatic security for hidden data, and
 ▷ the possibility to provide different views to different users, thus ease of reuse of existing databases.

Most of these arguments apply to object-oriented systems as well, with the modification that the discrimination between (external) users and other (internal) objects is no longer valid, because in object-oriented systems users are objects of the same kind as internal objects. Thus views should also be applicable inside the system.

Since reusability is a major goal of object-orientation, views come into account naturally. Given a powerful object class, a specific application might want to use a considerably smaller variant. In this case, an abstraction mechanism is needed which allows the necessary simplifications without reimplementation.

For instance, given a buffer object a producer client uses other operations and sees another part of its behaviour, than a consumer. In order to keep interfaces minimal (which is good engineering practice), there is the need to hide parts of given objects by defining client-dependent views.

Other practical examples of views are the accessibility of objects to given software engineering tools. E.g. one might expect that all objects have a *debugging view* including low level operations like *get* or *set* on its attributes to a debugging tool, or a *visualizing view* including operations like *draw*, *redraw*, *erase* for animation tools.

Another reason for views comes from the security area. The accessability of an object might depend on the security level of the client.

This concept of a view should not be confused with the concept of a *role*, which denotes the specialization of a model for special purposes. In our approach a view is a kind of projection, whereas a role is a kind of extension of a class.

The purpose of this paper is twofold. First, we give a formal definition of object-oriented systems, including object values and object behaviour in section 2. Then, we define classes and inheritance in section 3. The object model and the dynamic model are integrated into a compatible high-level approach to their dynamics in section 4. Then, in section 5 we define a simple concept of views on classes and investigate the relationship between a class and a view on it. We show that views fit into our framework as a kind of virtual generalizations of objects. Furthermore, we show how views fit to the integration of the object model with the dynamic model. The paper ends with a discussion of related work in section 6.

2 Objects

To be able to reason about object-oriented designs, a formal model of objects and classes is needed. The static structure of an object o is given by its *attributes*. An object might perform operations, called *methods*. The methods export services from an object o to other objects o', called *clients*, which use these services by *method calls*[1] Finally, the restrictions on the *execution order* of the methods on a given object is described by a state transition diagram.

The attributes and the methods define the *static* part of an object, and the state transition diagram gives its *dynamics*.

In OMT the value of objects at a given point of time consists of the association of elementary values to the attribute identifiers that an object is described by. In this definitional context the *set of all elementary values* is abstracted to a universe $\mathcal{U}$ of all possible data values. Here, "elementary" means that the structure does not matter in the context of this definition. Of course, elementary values need not be atomic, but may also be sets, lists, mappings and the like, but they are assumed to be non-functional, i.e. equality should be decidable.

If Σ_A is a finite *set of attribute identifiers* of an object o the overall value of o is a mapping $f : \Sigma_A \to \mathcal{U}$ which associates an elementary value to each attribute identifier in Σ_A. The attributes are typed in the sense that there is a domain function[2]

$$domain : \Sigma_A \to \mathbb{P}\mathcal{U}$$

which associates the set of allowed elementary values to each attribute identifier. Given Σ_A, $\mathcal{U}$, and *domain* the *set of all object values* is given by the set of all such mappings which are compatible with the *domain*-function:

$$values_{domain} := \{f : \Sigma_A \to \mathcal{U} \mid (\forall\, a : \Sigma_A \bullet f(a) \in domain(a))\}$$

To illustrate our ideas and definitions we reuse the well-known example of an automatic teller machine (ATM), like e.g. [RuBlPr 91] or [JuSaHa 91]. An ATM accepts a cash card and then carries out a transaction while communicating with the user and the bank. If the transaction is successful and the ATM has sufficient money, it dispenses cash to the user.

Each ATM can be described by two attributes. These are a unique string-valued identification *ident* and the current amount of *cashOnHand*. According to our formal definitions, this can be denoted as follows (Here *STRING* and *INTEGER* are the appropriate subsets of the universe $\mathcal{U}$.):

$$\Sigma_A = \{ident, cashOnHand\}$$
$$domain = \{ident \mapsto STRING, cashOnHand \mapsto INTEGER\}$$

At a certain point in time, the overall value of an ATM might be

$$\{ident \mapsto "ANB\text{-}LEI\text{-}784", cashOnHand \mapsto 27.850\}$$

Thus, objects are just reduced to their pure record structure.

In OMT the dynamics of an object o is described by a state transition diagram, which corresponds to a finite state automaton as introduced and discussed in [HopUll 79], for instance. The dynamics of an object is the set of all sequences

---

[1] The semantics of these methods are not modeled explicitly in the following. Only their identifiers are included.

[2] Note, that a Z-like notation ([Spiv 92]) is used throughout this paper: $\mathbb{P}\mathcal{U}$ denotes the powerset of $\mathcal{U}$.

of methods that it may perform. The automaton describes the language of all possible executions in terms of method calls.

Let Σ_M be the finite *set of method identifiers* of an object. Then, the state of the object may be changed by calling any method $m \in \Sigma_M$ (i.e. by sending an m-message to o). From an abstract point of view such a call is an event, which causes a state change of o.

If Q is the set of states of o, the *dynamic behaviour* of o may be described by a non-deterministic finite ϵ-automaton ([HopUll 79]) which is depicted by a state transition diagram.

$$STD = (Q, \Sigma_M, \delta, q_0, F)$$

consisting of

▷ a finite set Q of *states*,
▷ the *input alphabet* Σ_M of method identifiers,
▷ a *transition relation* $\delta \subseteq (Q \times (\Sigma_M \cup \{\epsilon\})) \times Q$,
▷ an *initial state* $q_0 \in Q$, and
▷ a subset $F \subseteq Q$ of *final states*.

In this abstraction the initial state corresponds to the *birth* and final states correspond to the *death* of the respective object.

During its "life" an object passes through a sequence of states according to method calls, usually changing its value while performing a state change. In our running example, the methods which might be performed by an ATM are

▷ the (re)filling of the ATM with money (*refill*),
▷ the start of a service session (*readCard*),
▷ the request for checking a cash card (*checkCardWithBank*),
▷ the display of various messages to the user (*displayCardAccepted*, *displayBadPIN*, *displayBadAccount*, *displayTransactionFailed*),
▷ the issuing of a transaction request to the bank (*issueTransaction*),
▷ the ejection of the inserted card (*ejectCard*),
▷ the dispense of cash (*dispenseCash*),
▷ the termination of a service session (*cancel*), and
▷ the removal (*remove*) of an ATM.

The dynamic behaviour, i.e. the allowed sequences of method invocations may now be defined by a finite automaton having the method identifiers as its input alphabet. Figure 1 shows a graph representation of the ATM automaton.

The state s_0 indicates the initial state, where a new ATM is installed. This state is entered when an ATM-object is created (birth). As this ATM is totally empty in the beginning, it has to be filled before any service session may start. After a *remove* method call the ATM object reaches state s_8 which corresponds to the object's destruction (death).

Up to now, the static structure (attribute value pairs and known method identifiers) of objects, and their dynamics (sequences of possible method calls) have been introduced.

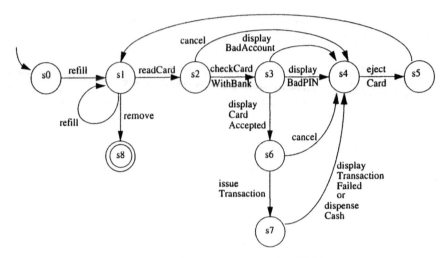

Figure 1: The Dynamics of the ATM

3 Class Descriptions

Normally, many similar objects share common properties. In object-oriented approaches the description of a system abstracts from concrete objects. It only consists of a set of *class descriptions*, which denote the possible static values, methods, and dynamic behaviour of all objects. Then, objects are concrete *instances* of these classes.

In OMT, it is assumed that states correspond to sets of object values, which are abstracted to being equivalent with respect to a special situation: "Sets of values are grouped together into a state according to properties that affect the gross behavior of the object." ([RuBlPr 91], p. 87). Thus, one may assume a function σ which associates a set of values to each state q of the behaviour automaton. Altogether this leads to the following definition of a class (let, again, $\mathcal{U}$ be the universe of all possible elementary data values):

A *class* $C = (\Sigma_A, domain, \Sigma_M, STD, \sigma)$ consists of
  ▷ a set Σ_A of *attribute identifiers*,
  ▷ a *domain function domain* $: \Sigma_A \rightarrow \mathbb{P}\mathcal{U}$,
  ▷ a set Σ_M of *method identifiers*,
  ▷ a *state transition diagram* $STD = (Q, \Sigma_M, \delta, q_0, F)$, and
  ▷ a *value function* $\sigma : Q \rightarrow \mathbb{P}\, values_{domain}$.

Here the attribute identifiers Σ_A and the domain function *domain* describe the static structure of objects of a class C. The dynamic behaviour is described by the method identifiers Σ_M and the state transition diagram STD. The function σ connects both parts.

Note that σ is dependent on the semantics of the method identifiers $m \in \Sigma_M$. Thus, on a very abstract level the interaction of the automaton STD and the function σ partially describes the semantics of the class. (If there is absolutely no knowledge about this, we have $\forall\, q \in Q \bullet \sigma(q) = values_{domain}$).

The static part of the class definition of an ATM consists of the set of attribute identifiers Σ_A, their domains $domain$, and the set of method identifiers Σ_M. Figure 2 gives a graphical representation of this class definition using the OMT notation. The dynamic behaviour of the class ATM is described by the STD given above in figure 1.

ATM
ident : STRING cashOnHand : INTEGER
cancel   issueTransaction remove   ejectCard refill   dispenseCash readCard checkCardWithBank displayBadAccount displayBadPIN displayCardAccepted displayTransactionFailed

Figure 2: Class Definition of the ATM

Within each state, the value of the attribute *ident* is identical, since no operation is assumed to change the identification of the ATM. The value of the attribute *CashOnHand* is known to be 0 in state s_0, while any other value is possible within the other states. Thus, the value function $\sigma : Q \rightarrow \mathbb{P}\, values_{domain}$ is restricted by

$$\exists\, x : STRING \bullet \forall s : Q \forall f : \sigma(s) \bullet f(ident) = x \;\wedge$$
$$\forall f : \sigma(s_0) \bullet f(cashOnHand) = 0$$

In an object model, the set of classes is arranged into a class hierarchy. Classes in a hierarchy are compatible to each other in the sense that "lower" classes are extensions of "higher" classes (*specialization*), and that objects of a "lower" class may be used wherever objects of the "higher" class are allowed (*substitutability*) ([KhoAbn 90]).

Substitutability may be described on the basis of class identifiers alone. Let $\mathcal{C}$ be the set of all classes Then, there is an acyclic relation

$$\_isSubClassOf\_ : \mathcal{C} \leftrightarrow \mathcal{C}.$$

Of course, if C is a subclass of C', then C' may also be called a superclass of

C. The intention of this definition is to state that whenever an object of C' is required, an object of C is also legal.

Specialization refers to the (static and dynamic) structure of classes. If C is a subclass of C', the description of C must be compatible with the description of C'. Whereas the subclass relation is prescribed by the class model, this relation is derivable from the properties of the classes. A class C is an extension of a class C' described by a relation

$\text{\_isExtensionOf\_} : C \leftrightarrow C,$

such that C isExtensionOf C' iff

▷ $\Sigma'_A \subseteq \Sigma_A,$
▷ $\forall a : \Sigma'_A \bullet domain(a) \subseteq domain'(a),$
▷ $\Sigma'_M \subseteq \Sigma_M,$
▷ STD' is a homomorphic picture of STD,
   i.e. there is a function $h : Q \to Q'$ s.t.
   ▷ $\forall q, \widehat{q} : Q; m : \Sigma_M \cup \{\epsilon\} \bullet$
      $((q, m), \widehat{q}) \in \delta$
      $\Rightarrow (m \in \Sigma'_M \wedge (((h(q), m), h(\widehat{q})) \in \delta')) \vee$
      $\quad (m \notin \Sigma'_M \wedge ((h(q), \epsilon), h(\widehat{q})) \in \delta' \vee h(q) = h(\widehat{q}))$
   ▷ $h(q_0) = q'_0$, and
   ▷ $\forall q : F \bullet h(q) \in F'$, and
▷ $\forall q : Q \bullet \{f : \sigma(q) \bullet \Sigma'_A \lhd f\} \subseteq \sigma'(h(q))$[3]

This definition assumes that extensions may have more attributes and operations and gives the exact compatibility conditions that dynamic class descriptions (STDs) must fulfill in this context[4].

In OMT both properties of inheritance are required, i.e. the condition

$\text{isSubClassOf} \subseteq \text{isExtensionOf}$

is posed on these relations.

Up to this point, a formal definition of classes and their subclass-relation has been given.

An example of a subclass is given by the definition of an extended ATM, which offers to the user the additional possibility to get information on the current balance of his account, either on the display or as printed output. Thus, the set of methods is extended by the three methods *showBalance*, *dispBalance*, and *printBalance*. Figure 3 shows the OMT notation of such a subclass definition. This leads also to an extension of the STD for the description of the dynamic behaviour as described in figure 4.

Objects are instances of classes, i.e. they are identifiable entities (e.g., given by an object identifier *oid*) which have a value and a behaviour according to the

---

[3] $X \lhd f$ denotes the restriction of the domain of f to the elements of X.
[4] This definition reflects multiple inheritance, but no overriding of attribute or operation identifiers.

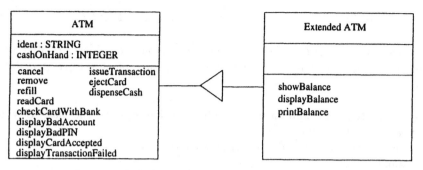

Figure 3: Subclass Definition of an Extended ATM

class description. More precisely, for each object o there is exactly one class. Thus, if $\mathcal{O}$ is the set of all objects there is a relation

$$\_\mathtt{isInstanceOf}\_ : \mathcal{O} \to \mathcal{C}$$

which is essentially a function associating exactly one class to each object. It is assumed here, that the function $\mathtt{isInstanceOf}$ is fixed.

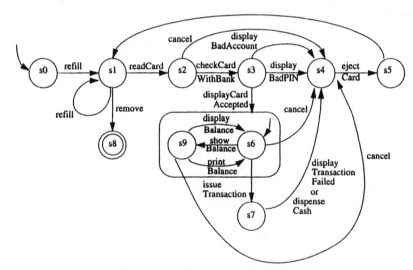

Figure 4: The Extended ATM

Since the relation $\mathtt{isSubClassOf}$ was introduced to model inheritance in object systems, it has to be assumed that an object o is not only a member of its class C with o $\mathtt{isInstanceOf}$ C but also of all superclasses C' of C.

Let $\mathtt{inheritsFrom}$ be the reflexive-transitive closure of $\mathtt{isSubClassOf}$:

$$\mathtt{inheritsFrom} := \mathtt{isSubClassOf}^*,$$

then we define the relation

$$\_\mathtt{isMemberOf}\_ : \mathcal{O} \leftrightarrow \mathcal{C}$$

by

o `isMemberOf` $C' \Leftrightarrow o$ (`isInstanceOf`; `inheritsFrom`) C'.

This definition integrates the *type-theoretic approach* of object-oriented programming languages with the *set-semantic approach* of object-oriented databases.

In the type-theoretic approach, each object o has exactly one class C with o `isInstanceOf` C and the sets
$$instances(C) := \{o : \mathcal{O} \mid o \text{ isInstanceOf } C\}$$
are disjoint.

In the set-semantic approach, each object is regarded as a member of all its superclasses. Thus the set
$$members(C) := \{o : \mathcal{O} \mid o \text{ isMemberOf } C\}$$
of a class C includes the instances of all descendants of C in the subclass hierarchy.

Through the definition of classes, objects are grouped in a fine-grained manner by their classes. These smaller sets are combined with others to larger sets, which include all members of subclasses, too. Of course, the behaviour of an object must be compatible with all classes that it belongs to.

4 Situations

At a given point in time, an object o is in a precisely defined situation os, i.e. it is in a concrete state q and it has a concrete value f[5]. Over time the object receives several method calls. Each method call may change the object's value and state. This leads to a new situation of o.

Thus, if C is a class, then an *object situation* $os = (q, f)$ with respect to C consists of[6]
  ▷ a state $q \in Q$, and
  ▷ a value $f \in \sigma(q)$.
Note, that the state alone does not determine the value of an object, and also the value alone does not determine the state. This is why both data are included into the definition of a situation.

The way the value of an object o may change depends on its situation, i.e. it depends on the value f that o has and on the state q that o is in.

A situation $os = (q, f)$ leads to a situation $\widehat{os} = (\widehat{q}, \widehat{f})$ with respect to a class C

---

[5] In automata theory this concept is often called *configuration*

[6] Here and in the following all symbols like Q, σ and so on are of course implicitly indexed by the appropriate class C.

(os `leadsTo` $\widehat{os}$) iff[7]
$$q = \widehat{q} \vee$$
$$\exists\, m : \Sigma_M \cup \{\epsilon\} \bullet ((q, m), \widehat{q}) \in \delta.$$

As defined above: if o is an object of class C and C `inheritsFrom` C', then also o `isMemberOf` C' is fulfilled. Thus, if $os = (q, f)$ is a situation of o with respect to C, then there is also a *derived situation* $os' = (h(q), \Sigma'_A \lhd f)$ of o with respect to C'. (As shown below, this situation may also be called a C'-*view* of os.) Thus, each object situation with respect to a class C determines a set of derived situations, one for each superclass of C.

The definitions given up to now assure, that the "life" of situations as described by the relation `leadsTo` on situations is compatible with the relation `inheritsFrom`.

More formally, for given situations $os = (q, f)$ and $\widehat{os} = (\widehat{q}, \widehat{f})$ we have:
If os `leadsTo` $\widehat{os}$ with respect to class C and
if C `inheritsFrom` C' then
$os' = (h(q), \Sigma'_A \lhd f)$ `leadsTo` $\widehat{os'} = (h(\widehat{q}), \Sigma'_A \lhd \widehat{f})$ with respect to class C'.

This follows easily from the definitions:
Since os `leadsTo` $\widehat{os}$ with respect to class C means
$$q = \widehat{q} \vee$$
$$\exists\, m : \Sigma_M \cup \{\epsilon\} \bullet ((q, m), \widehat{q}) \in \delta,$$
the definition of inheritance delivers
$$\exists\, m : \Sigma'_M \bullet ((h(q), m), h(\widehat{q})) \in \delta' \vee$$
$$((h(q), \epsilon), h(\widehat{q})) \in \delta' \vee$$
$$h(q) = h(\widehat{q})$$
which simplifies to the condition
$$h(q) = h(\widehat{q}) \vee$$
$$\exists\, m : \Sigma'_M \cup \{\epsilon\} \bullet ((h(q), m), h(\widehat{q})) \in \delta',$$
i.e. os' `leadsTo` $\widehat{os'}$ with respect to class C'

Thus, if an object passes over from one situation to another according to the description of its class, this passage is also compatible with all its ancestor classes.

In our running example of an ATM, this means that the dynamic behaviour of an extended ATM is compatible with the behaviour of a general ATM.

---

[7]Here, it is assumed, that $\widehat{f}$ is that value of o, which is computed by executing m starting with value f; but this fact is not modeled explicitly.
Since methods defined in subclasses of C may change the value, too, also spontaneous value changes are allowed in `leadsTo`. This can be avoided, if new methods in extensions are only allowed to work on new attributes, whereas the old attributes have to be accessed via methods ([Snyd 86]).

5 Views

Methods which are common to all subclasses within the same layer of an inheritance hierarchy should be moved up to the common superclass. This decreases redundancy within an inheritance hierarchy, and localizes information at unique places, but it leads to large shopping lists of methods of classes (a term coined by Meyer [Meye 88]). Clients of those classes are often interested and using only a part of the offered functionality of a class. These clients need only a view on a restricted set of methods and accordingly on a restricted dynamic behaviour.

For instance, each ATM interacts with a customer on the one hand and with the (computer of a) bank on the other hand. This means that two different views on the ATM can be distinguished. These are the *CustomerToATM* view and the *BankToATM* view. Both views can be derived from the description of the complete ATM. Both are characterized by a subset of allowed attributes and methods and an implied observable subbehaviour of the complete behaviour of an ATM.

In order to model views to these kinds of applications, we define a view of a class C as a simplified variant C', which can be derived from C. The simplest case of a view to a class C is a class C', which has fewer attributes and methods than C:

  ▷ $\Sigma'_A \subseteq \Sigma_A$,
  ▷ $domain' = (\Sigma'_A \lhd domain)$, and
  ▷ $\Sigma'_M \subseteq \Sigma_M$,

and whose behaviour can be derived from the behaviour of C by a projection on the restricted alphabets:

  ▷ STD' is the projection of STD on Σ_A, and
  ▷ $\forall q : Q \bullet \sigma'(q) = \Sigma'_A \lhd \sigma(q)$.

The projection
$$STD' = \pi_{\Sigma'_M}(STD) = (Q, \Sigma'_M, \delta', q_0, F)$$

of an automaton $STD = (Q, \Sigma_M, \delta, q_0, F)$ on a subalphabet $\Sigma'_M \subseteq \Sigma_M$ is defined by

$$\delta' = \{q, \hat{q} : Q; m : (\Sigma_M \cup \epsilon) \mid ((q, m), \hat{q}) \in \delta \bullet$$
$$\text{if } m \in \Sigma'_M \text{ then } ((q, m), \hat{q}) \text{ else } ((q, \epsilon), \hat{q}))\}$$

It can easily be seen, that $\pi_{\Sigma'_M}(STD)$ is a homomorphic picture of STD using the identity function on Q as the homomorphism.

Since these conditions for defining C' as a view of C imply that C is an extension of C', it follows immediately that restriction views are nothing else than (virtual) superclasses. Consequently, we have isViewOf $\subseteq$ isExtensionOf$^\sim$ (the transposed of isExtensionOf)

Thus, the concepts of view and superclass coincide. Whereas superclasses in the strong sense are part of the object model in OMT, views are additional superclasses which exist only virtually.

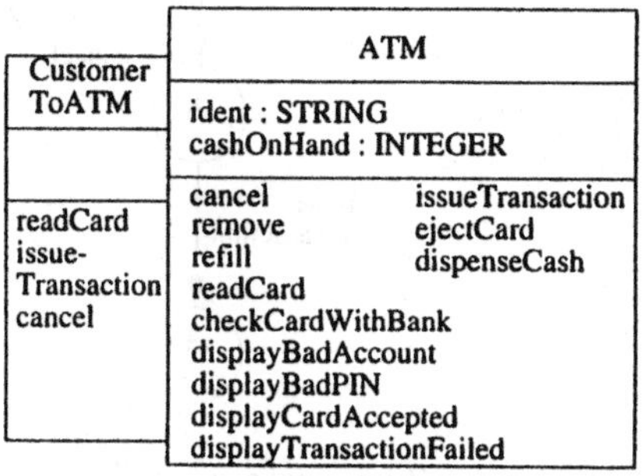

Customer ToATM	**ATM**	
	ident : STRING cashOnHand : INTEGER	
readCard issue- Transaction cancel	cancel remove refill readCard checkCardWithBank displayBadAccount displayBadPIN displayCardAccepted displayTransactionFailed	issueTransaction ejectCard dispenseCash

Figure 5: The CustomerToATM View

In our running example of an ATM a customer is only allowed to start a service session (*readCard*), to issue a withdrawal transaction (*issueTransaction*), or to terminate the service session (*cancel*). This means that the subset of methods visible to a customer comprises only
$\Sigma'_M = \{readCard, issueTransaction, cancel\}$.
The attributes are hidden to the user:
$\Sigma'_A = \varnothing$.
This CustomerToATM view may graphically be noted in an extended OMT notation as given in figure 5.

The observable behaviour can then be derived as described in figure 6. Within this STD, a lot of transitions occur without a specific method as label. This indicates that something has to happen to the ATM, which can not be influenced by the customer. For instance, in the beginning the ATM has to be set up and filled with some money before the customer may start a service session.

Note, that in this model ϵ-transitions are intended to represent spontaneous actions. This pragmatic interpretation lets the automaton of figure 6 be (pragmatically) different from a formally equivalent ϵ-free automaton.

6   Related Work

The connection between inheritance and dynamic models (given by state transition diagrams) is also discussed by Lopes and Costa ([LopCos 93]) in a category theoretic framework. In principle, their intention is similar to ours, but they

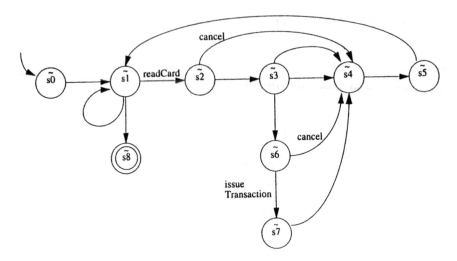

Figure 6: The Customer STD

use an operational approach based on graph grammars and they do not regard integration of the static and the dynamic model. [SaHaJu 94] give also a set basic operations on STDs aiming at the transformation of the dynamic model of superclasses into those of subclasses and vice versa.

In [McGDye 93] more loose restrictions are imposed on the connection between the different dynamic models, but they do not give a formalization or compatibilty proof of their approach.

The notion of view is a well known concept in database literature. The classical ANSI/SPARC architecture was largely motivated by the intention to allow different views of a database to different users. In relational databases (e.g. in SQL [Date 90]) views exist as a means to define "virtual" tables, i.e. as tables that do not really exist in their own right, but are instead derived from one or more underlying base tables by a query.

For object-oriented systems there is another approach to views. The first one to criticize that inheritance and information hiding are in conflict with each other was Snyder ([Snyd 86]). Subclasses should have a view on their parent classes which is different from that of other objects. On one hand, the subclass must be able to access some internal attributes or hidden methods, on the other hand not all internal design decisions of parent classes should be known, in order to allow independent maintenance.

Hailpern and Ossher ([HaiOss 90]) define views on an object-to-object basis. They define views as triples of server sets, client sets, and operation sets. With their approach visibility may be manipulated dynamically by maintaining these sets, thus allowing the addition or removal of certain operations at run time. In contrast to this approach, our proposal is intended to supply a view mechanism at a coarser granularity. Views are a concept at the schema level, thus allowing static analysis of object systems.

In TROLL ([JuSaHa 91]) restriction views appear as interface classes. In the paper [ScLaTr 91] they transfer the classical database concept of views into the context of object-oriented databases. These works resemble ours, but they do not discuss inheritance of behaviour.

7 Conclusion

In this paper, we gave an integrated formalization of object-oriented systems pertaining to the static and the dynamic (syntactical) aspects, including the notions of object values, object behaviours, classes, and inheritance. On the basis of state-transition semantics we showed the consistency of these definitions.

In this context, we gave an appropriate definition of a concept of view in the sense of hiding parts of the class description. It turned out, that a view has the same properties as a superclass.

Acknowledgements. We thank Martin Carstensen, Angelika Franzke, and Andreas Winter (Koblenz University), and Gunter Saake (Magdeburg University) for some interesting and stimulating discussions on the topics of this paper.

References

[Booch 91]   Grady Booch, *Object Oriented Design* , Benjamin/Cummings, Redwood City, 1991.

[Date 90]   C.J. Date, *An Introduction to Database Systems*, Reading, Ma.: Addison Wesley, 1990, 5th Edition.

[EbeEng 93] Jürgen Ebert, Gregor Engels, *Design Representation*, to appear in: J. Marciniak (Ed.), *Encyclopedia of Software Engineering*, Wiley, New York, 1993.

[HaiOss 90] Brent Hailpern, Harold Ossher, *Extending Objects to Support Multiple Interfaces and Access Control*, IEEE-SE 16 (1990, 11).

[HopUll 79] John E. Hopcroft, Jeffrey D. Ullman, *Introduction to Automata Theory, Languages, and Computation*, Addison-Wesley, Reading MA, 1979.

[Jaco 92]   Ivar Jacobson, *Object-Oriented Software Engineering*, Addison-Wesley, Wokingham, 1992.

[JuSaHa 91] R. Jungclaus, Gunter Saake, Thorsten Hartmann, Cristina Sernadas, *Object-Oriented Specification of Information Systems:*

The TROLL Language, TU Braunschweig, Technical Report 91-04.

[KhoAbn 90] Setrag Khoshafian, Razmik Abnous, *Object Orientation - Concepts, Languages, Databases, User Interfaces*, John Wiley, New York, 1990.

[LopCos 93] A.Lopes, J.F.Costa, *Rewriting for Reuse* in *Proceedings ERCIM Workshop on Development and Transformation of Programs*, INRIA, Nancy, Nov. 1993, pp.43-55.

[Meye 88] Bertrand Meyer, *Object-Oriented Software Construction*, Prentice Hall, Englewood Cliffs, 1988.

[McGDye 93] J.D.McGregor, D.M. Dyer, *A Note on Inheritance and State Machines*, *ACM Software Engineering Notes*, Vol. 18, No. 4, Oct. 1993, pp. 61-69.

[RuBlPr 91] J.Rumbaugh, M.Blaha, W.Premerlani, F.Eddy, W.Lorensen, *Object-Oriented Modeling and Design*, Prentice Hall, Englewood Cliffs NJ, 1991.

[SaHaJu 94] Gunter Saake, Peter Hartel, Ralf Jungclaus, Roel Wieringa, Remco Feenstra, *Inheritance Conditions for Object Life Cycle*, in Udo W. Lipeck, Gottfried Vossen (Hrsg.), *Formale Grundlagen für den Entwurf von Informationssystemen*, Universität Hannover, Informatik-Bericht 03/94, 79-88.

[ScLaTr 91] Marc H. Scholl, Christian Laasch, Markus Tresch, *Updatable Views in Object-Oriented Databases*, in C. Delobel, M. Kifer, Y. Masunaga (Eds.), *Deductive and Object-Oriented Databases DOOD '91*, Berlin: Springer-Verlag, LNCS 566, 1991, 189-207.

[ShlMel 92] S. Shlaer, St.J. Mellor, *Object Lifecycles: Modeling the world in state*, Yourdon Press, Englewood Cliffs NJ, 1992.

[Snyd 86] A. Snyder, *Encapsulation and inheritance in object-oriented programming languages*, in *Conf. Object-Oriented Programming Systems, Languages, and Applications*, Portland, OR, ACM, Sept. 1986, pp. 38-45.

[Spiv 92] J.M. Spivey, *The Z Notation (2nd Edition)*, Prentice Hall, New York, 1992.

Combining two Approaches to Object-Oriented Analysis

L. Mathiassen*   A. Munk-Madsen[t]   P.A. Nielsen*   J. Stage*

Abstract: There has been an immense growth in object-oriented methods to analysis and design. Many of these methods differ only on insignificant points and it is often difficult to deduce what the exact characteristics of the methods are before having tried them out in practice. All the more, there is a need for examining these characteristics and discussing fundamental aspects of object-oriented analysis and design. We believe that one such fundamental discussion is *the handling of events* in analysing the problem domain.

Coad & Yordon's method, OOA, forcefully models structure in the problem domain. Yet it fails significantly in modelling its dynamics. On the other hand, Jackson's method, JSD, provides an elegant way of modelling the dynamics of objects in the problem domain, but structure is to a large extend ignored. We have developed a new method, OOA&D, which takes the best elements of OOA and of JSD and integrates them into a coherent set of guidelines for analysis and design. In this paper we focus solely on how events are handled by OOA, JSD and OOA&D. The strengths and limitations of OOA and JSD are identified and discussed. The handling of events in OOA&D is described and illustrated and it is argued in which way it is an improvement compared to OOA and JSD.

1 Introduction

The growth in numbers of object-oriented methods for analysis and design has been immense over the last couple of years. Nevertheless, there is still a need for new methods. A number of methods stems from old methods from other paradigms that are made more object-oriented; some of them still adhere to the old paradigm despite the new image. Other methods starts from object-oriented programming seeking to deal more systematically with design as well as analysis.

There are difference between the new methods, but some of them are quite insignificant. The variety of background, style of presentation and focus makes it very difficult to deduce their characteristics by looking at the methods only. Two

---

*L. Mathiassen, P.A. Nielsen, and J. Stage are with the Department of Mathematics and Computer Science, Aalborg University, Fredrik Bajers Vej 7, DK-9220 Aalborg East, Denmark.

[t]A. Munk-Madsen is with the Metodica, Nyvej 19, DK-1851 Frederiksberg C, Denmark.

things are needed. First, it is necessary to base any discussion of methods on the features they show when they are taught and used. Second, it is necessary to discuss aspects of analysis and design which are fundamental irrespective of the methods considered. If these two things are present we may evaluate methods and new methods may be developed which are significantly different from the existing methods.

In this article we have chosen to discuss how events in the problem domain are handled by two well-known object-oriented methods, OOA by Coad & Yourdon [2] and JSD by Jackson[4]. The examination focusses solely on this fundamental aspect of the two methods. We shall argue that none of them deals properly with events. We illustrate how they may be combined and integrated forming a coherent set of guidelines in a method we recently developed, named OOA&D.

Object-oriented analysis has been presented as a 'natural' way of understanding and describing the problem domain of a computer system. Coad & Yourdon's method, OOA, is an example of a recent object-oriented analysis method. They argue that the techniques and notation of OOA is based on the methods of organization that pervade all of human thinking. OOA supports selection and definition of classes modelling objects in the problem domain. It also guides selection and definition of structural relationships between classes.

Murphy [7] reports from a software development project in which the OOA method was used. He states that the OOA method provides an excellent set of general guidelines for approaching object-oriented analysis. However, portions of the approach still remain undefined. Murphy classifies OOA as a data-driven approach to analysis that originates from the area of information modelling. He argues that this is a questionable approach since it ignores the dynamics of objects.

Jackson's method, JSD, includes a simple and elegant way of describing the dynamics of problem domain objects. An object is characterized by the structured set of actions in which it is involved throughout its lifetime. An action in JSD is what in this paper is termed an event. A major drawback of JSD is that structural relations between classes are ignored. The only relationship between objects is caused by transferring data about events from one object to another.

This paper describes how an object-oriented analysis method, OOA&D, has been developed by taking the best of OOA's handling of structure of the problem domain and combine it with JSD's handling of actions of objects. Our basis for this paper is: (i) our teaching of first JSD and later OOA to both undergraduate students and practioners for almost ten years, (ii) our own practicing of JSD on a few cases and OOA on a larger number of cases, (iii) our consultancy where we engaged in a substantial number of project group efforts in applying OOA in practice, and (iv) for the last three years we have through our research developed a method for object-oriented analysis [6].

Section 2 introduces our basic understanding of object-oriented analysis. Section 3 discusses modelling of problem domain dynamics and events in particular in OOA and JSD. The basics of OOA and JSD are outlined and their major strengths and drawbacks concerning structural relations and dynamics are emphasized. Section 4 presents our combined approach to problem domain modelling. Its use is illustrated by an example. Finally, Section 5 discusses directions for further improvement of methods for object-oriented analysis.

2   Basic Concepts of Object-Oriented Analysis

Object-oriented methods reflect a broad variety of basic concepts and approaches to analysis. The OOA method introduces two basic concepts: the problem domain is "a field of endeavor under consideration," and the system's responsibilities is "an arrangement of things accountable for, related together as a whole." Object-oriented analysis is defined as "the challenge of understanding the problem domain and then the system's responsibilities in that light," [2, pp. 8-9].

Booch defines object-oriented analysis as an approach that "examines requirements from the perspective of the classes and objects found in the vocabulary of the problem domain," [1, p. 37].

Our aim is to improve object-oriented analysis by combining techniques from different methods. In doing so, we have benefitted from a conceptual framework for object-oriented analysis based on the relationships between the computer system and its context.

A computer system's *application domain* contains the computer system, its users and their way of using the computer system in their work tasks. A computer system's *problem domain* denotes what the computer system is about. It contains that part of reality that the computer system is used to administer, monitor or control. For a car rental system the application domain may be the desk clerks taking care of customers utilizing the computer system to register customers, booking, printing contracts, etc. The corresponding problem domain may then consist of cars, prizing, contracts, and what may happen to cars, prizing, and contracts, e.g. cars are rented, cars are returned, cars are moved from one station to another, etc. The things in the problem domain are called objects and what happens to objects are called events.

The idea of a *computer system* that we are promoting is that it must contain a model that keeps track of what happens in the problem domain [6, p. 7-8]. Simply, if the desk clerk wants to know whether a particular car is available he only has to look at the state of the model and not at reality. It requires, of course, that the track-keeping is accurate and reliable. If the track-keeping is to be relevant to the desk clerks it must match their perception of the real-world problem domain. Objects and events do not exist in the real-world. In the real-world there are phenomena, and only when someone is making an abstraction may we speak of objects and events.

In Figure 1, it is illustrated that the application and problem domains *may* be overlapping. This only happens in rare cases.

The purpose of *analysis* is to understand and describe the users' requirements to the computer system. This involves building the model of the problem domain in object-oriented terms. In order to do this, objects and events must be described

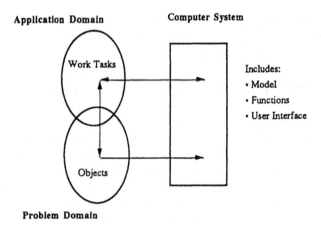

Figure 1: The computer system in context.

coherently. Analysis of the applicaton domain is not particularly object-oriented as it must at least involve description of the functionality provided by the system to support users in carrying out work tasks.

It should be noticed that what is termed an event in modern structured analysis, cf. [9], is not an event in the problem domain. It is merely denoting a request for information in the aplicaton domain.

3 Approaches to Modelling Events

Problem domain modelling is a key activity of object-oriented analysis. Event modelling, which we focus on in this paper, is a major part of this.

3.1 Event Modelling with OOA

Coad & Yourdon's object-oriented analysis method, OOA, comprises the following five activities, cf. [2]:

1. Finding Classes and Objects

   The main criterion for selecting an object is either that the system need to remember something about the object or the object need to provide some behaviour.

2. Identifying Structures

3. Identifying Subjects

4. Defining Attributes

5. Defining Services

A service is the processing to be performed upon receipt of a message.

OOA is a constructive contribution to the application of object-oriented concepts and ideas in problem domain modelling. The strength of OOA is the simple but powerful way in which it guides selection and definition of classes and their structural relations. A main weakness is its limited emphasis on problem domain dynamics.

Murphy [7] reports from a project in which an improved version of OOA was applied to analyze a network management application. OOA was initially selected through a review of ten object-oriented analysis methods. Yet this review also indicated areas in which OOA had to be supplemented with with other techniques. A major problem with OOA was its predominant focus on data as opposed to object behaviour.

In our experience, OOA handles events in two ways. If an event is worth remembering it is modelled as a class. It is part of activity 1 to identify events and classify these by finding a common denominator for a group of events which acts like a whole. It is even part of a checklist to look at the problem domain for events, locations, organisations, devices amongst other things. Looking through a vast number of OOA models shows that events are common in these models and any significant event is modelled as a class.

Minor events may, instead, be treated as services. A service on an object can be used to register that something has happened to the object. For example, the services on an event-remembering class will typically be representing events, e.g. renting a car may be a service on a contractual event and so may returning a car be. While this is in principle a possibility it is rarely used during analysis. Certainly, it is not mentioned and encouraged by OOA.

None of these two way are satisfactory. Events are intrinsically dynamic properties of the problem domain and it is truly misleading to model these as though they were objects. Objects and events are dual in nature and too much is lost if events are reduced to mere objects. To model events as services is to take the dynamic nature seriously, but a service is a computer construct which is not found outside the computer. The construct is useful in design where the computer is being modelled. In analysis it is a source of making the mistake of thinking that the real-world outside the computer is acting exactly like a computer. The dynamics of the problem domain cannot usefully be thought of as processing carried out upon receipt of a message—no message is passed from a customer to a car and a car does certainly not process anything but gas.

3.2   Event Modelling with JSD

JSD [4] was presented in 1983 as a reaction to the function-oriented approach of most contemporary analysis and design methods.

In many regards, Jackson's ideas are corresponding to the idea of a track-keeping system in a context of problem domain and application domain. Jackson argues that every computer system is concerned with the real-world, a part of reality outside itself, and the fundamental principle of JSD is that this reality should be modelled as an integrated part of developing the computer system.

JSD is based on the notions of entities and actions in the problem domain. An *action* is a process that occurs in the real-world outside the computer system. An action must be regarded as being instantaneous and atomic in the sense that it is not relevant to decompose it into subactions. An *entity* is something that can be identified individually in the real-world. An entity must perform or suffer actions in a significant time-ordering. Ideally, each entity is thought of as a sequential proces and a model as communicating, sequential processes.

The domain modelling of Jackson System Development comprises the following four activities, cf. [4]:

1. Entity Action Step: That which is relevant to the track-keeping model is listed as entities and actions.

2. Entity Structure Step: The lifetime of each entity is described by structured actions according to their ordering in time.

3. Initial Model Step: The problem domain is described as a process model consisting of connected entities.

4. Function Step: The functions that produce the desired output of the computer system are defined in terms of data processing and access to the entities of the model.

The JSD method was not originally presented as an object-oriented method. For that reason, some of the concepts used are different from conventional concepts of object-oriented thinking. On the other hand, most of the concepts resembles the same meaning as similar object-oriented concepts. To avoid this potential for mis-understanding, we exchange the concepts of JSD with their object-oriented equiv-alents. We will use the more common notion of 'object' as a substitute for 'entity'. We have chosen to use the notion of 'event' to denote the mechanism by which a model object registers an action that involves the corresponding problem domain object.

Events and objects are equally important in JSD. They are both identified in the very first step of the method. Objects and events are related closely in step 2 where objects are expressed in terms of events. What we know about an object is which events it is involved in and in which order these event are happening. There is a notation and a whole range of hints, experience and and guidelines to help ordering these events.

Regarded as a method for problem domain modelling, the main drawback of JSD is that its notion of object is too simple. JSD's notion of object is not benefitting from the advantages of abstract data types and the possibility to describe structural relations between objects and classes. In fact, JSD never introduces a class concept. It only deals with individual objects. In this respect, OOA offers a much more powerful approach.

3.3 Event Modelling in Other Methods

We have chosen to focus on OOA and JSD in our examination of how events are handled because they have been the main inspiration in providing the combined method in Section 4. But other methods also deal with events one way or another.

Our discussion addresses the modelling of a problem domain during object-oriented analysis and in particular the intrinsic relation between the description of classes and their structural relations (static view) and the description of object dynamics (dynamic view).

Concerning the static view, we could have chosen other methods by Rumbaugh et al., Martin et al. or Booch [8, 5, 1]. There are differences as to how these methods support the modelling of the static aspects of the problem domain, but these differences are of minor importance in relation to our discussion.

Concerning the dynamic view, the ideas of JSD are still quite unique and not expressed or utilized in contemporary object-oriented analysis methods. Object-oriented analysis methods do, of course, all address the dynamic aspects of objects as this is an inherent part of taking an object-oriented approach to modelling. JSD is, however, unique in its approach to modelling the dynamic aspects of the problem domain as we will illustrate by briefly reviewing two well-known methods, which both emphasize the concept of event.

Rumbaugh et al. [8] distinguishes, amongst other things, between object modelling and dynamic modelling. The object model describes the possible patterns of objects, attributes, and links that can exist in a system. This corresponds to the static view represented by OOA in our discussion. The dynamic model consists of multiple state diagrams, one state diagram for each class, and shows the pattern of activity for an entire system via shared events. The view provided by this dynamic model corresponds quite closely to the view provided by JSD. But the concern is quite different. Rumbaugh et al. propose to make a dynamic model of the computer system, whereas JSD propose to make a dynamic model of the problem domain later to be used as a basis for designing the computer system.

A similar difference can be found by reviewing Martin et al. [5]. Here, a distinction is made between object structure analysis and object behavior analysis. Object structure analysis defines the classes we perceive and the ways in which we associate them. This corresponds to the object model of Rumbaugh et al. and the static view represented by OOA in our discussion. The object behavior analysis takes an approach that is quite comparable to Rumbaugh et al., i.e. the view taken is similar to JSD, but the concern is again quite different. Even though a distinction is made between events in general and external (to the system) sources of events, Martin et al. basically proposes to model the dynamics of the computer system, not the problem domain as suggested by JSD.

4 The Combined Approach

We have conducted several analysis and design projects based on a method that combines the respective strengths of the two approaches described above. Below, we describe the domain modelling activities of this combined approach and illustrate its results by means of an example. Finally, we outline how these results are used in design.

4.1 Problem Domain Modelling Activities

The combined approach to problem domain modelling comprises the following three activities:

1. Classes and Events

   Selection and definition of the classes and events that are relevant to model the problem domain. All events that are considered relevant to a class is listed with it.

2. Structure

   Description of structural relations between classes in terms of generalization structures and between objects in terms of aggregation and association structures.

3. Dynamics

   Arrangement of the events in which an object is involved according to their potential occurence in time. This also includes definition of the attributes that are necessary to register certain states in the lifetime of an object.

These activities are carried out in a strongly iterative manner. Thus the ordering used here is mainly a matter of presentation.

4.2 A Problem Domain Model

To illustrate the results of this combined approach, we have chosen a small example: a car rental company. The classes and structures of this example are shown in the structure diagram, cf. Figure 2.

The structure diagram[1] illustrates the four classes that are used to describe the problem domain of the car rental company: Customer, Agreement, Price Group, and Car. The Customer and Car classes reflect the physical objects appearing in this case. The Agreement class is relevant as a single customer may rent more than one car, and the Price Group class is necessary because reservations are made on a collection of cars; the physical car is not allocated to a customer until he actually arrives to pick it up.

In the structure diagram, we have also outlined four clusters of classes; in [2] collections of claaes are denoted as subjects. Instead, we prefer the notion of clusters, but with the same meaning. The clusters depicted here reflects the heart of the car rental case: resources are allocated dynamically to customers by means of

---

[1]The notation used in this diagram is presented in [2].

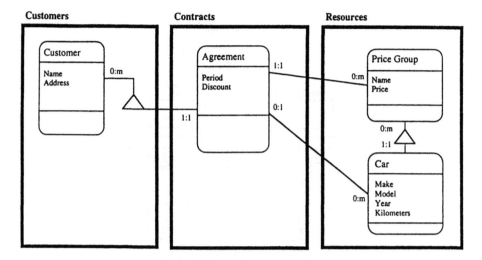

Figure 2: Structure diagram

contracts. The model we present here is as simple as possible. In more elaborate version, ech of these clusters contains more classes.

The dynamics of each class is described by a behaviour diagram. Figure 3, 4, 5, and 6 show the behaviour diagrams of the car rental case.

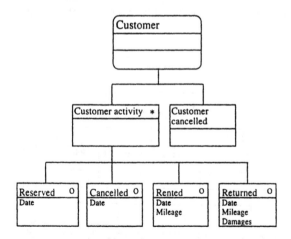

Figure 3: Behaviour diagram for Customer

Figure 3 shows a quite unrestricted way of describing object behavior. This diagram shows that a customer object can be involved in any sequence of the four events described as options. Moreover, it describes that customer objects disappear beyond the problem domain boundary, once the clerks decide to cancel them; in the case, this usually happens if a customer is inactive for more than a year.

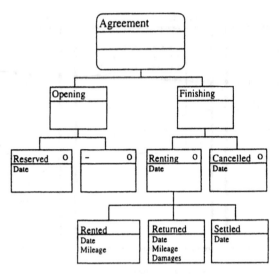

Figure 4: Behaviour diagram for Agreement

Figure 4 is much more structured. It shows that an agreement object is created either when a reservation is made or when the empty event occur. The latter situation reflects that a customer rents a car without any prior reservation. The next event is either that the car is rented or the reservation cancelled. If the car is rented a simple sequence occurs, involving that the car is returned and the customer's account is settled.

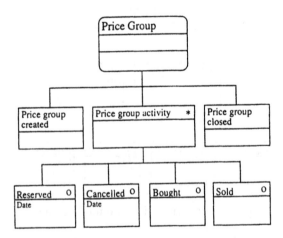

Figure 5: Behaviour diagram for Price Group

Figure 5 describes the ordering of events involving a price group object. Objects from this class are also characterised by a quite unrestricted behaviour. Price groups are explicitly created and deleted in the problem domain, and this implies that these actions of the car rental company are modelled here as events. Otherwise, a price group can be involved in any sequence of reservation, cancellation, buying, and selling.

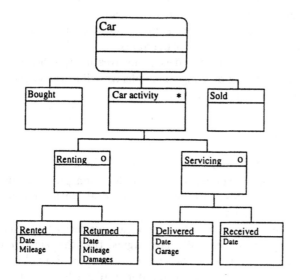

Figure 6: Behaviour diagram for Car

Finally, Figure 6 shows the behaviour of car objects.

4.3 Private and Common Events

Figure 3 and 4 illustrate a situation in which the behaviour diagrams of two different classes include events with the same names, e.g. 'reserved'. The meaning of this is that the occurrence of such an event in the problem domain involves exactly one object from each of these two classes. In this sense, the event is common to objects from these classes. This use of common events implies that events have to be named globally, as opposed to local naming within each class. Events that occur only in the behaviour diagram of one class are private to objects from that calss.

The purpose of introducing common events is to enable description of dynamic relations between objects from different classes.

4.4 Object-Oriented Design

In Section 2, the computer system was characterised as including a dynamic model of the problem domain. The purpose of design is to prescribe an overall framework for programming. This involves decisions about the specific implementation of the model.

As an integrated part of design, i must be decided how the structural relations will be implemented. Especially, object relation or links may impose serious problems on this activity.

The problem domain dynamics, described by the collection of behavior diagrams, raises separate implementation considerations. First, we must make sure that the information depicted in these diagrams is registered. Second, the the computer system, once it is in opration, must support its users in controlling that objects behave as prescribed by the behavior diagrams.

In addition to these problems, design involves many other issues. Design of functions that are updating or using the model as well as the interface to users and toher systems are key issues in this context.

5 Discussion

This paper has discussed and illustrated how the focus on structural relations of the OOA method can be combined with the focus on problem domain dynamics of the JSD method. In this sense, we have only dealt with the computer system's model of the problem domain.

In section2 we emphasized functions and user interface as two equally important elements of a computer system. We have argued that the selection of objects and events defines our perspective on the problem domain and its objects respectively. In a similar way, the functions of the computer system defines our perspective on the application domain. The application domain was defined as the collection of work tasks in the user organization in which the computer system will be used as a tool to support monitoring, administration, and management of the problem domain. Hence the set of functions implemented by the computer system defines the set of work tasks that are supported and the way in which this support is achieved. And this in turn defines the application domain.

The implication of this is that functional considerations has to be included in analysis. The simple approach to this is to claim as OOA and JSD that functional definitions should be made after the problem domain model is defined. This principle is theoretically sound. But in practice, it is impossible to observe. Especially, if you are a novice analyst, such as a student being in the process of learning the method.

Without any concern for computer system functionality, we have no criterion for defining the model of the problem domain. The key point is that an object should be integrated in the problem domain model if and only if it is administrated, monitored or controlled by at least one function of the computer system. Otherwise, it is outside the boundary of the problem domain. In this sense, the functionality of the computer system provides the only criterion of relevance for selection of objects.

With OOA and JSD this process of selection is based on a simple naming of the problem domain. Both methodologies suggest strongly that the problem domain is described before any systematic consideration of relevant functions. In this way, they pretend that the simple naming of the problem introduces a logic facilitating the selection of elements that are relevant to integrate in the model. Our experience is that the process of selection is more complicated.

Description of functions as part of object-oriented analysis serves two purposes. First, it contributes to define the application domain more precisely, similar to the way classes are used to define the problem domain. Second, the description of functions facilitates a check of the completeness of the problem domain model. The model should only contain the information that is necessary to produce the required output of each function.

OOA and JSD both reflect a lack of emphasis towards the user interface. In JSD, it is denoted as the input subsystem and it is pretended that this can be added subsequent to the definition of model and functions. In OOA, it is postponed to design, cf. [3]. Our experience that software development with inexperienced users requires early emphasis on the user interface, for example through development and evaluation of early prototypes. The user interface is our only means to verify the contents and structure of the model when we are cooperating with users who are unable to cope with the abstract nature of object-oriented descriptions.

References

[1] G. Booch. *Object-Oriented Design with Applications.* Benjamin/Cummings, Redwood City, California, 1991.

[2] P. Coad and E. Yourdon. *Object-Oriented Analysis.* Prentice-Hall, Englewood Cliffs, New Jersey, 2nd edition, 1991.

[3] P. Coad and E. Yourdon. *Object-Oriented Design.* Prentice-Hall, Englewood Cliffs, New Jersey, 1991.

[4] M. Jackson. *System Development.* Prentice-Hall, Englewood Cliffs, NJ, 1983.

[5] J. Martin and J. J. Odell. *Object-Oriented Analysis and Design.* Prentice-Hall, Englewood Cliffs, New Jersey, 1992.

[6] L. Mathiassen, A. Munk-Madsen, P. A. Nielsen, and J. Stage. *Objektorienteret analyse.* Marko, Aalborg, 1993.

[7] G.C. Murphy. Experiences applying ooa. In *TOOLS USA '91*, 1991.

[8] J. Rumbaugh, M. Blaha, W. Premerlani, F. Eddy, and W. Lorensen. *Object-Oriented Modelling and Design.* Prentice-Hall, Englewood Cliffs, New Jersey, 1991.

[9] E. Yourdon. *Modern Structured Analysis.* Prentice-Hall, 1989.

A Rewriting Technique for Implementing Active Object Systems

Danilo Montesi[1]* and Riccardo Torlone[2]

[1] Departamento de Informatica, Universidade de Lisboa
Campo Grande C5, 1700 Lisboa, Portugal
[2] IASI–CNR, Viale Manzoni 30, 00185 Roma, Italy

Abstract. We propose a novel approach to active rule processing based on a rewriting technique in the context of object database systems. A user defined transaction, which is viewed here as a sequence of basic update operations on objects forming an atomic unit, is transformed by means of active rules into induced one(s). These transactions embody the active rule semantics which can be either immediate or deferred. Then, rule semantics, confluence, equivalence and optimization are investigated in a solid framework that naturally extends a well known setting for relational database transactions.

1 Introduction

Object orientation and rule-based languages are two of the most promising features of new generation database systems [5]. The object-oriented paradigm allows us to express in an intuitive way the universe of discourse, to distinguish objects by means of their identities, to collect object with the same behavior into classes and to relate different classes by means of inheritance [15]. Rule languages are instead easy to understand and intuitive to use. Moreover, they provide a framework that allow us to formally investigate important concepts like expressive power and complexity.

Informally, and in very general terms, a rule connects a *cause* with an expected *effect*. In the framework of database systems, we are basically interested in manipulating data. Hence, cause and effect in a database rule are queries and updates, and it has been shown that this simple language schema allows us to express important database concepts like views, constraints and methods [6]. The notion of database rule is extended in the context of *active databases*. Specifically, the cause of an *active* rule (also called *ECA* rule [26]) can be more elaborate and include events that should trigger the rule automatically, without an explicit request done by users. Thus, the most general form of an active rule consists of three parts: the event part, which specify the event triggering the rule, the condition part, which states the conditions under which the rule has to be activated, and the action part, which contains the operations that dictate the

---

* The work of this author has been partially supported by the ERCIM fellowship *Information and Knowledge Systems*.

effect of rule execution. There are many applications that can be naturally modeled by exploiting the features of an active object systems [8, 9]. For instance, applications devoted to monitor a network of power stations. Each station can be expressed as an active object that is able to react to the failure of one or more stations by increasing its energy production.

Active rules have been extensively investigated both in term of expressiveness and semantics [3, 11, 14, 18, 23, 25]. Many active rule languages have been proposed in different data models [4, 3, 7, 12, 20, 21, 22, 24, 26], and some attempt has been carried out to provide tools for testing confluence, termination, equivalence and optimization [2]. However, the various proposals generally suffer from a lack of formal semantics. As a matter of fact, the basic motivations to use rule languages, namely, easiness and intuitiveness, are no more justified without a formal, simple model. Very often, active rule processing is difficult to understand and also to follow even when few rules are considered.

The goal of this paper is to provide a simple formal model to active rule processing in the framework of an object database systems that relies on a transaction rewriting technique. The basic idea is to rewrite a transaction[3] defined by users before executing it. The transformation process considers the active rules and produces a new transaction that explicitly includes the additional updates due to reactive processing. Other approaches consider transformation, but usually they apply in a restrictive context or are not formal [24]. Conversely, we believe that this formal and simple approach can improve the understanding of several active concepts and makes it easier to show results.

We start by introducing a simple object based data model whose schemes have instances composed of classes of (complex) objects with identity. We will not address in this paper other object-oriented issues (like encapsulation and inheritance) but our method can be easily extended to take them into account. We then define a quite general active rule language within this model. We consider two different semantics for active rules: immediate and deferred. Under the deferred semantics, the transformed transaction is the original one augmented with some induced actions, whereas, under the immediate semantics, the new transaction interleaves original updates and actions defined in active rules. The execution model of those induced transactions is defined by extending a model for relational transactions [1] which has been extensively investigated. The reason for this choice is twofold. Firstly, we wish to use a well know model with a formal setting and a solid transaction execution model. Secondly, we wish to take full advantages of the results already available on transaction equivalences and optimization [1, 16]. In fact, by using this model, we can investigate several interesting property at compile time. First, we can check if two transactions are equivalent. Then, due to the results on transaction equivalence, we are also able to provide results on confluence. Finally, some optimization issues can be addressed.

The primary aim of our research is to provide compile time tools for the

---

[3] In the rest of this paper, we use the term "transaction" to mean a sequence of basic update operations on objects viewed as a semantics unit.

analysis of transaction properties in an active object system. The main justification of the required extra-computation is that, as discussed above, it allows us to apply certain optimizations. However, since the approach is simple and easy to implement (it does not require any specific run-time support), it seems also promising for implementing such active object system. In particular, the rewriting technique can be effectively used for adding with minimal effort some active capabilities to a passive object system. Thus, the above system of power stations should be managed by extending a passive environment where failure of a station is just detected.

The remind of this paper is organized as follows. Section 2 introduces some background on active rule concepts. In Section 3, an overview of the approach is presented by using several practical examples. In Sections 4 and 5 we formally define the basic framework and the transformation process respectively. Results on active rule processing are discussed in Section 6, and finally, in Section 7, we draw some conclusion and sketch further research issues. Because of space limitation, we mention only the main results whose proofs are omitted.

2 Active Rule Languages

Active rule languages are based on active rules. According to [26] an *active rule* has the following form:

$$\text{when } E \text{ if } C \text{ then } A$$

where E, C an A are called *event part*, *condition part* and *action part*, respectively.

The computation of an active rule is characterized by three basic steps:

- rule *triggering*: it is the process of checking for the occurrence of the events to which a rule is sensitive.
- rule *evaluation*: it is the process of verifying if the condition part is satisfied.
- rule *firing*: it is the process of executing the action part.

Various active rule languages have been proposed (see [23] for an extensive bibliography). The various proposals generally differ in the data model of reference and in the rule format. Events to which a rule is sensitive may be queries, insertions, deletions, updates and their composition, plus special external events. Moreover, events may contain parameters or not. The condition may be an SQL statement or a logical query (e.g., a first-order formula, or a conjunction of atoms) and may take variable bindings from the event part. Finally, actions may be queries, insertions, deletions, updates and their composition, and may take variable bindings from the condition part and the event part. In the sequel, we will consider a specific but at the same time quite general rule language in which: *(i)* events are simple updates (i.e., no composition) which may contain parameters, *(ii)* conditions are expressed by means of a conjunction of literals which may take variable bindings from the event part, and *(iii)* actions are simple updates which may take variable bindings from both the event and condition parts. We believe however that the approach can be extended to more general frameworks without so much difficulty.

2.1 Triggering, Evaluation and Firing

Triggering, evaluation and firing are important notions related to the temporal relationship among the triggering of the event part, the evaluation of the condition part and the execution of the action part. The relationship between event triggering and condition evaluation may be: immediate [*EC.Imm*] or deferred [*EC.Def*]. Similarly, the relationship between condition evaluation and action execution may be: immediate [*CA.Imm*] or deferred [*CA.Def*]. (Those relationship are called coupling modes in HiPAC [20]). The importance of the temporal relationship resides in the fact that event triggering, condition evaluation and action execution may be done at different times and thus on different database states, hence with different resulting semantics.

Several of the proposed rule execution semantics, described in the literature (see [2] for a survey), refer to different combinations of the above options, as summarized in the following table. In the table, ";" denotes the (possibly delayed) sequential concatenation of two processes, whereas "∧" denotes simultaneous occurrence. For example $A; B$ means that B is considered after than A, whereas $A \wedge B$ means that A and B are considered simultaneously. The above informal notion "after than" hides several choice about operation granularity which can range from the execution of a single action to the execution of a transaction. We will not go forward in this direction because this is behind our goal and increases the complexity of the resulting semantics.

RELATIONSHIP	COMBINATIONS	SEMANTICS
$E \wedge C \wedge A$	[*EC.Imm*] and [*CA.Imm*]	*Immediate* [7, 10, 24]
$E; C \wedge A$	[*EC.Def*] and [*CA.Imm*]	*Deferred* [7, 25, 26]
$E \wedge C; A$	[*EC.Imm*] and [*CA.Def*]	*Deferred action* [20]
$E; C; A$	[*EC.Def*] and [*CA.Def*]	*Decoupled* [12, 20]

We point out that there are other differences between the various proposed semantics that we have not discussed here. For instance, some are tuple-oriented (e.g., [24]) while others are set-oriented (e.g., [26]). In this paper, we will focus our attention on the immediate and the deferred cases corresponding to the first two rows of the table above. We believe however that the other modalities can be also modeled with our approach.

2.2 Active rule applications

Active rules have been used to manage a large set of database activities. Specifically, due to their capabilities, they have been used primarily for integrity constraints enforcement [8] and view materialization [9]. The former activity consists in performing actions in order (to try) to repair some constraint violation and the latter provide a way to compute a stored derived relation in relationship with updates that can affect the view itself. Within those applications, deferred semantics is generally used to express concepts where it is possible that something change before the end of transaction. For instance, with respect to integrity constraint enforcement, under the deferred semantics a constraint violation is checked during transaction execution but the action to repair it is postponed to the end of the transaction itself. So, if during transaction execution some operations have recovered the violation, the action is no more applied. Instead, under the immediate semantics, a repairing action is executed in the middle of transaction execution even if the next update in the transaction repairs itself. In addition, active rules have been used to express *methods* in object-oriented rule languages [7, 12, 20] *triggers* [7] and deductions [7, 10]. Immediate rules semantics is often used whenever rules express methods. The computation of a method, indeed, must be immediate. Thus, the choice of rule semantics should be related to the specific application.

In this paper we do not consider the different concepts which can be expressed with active rules. Rather, we address a more general issue related to the semantics traditionally provided for active rules and the characterization of various properties of active rule processing (namely, equivalence, confluence and optimization).

3   An overview of the approach

In this section we informally present our approach. The basic idea is to express active rule processing as a three steps computation. The first step takes the user defined transaction and transform it into an induced one(s) that "embody" the active rule semantics. In general, during this step several transactions may be generated. These different induced transactions take into account the fact that an update of the original transaction may trigger several rules at the same time, and so the corresponding actions can be executed in different orders. In the second step, confluence and optimization issues of active rule processing are investigated by analyzing the transactions obtained at the first step. This is done by using (extensions of) techniques for testing equivalence of database transaction [1, 16]. Then, in the last step, according to the results of this analysis, one transaction is finally executed. There are two important points in this plan. The former is that the overall approach relies on a formal basis that allows to derive solid results. The latter is that the first two steps can be performed statically, without accessing the underlying database and therefore they can be performed efficiently at compile time.

As we have said, we are interested in the immediate and deferred active rule semantics: the immediate semantics reflect the intuition that rules are processed as soon as they are triggered, while deferred semantics suggests that a rule is evaluated and executed after the end of the original transaction [20]. Thus, two different transformation procedures will be given. For sake of simplicity, we will consider two basic update operations on objects: one to create objects (with implicit oid invention) and another one to destroy objects. Now, let us consider a user defined transaction as a sequence of updates of this kind:

$$T = U_1; \ldots; U_k.$$

This transaction is transformed under the deterministic immediate semantics into an induced one:

$$T^I = U_1; \bar{U}_1^P; \ldots; U_k; \bar{U}_k^P.$$

where $\bar{U}_i^P$ denotes the sequence of updates computed as *immediate reaction* of the update U_i with respect to a set of active rules P. This reaction can be derived by "unifying" the updates U_i with the event part of the active rules. Clearly the obtained updates can themselves trigger other rules, hence this reaction is computed recursively. As noted above, several transactions can be obtained in this way. Note that under the immediate semantics the induced transaction is an interleaving of the user defined updates with rule actions.

Under the deferred semantics, the induced transaction has the form:

$$T^D = U_1; \ldots; U_k; \bar{U}_1^P; \ldots; \bar{U}_k^P.$$

Hence the *reaction is deferred* (or postponed) until the end of the user transaction. Here again the induced updates can themselves trigger other rules, and so the reactions of the original updates are recursively computed, but using the immediate semantics.

We now give some examples to clarify the above discussion. Consider the following active database program (whose syntax should be self-explanatory) where active rules react to updates to a personnel database composed of three classes of objects: Emp, Dep and Man. We assume that the type associated with the class Emp is [ename:string,dept:Dep,sal:integer], the type associated with the class Dep is [dname:string,budget:integer], and that Man is a specialization of Emp. The variables denote object identifiers.

R_1 : WHEN $-$dep(X)
    IF   emp(Y) AND Y.dept.dname $=$ X.dname
    THEN $-$emp(Y).
R_2 : WHEN $+$emp(X)
    IF   man(Z) AND Z.dept.dname $=$ X.dept.dname AND X.sal $>$ Z.sal
    THEN $-$man(Z).
R_3 : WHEN $+$emp(X)
    IF   X.sal $>$ 50k
    THEN $+$man(X).

The first rule states that when a department is deleted then all the employees working in such a department have to be removed (cascading delete). The second one states that when an employee object is inserted into the class emp, and its salary is greater than the salary of his manager, then such a manager is no more entitled to be a manger. Finally, the last rule states that when an employee is inserted with a salary greater than 50k, then is eligible to be a manger of the department in which he works.

Now, we provide the following simple user-defined transaction where first the toy department is removed and then a new employee is added to the book department with a salary of 60K.

$$T_1 = -\text{dep}(X)[X.\text{dname} = \text{toy}];$$
$$+\text{emp}(Y)[Y.\text{ename} = \text{jim}, Y.\text{dept.dname} = \text{book}, Y.\text{sal} = 60K].$$ [4]

Under immediate semantics this transaction can be translated by means of an "unfolding" technique that takes into account the active rules, into the following transaction (the superscript $*$ denotes an induced update).

$$T_1^I = -\text{dep}(X)[X.\text{dname} = \text{toy}];$$
$$-\text{emp}(Z)[Z.\text{dept.dname} = \text{toy}]^*;$$
$$+\text{emp}(Y)[Y.\text{ename} = \text{jim}, Y.\text{dept.dname} = \text{book}, Y.\text{sal} = 60K];$$
$$-\text{man}(V)[V.\text{dept.dname} = \text{book}, V.\text{sal} < 60K]^*;$$
$$+\text{man}(W)[W.\text{ename} = \text{jim}, W.\text{dept.dname} = \text{book}, W.\text{sal} = 60K, 60K > 50K]^*.$$

Thus, the above transaction describes the behavior of the transaction T_1 taking into account the active rules under the immediate semantics. Note that there is another possible translation in which the last two updates are switched. This is because the second update of the original transaction triggers two rules at the same time (namely R_2 and R_3) and therefore we have two possible execution orders of the effects of these rules. It follows that in general, a user defined transaction induce indeed a *set* of transactions. One of the goal of this paper is to show that in many cases it is possible to statically check whether these transactions are equivalent (like in the example at hand). If all the induced transactions are equivalent we can state that the active program is "confluent" with respect to the transaction T_1. We recall that an active program is said confluent if for any database state and for any transaction the final database state is the same. In [2] a partial confluence notion is provided relaxing the above definition allowing to be non-confluent for certain unimportant relations. In this paper, we provide a new confluence notion: we say that an active program is *weakly* confluent if for a fixed transaction and for any database state the final database state is the same. This notion can be useful in many cases. Indeed, very often, the database designer is interested to check the confluence only over a fixed set of user transactions. It turns out that if the program is confluent, the execution of one of the obtained transaction implements the expected behavior of the user defined transaction in this framework.

Let us now turn our attention to the deferred execution model. Assume that we want to move the employee Tom from the toy to the book department. This can be implemented by means of the following transaction.

$$T_2 = -\text{emp}(X)[X.\text{ename} = \text{tom}, X.\text{dept.dname} = \text{toy}];$$
$$+\text{emp}(Y)[Y.\text{ename} = \text{tom}, Y.\text{dept.dname} = \text{book}, Y.\text{sal} = 50K].$$

---

[4] The notation $U[Q]$ can be read: "perform the update U where the condition Q holds".

If we transform this transaction taking into account the active rules under the deferred semantics we have the following possible translation in which the effect of the rules is postponed to the end of the transaction.

$$T_2^D = -\text{emp}(X)[X.\text{ename} = \text{tom}, X.\text{dept.dname} = \text{toy});$$
$$+\text{emp}(Y)[Y.\text{ename} = \text{tom}, Y.\text{dept.dname} = \text{book}, Y.\text{sal} = 50K];$$
$$-\text{man}(Z)[Z.\text{dept.name} = \text{book}, Z.\text{sal} < 50K]^*;$$
$$+\text{man}(W)[W.\text{ename} = \text{tom}, W.\text{dept.dname} = \text{book}, W.\text{sal} = 50K, 50K > 50K]^*.$$

Note that we can decide in this case that the third update will be not executed, since it depends on the condition $50K > 50K$ which is false. Again, the obtained transaction implements the expected behavior. Interestingly, it turns out that some optimizations can be done on those induced transactions.

There are however several problems related to the activity of transaction transformation and execution. First of all, if there is some sort of recursion in the active program (e.g., a rule that trigger itself) termination of the transformation process is not guaranteed. Moreover, differently from a user-defined transaction, the updates in the derived transactions are not independent as some updates are indeed "induced" from others. This fact has a consequence on the execution semantics of an induced transaction. Assume for instance that at run-time the execution of an update U in a transformed transaction T has a null effect on the current instance (because, for example, its condition is not verified). What about of the updates in T induced (directly or indirectly) by U in this case? Clearly, it is reasonable that the induced updates are not executed as well. Under this interpretation, we need to define a new transaction semantics that takes into account the relationship among updates. Moreover, the methods to achieve confluence and optimization must take into account this fact. To clarify this point, consider the following transaction under the deferred semantics.

$$T_3 = +\text{emp}(X)[X.\text{ename} = \text{john}, X.\text{dept.dname} = \text{toy}, X.\text{sal} = 60K];$$
$$-\text{dep}(Y)[Y.\text{dname} = \text{toy}].$$

According to the previous discussion, the transformation process should generate the following induced transaction.

$$T_3^D = +\text{emp}(X)[X.\text{ename} = \text{john}, X.\text{dept.dname} = \text{toy}, X.\text{sal} = 60K];$$
$$-\text{dep}(Y)[Y.\text{dname} = \text{toy}];$$
$$-\text{man}(Z)[Z.\text{dept.dname} = \text{toy}, Z.\text{sal} < 60K]^*;$$
$$+\text{man}(V)[V.\text{ename} = \text{john}, V.\text{dept.dname} = \text{toy}, V.\text{sal} = 60K, 50K < 60k]^*;$$
$$-\text{emp}(W)[W.\text{dept.dname} = \text{toy}]^*.$$

However, it is easy to see that the last update invalidates the effect of first one. It follows that the two updates of the transaction T_3^D, which are induced by such an update, must not be executed at run time. Thus, the correct translations of the transaction T_3 under the deferred semantics can be simplified as follows:

$$T_3^D = -\text{dep}(Y)[Y.\text{dname} = \text{toy}]; -\text{emp}(W)[W.\text{dept.dname} = \text{toy}]^*.$$

Hence, we need to develop novel techniques to check equivalence and to optimize induced transactions. This will be done by extending the already existing framework for equivalence and optimization in relational databases [1].

The rest of the paper is devoted to the formalization and characterization of the issues discussed in this section. In the following two sections we will formally fix our framework of reference and the transformation process respectively. Then, we will provide in this context several results on active rule processing.

4 Active rules and transactions

In this section we briefly present our data model of reference which we will call $\mathcal{ODM}$ and we introduce our notion of active object database and a user defined transaction. The $\mathcal{ODM}$ data model can be considered as a simple *Object Data Model* in that it includes the notions of class, abstract type, and object identity. We point out that our aim here is just to define a generic but at the same time quite general framework in which to tackle our study.

Fixed a set of base types (integers, strings, and so on), with associated sets of base values, an $\mathcal{ODM}$ *type* is a structure built as usual from the base types using a fixed set of *type constructors* $\mathbf{T}$: the tuple, the set, and the sequence ones. An $\mathcal{ODM}$ *scheme* is defined as a pair $\mathbf{S} = (\mathbf{C}, \mathrm{TYP})$ where $\mathbf{C}$ is a finite set of *class names*, and TYP is a function that associates to each symbol in $\mathbf{C}$ an $\mathcal{ODM}$ type. We also allow to express explicit references among classes through object identifiers (oid's) [19]. At the schema level, this is implemented by augmenting the set of types with the set $\mathbf{C}$, that is, by allowing the use of class names in defining types.

Given a countable set $\mathcal{O}$ of oid's we can associate with each type τ of $\mathbf{S}$ the set $\mathrm{DOM}(\tau)$ of its possible values, called the *domain* of τ, which is built as usual from base values and oid's according to the definition of τ. In particular, if τ is a class name, then $\mathrm{DOM}(\tau) = \mathcal{O}$. Then, a $\mathcal{ODM}$ *object instance* $\mathbf{s}$ of a scheme $\mathbf{S} = (\mathbf{C}, \mathrm{TYP})$, is defined as a pair of functions $\mathbf{s} = (\mathbf{c}, \mathbf{o})$, where: $\mathbf{c}$ associates with each $C \in \mathbf{C}$ a finite set of oid's, and $\mathbf{o}$ is a partial function from $\mathcal{O}$ to the union of all the domains of the types, such that, for every $C \in \mathbf{C}$ and every $o \in \mathbf{c}(C)$, $\mathbf{o}(o) \in \mathrm{DOM}(\mathrm{TYP}(C))$. Thus, in our model, an *object* belonging to a class C in an instance $\mathbf{s} = (\mathbf{c}, \mathbf{o})$ can be represented as a tuple $(o, \mathbf{c}(o))$ where o denotes its oid and allows to distinguish it from the other objects stored in the database, whereas $\mathbf{c}(o)$ denotes its *extension*, that is, the actual values associated with it. An object instance can be viewed as a set of objects of this kind grouped in classes. In the following, we will denote the extension of an object by using particular delimiters to represent the various type constructors. We will denote with $\mathit{Inst}(\mathbf{S})$ the set of all possible instances over a scheme $\mathbf{S}$.

A *term* is a variable or a value taken form a domain. An *object atom* over a class $C \in \mathbf{C}$ with type $\tau = (A_1 : \tau_1, \ldots, A_k : \tau_k)$ has the form $C(self : t_0, A_1 : t_1, \ldots, A_k : t_k)$ where t_0 is a term denoting an oid, and t_i, for $i = 1, \ldots, k$, is a term of type τ_i. An object atom will be also denoted with $C(t_0, t_1, \ldots, t_k)$ when the correspondence between the terms and the attributes is clear. If every term is a constant then the object atom is *ground*. A ground object atom is also called *tuple*. Together with the object atoms, we will also use *built-in* atoms based on traditional *comparison predicates* $(=, >, <, ...)$. A *literal* is an atom (*positive* literal) or a negated atom (*negative* literal). A *condition* is a set of literals. A *substitution* is a function $\theta : V \rightarrow D$, which associates with each variable a constant. Given an object atom B, an object instance s and a substitution θ, we say that θ is a *valuation* of the positive object literal B (resp. the negative object literal $\neg B$) on s if there is (there is not) a class $C \in \mathbf{C}$ such that $o \in c(C)$ and $\theta(B) = (o, o(o))$. Similarly, a substitution θ is a valuation of a built-in atom B if $\theta(B)$ is true according to the usual interpretation of the corresponding comparison predicate. A substitution θ is a valuation of a condition Q on an object instance s if it is a valuation of each $L_i \in Q$ on s. We assume that an empty condition has always one valuation on any object instance which is the identity. Clearly, the set of valuations of a condition is finite only if the condition is *safe*, that is, each variable that occurs in a negative object literal also occurs in a positive object literal, and each variable that occurs in a built-in literal also occurs in an object literal. We will consider only safe conditions.

Definition 4.1 *An* action *is an object atom preceded by one of the symbols* $\{+, -\}$. *A* conditional update U *(or simply an* update*) has the form:* $A[Q]$, *where Q is a condition and A is an action such that all the variables occurring in it, except the oid variable, also occur in Q.*

A conditional update is executed for those objects (if any) that verify the specified condition. The *effect* of an update U is a function $\mathrm{EFF}(U) : Inst(\mathbf{S}) \rightarrow Inst(\mathbf{S})$ defined as follows:

- $\mathrm{EFF}(+B[Q])(s) = s \cup \{\theta(B) : \theta$ is a valuation of Q in $s\}$;
- $\mathrm{EFF}(-B[Q])(s) = s - \{\theta(B) : \theta$ is a valuation of Q in $s\}$.

Note that, for sake of simplicity, we do not consider here modify operations. They can be however introduced without much difficulty.

In databases update operations are generally executed within *transactions*, that is, collections of data manipulation operations viewed as a semantics atomic unit for recovery and concurrency purposes.

Definition 4.2 *A user defined transaction is a sequence of updates of the form:*

$$U_1; \ldots; U_k$$

The effect of a transaction $T = U_1; \ldots; U_k$ is defined as:

- $\mathrm{EFF}(T)(s) = \mathrm{EFF}(U_1) \circ \ldots \circ \mathrm{EFF}(U_k)(s)$.

Definition 4.3 *An* event *is an object atom preceded by one of the symbols* $\{\oplus, \ominus\}$.

An event denotes the fact that a certain update operation has been performed on a object instance. We can say that the execution of an update *generates* an event which therefore can be viewed as an object tracing update executions.

Definition 4.4 *An* active rule *has the form:*

$$E \circ Q \to A$$

where E is an event, Q is a condition and A is an action such that: (1) each variable that occurs in a negative literal in the condition also occurs in a positive literal or in the event part, and (2) each variable that occurs in the action also occurs in the event or in the condition part. An active program *P is a set of active rules. An* active database *is a pair (s, P) where s is an object instance and P is an active program.*

The intuitive semantics of an active rule is: "when E is executed, evaluate the condition Q and if it is true then perform the action A using the bindings of the event and the condition parts". As we have said, one important point here is the temporal relationship between the execution of the various components of a rule. The event part and the condition part have a temporal decoupling if the program has deferred semantics, whereas, if it has immediate semantics there is no temporal decoupling. In any case, the above informal meaning shows that the execution of a transaction over a certain instance generate events which in turn trigger active rules. Hence, the behavior of an active database always depends on the given user defined transaction. In our approach, the semantics of an active database with respect to a transaction T is given in terms of execution of a transaction T' induced by T. So, this semantics will be defined along with the definition of the transformation technique.

We note that for technical reason, the notation used in this section is slightly different from the one used in Section 3 in which, for sake of simplicity, the dot notation has been heavily used. It is obvious however that one can be reduced to the other in a straightforward way.

5 Transaction transformation

In this section we present the algorithms that transform a user defined transaction into an induced one which embodies the active rules behavior. We consider both the immediate and deferred cases.

5.1 Immediate and deferred transaction transformations

Let us start with some preliminary notion. Let U be an update $A[Q]$ and R be an active rule $E \circ Q' \to A'$ that does not contain any variable in U. Then, we say that U *triggers* R if: (1) $A = +B$ and $E = \oplus B'$, or $A = -B$ and $E = \ominus B'$, and (2) there is a substitution θ, called *unifier*, such that $B = \theta(B')$. If an update U triggers a rule $E \circ Q' \to A'$ with θ as unifier, then we say that U *induces* the update $\theta(A'[Q'])$

As we said, in our translation technique we need to keep trace of the relationship between inducer and induced update. This is done by subscribing the induced updates in order to encode the inducer, the inducer of the inducer and so on. For instance the update $U_{3;2;1}$ means that it was induced by the update $U_{3;2}$ that in turn was induced by U_3. Thus the original update U_3 induces $U_{3;2}$ that induces $U_{3;2;1}$. In other words, we trace the history of the inducers in the update indexes. Note that this is sufficient to encode all the possible relationships between updates in a transaction.

The following is a recursive algorithm that computes the reaction of a single update.

Algorithm REACTION
Input: *The program P and the update U_j.*
Output: *A sequence $\bar{U}_j^P$ of updates induced by U_j and P.*
begin

    $\bar{U}_j^P :=<>$;
    $i := 1$;
    $index := j$;
    $Triggered(U_j, P) := \{R \in P : R$ *is triggered by* $U_j\}$;
    while *Triggered(U_j, P) is not empty* **do**
        pick a rule $E \circ Q \rightarrow A$ *from Triggered(U_j, P)*;
        $\theta :=$ *the unifier of E and U_j*;
        $index :=$ APPEND$(index, i)$;
        $U_{index} := \theta(A[Q])$;
        $\bar{U}_j^P :=$ APPEND$(\bar{U}_j^P, U_{index})$;
        $\bar{U}_j^P :=$ APPEND$(\bar{U}_j^P,$ REACTION$(P, U_{index}))$;
        $i := i + 1$;
    endwhile
    output $\bar{U}_j^P$
end.

It is easy to see that the above algorithm may not terminate if there is some sort of recursion in the active program. However, syntactical restriction can be given so that the algorithm is guaranteed to terminate. The following result is based on the construction of a graph G_P such that the nodes represent the rules in P and there is an edge from a rule $R : E \circ Q \rightarrow A$ to a rule $R' : E' \circ Q' \rightarrow A'$ if $A[Q]$ triggers E'.

Lemma 5.1 *If the graph G_P is acyclic then the algorithm REACTION is guaranteed to terminate over P and any update U_j.*

Actually, less restrictive conditions can be given to achieve termination. This is subject of current investigation.

Now we built from this reaction the immediate and deferred transformations. The resulting transactions, under the immediate or deferred transformations, embody the active rule behavior. Thus, we can forget that it was induced by active rules processing. This is an important step that allow us to consider only transactions. All the necessary information on the relationship between the user defined updates and the updates generated by the rules are encoded into update indexes.

The following immediate and deferred transformation algorithms reflect the informal expected behavior of rule execution under immediate and deferred semantics respectively.

Algorithm IMMEDIATET
Input: *The active program P and the user defined transaction $U_1; \ldots; U_k$.*
Output: *The induced transaction T^I.*
begin
$\quad T^I := U_1; \text{REACTION}(P, U_1); \ldots; U_k; \text{REACTION}(P, U_k)$
end.

Algorithm DEFERREDT
Input: *The active program P and the user defined transaction $U_1; \ldots; U_k$.*
Output: *The induced transaction T^D.*
begin
$\quad T^D := U_1; \ldots; U_k; \text{REACTION}(P, U_1); \ldots; \text{REACTION}(P, U_k)$
end.

Note that, for sake of clarity, the above algorithms provide just one transaction for any user defined transaction. However, in general, different transaction can be generated depending on the order in which the available rules are selected in the first step of the loop in algorithm REACTION. The algorithms can be generalized in such a way that all the possible induced transaction are generated. It should be noted that even if the number of those induced transactions is always finite, it may be very large. However, this number can be reduced by checking for instance when certain ones are "obviously" equivalent, e.g., when certain rules trivially commute. This is an important problem that will be subject of future investigation.

In the following, we will denote by $Imm(T, P)$ (respectively $Def(T, P)$) the set of all possible transactions that can be generated by a transaction T and an active program P using Algorithm IMMEDIATET (DEFERREDT).

5.2 Semantics of induced transaction

Let $T' = U_1; \ldots; U_k$ be an *induced transaction*, that is, a sequence of updates obtained as output of algorithms IMMEDIATET or DEFERREDT. Two possible effect semantics can be given for the transaction T'. The former considers T' like a user defined transaction independently from the fact that some inducing update has no effect at run time (as we said in Section 3 this is reasonable in some particular application). In this case the effect of T' coincides with the function EFF defined in Section 4. In the latter approach, an induced update is executed only if the update inducing it has been effectively executed. Then, a new effect semantics EFF' needs to be defined according to that. Let U be an update, and s be an object instance. We denote with $\Delta^+(U, s)$ and $\Delta^-(U, s)$ the *changes* induced by U on s, that is, the objects that U adds to and deletes from s, respectively. Now, let s' be another object instance. We say that the effect of

U on s is *visible* on s', if $\Delta^+(U, s) \subseteq s'$ and $\Delta^-(U, s) \cap s' = \emptyset$. Then, we have the following definition of the function EFF$'$, in which $0 \leq i < j \leq k$.

$$\text{EFF}'(U_1; ..; U_j)(s) = \begin{cases} \text{EFF}'(U_1; ..; U_{j-1})(s) & \text{if } U_j \text{ is induced by } U_i \\ & \text{and the effect of } U_i \\ & \text{is not visible on} \\ & \text{EFF}'(U_1; ..; U_{j-1})(s) \\ \text{EFF}(U_j) \circ \text{EFF}'(U_1; ..; U_{j-1})(s) & \text{otherwise} \end{cases}$$

Note that the above "induced by" relationship between updates can be easily derived on the basis of the indexes associated with the updates. We are now ready to give the semantics of an active transaction with respect to an active database.

Definition 5.1 *An* immediate effect *of user defined transaction T over an active database (P, s) coincides with* EFF$'$(IMMEDIATE $T(P, T))(s)$.

Definition 5.2 *A* deferred effect *of user defined transaction T over an active database (P, s) coincides with* EFF$'$(DEFERRED $T(P, T))(s)$.

6 Results on rule processing

We believe that many interesting problems can be systematically studied in the above formal setting. Among others, termination, equivalence, optimization, confluence of transactions in an active object databases. We show how they can be tackled taking full advantages of rewriting technique presented in the previous section. Let us go through some of these issues.

6.1 Transaction equivalence

Transaction equivalence has been extensively investigated in the relational model [1]. The major results of this study are about deciding if two transaction are equivalent and transforming a transaction into an equivalent but less expensive one. Unfortunately, these results cannot be directly used in our framework. The difference between the relational and the object data model are not relevant for our purpose. Thus, we need to define a new notion of equivalence based on the effect provided by means of the function EFF$'$.

As soon as the equivalence notion is fixed we provide a method for testing equivalence of induced transaction. The method is based on a set of transformation rules that allows to transform an induced transaction into a new, equivalent one. According to [1], we restrict our attention to the important class of *domain-based* transactions, where the conditions involve only atoms of the form $X = a$ and $X \neq a$. Moreover, we assume that the transaction is in *first normal form*, that is, every condition in a transaction has a disjoint valuation over any instance. It is possible to show that, similarly to [1], each transaction can be transformed into an equivalent 1NF transaction by "splitting" each update by means of opportune reduction rules.

In the transformation rules we are going to present, we use the notation $S \,\widehat{\in}\, T$ to denote that a sequence of updates S occurs in a transaction T. Moreover, $Ind(i)$ denotes the set of updates induced by the update with index i (note that this set can be built by simply inspecting the update indexes). Finally, we make use of the operators RM and SW: the former takes as input a transaction T and a set of indexes I, and removes from T the updates with index in I, the latter takes as input a transaction T and a pair of indexes (i, j), and switches the updates in T with those indexes.

Let $\mathcal{R}$ be the following set of transformation rules.

$(1)\ -A[C_1]_i; -A[C_2]_j \,\widehat{\in}\, T \Rightarrow \text{SW}(T, (i, j)) \qquad\qquad\qquad\quad \text{if } j \notin Ind(i)$
$(2)\ -A[C_1]_i; -A[C_1]_j \,\widehat{\in}\, T \Rightarrow \text{RM}(T, \{i\} \cup Ind(i))$
$(3)\ +A[C_1]_i; +A[C_2]_j \,\widehat{\in}\, T \Rightarrow \text{SW}(T, (i, j)) \qquad\qquad\qquad\quad \text{if } j \notin Ind(i)$
$(4)\ +A[C_1]_i; +A[C_1]_j \,\widehat{\in}\, T \Rightarrow \text{RM}(T, \{i\} \cup Ind(i))$
$(5)\ -A[C_1]_i; +A[C_2]_j \,\widehat{\in}\, T \Rightarrow \text{SW}(T, (i, j)) \qquad\qquad\qquad\quad \text{if } C_1 \neq C_2 \text{ and}$
$\qquad\qquad\qquad\qquad\qquad\qquad\qquad\qquad\qquad\qquad\qquad\qquad\qquad\qquad\qquad j \notin Ind(i)$

$(6)\ -A[C_1]_i; +A[C_1]_j \,\widehat{\in}\, T \Rightarrow \text{RM}(T, \{i, j\} \cup Ind(i) \cup Ind(j))$
$(7)\ +A[C_1]_i; -A[C_1]_j \,\widehat{\in}\, T \Rightarrow \text{RM}(T, \{i, j\} \cup Ind(i) \cup Ind(j))$

Intuitively, rules $(1), (3)$ and (5) state that if the updates are not related, then they can be switched. Rules (2) and (4) state that the execution of the same two updates can be done once only and so we can remove the former and the corresponding induced updates. Finally, rules (6) and (7) state that the execution of complementary updates can be avoided by removing them and the induced ones. We have the following result that allows us to check for equivalence of transaction, and it is possible to show that this can be done in polynomial time.

Theorem 6.1 *Let T be an induced transaction and T' be a transaction obtained from T by applying rules in $\mathcal{R}$. Then, T is equivalent to T'.*

6.2 Confluence

Confluence is a strong property and some applications may need a weaker notion. It is sometimes useful to allow an active program P to be non-confluent for certain unimportant relations in the database, but ensure that P is confluent for other important relations. This was called partial confluence in [2]. We propose another notion that can be useful in many cases and turn to be a practical one. We say that an active program P is *weakly confluent* under the immediate semantics (resp. the deferred semantics) with respect to a user transaction T if each pair of induced transaction T_1 and T_2 in $Imm(T, P)$ $(Def(T, P))$ have the same immediate (deferred) effect on any active object database over P. Obviously, confluence implies weaker confluence. From the definition of weak confluence and the above result on equivalence, it follows that weak confluence can be checked in polynomial time.

Theorem 6.2 *Let P be an active program and T a user defined transaction. Then, P is weakly confluent under the immediate semantics (resp., deferred semantics) with respect to T if an induced transaction in $Imm(T, P)$ $(Def(T, P))$ can be transformed in each other transaction in $Imm(T, P)$ $(Def(T, P))$ using the rules in $\mathcal{R}$.*

6.3 Optimization

One objective of our research is to provide tools for optimizing induced transactions. This is particularly important since, with our approach, an optimization technique for induced transaction yields a method for optimizing the overall activity of active rule processing.

According to [1], two types of optimization criteria for transaction can be considered. The first is related to syntactic aspects (e.g., length and complexity of updates) of the transaction, whereas the second is related to operational criteria such as the number of atomic updates performed by a transaction. The notion of optimality that we use in this section is based on the first criteria ($|T|$ denotes the length of the transaction $|T|$) but it turns out to be appealing also for the latter. Given two equivalent induced transaction T and T', we say that T is *simpler* than T' if $|T| < |T'|$

The transformation rules $\mathcal{R}$ introduced in the previous subsection can be grouped into two sets. The former contains commutativity rules (namely, rules (1), (3) and (5)) whereas the latter consists of simplification rules (namely, rules (2), (4), (6) and (7)). The application of a simplification rule yields a strictly simpler transaction, whereas commutativity rules do not affect the complexity of the translation, but are however useful in order to apply simplification rules. This observation leads to a method for optimizing induced transaction based on the rules $\mathcal{R}$. This method consists of applying a sequence of commutativity rules followed by one simplification rule, until no modification can be performed. We say that a *reduction* of transaction T based on $\mathcal{R}$ is the transaction obtained from T by applying rules in $\mathcal{R}$ alternating simplification and commutativity rules as long as some simplification rule can be applied. The following result states that the reduction process always terminates (in polynomial time) and is essentially deterministic regardless of the order of application of the rules.

Theorem 6.3 *Let T be an induced transaction. Then, (i) a reduction of T based on $\mathcal{R}$ is simpler than T, (ii) each reduction of T based on $\mathcal{R}$ can be generated in polynomial time, and (iii) for each pair of reductions T' and T'' of T based on $\mathcal{R}$, T' can be transformed into T'' by using only commutativity rules in $\mathcal{R}$.*

7 Conclusions and Future Work

We have presented a formal technique that allows us to reduce active rule processing to transaction execution. User defined transactions are translated into new transactions that embody the expected rule semantics under the immediate and deferred execution modality, so that active rules must not to be inspected at execution time. All the interesting properties are encoded into the novel transactions by means of an indexing technique. We have shown that many problems are easier to understand and to investigate from this point of view, as they can be tackled in a formal setting that naturally extends an already established framework for relational transactions. In fact, it turns out that several important results derived for transaction in a passive environment can be taken across to an active one. Firstly, we can formally study transaction equivalence in the framework of an active object database. Secondly, results on transaction equivalence can be used to check for interesting and practically useful notions of confluence. Finally, optimization issues can be also addressed.

We believe that this approach to active rule processing is quite general and promising for further formal investigations. We would like to include in the framework specific transaction operators and provide an efficient way to generate and keep induced transactions. We intend to extend the results on equivalence and confluence and provide more powerful tools for testing termination, for instance run-time checking of termination. Moreover, the area of optimization remains to be extensively investigated. We believe that several optimization criteria can be studied and formally characterized in the framework we have created.

Acknowledgment

We would like to thank the anonymous referees, who provided very helpful comments and suggestions.

References

1. S. Abiteboul and V. Vianu. Equivalence and Optimization of Relational Transactions. *Journal of the ACM*, 35(1):70–120, January 1988.
2. A. Aiken, J. Widom, and J. M. Hellerstein. Behavior od Database Production Rules: Termination, Confluence, and Observable Determinism. In M. Stonebraker, editor, *Proc. Int'l Conf. ACM on Management of Data*, pages 59–68, 1992.
3. C. Beeri and T. Milo. A model for active object-oriented database. In *Seventeenth International Conf. on Very Large Data Bases, Barcelona*, pages 337–349, 1991.
4. E. Bertino, B. Catania, G. Guerrini and D. Montesi. Transaction Optimization in Rule Databases. In *Fourth IEEE Research Issues in Data Engineering: Active Database Systems (RIDE-ADS'94)*, IEEE Computer Society Press, 1994.
5. E. Bertino, G. Guerrini and D. Montesi. Deductive Object Databases. To appear In *Proc. European Conference on Object-Oriented Programming*, Bologna, 1994.
6. S. Ceri, G. Gottlob, and L. Tanca. *Logic Programming and Data Bases*. Springer-Verlag, 1989.
7. S. Ceri and R. Manthey. First Specification of Chimera, the Conceptual Interface of Idea. Technical report, Eprit project 6333 IDEA.
8. S. Ceri and J. Widom. Deriving production rules for constraint maintenance. In *Sixteenth International Conf. on Very Large Data Bases, Brisbane*, pages 566–577, 1990.

9. S. Ceri and J. Widom. Deriving production rules for incremental view mainte-nance. In *Seventeenth International Conf. on Very Large Data Bases, Barcelona*, pages 577–589, 1991.

10. C. de Maindreville and E. Simon. A Production Rule based approach to Deductive databases. In *Proc. Fourth Int'l Conf. on Data Engineering*. IEEE Computer Society Press, 1988.

11. P. Fraternali, D. Montesi, and L. Tanca. Active Database Semantics. In *Australasian Database Conference*, 1994.

12. N. Gehani and H. V. Jagadish. ODE as an active database: constraints and triggers. In *Proc. Seventeenth International Conf. on Very Large Data Bases, Barcelona*, pages 327–336, 1991.

13. G. Guerrini, D. Montesi, and G. Rodrigues. Specification of the Run-Time Sup-port for Chimera (algres testbed). Technical Report IDEA.DE.3P.007.02, Eprit project 6333 IDEA, December 1993.

14. E. N. Hanson and J. Widom. Rule Processing in Active Database Systems. In L. Delcambre and F. Petry, editors, *Advances in Databases and Artificial Intelli-gence*. JAI Press, 1992.

15. R. Jungclaus, G. Saake and C. Sernadas. Formal Specification of Object Sys-tems. In *Proc. TAPSOFT'91*, pages 60–82, 1991.

16. A. Karabeg, D. Karabeg, K Papakonstantinou and V. Vianu. Axiomatisation and Simplification for Relational Transactions. In *ACM SIGACT SIGMOD SIGART Symp. on Principles of Database Systems*, pages 254–259, 1987.

17. D. Karabeg and V. Vianu. Simplification rules and complete axiomatisation for relational update transactions. In *ACM Transactions on Database Systems*, 16(3):439–475, September 1991.

18. A. Karadimce, S. Urban. Conditional Term Rewriting as a Formal Basis for Ac-tive Database Rules. In *Fourth IEEE Research Issues in Data Engineering: Active Database Systems (RIDE-ADS'94)*, IEEE Computer Society Press, 1994.

19. S. Khoshafian and G. Copeland. Object identity. In *ACM Symp. on Object Ori-ented Programming Systems, Languages and Applications*, pages 406–416, 1986.

20. D.R. McCarthy and U. Dayal. The architecture of an Active Data Base Manage-ment System. In *Proc. Int'l Conf. ACM on Management of Data*.

21. L. Palopoli, R. Torlone. Modeling Database Application Using Generalised Produc-tion Rules. In *Fourth IEEE Research Issues in Data Engineering: Active Database Systems (RIDE-ADS'94)*, IEEE Computer Society Press, 1994.

22. T. Sellis, C.C. Lin, and Raschid L. Implementing large production systems in a DBMS environment: concepts and algorithms. In *ACM SIGMOD International Conf. on Management of Data*, pages 404–412, 1988.

23. M. Stonebraker. The integration of rule systems and database systems. *IEEE Trans. on Knowledge and Data Eng.*, 4(5):415–423, October 1992.

24. M. Stonebraker, A. Jhingran, J. Goh, and S. Potamianos. On rules, procedures, caching, and views in data base systems. In *Proc. ACM SIGMOD International Conf. on Management of Data*, pages 281–290, 1990.

25. J. Widom. A Denotational Semantics for the Starburst Production Rule Language. *SIGMOD Record*, 21(3):4–9, September 1992.

26. J. Widom and S. J. Finkelstein. Set-Oriented Production Rule in Relational Databases Systems. In H. Garcia-Molina and H.V. Jagadish, editors, *Proc. Int'l Conf. ACM on Management of Data*, pages 259–270, 1990.

Beyond Coupling Modes
Implementing Active Concepts on Top of a Commercial ooDBMS

G. Kappel, S. Rausch-Schott, W. Retschitzegger

Institute of Computer Science, Department of Information Systems
University of Linz, AUSTRIA
email: {gerti, stefan, werner}@ifs.uni-linz.ac.at

Abstract. Active object-oriented database systems are especially useful in the area of nonstandard applications in order to implement an event-driven and constraint-driven system environment. Several approaches exist in literature integrating active concepts into object-oriented databases. For most systems, their knowledge model is based on Event/Condition/Action rules, and their execution model is based on coupling modes, specifying the temporal relationships between rule triggering and condition evaluation, and between condition evaluation and action execution, respectively. The expressive power of coupling modes, however, is insufficient for specifying certain execution semantics required by nonstandard applications. The system TriGS (=Trigger system for GemStone™) fills this gap. Instead of exploiting coupling modes TriGS uses an event specification mechanism not only for defining the points in time for rule triggering but also the points in time for condition evaluation and action execution. A first prototype of TriGS implemented in Smalltalk and GemStone on SUN™ workstations is operational.

1. Introduction

The paper reports on the development of TriGS, an active extension to the commercial object-oriented database system GemStone. Concerning the underlying concepts of active object-oriented database systems it is commonly accepted that the pioneering work of HiPAC [Daya88] in terms of its knowledge model and execution model has influenced a whole fleet of active object-oriented database system proposals, e.g., [Anwa93, Chak90, Diaz91, Gatz91, Geha91, Kotz93, Mede91]. TriGS also builds on this work. Like in most systems the knowledge model of TriGS comprises Event/Condition/Action (ECA) rules. Unlike most systems, however, TriGS does not exploit coupling modes to describe the execution model of the rule scheduler. Instead, the event specification mechanism is used again for specifying the points in time when conditions are evaluated and actions are executed. This idea has been described the first time by Beeri and Milo in [Beer91]. TriGS extends their approach in several directions, most importantly, conditions are considered in addition to events and actions, and a flexible event specification mechanism including both class level specification

---

™GemStone is a registered trademark of Servio Corporation
™SUN is a registered trademark of Sun Microsystems

and object level specification is provided. The advantages of the approach compared to coupling modes are twofold. Firstly, fewer concepts are employed, thus higher uniformity and (hopefully) improved understandability is reached. Secondly, the event specification mechanism for describing the execution behavior of the rule scheduler is more general than using coupling modes, thus higher expressive power is reached.

Note, TriGS emphasizes the development of advanced active concepts on top of some existing object-oriented data model and system. In this way, a useful migration path from non-active database systems to systems that have some active capability is provided [Chak92]. This is extremely important, since it is unlikely that currently used non-active database systems will be replaced by brand new active systems in the near future. The choice of GemStone [Butt91] as underlying research vehicle has been influenced by at least two reasons. Firstly, it provides an interpretative environment, thus supporting experiments with various system features. Secondly, system defined classes are available in source code, thus it is easy to extend system behavior for the purpose of event detection. Nevertheless, the concepts of TriGS are general in the sense that they can be applied to other object-oriented database systems as well.

The rest of the paper provides a detailed account of the execution model and implementation aspects of TriGS. To make the paper self-contained the underlying knowledge model is shortly summarized in the next section. For an in-depth discussion of the knowledge model we refer to [Kapp94a]. A comparison with related approaches and an outlook on further work concludes the paper. The work on TriGS is part of the EC ESPRIT project "Design, Development and Implementation of a Knowledge-Based Leitstand" (KBL No. 5161)[1] aiming at the development of next generation production scheduling and control systems.

2. Underlying Knowledge Model

TriGS is based on the ECA paradigm [Daya88], i.e., rules are specified as event-condition-action triplets. Rules and its components are implemented as first-class objects in GemStone allowing both the definition and modification of rules during run time. The event part of a rule is represented by an *event selector* determining the event(s) which is (are) able to trigger the rule (e.g., a machine breakdown). Triggering a rule implies that its condition has to be evaluated and if true, its action has to be executed. In object-oriented databases, an event may be the sending of a message to some object. In TriGS, any message sent to an object may be associated with a *message event*. Note that other kinds of events such as time events and external events [Geha92] are not considered in this paper. The condition part of a rule is specified by a boolean expression, possibly based on the result of a database query (e.g., are there some scheduled jobs on the damaged machine?). The action part is specified again in terms of messages (e.g., display all jobs scheduled on the damaged machine and reschedule them on another machine). Considering rules in the context of the class hierarchy of an

---

[1] The research described in this paper is supported by FFF (Austrian Foundation for Research Applied to Industry) under grant No. 2/279

object-oriented database schema they may be attached to a specific class or defined apart from any class. According to this distinction TriGS supports two categories of rules, called local rules and global rules, each of them having a specific *scope*. The scope of a rule determines the set of classes which may be involved in triggering a rule.

A *local rule* allows to monitor specific behavior of certain classes. Thus the event selector of a local rule consists of a triggering class in addition to a triggering method. The *triggering class* denotes the class which the rule is attached to. The *triggering method* denotes, in terms of GemStone, a class method or an instance method (default) which raises the event before or after its execution (cf. keywords CLASS_METHOD/ INSTANCE_METHOD and PRE/POST in Figure 2). Since a local rule is attached to a specific class it is subject to inheritance. This implies that a local rule is triggered not only by invoking the triggering method on any object of the triggering class but also by invoking this method on any object of its subclasses. Therefore, the scope of a local rule is defined as the part of the class hierarchy rooted at the triggering class. Due to the design goal of TriGS, which is the seamless integration of rules in the underlying object-oriented data model, TriGS allows to override inherited rules in subclasses.

In contrast to a local rule, a *global rule* allows to monitor specific behavior of arbitrary classes. Thus the event selector of a global rule consists of a triggering method only. Consequently, the scope of a global rule covers all classes which know the triggering method. Without the concept of global rules, it would be necessary to define several local rules redundantly, each of them attached to a root of the class hierarchy knowing the triggering method. Since a global rule is attached to a specific method only, it is neither subject to inheritance nor overriding. Both local and global rules may be (de-)activated at different levels of granularity ranging from object level to class level. Class level granularity implies (de-)activating a rule for all instances within its scope. Object level granularity allows (de-)activating a rule for specific instances, thus supporting a powerful exception handling mechanism. Note, the notion of global and local rules doesn't influence the semantics of condition evaluation and action execution.

Example:

As running example throughout the paper we select a simple production control system. Considering our universe of discourse, a schedule reserves a machine for the purpose of executing a certain operation within a specific start time and end time. Machines and Buffers are two kinds of resources that each have a certain state (for a machine, e.g., "WORKING" or "IDLE"). In Figure 1 the application of local rules and global rules is demonstrated. Three local rules, R1, R2,and R1', and one global rule Rg1 are shown. Since the event selector of R1 includes the triggering class Machine, R1 is attached to class Machine and consequently inherited to Machine's subclasses MillingMachine and MMWithout-Buffer. In class MMWithoutBuffer, however, R1 is overridden by R1' reflecting the fact that machines of that kind don't have a buffer. In class Milling-Machine, an additional rule R2 is defined and inherited to MMWithout-Buffer. The global rule Rg1 is defined on the triggering method `changeState`. The scope of `Rg1`, thus, covers the whole class hierarchy except the classes `Object` and `MachineSet`.

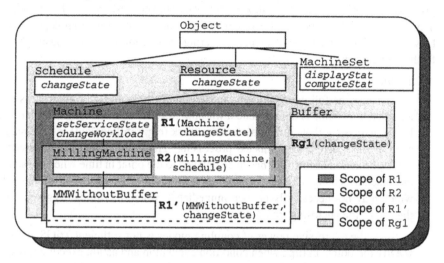

Figure 1. Local Rules and Global Rules

3. Execution Model

In this section we focus on relevant aspects concerning the execution of rules. These comprise the definition of points in time when rule processing takes place and how rule execution is embedded into the underlying transaction model. In addition, we specify the semantics of multiple rule processing by analyzing their execution order. Other components of the execution model such as rule cascading and termination of rule execution are not treated in this paper. They are subject of ongoing research.

3.1 Single Rule Processing

In Section 2 we've introduced the concept of event selectors. From the point of view of the rule system, the event selector determines the events able to trigger a rule. From the application's point of view the event selector determines the point in time when the rule should be triggered with respect to the execution of the application. The latter is called *Rule Triggering Point (RTP)*. After triggering a rule its condition has to be evaluated and if true, the corresponding action has to be executed. The point in time when the condition should be evaluated is called *Condition Evaluation Point (CEP)*. Analogously, the point in time when the corresponding action should be executed is called *Action Execution Point (AEP)*. In most existing systems two coupling modes are used for specifying CEP and AEP. Firstly, *immediate coupling* that is evaluating/executing the condition/action immediately after the RTP/CEP. And secondly, *deferred coupling* that is evaluating/executing the condition/action at the end of the transaction where the rule has been triggered. Note, a third coupling mode called *separate* and introduced in many systems [Geha92, Daya88, Beer91] does not specify a point in time. It rather defines the degree of parallelism for rule execution and thus, is not subject of this section. A more detailed discussion concerning parallelism in TriGS is given in Section 3.1.2. Coupling modes, however, are very restrictive. They prohibit to define CEPs and AEPs beyond the points in time stated above, for example, some time between the RTP and the end of the triggering transaction or on the basis of some forthcoming events.

Example:

Consider the following situation in our running example. During processing of an order, a machine is able to send a warning (e.g. the coolant falls below a certain level), indicating that some maintenance work (e.g. refill coolant) is necessary as soon as the machine has finished processing. This implies that the maintenance work (the action of the rule) has to be delayed to the point in time when the state of the machine changes from "WORKING" to "IDLE" (the condition of the rule), which may not necessarily happen immediately when the rule is triggered nor at the end of the enclosing transaction.

Since the expressive power of coupling modes is not sufficient TriGS allows to specify the points in time when condition evaluation and action execution, respectively, have to take place by means of an event based approach. This idea has been described the first time by Beeri and Milo in [Beer91]. TriGS extends their approach in several directions, most importantly, conditions are considered in addition to events and actions, and the event specification mechanism originally introduced for rule triggering (cf. Section 2) is reused for defining CEPs and AEPs. Note, due to the possibility of different times of condition evaluation and action execution it might be problematic to pass the values retrieved in condition evaluation to the corresponding action. Thus, for the first prototype we decided to re-evaluate the condition if necessary. A more sophisticated solution is subject of ongoing research.

3.1.1 Event-Based Approach

The event-based definition of CEPs and AEPs is realized by introducing two event selectors for defining the events for triggering condition evaluation, called *condition event selector*, and for triggering action execution, called *action event selector*, in addition to the event selector for triggering the rule in the first place, called *rule event selector*. Figure 2 depicts the relevant parts of the syntax for specifying event selectors in TriGS using the Backus-Naur Form (BNF). The symbols : := | [ ] { } are meta symbols belonging to the BNF formalism.

```
<rule_definition>  ::=
   DEFINE RULE <rule_name>
   ON <rule_event_selector> DO                        /*event part*/
   ON <cond_event_selector> IF <bool_expr> THEN /*condition part*/
   ON <act_event_selector> EXECUTE [ONCE] <action> /*action part*/
   ...

<rule_event_selector>::=
   {PRE|POST} ([<class_name>,]
```

```
[CLASS_METHOD|INSTANCE_METHOD] <method_signature>)
<cond_event_selector>::=
  <rule_event_selector> |
  {PRE|POST} (rule_trgO[.<path_expr>], <method_signature>)
<act_event_selector>::=
  <cond_event_selector> |
  {PRE|POST} (cond_trgO[.<path_expr>], <method_signature>)
<path_expr> ::=
  <instance_var>[.<path_expr>]
```

Figure 2. BNF of Event Selector Specification

The basic idea is that condition event selectors and action event selectors are specified like rule event selectors defining a triggering method together with one of the keywords PRE/POST and optionally a triggering class to restrict the set of events able to trigger condition evaluation and action execution, respectively. To restrict the set of events able to trigger condition evaluation and action execution even further, TriGS provides *object binding* between event selectors by introducing the keywords rule_trgO denoting the rule triggering object and cond_trgO denoting the condition triggering object. The keyword rule_trgO is used for specifying that the object involved in triggering condition evaluation and/or action execution has to be the same (directly or indirectly referenceable from the same) object which is involved in triggering the corresponding rule. The keyword cond_trgO provides a binding between the object involved in triggering condition evaluation and the one involved in triggering action execution. Note, that these two keywords can also be used in the condition part and the action part of the rule in order to reference the objects triggering rule or triggering condition, respectively. In order to reference the action triggering object, the additional keyword act_trgO may be used in the action part of the rule (not shown in the BNF of Figure 2).

Example:

The rule R_Service specifies the required behavior stated in the previous example. If during processing of an order a machine (triggering class Machine) receives the message setServiceState (triggering method) the rule R_Service is triggered. Condition part and action part of the rule are triggered not before the machine has finished processing indicated by the triggering method changeState. To ensure that condition evaluation and action execution are triggered by the same machine object as the corresponding rule the keyword rule_trgO is employed for object binding.

```
DEFINE RULE R_Service
  ON POST(Machine,setServiceState) DO
  ON POST(rule_trgO,changeState) IF rule_trgO state='IDLE' THEN
  ON POST(rule_trgO,changeState) EXECUTE /*start maintenance*/
```

3.1.2 Transaction Semantics

So far we have discussed when conditions may be evaluated and actions may be executed. We will now turn to the transaction semantics of rule processing. This effects the triggering transaction, the condition transaction, and the action transaction. The *triggering transaction* is the transaction in which the event is raised which triggers rule processing in turn. The *condition transaction* embodies condition evaluation, and the *action transaction* includes action execution. TriGS supports both serial and parallel execution of condition transactions and action transactions. The kind of transaction execution is specified as part of the corresponding rule's definition. (The respective keyword is not shown in Figure 2. For a complete discussion we refer to [Kapp94b].) In case of serial transaction execution a parent transaction invokes a child transaction as nested transaction and blocks until the child transaction has finished. In case of parallel transaction execution a parent transaction invokes a child transaction as new top level transaction and continues its own execution immediately. Serial as well as parallel child transactions may be rolled back independently of the parent transaction. As GemStone provides neither nested nor parallel transactions these features have to be simulated. Nested transactions are realized by means of safepoints and parallel transactions are realized by starting a concurrent GemStone session [Butt91].

3.1.3 Event-Based Approach versus Coupling Modes

We now turn to the question of how the event-based approach for specifying rule processing points compares to the coupling mechanism originally introduced in [Daya88]. The event-based approach for defining CEPs and AEPs reuses the event selector mechanism originally used for triggering a rule, thus higher uniformity is reached. Furthermore, the event-based approach is more general and more flexible than coupling modes are resulting in a high expressive power.

Example:

Figure 3 shows a sequence of method calls m_1 to m_n executing within a sequence of transactions. Method m_2 is defined to be a triggering method (PRE) determining the RTP of a rule.

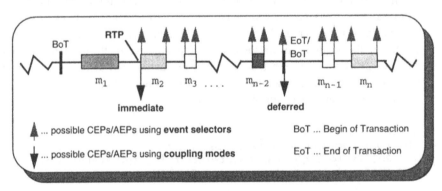

Figure 3. Event-Based Approach versus Coupling Modes

It is shown that the traditional coupling mechanism supports only two possible CEPs and AEPs (immediate coupling or deferred coupling). In TriGS, the begin and end of every method following m_2 irrespective of transaction boundaries may be defined as triggering method for condition evaluation and action execution.

In the following we demonstrate how coupling modes are simulated in TriGS for event-condition coupling. The same applies to condition-action coupling. To simulate the semantics of *immediate* coupling, the rule event selector and the condition event selector have to be defined by the same triggering method, and, in case of a local rule, by the same triggering class. The *deferred* event condition coupling mode is simulated by simply using the commit or abort method of GemStone as triggering method of the condition event selector. Whereas immediate coupling and deferred coupling implicitly assume the condition transaction to be serial to the triggering transaction, the *separate* event condition coupling mode defines the condition transaction to be parallel to the triggering transaction but without specifying a distinct point in time. In TriGS, however, transaction semantics is orthogonal to the definition of CEPs and AEPs allowing the specification of serial or parallel transaction semantics in addition to the specified CEP and AEP. Thus, a clear separation between transaction semantics and points in time for processing rules is achieved.

3.1.4 A More Complex Example

Consider the following situation in our running example. Suppose that a production controller is able to query statistical data about the utilization of machines, which is represented graphically. Every change concerning the workload of any of these machines has to be reflected in the graphics, i.e., the statistics have to be recomputed. This computation is a very complex and time consuming task resulting in a high overhead. Usually, the workload of machines changes very often compared to the occurrences of user queries about statistical information. Thus it is desirable that the time consuming task of computing workload statistics is delayed to the latter operation. The rule R_ComputeStat ensures this behavior:

```
DEFINE RULE R_ComputeStat
  ON POST(Machine,changeWorkload) DO
  ON PRE (MachineSet,displayStat)
          IF cond_trgO includes: rule_trgO THEN
  ON PRE (cond_trgO,displayStat)
          EXECUTE ONCE cond_trgO computeStat
```

The semantics of the rule R_ComputeStat is as follows. After executing the method changeWorkload on an instance of class Machine or of one of its subclasses, the rule R_ComputeStat is triggered. The corresponding condition is triggered when the message displayStat is sent to an instance of MachineSet. Since the action event selector is identical to the condition event selector, action execution responsible for computing the desired statistics is immediately triggered assuming the condition evaluates to true, i.e., the concerned machine (rule_trgO) is element of the instance of MachineSet receiving the message displayStat (cond_trg0). An invocation of displayStat without a former change of work-load does not trigger the action since the rule itself has not been triggered at all. The rule R_ComputeStat is triggered every time the workload of a Machine changes although the action of the rule (computeStat) should be executed only once for a specific machine set. This semantics is expressed by the keyword ONCE specified in the action part of the rule. The keyword ONCE ensures that given a particular rule is triggered several times and thus the corresponding action is triggered several times by the same action triggering object the action is executed only once.

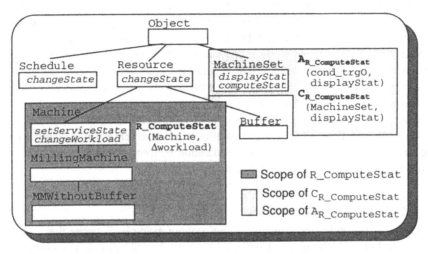

Figure 4. Different Scopes of a Rule and its Components

Considering the class hierarchy of our running example, note that the specifications of different event selectors for the various components of a rule lead to different scopes for triggering these components. Figure 4 illustrates the different scopes of the rule R_ComputeStat and its components, respectively. The scopes of the condition event selector, denoted as $C_{R\_ComputeStat}$, and of the action event selector, denoted as $A_{R\_ComputeStat}$, are the same. This is due to the fact that the action is to be executed immediately after the condition has been evaluated. The scope of the rule event selector, denoted as R_ComputeStat, is different to the other scopes since its triggering class does neither belong to the scope of the condition event selector nor to the scope of the action event selector.

3.2 Execution Order of Multiple Rules

In TriGS the execution order of multiple rules is defined by the following algorithm. It is assumed that C_Set denotes a set of conditions C_i, i=1..n, A_Set denotes a set of actions A_i, i=1..n, $R(C_i)$ denotes the rule containing C_i, $R(A_i)$ denotes the rule containing A_i, CEP_i denotes the condition evaluation point of $R(C_i)$, AEP_i denotes the action execution point of $R(A_i)$, and Prio(R) denotes the priority of a rule R.

(1) Condition evaluation of triggered rules and action execution of triggered rules with conditions evaluated to true are ordered on the basis of their CEPs and AEPs:

$$\forall C_i, C_j \in C\_Set, A_i, A_j \in A\_Set, C_i \neq C_j \wedge A_i \neq A_j$$
$$. (CEP_i < CEP_j \Rightarrow C_i \text{ before } C_j) \wedge (AEP_i < AEP_j \Rightarrow A_i \text{ before } A_j) \wedge$$
$$(CEP_i < AEP_j \Rightarrow C_i \text{ before } A_j) \wedge (AEP_i < CEP_j \Rightarrow A_i \text{ before } C_j).$$

(2) Conditions and actions having the same CEPs and/or AEPs, i.e., they are triggered by the same event on the same triggering object, are ordered by means of priorities similar to other systems [Kotz93, Mede91]:

$$\forall C_i, C_j \in C\_Set, A_i, A_j \in A\_Set, C_i \neq C_j \wedge A_i \neq A_j$$
$$. (CEP_i = CEP_j \wedge Prio(R(C_i)) < Prio(R(C_j)) \Rightarrow C_i \text{ before } C_j) \wedge$$
$$(AEP_i = AEP_j \wedge Prio(R(A_i)) < Prio(R(A_j)) \Rightarrow A_i \text{ before } A_j) \wedge$$
$$(CEP_i = AEP_j \wedge Prio(R(C_i)) < Prio(R(A_j)) \Rightarrow C_i \text{ before } A_j) \wedge$$
$$(AEP_i = CEP_j \wedge Prio(R(A_i)) < Prio(R(C_j)) \Rightarrow A_i \text{ before } C_j).$$

By default all rules have the same priority, which may be increased or decreased for any rule dynamically.

Example:

Suppose that two rules R1 and R2 have been specified to enforce some integrity constraint, where R2 should be processed only if the more restrictive rule R1 did not solve the problem. For this purpose R1 is assigned a higher priority than R2. The conditions of both rules check if the integrity constraint is violated, and their actions correct the database state. If the more restrictive rule R1 was successful, i.e., the incorrect database state could be corrected, the condition of rule R2 is evaluated to false and its action, now superfluous, is not taken.

(3) For conditions and actions which have the same CEPs/AEPs and the same priority the following rules are applied:

- In order to ensure the semantics of ECA rules the condition of a rule is evaluated always before the action of the same rule is executed provided that the condition evaluated to true:

$$\forall R(C_i, A_i), C_i \in C\_Set, A_i \in A\_Set, .C_i \text{ before } A_i.$$

- If a rule has been triggered several times, i.e., there exist several instantiations of the rule, all rule instantiations are processed as *atomic units*, i.e., the action of each rule instance is executed immediately after condition evaluation.

- Remaining conditions and actions, which are all part of different rules, are processed in arbitrary order. This is due to the assumption that the assignment of the same priority to a number of rules expresses independence between these rules in the sense that their actions are not able to negate each others condition (because they work on disjoint subsets of the database, for example).

Example:

Figure 5 illustrates the execution order of multiple rules according to the specified criteria. During an application transaction three different events occur sequentially (E1, E2, E3) triggering a number of conditions C2-C9 and a number of actions A1-A8 of already triggered rules. These rules are assigned two different priorities where priority 1 being higher than priority 2.

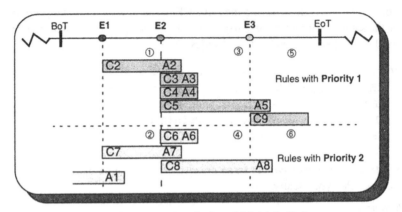

Figure 5. Execution Order of Multiple Rules

The scheduling algorithm of TriGS produces a partially ordered schedule which is indicated by the numbers ①-⑥ in Figure 5. Conditions and actions located within the same numbered area are processed in an arbitrary order provided that a condition is processed before its corresponding action. In the following, a possible schedule is shown:

$$C2 < (C7 \| A1) < (C3 \| C5 \| A3 \| C4 \| A4 \| A2) < (A7 \| C6 \| C8 \| A6) < (A5 \| C9) < A8$$

| E1 | E2 | E3 |

The symbol "<" denotes the temporal relation *before* between two rule components. The symbol " $\|$ " denotes the temporal relation *concurrent* between two rule components. The event E_i, $i=1..3$ denotes the triggering event which causes the corresponding conditions to be evaluated and actions to be executed, respectively.

4. Implementation Aspects

The architecture of TriGS shown in Figure 6 consists of four main components, namely *Event Detector, Rule Scheduler, Condition Evaluator* and *Action Executor.* The Event Detector is responsible for signaling detected events and passing them to the Rule Scheduler. The tasks of the Rule Scheduler are to collect rules (denoted by ① in Figure 6), conditions (denoted by ②), and actions (denoted by ③), all triggered by the signaled event, and to pass collected conditions and actions to the Condition Evaluator and Action Executor, respectively. Rules are transferred between components by means of persistent dictionaries.

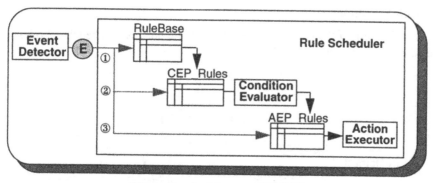

Figure 6. Architecture of TriGS

In the remainder of this section, a more detailed description of the tasks executed by the different components is given.

4.1 Event Detection

In TriGS, event detection is realized by means of method wrappers. At the first time a method m1 is defined to be part of an event selector, m1 is transformed into a triggering method by, firstly, renaming m1 to m1_original and recompiling it within the class where it has been defined in the first place and, secondly, adding a wrapper, i.e. a new method named m1, to that class. The body of the wrapper consists of a call of m1_original and a call of the scheduler responsible for scheduling all triggered rules, conditions, and actions. In case of pre method detection the rule scheduler is called before the original method is executed. In case of post method detection it's the other way round. On event detection, a so called event object is generated which holds all information concerning the occurred event such as the triggering object and actual parameters.

4.2 Rule Storage

Rules are stored in a persistent dictionary representing the *rulebase* of TriGS. Every entry in this dictionary consists of a key represented by the appropriate event selector of the rule and a value consisting of references to all rules containing that event selector. Thus rules can be indexed by their event selectors, which allows speeding up the process of scheduling all rules triggered by a specific event. Besides the rulebase, two additional persistent dictionaries having the same structure as the rulebase are used to store rules waiting for condition evaluation (*CEP dictionary*) and action execution (*AEP dictionary*). The keys of these dictionaries are the event selectors of the conditions and actions, respectively. Finally, a transient dictionary (*triggered_Rules*) is used to implement overriding of rules by storing rule references indexed by their names.

4.3 Rule Scheduling

The first task of the Rule Scheduler shown in Figure 7 is to schedule all rules triggered by a signaled event.

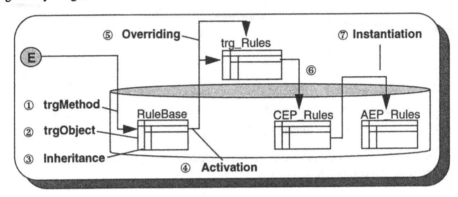

Figure 7. Rule Scheduling

In a first step (denoted by ① in Figure 7) the Rule Scheduler looks for an entry in the rulebase corresponding to the triggering method to find global rules. This can be done by only one access since the dictionary is indexed by the triggering method. Next, the Rule Scheduler looks for local rules within the rulebase (denoted by ② in Figure 7). Since local rules are subject to inheritance, a lookup mechanism (denoted by ③ in Figure 7) based on metaclass information is used starting at the class of the object where the event was signaled, and ending at the class where the triggering method is defined (in the worst case at the root of the class hierarchy). For each collected rule the Rule Scheduler has to check its activation status (denoted by ④ in Figure 7). If the rule is activated it is stored in the CEP dictionary if not overridden by another rule. To recognize overriding of rules (denoted by ⑤ in Figure 7) a mechanism based on the equality of rule names is used. Since overriding has to be checked for each specific event and since the CEP dictionary may still hold rules triggered by former events, the transient triggered_Rules dictionary having the rule name as key is used to filter overridden rules. Before making a triggered rule persistent within the CEP dictionary, its name is compared to the keys of rules already inserted into the triggered_Rules dictionary. Equality means that the rule has been overridden, and consequently the rule is rejected, otherwise it is inserted. After having grouped all rules triggered by one specific event into the transient dictionary they are transferred to the persistent CEP dictionary (denoted by ⑥ in Figure 7).

Right after a certain event has been used for scheduling all corresponding rules the same event is used to schedule conditions and actions. Firstly and similar to collecting rules (denoted by ① and ② in Figure 7), it is determined if the conditions stored within the CEP dictionary are ready for evaluation or not, no matter whether their corresponding rules have been scheduled by the same or by a former event. Secondly, the Condition Evaluator is started to evaluate the conditions of the collected rules according to their priority. The condition evaluator treats all conditions whose condition transaction is defined to be serial within the triggering transaction. All conditions whose condition transaction is defined to be parallel are evaluated in independent top-level transactions (cf. also Section 3.1.2). If condition evaluation returns true and - in case of actions which should be executed only once - if no instance of the same rule already exists in the AEP dictionary the rule is transferred to the persistent AEP dictionary (denoted by ⑦ in Figure 7). If the rule has to be processed as atomic unit (cf. section 3.2) the Action Executor is started immediately and executes the corresponding action. Otherwise, the Condition Evaluator continues evaluating the next condition. Finally, the Action Executor has to execute all actions still waiting for execution within the AEP dictionary according to the specified priorities and according to the specified transaction semantics.

5. Comparison and Outlook

Almost all active systems [Daya88, Diaz91, Gatz91, Geha91, Mede91, Kotz93] use coupling modes to define CEPs and AEPs, which implies that the condition has to be evaluated either immediately after the signaled event (=immediate coupling), or at the end of the triggering transaction (= deferred coupling), or in a separate transaction (=separate coupling). The same applies for action execution. [Beeri91], who supports EA-rules only, defines an execution interval instead wherein the triggered action must be executed. The endpoints of the execution interval are specified by events. Since TriGS adheres to the paradigm of ECA rules Beeri's approach has been extended by distinguishing between two events for condition evaluation and action execution, respectively. TriGS dispenses execution intervals in order to be able to use one mechanism, namely the concept of event selectors. Event selectors are used to define the points in time for rule triggering, condition evaluation, and action execution. A somewhat similar approach is taken in [Geha92] with the distinction that in [Geha92] also composite events are supported. In many active systems [Daya88, Geha91, Mede91] coupling modes determine not only the condition evaluation and action execution point but also the semantics of condition transaction and action transaction. In HiPAC [Daya88], for example, immediate and deferred coupling modes implicitly imply a closed nested transaction whereas separate coupling implies an open nested transaction model. To the contrary, in TriGS, similar to [Kotz93], the transaction semantics is orthogonal to rule firing. In case that multiple actions have to be executed simultaneously in the same transaction their execution order is determined by means of priorities, similar to many other systems.

Like [Kotz93, Daya88] TriGS realizes event detection by using method wrappers. Unlike in these systems wrappers may be defined dynamically for any method to reduce the overhead of event detection. Method wrappers are transparent to the user in order to avoid confusing him or her. To speed up collecting rules, conditions, and actions triggered by one specific event they are all indexed by their event selectors and stored within persistent dictionaries. Concerning the inheritance of rules only O_2 provides more detail in the literature [Mede91]. In O_2 inheritance is realized by using a flattening mechanism. This means that for each "external" rule attached to a specific class a set of internal rules is created, one for the class itself and one for each subclass.

This approach causes much overhead in case of updating rules, e.g., deactivating a rule. To avoid this overhead, TriGS uses a lookup mechanism based on metaclass information to realize inheritance of rules. Unlike other systems, TriGS supports overriding of rules by using a mechanism based on the equality of rule names, allowing to adapt the semantics of certain rules in order to monitor the specific behavior of subclasses. A first prototype of TriGS implemented on top of GemStone on SUN workstations is operational. Future research will focus on the problem of cascading rules and their termination. In addition, further possibilities to embed the evaluation of conditions and the execution of actions into the transaction model of GemStone have to be explored. Last but not least, the applicability of TriGS will be evaluated within the framework of production planning and control systems and of workflow management systems.

References

[Anwa93]   E. Anwar, L. Maugis, S. Chakravarthy, *A new Perspective on Rule Support for Object-Oriented Databases*, Proc. of the ACM-SIGMOD Int. Conference on Managment of Data, SIGMOD Record, Vol.22. No.2, pp. 99-108, June 1993

[Beer91]   C. Beeri, T. Milo, *A Model for Active Object Oriented Database,* Proc. of the 17th Int. Conference on VLDB, Barcelona, pp. 337-349, 1991

[Butt91]   P. Butterworth, A. Otis, J. Stein, *The GemStone Object Database Management System,* Communications of the ACM, Vol. 34, No. 10, pp. 64-77, October 1991

[Chak90]   S. Chakravarthy, S. Nesson, *Making an Object-Oriented DBMS Active: Design, Implementation, and Evaluation of a Prototype,* Proc. of the Int. Conference on Extending Database Technology (EDBT), Venice, Springer LNCS 416, pp. 393-406, March 1990

[Chak92]   S. Chakravarthy, *Architectures and Monitoring Techniques for Active Databases: An Evaluation,* UF-CIS-TR-92-041, University of Florida, 1992

[Daya88]   U. Dayal et al., *The HiPAC Project: Combining Active Databases and Timing Constraints,* ACM SIGMOD Record, Vol. 17, No. 1, pp. 51-70, March 1988

[Diaz91]   O. Diaz, N. Paton, P. Gray, *Rule Management in Object Oriented Databases: A Uniform Approach,* Proc. of the 17th Int. Conference on VLDB, Barcelona, pp. 317-326, 1991

[Gatz91]   S. Gatziu, A. Geppert, K.R. Dittrich, *Integrating Active Concepts into an Object-Oriented Database System,* Proc. of the 3rd Int. Workshop on Database Programming Languages, Nafplion, 1991

[Geha91]   N. H. Gehani, H. V. Jagadish, *Ode as an Active Database: Constraints and Triggers*, Proc. of the 17th Int. Conference on VLDB, Barcelona, 1991

[Geha92]   N. H. Gehani, H. V. Jagadish, O.Shmuheli, *Composite Event Specification in Active Database Systems*, Proc. of the 18th Int. Conference on VLDB, August 1992

[Kapp94a] G. Kappel, S. Rausch-Schott, W. Retschitzegger, S. Vieweg, *TriGS - Making a Passive Object-Oriented Database System Active*, to be published in: Journal of Object-Oriented Programming (JOOP), 1994

[Kapp94b] G. Kappel, S. Rausch-Schott, W. Retschitzegger, A M. Tjoa, S. Vieweg, R. Wagner, *Active Object-Oriented Database Systems For CIM Applications*, in: V. Marik (ed.), CIM-Textbook (TEMPUS-Project), Springer LNCS, (in print), 1994

[Kotz93]   A. Kotz-Dittrich, *Adding Active Functionality to an Object-Oriented Database System - a Layered Approach*, Proc. of GI-Conference on Database Systems for Office, Technology and Science, Braunschweig (BRD), W. Stucky, A. Oberweis (eds.), Springer, pp. 54-73, March 1993

[Mede91]   C. B. Medeiros, P. Pfeffer, *Object Integrity Using Rules*, European Conference on Object-Oriented Programming (ECOOP), P. America (ed.), Springer LNCS 512, pp. 219-230, 1991

Testing of Object-Oriented Programming Systems (OOPS): A Fault-Based Approach

Jane Huffman Hayes

Science Applications International Corporation
1213 Jefferson-Davis Highway, Suite 1300
Arlington, Virginia 22202

Abstract. The goal of this paper is to examine the testing of object-oriented systems and to compare and contrast it with the testing of conventional programming language systems, with emphasis on fault-based testing. Conventional system testing, object-oriented system testing, and the application of conventional testing methods to object-oriented software will be examined, followed by a look at the differences between testing of conventional (procedural) software and the testing of object-oriented software. An examination of software faults (defects) will follow, with emphasis on developing a preliminary taxonomy of faults specific to object-oriented systems. Test strategy adequacy will be briefly presented. As a result of these examinations, a set of candidate testing methods for object-oriented programming systems will be identified.

1 Introduction and Overview

Two major forces are driving more and more people toward Object-Oriented Programming Systems (OOPS): the need to increase programmer productivity, and the need for higher reliability of the developed systems. It can be expected that sometime in the near future there will be reusable "trusted" object libraries that will require the highest level of integrity. All this points to the need for a means of assuring the quality of OOPS. Specifically, a means for performing verification and validation (V&V) on OOPS is needed. The goal of this paper is to examine the testing of object-oriented systems and to compare and contrast it with the testing of conventional programming language systems, with emphasis on fault-based testing.

1.1 Introduction to Object-Oriented Programming Systems (OOPS)

Object-Oriented Programming Systems (OOPS) are characterized by several traits, with the most important one being that information is localized around objects (as opposed to functions or data) [3]. Meyer defines object-oriented design as "the construction of software systems as structured collections of abstract data type implementations" [15]. To understand OOPS, several high level concepts must be introduced: objects, classes, inheritance, polymorphism, and dynamic binding.
Objects represent real-world entities and encapsulate both the data and the functions (i.e., behavior and state) which deal with the entity. Objects are run-time instances of classes. *Classes* define a set of possible objects. A class is meant to implement a user-defined type (ideally an Abstract Data Type (ADT) to support data abstraction). The goal is to keep the implementation details private to the class (information hiding). *Inheritance* refers to the concept of a new class being declared as an extension or restriction of a previously defined class [15].

Polymorphism refers to the ability to take more than one form. In object-oriented systems, it refers to a reference that can, over time, refer to instances of more than one class. The static type of the reference is determined from the declaration of the entity in the program text. The dynamic type of a polymorphic reference may change from instant to instant during the program execution. *Dynamic binding* refers to the fact that the code associated with a given procedure call is not known until the moment of the call at run-time [12]. Applying the principles of polymorphism and inheritance, it can be envisioned that a function call could be associated with a polymorphic reference. Thus the function call would need to know the dynamic type of the reference. This provides a tremendous advantage to programmers over conventional programming languages (often referred to as procedural languages): the ability to request an operation without explicitly selecting one of its variants (this choice occurs at run-time) [16].

1.2 Introduction to Verification and Validation (V&V)

Verification and validation refers to two different processes that are used to ensure that computer software reliably performs the functions that it was designed to fulfill. Though different definitions of the terms verification and validation exist, the following definitions from *ANSI/IEEE Standard 729-1983* [10] are the most widely accepted and will be used in this paper:

Verification is the process of determining whether or not the products of a given phase of the software development cycle fulfill the requirements established during the previous phase. *Validation* is the process of evaluating software at the end of the software development process to ensure compliance with software requirements.

1.3 Introduction to Testing

Testing is a subset of V&V. The IEEE definition of testing is "the process of exercising or evaluating a system or system component by manual or automated means to verify that it satisfies specified requirements or to identify differences between expected and actual results." [10]. Conventional software testing is divided into two categories: static testing and dynamic testing. Static testing analyzes a program without executing it while dynamic testing relies on execution of the program to analyze it [5]. The focus of this paper will be dynamic testing. Dynamic testing is often broken into two categories: black-box testing and white-box testing. Black-box testing refers to functional testing which does not take advantage of implementation details and which examines the program's functional properties. White-box testing, on the other hand, uses information about the program's internal control flow structure or data dependencies.

1.4 Research Approach

Figure 1.4-1 depicts the research approach to be taken in this paper. The examination of conventional system testing, object-oriented system testing, and the application of conventional testing methods to object-oriented software will be the first area of concern (sections 2.1 and 2.2). The differences between testing of conventional (procedural) software and the testing of object-oriented software will be examined next (section 2.3). An examination of software faults (defects) will follow, with emphasis on developing a preliminary taxonomy of faults specific to object-oriented systems (section 3). Test strategy adequacy will briefly be presented (section 4). As a result of these examinations, a set of candidate testing methods for object-oriented programming systems will be identified (section 5). It is also possible that some object-oriented software faults which are not currently detected by any testing methods (conventional or object-oriented specific) will be uncovered. It should be noted that despite the future research that is needed, a preliminary recommendation on test methods can be made based on the similarities between OOPS and procedural language systems.

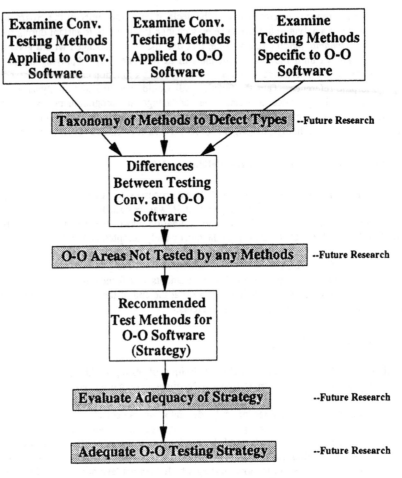

Figure 1.4-1. Research Approach.

2 Testing Methods

An examination of testing methods for conventional programming language systems follows as well as a look at the applicability of these testing methods to object-oriented programming systems. A discussion of testing methods specific to OOPS will then be presented.

2.1 Conventional Programming Language System Testing Methods

2.1.1 Testing Methods. Much has been written concerning the testing of conventional (or procedural) language systems. Some of the earlier works include The Art of Software Testing by Myers [22], "Functional Program Testing" by Howden [9], and more recently <u>Software Testing Techniques</u> by Boris Beizer [2]. The first reference [22] focused on explaining testing and leading the reader through realistic examples. It also discussed numerous testing methods and defined testing terminology. Howden's reference focused on functional testing, which is probably the most frequently applied testing method. Finally, Beizer's text provided a veritable encyclopedia of information on the many conventional testing techniques available and in use.

For this paper, the test method taxonomy of Miller is used [19]. Testing is broken into several categories: general testing; special input testing; functional testing; realistic testing; stress testing; performance testing; execution testing; competency testing; active interface testing; structural testing; and error-introduction testing.

General testing refers to generic and statistical methods for exercising the program. These methods include: unit/module testing [24]; system testing [7]; regression testing [23]; and ad-hoc testing [7]. Special input testing refers to methods for generating test cases to explore the domain of possible system inputs. Specific testing methods included in this category are: random testing [1]; and domain testing (which includes equivalence partitioning, boundary-value testing, and the category-partition method) [2].

Functional testing refers to methods for selecting test cases to assess the required functionality of a program. Testing methods in the functional testing category include: specific functional requirement testing [9]; and model-based testing [6].

Realistic test methods choose inputs/environments comparable to the intended installation situation. Specific methods include: field testing [28]; and scenario testing [24]. Stress testing refers to choosing inputs/environments which stress the design/implementation of the code. Testing methods in this category include: stability analysis [7]; robustness testing [18]; and limit/range testing [24].

Performance testing refers to measuring various performance aspects with realistic inputs. Specific methods include: sizing/memory testing [33]; timing/flow testing [7]; and bottleneck testing [24]. Execution testing methods actively follow (and possibly interrupt) a sequence of program execution steps. Testing methods in this category include: thread testing [11]; activity tracing [7]; and results monitoring [23].

Competency testing methods compare the output "effectiveness" against some pre-existing standard. These methods include: gold standard testing [28]; effectiveness procedures [13]; and workplace averages [28]. Active interface testing refers to testing various interfaces to the program. Specific methods include: data interface testing [24]; user interface testing [25]; and transaction-flow testing [2].

Structural testing refers to testing selected aspects of the program structure. Methods in this category include: statement testing [2]; branch testing [17]; path testing [30]; test-coverage analysis testing [2]; and data-flow testing [2]. Error introduction testing systematically introduces errors into the program to assess various effects. Specific methods include: error seeding [7]; and mutation testing [24].

When utilizing conventional programming languages, software systems are usually tested in a bottom-up fashion. First, units or modules are tested and debugged (unit testing). This is followed by integration testing, which exercises sets of modules. Testing of the fully integrated system (system testing) is accomplished next. In some cases system testing is followed by acceptance testing (usually accomplished by/for the customer and/or end user).

2.1.2 Applicability to Object-Oriented Systems. To understand the applicability of conventional testing methods to object-oriented programming systems, it is vital to examine the components of these systems. OOPS can be seen as having five components: (1) objects, (2) their associated messages and methods, (3) hierarchically-organized classes of objects, (4) external interfaces, and (5) tools and utilities. *Objects* are code modules that contain both data and procedures. The *methods* are one type of object-procedure and are responsible for actions of computation, display, or communication with other objects. Communication is accomplished through the sending of *messages*. Objects are described by abstract *classes* (or types). Specific objects are created as instances of a class. Inheritance is used to pass down information from parent classes to their sub-classes. *External interfaces* deal with the connection of OOPS systems to the databases, communication channels, users, etc. *Tools and utilities* refers to general application programs which may be used in building the objects or assisting in any other features of the OOPS [20].

As one might expect, certain OOPS components can be handled very easily by applying conventional testing methods to them, while other components will require distinctive treatment. The hierarchically-organized classes can be viewed as declarative knowledge structures. These components use syntax and naming conventions to explicitly represent details of application knowledge. They are therefore very amenable to a verification and validation philosophy of formal verification. Formal verification refers to the use of formal mathematical theorem-proving techniques to prove a variety of properties about system components, such as redundancy, incompleteness, syntax violations, and inconsistencies [20]. Although this approach is not yet mature, it is the most effective approach for the class component. Formal methods are static methods, and therefore are outside the scope of this paper.

The tools and utilities component is seen as an example of a highly reusable component. Certain objects will also fall into this category (this must be evaluated on a case-by-case basis). A highly reusable component can be reused over a wide variety of applications without needing any customization to specific systems. A certification procedure is recommended for these components which establishes the functional and performance characteristics of the component, independent of the application. Software certification, like formal methods, could easily be the subject of an entire paper and will not be addressed here. The remaining components, including the integrated system itself, some objects, messages and methods, and external interfaces, fall into a third, catch-all category. The traditional set of conventional testing methods can be applied to these components.

In summary, OOPS can be seen as comprising of five components. Of these components, objects which are not highly reusable, messages and methods, and external interfaces can be tested using conventional testing methods. Formal methods should be applied to the class component. Certification procedures should be applied to the tools and utilities component and to highly reusable objects.

2.2 Object-Oriented System Specific Test Methods

In examining the literature on object-oriented programming systems and testing, several testing methods were discovered which are specific to OOPS. The unit repeated inheritance hierarchy testing method, inheritance method, identity method, the set and examine method, and the state-based testing method will be described below.

2.2.1 Unit Repeated Inheritance (URI) Hierarchy Method. Repeated inheritance is defined as a class (e.g., class D) that multiply inherits from two or more classes (e.g., classes B and C), and these classes (B and C) are descendants of the same parent class (e.g., class A). Repeated inheritance is depicted in Figure 2.2.1-1 using the classes described in the preceding sentence.

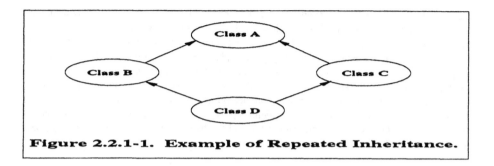

Figure 2.2.1-1. Example of Repeated Inheritance.

Chung and Lee [5] assert that errors such as name-confliction will arise when repeated inheritance is used. They build a directed graph and then apply an algorithm to find all unit repeated inheritances. The graph consists of classes and inheritance edges. A breadth-first traverse algorithm is used to traverse all the root classes. Parent classes are added to the children ancestor sets. The ancestor sets are then examined for unit repeated inheritance. Since there may be too many unit repeated inheritance instances to test, they classify all the repeated inheritances according to their euler region numbers (r) [4]. A hierarchy is built by dividing all the repeated inheritances into a set of closed regions denoted as URIs(n) where $1 <= n <= r$. For example:

URIs(1): require every class in a repeated inheritance graph to be exercised at least once.

URIs(2): require every unit repeated inheritance with $r = 2$ to be exercised at least once

URIs(3): require every closed region with $r = 3$ to be exercised at least once

[5]. After finding the hierarchy, McCabe's cyclomatic testing strategy is applied (a structural test method) [14].

2.2.2 Inheritance Method. Smith and Robson [29] have identified a framework for testing object-oriented systems which uses seven different testing strategies (test methods in the terminology of this paper). Though not all these strategies are specific to object-oriented systems, the inheritance method is. The inheritance method uses regression analysis to determine which routines should be tested (when a change has been made to the system) and then performs the tests based upon how the superclass was successfully tested. This applies to sub-classes inherited from the parent class. The sub-class under test is treated as a flattened class except that the routines from the parent that are unaffected by the subclass are not retested [29].

2.2.3 Identity Method. Another method proposed by Smith and Robson is the identity method. This method searches for pairs (or more) of routines that leave the state as it was originally (before any routines were invoked). This list of routines is reported to the tester who can examine the pairs and ensure that the unaltered state is the desired result [29].

2.2.4 Set and Examine Method. This Smith and Robson method is similar to the identity method. Pairs of routines that set and examine a particular aspect of the state are related and are used in conjunction to run tests. For example, a clock object may have one routine that sets the time then another that checks the time. The time can be set, then immediately checked using this pair of routines. Boundary and error values can be checked using this method [29].

2.2.5 State-Based Testing Method. Turner and Robson [31] have suggested a new technique for the validation of OOPS which emphasizes the interaction between the features and the object's state. Each feature is considered as a mapping from its starting or input states to its resultant or output states affected by any stimuli [31]. Substates are defined which are the values of a data item at a specific point in time. These are then analyzed for specific and general values. Next, the set of states that the Ith feature actually accepts as input (I_i) and the set of states it is able to generate as output (O_i) are determined for all the features of the class. Test cases are then generated using general guidelines provided. For example, one test case should allocate one substate per data item. Turner and Robson have found this technique to work best for classes which have many interacting features.

2.3 Differences Between Testing Conventional and Object-Oriented Software

Some of the differences between testing conventional and object-oriented software were examined in Section 2.1.2 above. Firesmith [8] has examined these differences in some depth. Table 2.3-1 summarizes the differences noted by Firesmith.

The difference between unit testing for conventional software and for object-oriented software, for example, arises from the nature of classes and objects. Unit testing really only addresses the testing of individual operations and data. This is only a subset of the unit testing that is required for object-oriented software since the meaning and behavior of the resources encapsulated in the classes depend on other resources with which they are encapsulated [8]. Integration testing (for conventional software) then is truly the unit testing of object-oriented software. The points made by Firesmith about boundary value testing and basis path testing are debatable in this author's opinion. Even with strongly typed languages, poor usages can still occur, and testing should be used to ensure that data abstraction and value restriction are implemented properly. Similarly, an argument that the object-oriented paradigm lowers complexity and hence lessens the need for basis path testing could be made just as easily for many structured languages such as Ada.

In summary, there are differences between how conventional software and object-oriented software should be tested. Most of these differences are attributable to the class component of object-oriented systems, and to the fact that these classes are not comparable to a "unit" in conventional software. However, the differences are minor and it is apparent that conventional testing methods can readily be applied to object-oriented software. As a minimum, a tester of an OOPS would want to apply the unit testing, integration testing, and black box testing methods discussed here. One or more of the OOPS-specific test methods would also be advisable to complete the test strategy.

Table 2.3-1. Differences Between Testing of Procedural and Object-Oriented Software [8].		
Test Method	With Procedural Software	With Object-Oriented Software
Unit Testing	Test individual, functionally cohesive operations	Unit testing is really integration testing, test logically related operations and data
Integration Testing	Test an integrated set of units (operations and common global data)	Object-oriented's unit testing. No more bugs related to common global data (though could have errors associated with global objects and classes)
Boundary Value Testing	Used on units or integrated units and systems	Of limited value if using strongly typed object-oriented languages and proper data abstraction is used to restrict the values of attributes
Basis Path Testing	Generally performed on units	Limited to operations of objects. Must address exception handling and concurrency issues (if applicable). Lowered complexity of objects lessens the need for this
Equivalence and Black-Box Testing	Used on units, integrated units and systems	Emphasized for object-oriented: objects are black boxes, equivalence classes are messages

3 OOPS-Specific Software Faults

A fault is defined as a textual problem with the code resulting from a mental mistake by the programmer or designer [10]. A fault is also called a defect. Fault-based testing refers to the collection of information on whether classes of software faults (or defects) exist in a program [32]. Since testing can only prove the existence of errors and not their absence, this testing approach is a very sound one. It is desirable to be able to implement such a testing approach for object-oriented systems. Although lists of error types can be found in the current object-oriented literature, at present there does not exist a comprehensive taxonomy of defect types inherent to object-oriented programming systems. This paper takes a first step toward such a taxonomy by consolidating the fault types found in the literature.

Three major sources of object-oriented faults were examined: [8], [21], and [27]. Each source examined object-oriented faults and attempted to describe the types of test methods that could be applied to detect the faults. Firesmith concentrated on conventional test methods such as unit testing and integration testing, while Miller et al concentrated on a prototype static analyzer called Verification of Object-Oriented Programming Systems (VOOPS) for detecting faults. Purchase and Winder [27] presented nine types of faults, seven which are detectable using debugging tools. A preliminary list of object-oriented software defects (faults) is presented in Table 3.0-1. For each defect, a proposed test method for detecting the defect is provided.

In order to cull the list of faults in Table 3.0-1 into a workable taxonomy, more fault types must be identified. Duplicate/related fault types must be eliminated or grouped. Dynamic testing methods should be identified to detect each of the faults currently detected by VOOPS (this is not mandatory, one can simply broaden the definition of testing to include static and dynamic methods). Similarly, static testing methods should be identified for as many fault types as possible. The taxonomy must then be organized to either address OOPS components (as does Firesmith), the object-oriented model (as does Miller), or causal and diagnostic fault types (as does Purchase and Winder). These are all areas for future research.

The approach proposed in this paper differs from that of Miller, Firesmith, Purchase & Winder in that it looks not only at object-oriented faults (as does Miller and Purchase & Winder) and not only at conventional methods applied to these faults (as does Firesmith). It looks at both of these items plus examines methods specific to OOPS. It is therefore a step toward a more comprehensive approach.

4 Test Adequacy

After examining the many test methods available for application to OOPS, the faults specific to OOPS, and the test methods that can be applied to detect these faults, a tester should be able to devise a set of suggested methods to apply to a given OOPS (some suggestions were made regarding this in Section 2.3). This set of test methods is termed a testing strategy or approach. The tester should then wonder whether or not this set of test methods is adequate to thoroughly exercise the software. Section 4 examines the topic of test strategy adequacy.

4.1 Test Adequacy Axioms

Elaine Weyuker has postulated eleven axioms for test set adequacy. The first axiom, *applicability*, states that for every program there exists an adequate test set. The axiom of *non-exhaustive applicability* states that there is a program P and a test set T such that P is adequately tested by T and T is not an exhaustive test set. The *monotonicity* axiom asserts that if T is adequate for P, and T is a subset of T', then T' is adequate for P. The *inadequate empty set* axiom postulates that the empty set is not an adequate test set for any program [34].

The *renaming* axiom states that if P is a renaming of Q, then T is adequate for P if and only if T is adequate for Q. The *complexity* axiom postulates that for every n, there is a program P such that P is adequately tested by a size n test set, but not by an size n - 1 test set.

Table 3.0-1. Preliminary Taxonomy of Object-Oriented Software Faults.

Faults \ Test Methods	Assertions	Exceptions	Black-Box Testing	Inspection	White-Box Testing	Integration Testing	Performance Testing	Compilation Testing	Unit Testing	Acceptance Testing	Regression Testing	VOOPS	Debugging Tools
Errors Associated with Objects [Firesmith]													
Abstraction violated	X	X	X										
Persistence problems			X										
Documentation out of sync with code				X									
Incorrect state model			X	X	X								
Invariants violated	X				X								
Failures linked to instantiation & destruction			X										
Concurrency problems					X	X	X						
Failure to meet requirements of the object			X										
Syntax errors								X					
Failures associated with messages, exceptions, attributes, or operations			X				X		X	X			
Errors Associated with Classes [Firesmith]													
Abstraction violated	X	X	X										
Documentation out of sync with code				X									
Incorrect state model			X	X	X								
Invariants violated	X				X								
Failures linked to instantiation & destruction			X										
Failures associated with inheritance						X					X		
Failure to meet requirements of the class			X										
Syntax errors								X					
Failures associated with messages, exceptions, attributes, or operations			X				X		X	X			
Errors Associated with Scenarios [Firesmith]													
Failure to meet requirements of the scenario						X							
Correct message passed to the wrong object						X							
Incorrect message passed to the right object						X							
Correct exception raised to wrong object						X							
Incorrect exception raised to right object						X							

Table 3.0-1. Preliminary Taxonomy of Object-Oriented Software Faults (Continued).

Faults	Assertions	Exceptions	Black-Box Testing	Inspection	White-Box Testing	Integration Testing	Performance Testing	Compilation Testing	Unit Testing	Acceptance Testing	Regression Testing	VOOPS	Debugging Tools
Failures linked to instantiation & destruction			X										
Concurrency problems				X		X	X						
Inadequate performance & missed deadlines							X						
Errors with Abstraction [Miller, 1993b]													
Class contains non-local method												X	
Incomplete (non-exhaustive) specialization												X	
Errors with Encapsulation [Miller, 1993b]													
Public interface to class not via class methods												X	
Implicit class to class communication												X	
Access module's data structure from outside												X	
Overuse of friend/protected mechanisms												X	
Errors Associated w/Modularity [Miller, 1993b]													
Method not used												X	
Public method not used by object users												X	
Instance not used												X	
Excessively large # of methods in class												X	
Too many instance variables in class												X	
Excessively long method												X	
Module/class/method/instance var. not used												X	
Module contains no classes, method no code												X	
Class contains no method/no instance var.												X	
Excessively large instance variable												X	
Excessively large module												X	
Errors with Hierarchy [Miller, 1993b]													
Branching errors												X	
Dead-ends and cycles												X	
Multiple inheritance errors												X	
Improper placement												X	

Table 3.0-1. Preliminary Taxonomy of Object-Oriented Software Faults (Continued).

Faults / *Test Methods*	Assertions	Exceptions	Black-Box Testing	Inspection	White-Box Testing	Integration Testing	Performance Testing	Compilation Testing	Unit Testing	Acceptance Testing	Regression Testing	VOOPS	Debugging Tools
O-O Bug Types [Purchase & Winder, 1991]													
Perceptual Bugs													X
Specification Bugs													X
Abstraction Bugs													X
Algorithmic Bugs													X
Reuse Bugs													X
Logical Bugs													X
Semantic Bugs													X
Syntactic Bugs													X
Domain Adherence Bugs													X

The *statement coverage* axiom states that if T is adequate for P, then T causes every executable statement of P to be executed. The *antiextensionality* axiom asserts that there are programs P and Q such that P computes the same function as Q (they are semantically close), and T is adequate for P but is not adequate for Q [34].

The *general multiple change* axiom states that there are programs P and Q which are the same shape (syntactically similar), but a test set T that is adequate for P is not adequate for Q. The *antidecomposition* axiom asserts that there exists a program P and component Q such that T is adequate for P, T' is the set of vectors of values that variables can assume on entrance to Q for some t of T, and T' is not adequate for Q. Finally, the *anticomposition* axiom postulates that there exist programs P and Q and test set T such that T is adequate for P, and the set of vectors of values that variables can assume on entrance to Q for inputs in T is adequate for Q, but T is not adequate for P;Q (where P;Q is the composition of P and Q) [34].

4.2 Evaluation of Adequacy of Test Strategies

It is desirable to apply these axioms to a set of test methods (test strategy or test set) to determine their adequacy. As one can imagine, this is not a simple task. Perry and Kaiser applied Weyuker's axioms to a test strategy pertaining to inherited code. They examined the popular philosophy that inherited code need not be retested when reused. Using the adequacy axioms, they found this philosophy to be erroneous. For example, if only one module of a program is changed, it seems intuitive that testing should be able to be limited to just the modified unit. However, the anticomposition axiom states that every dependent unit must be retested as well. Therefore one must always perform integration testing in addition to unit testing [26]. Another interesting observation made by Perry and Kaiser pertains to the testing of classes. When a new subclass is added (or an existing subclass is modified) all the methods inherited from each of its ancestor superclasses must be retested. This is a result of the antidecomposition axiom.

4.3 Future Research on Test Set Adequacy

Unfortunately, the work to date in this area has either been highly generic (as in the case of Weyuker's axioms) or has been too specific (Perry and Kaiser examined but one scenario of the object-oriented paradigm). In order for a tester to evaluate the set of test methods selected for use with an OOPS, there must be a way of easily examining each of the methods in the strategy, as well as the synergism of these methods. The adequacy evaluation should not depend on assumptions such as the system having previously been fully tested (e.g., the Perry and Kaiser scenario only examined the adequacy of test sets in testing changed code). Translating the very solid axioms of Weyuker into a usable method for evaluating actual test strategies is an area for further research.

5 Recommended Test Strategy for OOPS

There is much research that remains before well informed decisions can be made regarding which test methods to apply to OOPS. However, noting the great similarities between OOPS and procedural language systems, a preliminary set of methods can be recommended. Based on the conventional testing methods available which are applicable to object-oriented software, the object-oriented software specific testing methods available, the taxonomy of object-oriented software faults, and largely the author's personal testing experience, the following general test strategy (set of test methods) is recommended for object-oriented software:

Compilation Testing
Unit Testing
Unit Repeated Inheritance (URI) Hierarchy Method
Integration Testing
Boundary Value Testing
Basis Path Testing
State-Based Testing
Equivalence Partitioning Testing
Black-Box Testing
Acceptance Testing
Performance Testing

Note that Smith and Robson's identity, inheritance, and set and examine test methods were not selected. In the author's opinion, these methods are superseded by other selected methods such as the URI hierarchy method and unit testing.

The test methods are listed in the suggested execution order, with compilation testing being the obvious method to run first. It is also obvious that unit testing must precede integration testing which must precede acceptance testing. The order of the other methods is not as obvious and can be changed to suit the tester's needs. This test strategy is highly generic and should be tailored for the specific object-oriented system which is the subject of testing.

6 Summary and Conclusions

This paper first examined object-oriented programming systems, verification and validation, and testing. The research approach was presented next. Conventional system testing was examined, followed by object-oriented system testing, and a comparison of the testing of conventional and object-oriented software. Over sixty conventional testing methods were identified, but only four object-oriented software specific methods were discovered. The need for further research in the area of object-oriented software specific testing methods is apparent. The result of this examination was that conventional methods are highly applicable to object-oriented software, with classes and tools and utilities being OOPS components which may require special attention. Unit testing, integration testing, and black-box testing were found to be especially useful methods for application to OOPS.

A proposed taxonomy of object-oriented defects (faults) was then presented, with an emphasis on the testing methods which could be applied to detect each fault. This is an area where further research is required. A discussion of test set adequacy followed. Though sound axioms for test set adequacy exist, there is not a usable means of applying these axioms to a set of test methods (such as those presented in Section 5.0). This presents another area for future research. Finally, a generic set of suggested test methods (a test strategy) for OOPS was proposed. This test strategy must be customized for the specific OOPS to be tested.

Acknowledgment

I would like to thank Dr. David Rine and Dr. Bo Sanden of George Mason University for their helpful comments and suggestions about this paper.

References

1. Barnes, M., P. Bishop, B. Bjarland, G. Dahll, D. Esp, J. Lahti, H. Valisuo, P. Humphreys. "Software Testing and Evaluation Methods (The STEM Project)." OECD Halden Reactor Project Report, No. HWR-210, May 1987.

2. Beizer, Boris. Software Testing Techniques. Second Edition. New York, Van Nostrand Reinhold, 1990.

3. Berard, Edward V. Essays on Object-Oriented Software Engineering. Prentice-Hall, Englewood Cliffs, New Jersey, 1993, p. 10.

4. Berge, C. Graph and Hypergraphs. North-Holland, Amsterdam, The Netherlands, 1973.

5. Chung, Chi-Ming and Ming-Chi Lee. "Object-Oriented Programming Testing Methodology", published in Proceedings of the Fourth International Conference on Software Engineering and Knowledge Engineering, IEEE Computer Society Press, 15 - 20 June 1992, pp. 378 - 385.

6. Davis, A. Software Requirements: Analysis and Specification. New York, Prentice-Hall, Inc., 1990.

7. Dunn, R.H. Software Defect Removal. New York, McGraw-Hill, 1984.

8. Firesmith, Donald G. "Testing Object-Oriented Software," published in Proceedings of TOOLS, 19 March 1993.

9. Howden, W. E., "Functional Program Testing," IEEE Transactions on Software Engineering, SE-6(2): March 1980, 162-169.

10. IEEE 729-1983, "Glossary of Software Engineering Terminology," September 23, 1982.

11. Jensen, R.W. and C.C. Tonies. Software Engineering. Englewood Cliffs, NJ, Prentice-Hall, 1979.

12. Korson, Tim, and John D. McGregor. "Understanding Object-Oriented: A Unifying Paradigm." Communications of the ACM, Volume 33, No. 9, September 1990, pp. 40-60.

13. Llinas, J., S. Rizzi, and M. McCown, "The Test and Evaluation Process for Knowledge-Based Systems." SAIC final contract report, Contract #F30602-85-G-0313 (Task 86-001-01), prepared for Rome Air Development Center, 1987.

14. McCabe, T.J. "Structured Testing: A Testing Methodology Using the McCabe Complexity Metric," NBS Special Publication, Contract NB82NAAK5518, U.S. Department of Commerce, National Bureau of Standards, 1982.

15. Meyer, Bertrand. Object-oriented Software Construction. Prentice-Hall, New York, NY, 1988, p. 59, 62.

16. Meyer, Bertrand. Eiffel: The Language. Prentice-Hall, New York, NY, 1992, p. 17.

17. Miller, Edwin. "Better Software Testing" Proceedings of Third International Conference on Software for Strategic Systems, 27-28 February 1990, Huntsville, AL, 1-7.

18. Miller, Lance A., "Dynamic Testing of Knowledge Bases Using the Heuristic Testing Approach." in Expert Systems with Applications: An International Journal, 1990, 1, 249-269.

19. Miller, Lance A., Groundwater, Elizabeth, and Steven Mirsky. Survey and Assessment of Conventional Software Verification and Validation Methods (NUREG/CR-6018). U.S. Nuclear Regulatory Commission, April 1993, p. 9, 33, 35.

20. Miller, Lance A., Hayes, Jane E., and Steven Mirsky. Task 7: Guidelines for the Verification and Validation of Artificial Intelligence Software Systems. Prepared for United States Nuclear Regulatory Commission and the Electric Power Research Institute. Prepared by Science Applications International Corporation, May 28, 1993.

21. Miller, Lance A. Personal communication. September 1993.

22. Myers, G.J. The Art of Software Testing. Wiley, New York, New York, 1979.

23. NBS 500-93, "Software Validation, Verification, and Testing Technique and Tool Reference Guide," September 1982.

24.   Ng, P. and R. Yeh (Eds.). Modern Software Engineering: Foundations and Current Perspectives. New York, Van Nostrand Reinhold, 1990.

25.   NUREG/CR-4227, Gilmore, W., "Human Engineering Guidelines for the Evaluation and Assessment of Video Display Units." July 1985.

26.   Perry, DeWayne E. and Gail E. Kaiser. "Adequate Testing and Object-Oriented Programming," Journal of Object-Oriented Programming, 2(5):13-19, 1990.

27.   Purchase, J.A. and R.L. Winder. "Debugging Tools for Object-Oriented Programming," Journal of Object-Oriented Programming, Volume 4, Number 3, June 1991, pp. 10-27.

28.   Rushby, J., "Quality Measures and Assurance for AI Software." NASA Contractor Report No. 4187, prepared for Langley Research Center under Contract NAS1-17067, October 1988.

29.   Smith, M.D. and D.J. Robson. "A Framework for Testing Object-Oriented Programs," Journal of Object-Oriented Programming, June 1992, pp. 45-53.

30.   Tung, C., "On Control Flow Error Detection and Path Testing," Proceedings of Third International Conference on Software for Strategic Systems, Huntsville, AL, 27 - 28 February 1990, 144-153.

31.   Turner, C.D. and D.J. Robson. "The State-based Testing of Object-Oriented Programs," Proceedings of the 1993 IEEE Conference on Software Maintenance (CSM-93), Montreal, Quebec, Canada, September 27 - 30, 1993, David Card - editor, pp. 302-310.

32.   Voas, Jeffrey M. "PIE: A Dynamic Failure-Based Technique," IEEE Transactions on Software Engineering, Volume 18, No. 8, August 1992.

33.   Wallace, Dolores R. and Roger U. Fujii. "Software Verification and Validation: An Overview." IEEE Software, Vol. 6, No. 3, May 1989.

34.   Weyuker, Elaine J. "The Evaluation of Program-Based Software Test Data Adequacy Criteria," Communications of the ACM, 31:6, June 1988, pp. 668-675.

An Ambiguity Resolution Algorithm

Chandra Shrivastava †   **Doris L. Carver** †   **Rajendra Shrivastava** ‡
† Dept. of Computer Science, Louisiana State University
Baton Rouge, LA-70803
Telephone : (504) 388-1406, (504) 388-1495
‡ Dept. of Computer Science, Southern University
Baton Rouge, LA-70813
Telephone : (504) 771-2060
Email : (chandra,carver,rajendra)@bit.csc.lsu.edu

Abstract

Compilers for object-oriented languages must traverse an inheritance graph to locate the class to which an attribute belongs. The algorithm presented in this paper performs the ambiguity resolution check in one single traversal of the inheritance graph. It uses the *dominates-set* data structure which represents the dominance relationship between a derived class and its bases. The algorithm uses the dominates-set data structure to visit as few classes as possible in its search for the member.

Keywords : *Ambiguity, multiple inheritance, base class, derived class, dominance, dominates set, inheritance graph, virtual classes, most-derived-class.*

1 Introduction

The central notions of the object-oriented paradigm are *class* and *object* . An object models an entity or a concept and has state, behavior and identity; a class serves as a template for the common specification of the attributes of similar objects. A very lucid introduction to object-oriented concepts is provided in [Boo93].

Inheritance is a quintessential feature of the object-oriented paradigm [Weg87], and every object-oriented language designed in the past decade provides this mechanism implicitly or explicitly. Object-oriented programming languages view inheritance as a class composition mechanism that allows code sharing, code reuse and incremental programming [CJ89, Sny87, Weg87]. Inheritance is realized in object-oriented programming languages via *class derivation*. A class reuses code available in other classes by *inheriting* the attributes of the other classes. The class that inherits attributes is called a *child* class (also referred to as a *derived class, subclass,* or a *descendant*) and the classes that provide the attributes are called *parent* classes (also referred to as *base classes, superclasses,* or *ancestors*). *Single inheritance* is a model in which a child class is permitted to have only one parent class; *multiple inheritance* allows a child to have multiple parent classes. Smalltalk provides single inheritance [GR89] while Eiffel [Mey88] and C++ [Str91] support multiple inheritance.

One of the problems created by multiple inheritance is the *name conflicts problem* [BG90, Mey88]. Since a child class has multiple parents, it is possible for it to inherit an attribute with the same name from different parents. For example, say *class A* and *class B* each have *attribute x*; let *class C* inherit from both *A* and *B*. The name conflict problem arises when *attribute x* is desired from *class C* ; which *x* is the reference resolved to − *A's x* or *B's x* ? This example clearly illustrates an ambiguous reference to an inherited attribute.

The name conflict problem and the rules specified by an object-oriented programming language to resolve an ambiguous reference will be referred to as the *ambiguity resolution problem*. Ambiguity resolution does not arise in Smalltalk since it does not provide multiple inheritance. Eiffel solves the ambiguity resolution problem by providing a *rename construct* and prohibiting name clashes. However, an Eiffel compiler is still compelled to identify the ambiguous references. The rationale for such a restricted inheritance model is explained in [Mey88]. A more flexible inheritance model in which all available definitions of an attribute (method) in an inheritance hierarchy are accessible by a child class is given in [AHG93].

C++ has a complex set of rules for ambiguity resolution. Providing an analysis of the C++ rules and a complete ambiguity resolution algorithm for C++ is the basis of this paper.

1.1 Basic definitions

Child classes in C++ are referred to as *derived classes* and parent classes are called *base classes*. Since some of the base classes may themselves be derived classes, the term *most-derived-class* is used to refer to the class at the bottom of the inheritance hierarchy. The base classes from which a class inherits directly (ie an immediate parent class) are called *direct base classes*; classes from which a class inherits indirectly (ie grandparent and other ancestor classes) are called *indirect base classes*. An attribute of a class is called a *member* of the class. A *virtual base class* is a class that appears exactly once in the inheritance hierarchy, even though it may be the base class of several classes. The keywords *private*, *protected* and *public*, when appearing within the definition of a class, specify the access permissions associated with the members of a class. When appearing in the header of a class declaration, the keywords *private, protected, public* indicate the accessibility associated with the base class. This association of access control with inheritance leads to the three different kinds of inheritance in C++, *private inheritance, protected inheritance* and *public inheritance* [Boo93].

An inheritance graph [Sny87] is a directed acyclic graph, consisting of labeled vertices and directed edges. The vertex labels represent class names; a directed edge is from derived class to base class. Due to multiple inheritance, there may be more than one vertex with the same label in a graph, but cyclic inheritance is not permitted (ie a class cannot inherit from itself, directly or indirectly). Virtual base classes give rise to the acyclic nature of the graph.

An inheritance graph G(V,E) for a derived class D is defined as follows :

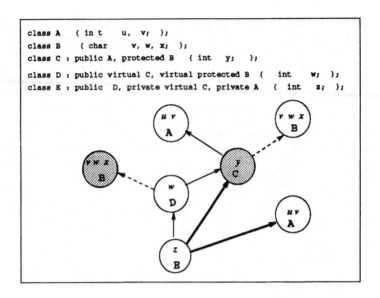

```
class A    ( in t      u,  v;  );
class B    ( char      v, w, x;  );
class C : public A, protected B  ( int   y;   );
class D : public virtual C, virtual protected B  ( int   w;  );
class E : public  D, private virtual C, private A  ( int   z;  );
```

Figure 1: Multiple Inheritance in C++

$$L_1 \quad = \quad \{\ Names\ of\ all\ non-virtual\ base\ classes\ \}$$

$$L_2 \quad = \quad \{\ Names\ of\ all\ virtual\ base\ classes\ \}$$

$$V \quad = \quad \{\ D\ \} \cup L_1 \cup L_2$$

$$E_1 \quad = \quad \{\ (c_1,\ c_2)\ |\ c_1 \in V,\ c_2 \in L_2,\ c_2\ is\ a\ direct\ base\ of\ c_1\ \}$$

$$E_2 \quad = \quad \{\ (c_1,\ c_2,p)\ |\ c_1 \in V,\ c_2 \in L_1,\ c_2\ is\ a\ direct\ base\ of\ c_1\ \}$$

$$E \quad = \quad E_1 \cup E_2$$

(1)

In the example in Fig. 1,

$$L_1 \quad = \quad \{\ A, B\ \}$$

$$L_2 \quad = \quad \{\ B, C, D\ \}$$

$$V \quad = \quad \{\ E\ \} \cup L_1 \cup L_2 = \{\ A, B, C, D, E\ \}$$

$$E_1 \quad = \quad \{\ (E, C),\ (D, C),\ (D, B)\ \}$$

$$E_2 \quad = \quad \{\ (C, A),\ (C, B),\ (E, D),\ (E, A)\ \}$$

$$E \quad = \quad E_1 \cup E_2$$

(2)

Sample C++ class declarations and the inheritance graph of the most-derived-

Class	Unambiguous	Ambiguous
A	u,v	-
B	v,w,x	-
C	u,w,x,y	v
D	u,w,y	v,x
E	w,y,z	u,v,x

Table 1: Ambiguous and Unambiguous references

class E are shown in Figure 1. Virtual base classes are shown as darkened circles, private inheritance is indicated with a dark solid arrow, protected inheritance with a dashed arrow, and public inheritance with a faint solid arrow. Characteristics of the inheritance graph in Fig. 1 are:

1. A occurs twice in the inheritance graph illustrating multiple occurrences of a class in a C++ inheritance graph.

2. B occurs twice in the graph; as a virtual base class and as a non-virtual base class. Hence B appears in L_1 and L_2.

3. Since C is a virtual base class of D and E, it occurs only once in the graph.

4. A and B are simple classes and hence no ambiguous reference to a member is possible for these classes (see Table 1). Reference to member v via class C is ambiguous since it can be resolved to A's v or B's v. Similarly v and x are ambiguous references for class D and u, v, x are ambiguous references via E. w is not an ambiguous reference for class D, since it is redefined in class D.

A reference to an attribute of a class is *valid* if the attribute can be located somewhere in the inheritance hierarchy; it is considered invalid otherwise. Such a locatable attribute is said to be *visible* in C++. The valid references to members of classes in Figure 1 are classified as ambiguous and unambiguous in Table 1.

The rules that determine ambiguous and unambiguous references to members of a base class in C++ are given in Section 2.

2 Ambiguity resolution

A member of a C++ class can be *an object, a type, an enumerator, or a function*. If more than one definition of the member can be reached in an inheritance graph, an ambiguous situation is said to have occurred. If only one definition is detected, it is an unambiguous reference. The goal of the ambiguity resolution algorithm is to search for all definitions of a particular member in the inheritance graph and determine an ambiguous situation if it exists.

The ambiguity resolution rules of C++ specify that the ambiguity check algorithm must perform a *breadth-first traversal* of the inheritance graph, visiting all base classes in a *left-to-right order*. The *dominance rule* should be applied, if necessary, to disambiguate between multiple occurrences.

The dominance rule as given in [Str91] is :

> "*A name B::f dominates A::f if its class B has A as a base class. If a name dominates another no ambiguity exists between the two; the dominant name is used when there is a choice.* "

The dominance rule essentially establishes an intuitive relationship between available member definitions; definitions in derived classes dominate definitions in base classes. In the case of a simple tree-graph model this rule is easily understood and implemented; however, due to virtual base classes, the inheritance graph is acyclic and a virtual base class can simultaneously be a direct and indirect base class of a derived class. For example, in Fig. 1, virtual base class C is a direct base of E as well as an indirect base of E via class D. A naive implementation of the ambiguity check algorithm would perform a breadth-first traversal of this graph, visiting the classes in the order { ⟨ D, C, A ⟩, ⟨ B, C ⟩, ⟨ A, B ⟩ }. If a definition is discovered in classes D, B and C, the dominance rule states that the reference should be resolved to the definition in D since it dominates B and C. The *dominates-set* data structure proposed in this algorithm captures the dominance relationship between classes in an inheritance graph. The order in which the classes are searched in the algorithm presented below is partially determined by the dominates-set. This data structure also ensures that fewer classes are visited in the average case.

The rules for determining ambiguity are explained by analyzing all possible situations that can arise in a C++ inheritance graph. The ambiguous and unambiguous situations are categorized below.

2.1 Unambiguous situations

1. Member occurs in the most-derived-class; eg. any reference to member z of class D is unambiguous.

2. Member occurs in exactly one base class in the inheritance hierarchy; eg. the member y occurs only in class C in Fig. 1.

3. The member occurs in a virtual base class and this is the only occurrence of the base class in the inheritance graph eg. member y occurs in the virtual base class C.

4. The member occurs in a dominant class; eg. member w occurs in B and in D, but D dominates B, so this is not an ambiguous reference.

2.2 Ambiguous situations

1. The member occurs in more than one base class; eg. member v occurs in classes A and B.

2. The member occurs in a non-virtual base class, which itself appears more than once in the inheritance graph; eg. member u appears in class A and there are two occurrences of A in the graph.

3. The member occurs in a base class; there is a virtual occurrence of this base class and one or more non-virtual occurrences. For example, member x of class B will always be an ambiguous reference.

Thus, the ambiguity check algorithm will first find all the occurrences of the member and categorize the situation as either ambiguous or unambiguous. The strategy proposed in this paper examines dominant classes before examining the dominated classes. The dominated classes are examined if and only if the member is not found in the dominant classes, thus reducing the number of classes that need to be examined. Moreover, by maintaining a data structure that stores information about the number of occurrences of a class in an inheritance graph, the algorithm can identify ambiguous situations 2 and 3 the moment the member is found.

The algorithm and the associated data structures are given below.

2.3   Data Structures

1. *Dominates set :*   This is a data structure that is associated with every class. Let C be a derived class. Then the dominates set associated with C is :

$$DOM(C) = \{\langle X, f \rangle \mid X \text{ is a base class of } C, f \in N \} \quad (3)$$

An element of this set is a tuple $\langle X, f \rangle$; X denotes the name of a base class, f is the frequency (number of occurrences) of the class in the inheritance graph. Frequency is actually a non-negative integer and is a key factor in all the algorithms given below. However, for pedagogical reasons, let frequency assume one of the values in {*virtual, single, multiple*} representing the occurrence of a single virtual base class, a single occurrence of a base class and multiple occurrences of a base class. The elements of the set do not occur in any particular order, and the construction of the dominates set is the union of all the dominates sets of its base classes, with appropriate adjustment of the frequencies. A simple class has an empty dominates set. The algorithm for creating a dominates set of a class is given in Figure 2.

The construction of the dominates set of class E is given below. Assume that the dominates sets of A, B, C and D have been constructed (see Table 2. Initially, Dom(E) is the same as Dom(D). Now we start adding the members of the dominates set of direct bases C and A. Since C is a base class of D, its dominates set is already present in E. When A is added to the dominates set of E, the final contents of Dom(E) are :

Dom(E) = {⟨ A,multiple ⟩, ⟨ B,multiple ⟩, ⟨ C,virtual ⟩, ⟨ D,virtual ⟩ }

Thus the dominates set of the most-derived-class is a union of the dominates sets of its base classes, with an appropriate adjustment of the frequencies. Adjusting the frequencies requires a set of rules which are complicated by the appearance of virtual base classes. The adjust_frequency algorithm can be found in [Shr92].

2. *Base Search Order list (BSOL) :*
The BSOL is an ordered list of direct base classes that should be searched to locate the definition of a member in a base class. This list is constructed so that direct bases which are dominated by other direct bases are eliminated from the list. This ensures that dominant base classes are searched before dominated classes, and if a definition is located in the dominant class, the dominated classes are not searched at all. The algorithm for creating the base search order list is given in Figure 3.

The BSOL of E is constructed, given the BSOL of A,B,C, and D (see Table 2.)

Create_Dom_Set (Class C) {
1 Let A be the first direct base of C.
   Dom(C) $\Leftarrow$ Dom(A);
2 if (A is a virtual base of C)   add $\langle$ A,*virtual*$\rangle$ to the set Dom(C);
   else add $\langle$ A,*single*$\rangle$ to the set Dom(C);
3 For all other direct base classes B of C {
   3.1 For all classes X, such that $\langle$ X,f $\rangle$ $\in$ Dom(B){
      if (X appears in Dom(C)) adjust_frequency of X in Dom(C) with f;
      else add $\langle X, f \rangle$ to the set Dom(C);
      } /** End of for-all-classes-x-loop **/
   3.2 if (B appears in Dom(C)) the adjust_frequency of B in Dom(C) with *single* or *virtual*.
   3.3 if (B is a virtual base of C) add $\langle B, virtual \rangle$ to the set Dom(C);
      else add $\langle B, single \rangle$ to the set Dom(C);
   } /**** End of for-all-direct-base-classes-loop ****/
}   /****   End   of   algorithm   ****/

Figure 2: Creating Dominates Set

Class	Dominates Set	BSOL
A	empty	empty
B	empty	empty
C	{$\langle$ A,single $\rangle$, $\langle$ B,single $\rangle$ }	{ A, B }
D	{$\langle$ A,single $\rangle$, $\langle$ B,multiple $\rangle$, $\langle$ C,virtual $\rangle$ }	{ B,C }

Table 2: Dominates Set and Base search Order Lists for classes A,B,C,D.

Create_Base_Search_Order(class C) {

1 **BSOL** ⇐ { all direct base classes of C }

2 **For all direct base classes A ∈ BSOL**
    if ((⟨ X,f ⟩ ∈ Dom(A)) and (X ∈ BSOL))
    if ((⟨ X,f1 ⟩ ∈ Dom(C)) and (f1 is the same as f))
    BSOL ⇐ BSOL − ⟨ X,f ⟩

}

Figure 3: Creating Base Search Order List

Initially, BSOL(E) ⇐ { D,C,A }. Since D dominates C, it is eliminated from BSOL(E), so that finally BSOL(E) = { D,A }

3. *Discard List :*
   This is a list of classes that should not be examined-either because they have been searched once or because a definition has been found in a class that dominates these classes. For example, after the member is located in class D, the discard list will consist of { D, B, C }. Class A is not in this list since there is one occurrence of A which is not dominated by class D.

2.4   Ambiguity algorithm

The input to this algorithm consists of:

- most-derived-class D and the member-name M

- Dominates set Dom(D) associated with D

- Base search order list of D BSOL(D)

The output of this algorithm consists of reporting if the reference is AMBIGUOUS or UNAMBIGUOUS. A class list containing the names of the classes in which the member was found is also returned. If the reference was determined to be unambiguous, class list will contain exactly one class name. If the reference was construed as ambiguous, class list will contain either one name (in the case when a base class occurs more than once) or a maximum of two names (in the case when the member is located in two different base classes).

The algorithm is presented in Figure 4. The algorithm first searches for the member M in the most-derived-class D (step 1). If the member is found, it stops the search identifying an unambiguous reference. If the member is not found the algorithm begins a breadth-first traversal, visiting the direct bases of the most-derived class . The base-search-order-list (BSOL) is initialized with the direct bases of D and the discard-list (DL) is initialized with the most-derived-class D. CL is a list of classes in which the member definition is located; it is initialized to empty. While an ambiguous situation has not been identified, and there are still some unexamined classes remaining, the algorithm examines each direct base class B of D (step 3). If M is found in B and there are multiple occurrences of B or M is found in B and some other class, an ambiguous situation is identified and the algorithm quits (step 3.1). If there is a single or virtual occurrence of

Ambiguity_Resolution_Algorithm(D,M,Dom(D),BSOL(D)) {
1   Search for M in D
    If M is a member of D then return (UNAMBIGUOUS,D);
2 If (M is not found in D) then
        BSOL ⇐ BSOL(D);
        DL ⇐ { D };
        CL ⇐ { };
3 while ((| CL | ≤ 1) and (BSOL has unexamined classes)) {
        for each unexamined base class B in BSOL {
        if (M is a member of B)
        3.0 add B to CL;
        3.1 if (frequency(B) is multiple in Dom(D))   return (AMBIGU-
            OUS,CL);
        3.2 else if (frequency(B) is virtual or single) {
            For all classes X such that ⟨ X,f ⟩ ∈ Dom(B)
            if (frequency of X in Dom(B) is the same as in Dom(D))
            add X to DL;
            } /** End of else part **/
        } /** End of for-loop **/
4   BSOL ⇐∪ BSOL(B) such that B ∈ BSOL
        } /** End of while loop ** /
5 if (| CL | ≰ 1) return (AMBIGUOUS, CL);
    else return (UNAMBIGUOUS, CL);
} /** End of algorithm **/

Figure 4: Ambiguity resolution algorithm

B in the graph, discard all the classes that B dominates (step 3.2). In step 4, the algorithm starts exploring the next level of base classes in a breadth-first traversal. An unexamined class is a class that is not in the discarded list.
The advantages and limitations of the algorithm are given below.

1. Dominates set is a concise representation of the inheritance graph.

2. The algorithm minimizes the number of classes that have to be visited in order to locate the member by using the dominates set to construct the base search order list.

3. The creation of the dominates set is a small space-time overhead.

A trace of the algorithm on the inheritance graph of E (see Figure 1) is given below.
   Case 1 : Member z is searched for in the inheritance graph of class E. Since z is located in E, the algorithm terminates immediately after step 1.
   Case 2 : Member w is searched for in the inheritance graph of class E. After executing steps 1 and 2, BSOL and DL have the following contents: BSOL = { D, A } and DL = { E }. Member w is located in class D in step 3 and since D is a virtual base, step 3.2 is executed and DL now has { E,D,B,C }. Since BSOL still has one more unexamined class A, which is not in DL, A

is the next class to be searched; w is not located in A, and A is added to DL. Since all classes have been added to the discarded list, the algorithm terminates having identified an unambiguous situation. Member y is located in class C and is identified as an unambiguous reference.

Case 3 : Member v is searched for in the inheritance graph of class E. After executing steps 1 and 2, BSOL and DL have the following contents: BSOL = { D, A } and DL = { E }. Member v is not found in classes D and A in step 3 and after two iterations of the for-loop for direct bases, BSOL and DL now have BSOL = { B, C } and DL = { E, D, A } Member v is located in B and since B has a frequency of multiple associated with it in the dominates set of E, it is identified as an ambiguous reference. Similarly for member x. Member u is also an ambiguous reference since class A occurs twice in the graph.

3   Conclusions

An analysis of the ambiguity resolution problem in C++ and a solution were presented in this paper. The solution uses the dominates set data structure to avoid visiting classes unnecessarily in its search for the member. The dominates set data structure serves as a concise and adequate (for the purposes of this particular check) representation of an inheritance graph. Its primary usefulness is in enabling the identification of an ambiguous situation when a base class occurs multiple times in the graph and in providing a means to capture the dominance relationship between classes. This dominance relationship is used by the algorithm presented here to visit dominant classes before visiting dominated classes. Indeed, if the member is located in a dominant class, the dominated classes are not examined at all, thus avoiding unnecessary visits to classes.

The ambiguity check algorithm is a necessary part of a compiler for an object-oriented languages; it also has value for determining dependency graphs of classes, browsers for class hierarchies and class restructuring. The algorithm presented here is part of an effort to integrate the ambiguity and accessibility checks and determine visibility and accessibility of a member in a single traversal. This integrated approach will then be compared with the other approach where a traversal is performed for ambiguity and another traversal is required for accessibility. Performing such a comparison involves the implementation of the front-end of a C++ compiler (ie. symbol table, scanner and parser) as well as the implementation of both types of algorithms. The implementation is ongoing. To the best of their knowledge, the authors have not come across any published work dealing exclusively with the algorithms that perform the semantic checks in a C++ compiler, though the existence of several C++ compilers proves that they do exist.

3.1   Future Work

The use and applicability of the dominates set data structure to other compiler-related problems is being investigated.

References

[AHG93] H. M. Al-Haddad and K. M. George. An implementation inheritance model for object-oriented programming. In *The Journal of Systems and Software*. North-Holland, January 1993.

[BG90] Carre B. and Jean-Marc Geib. The point of view notion for multiple inheritance. In *OOPSLA-ECOOP '90*. ACM Press, 1990.

[Boo93] Grady Booch. *Object-Oriented Design with Applications*. Benjamin Cummings, 2 edition, 1993.

[CJ89] William R. Cook and Palsberg Jens. A denotational semantics of inheritance and its correctness. In *OOPSLA-89*, 1989.

[GR89] Adele Goldberg and D. Robson. *Smalltalk-80: The Language*. Addison-Wesley, 1989.

[Mey88] Bertrand Meyer. *Object-Oriented Software Construction*. Prentice Hall, 1 edition, 1988.

[Shr92] Chandra Shrivastava. Ambiguity resolution. *Technical Report, Dept. Computer Science, LSU.*, May 1992.

[Sny87] Alan Snyder. Inheritance and the development of encapsulated software components. *Research Directions in Object-Oriented Programming*, 1987.

[Str91] Bjarne Stroustrup. *The C++ Programming Language*. Addison-Wesley, 2 edition, 1991.

[Weg87] Peter Wegner. Object-oriented classification. *Research Directions in Object-Oriented Programming*, 1987.

On Providing a High-Level C Interface for an Object-Oriented, C++ System

Sandeep Kochhar

Graphics Technology Group

Computervision

Abstract

We address the problem of providing a C language interface to a C++ system, with the explicit goals of keeping the cost of maintaining and extending the C interface low, and facilitating the transition of the C application to C++ in the long run. We describe an approach that satisfies these goals while efficiently using the C++ mechanisms of polymorphism and inheritance, and contrast our approach with the more traditional approach of creating a C binding by providing one C routine corresponding to every C++ method.

1 Introduction

Over the last few years, object-oriented technology has become widespread in a large number of application areas, with C++ [Stro91] becoming the language of choice in the majority of applications. However, despite the surge in the number of systems and class libraries—including fairly large ones—built using C++, C is still the more widely used language. Moreover, in large applications, we often find both C-and C++-based subsystems that need to share each other's functionality; in some cases, the subsystems are written in C only to satisfy immediate product requirements, with the intention of moving them to C++ in the long run.[1] Thus, the issue of providing a C language binding for a system or class library built using C++ is an important one; in addition, the C binding should facilitate the process of moving the application to C++.

The most common approach is to provide a C routine corresponding to every C++ method. This approach has several problems, including a large name space for functions, and the higher cost of maintaining consistency between the C and C++ bindings (this is explained later in the paper).

In this paper, we propose an alternative approach, in which the core C++ subsystem is accessible through a very small set of C routines, including creation and destruction of objects, and setting and getting attributes of objects (Section 3). In this approach, we

---

Author's address: 248 Hampshire St., Cambridge, MA 02138, USA. (Telephone: 617-876-2052, Electronic mail: kochhar@das.harvard.edu.)

[1]The issue of moving C projects to C++ is being faced by many large projects. See [Hans91] for a discussion of some of the issues involved in this transition.

view the invocation of a C++ method as the manipulation of the attributes (members) of objects. We also describe the implementation of this approach using efficiently the C++ mechanisms of polymorphism and inheritance (Section 4). This approach has several advantages that we discuss in Section 5.

2 Design Goals

We came across the problem of providing a C Binding with the goals mentioned below during the design and implementation of an object-oriented CAD/CAM graphics subsystem [Koch92]. This system has over 200 classes, with over 2500 methods; this functionality needs to be exposed to other subsystems and applications, some of which are written in C. Since the subsystem is under active development, we wished to minimize the cost of maintaining and extending the C interface. Moreover, many of the applications written in C will be moved to C++ in the long run; thus, we wished to provide the applications a simple and rapid approach to move from using our C binding to using our C++ binding.

Thus, we were faced with with following design goals for the C HLI and its implementation:[2]

- the C++ HLI must be a superset of the C HLI, so that C users could continue using the same approach while switching to C++;

- while CSS is extensible only in C++ (through derivation from existing classes), extensions should be easily available through the C HLI;

- the implementation of the C HLI should use C++ mechanisms (e.g. polymorphism, inheritance, etc.) efficiently (thus, for example, avoiding large switch statments or tables based on object/attribute types);

- as CSS is continuously being developed in C++, keep the cost of maintaining consistency in the C HLI low.

- facilitate the transtion of the C application to C++ in stages, without requiring that the entire C application be converted in one step.

We believe that these goals are general enough to be applicable to a large number of applications that contain both C and C++ subsystems.

To address the above goals, we designed a C-language HLI that provides access to the CSS functionality through a small and uniform set of routines. The routines allow the HLI user to manipulate various kinds of CSS objects, including creation, destruction, and setting of attributes. In this scenario, the invocation of a method on an object takes place through the manipulation of the object's attributes.

---

[2]In our discussion, we refer to the object-oriented, C++ subsystem or library as the Core Sub-System (CSS), and the interface or binding to this subsystem as the High-Level Interface (HLI). By definition, the C++ HLI consists of the public methods on the classes in the subsystem. The C HLI is the focus of this paper.

3 C-Language HLI

In this section, we describe briefly the structure of the C HLI and the routines that it contains. First, however, let us mention some conventions we use in the HLI routines. C functions that manipulate (set or get) attributes have variable-argument (*vararg*) and fixed-argument (*fixedarg*) equivalents.[3] In such cases, the names of the routines contain VA and FA respectively. For example, VASetAttr and FASetAttr are the variable- and fixed-argument variations to set attributes on an object.

Functions that perform operations on objects take the object handle as the first argument. All functions return a status code as the value of the function, which can be used to specify success, errors and warnings. The vararg functions take a list of attribute name/value pairs, terminated by a special argument (NULL_ARG). Functions that take fixed arguments replace the variable argument list with two arguments: a count indicating number of arguments, and an array containing the arguments that would have appeared in the varargs list. (A count of zero or a null array pointer indicate no arguments.) Each element in the array is a structure containing the actual attribute name and value.

In this paper, instead of describing our particular object-oriented, graphics subsystem, we use a very simple set of classes to illustrate our approach.[4] Basically, we consider three classes of objects: a root class, Root, from which all other classes derive; a PointD2 class that derives from Root, and provides X and Y coordinates to describe a two-dimensional point, and a PointD3 class that derives from PointD2, and adds a Z coordinate to describe a three-dimensional point (Figure 3 later shows these classes).

The C HLI can be structured as follows:

- *Error Handling:* As mentioned above, all routines return a status indicating whether the operation was successful. In addition, the C HLI allows its client (user) to specify an error-handling routine (the HLI provides a default one). This routine is then called when an error condition occurs, with arguments indicating other details (severity, message, etc.).

- *Initialization and Shutdown:* The routines allow the CSS to perform initialization and cleanup activities.

- *Common Object-Manipulation:* These routines allow the HLI client to manipulate *all* CSS objects through a small and uniform set of routines. These allow the client to create and destroy objects, and set and retrieve values for attributes of a given object. Most operations (methods) are invoked via the setting of attributes on

---

[3]We chose to provide both vararg and fixedarg versions of these functions in order to satisfy the needs of our applications: some of these preferred the vararg versions, some preferred the fixedarg versions, and some intended to use both with the idea that users often find it easier to program with vararg versions, while the fixedarg versions are more useful when automatically creating a list of attributes in the application. The X Window System Toolkit [Asen90] demonstrates the same notions: in X11R4, most attribute manipulation was done through fixedarg functions; in X11R5, varargs is supported as well.

[4]Readers interested in object-oriented, graphics systems are referred to [Cunn92, Koch92, Koch94, Wiss90].

Category	Variations
Create	Create(Class *type*, ObjectPtr *objRet*)
	VACreate(Class *type*, ObjectPtr *objRet*, Attr *attr*, ...)
	FACreate(Class *type*, ObjectPtr *objRet*, Int *count*, ArgPtr *args*)
	Duplicate(ObjectPtr *objRet*, Object *from*)
Destroy	Destroy(Object *obj*)
Copy	Copy(Object *from*, Object *to*)
	VACopy(Object *from*, Object *to*, Attr *attr*, ...)
	FACopy(Object *from*, Object *to*, Int *count*, ArgPtr *args*)
Set Attribute	VASetAttr(Object *obj*, Attr *attr*, ...)
	FASetAttr(Object *obj*, Int *count*, ArgPtr *args*)
Get Attribute	VAGetAttr(Object *obj*, Attr *attr*, ...)
	FAGetAttr(Object *obj*, Int *count*, ArgPtr *args*)

Legend

All routines return a status
Object refers to the (opaque) object handle used
by the C HLI client
Object *obj*: refers to the object on which the op-
eration is performed
Class *type*: type of object to be created

ObjectPtr *objRet*: to return object handle
Attr *attr*: type of attribute
... ... : list of value, type pairs
Int *count*: number of attributes
ArgPtr *args*: array of attribute type/value

Figure 1: Common Object-Manipulation Routines

---

some objects. For example, to highlight a **Rectangle**, one would set the *highlight* attribute for that **Rectangle** to *on*.[5]

- *Convenience Routines:* These include routines that are not available through the above set, for example, since they are specific to a certain object, or are needed very often. The convenience routines also include utility routines (e.g., routines that manipulate data structures such as object lists).

Common Object-Manipulation Routines

In this paper , we focus only on the routines comprising the *common-object manipulation* set above, since that is where the main contributions of our approach lie.

Figure 1 presents a summary of the routines available to manipulate all objects:

- *Create:* These functions create an initialized object and return (through one of the arguments) a handle to the object. **Create**, **VACreate**, and, **FACreate** create objects of the class specified by *type*; **Duplicate** creates an object of the same

---

[5]In many graphics and user-interface toolkits, getting and setting attributes is often the most common approach to manipulating objects; hence, our approach is particularly suitable for such toolkits.

class as *from*. Create initializes the object created with default values for all the attributes. VACreate and FACreate allow the user to specify an arbitrary number of pairs of Attribute Names (or Types) and Values; the specified attributes are be set to the provided values, and the rest given defaults.

- *Destroy:* This routine is used to destroy an object that was created using the C HLI.

- *Copy:* This routine copies object *from* into object *to* (both of the same class). VACopy and FACopy copy only the attributes specified in the argument list.

- *Set Attributes:* These functions set attributes (or data members) for an object. For VASetAttr, the attributes to be set are passed as a vararg list of type/value pairs, terminated by NULL_ARG. For FASetAttr, the attributes are passed in the attribute array *args*, with *count* indicating how many.

- *Get Attributes:* These functions retrieve attribute values (for an object); the attributes to be retrieved are passed in the first part of the type/value pairs (VAGetAttr) or first part of the array elements (FASetAttr), with the second part pointing to the right amount of storage for the return values.

We should emphasize that the routines in Figure 1 are not just a subset of the C HLI, but the *complete* set of common object-manipulation routines. An a simple example of their usage, Figure 2 shows how an application can use the C HLI to create and manipulate PointD3 objects.[6]

4 Design of the Implementation

In Section 2 above, we presented the goals that our implementation of the C HLI needed to satisfy. In this section, we give a high-level overview of the design of our implementation for the common object-manipulation routines described above.

The implementation of the C HLI consists of two parts:

- implementation of the C HLI (interface) routines, which make appropriate calls on the CSS objects, and,

- support provided by the Root and other CSS objects.

Let us examine these two parts separately, in Sections 4.1 and 4.2 respectively.

4.1 Interface Implementation

The implementation of the interface consists of two parts, header files (jointly referred to as HLI_C.h in Figure 2) that define the interface, and source files (referred to as HLI_C.c in this paper) that implement the routines listed in Figure 1. HLI_C.h is included by all applications wishing to use the C HLI; through the use of preprocessor macros, we ensure that file is accepted by both C and C++ compilers. HLI_C.c is a C++ source file.

---

[6]Note that the examples shown in this paper do not do error checking to keep the code simpler to read.

```
/* Example of creating PointD3 objects through the C HLI */

#include "HLI_C.h"

c_pointD3()
{
    Object pt1, pt2, pt3, pt4, pm;

    /* create some points ... */
    Create(CPointD3, &pt1);
    Create(CPointD3, &pt2);
    /* and set their attributes */
    VASetAttr(pt1, AXcoord, 0.0, AYcoord, 0.0, AZcoord, -1.0, NULL_ARG);
    VASetAttr(pt2, AXcoord, 0.0, AYcoord, 1.0, AZcoord, 1.0, NULL_ARG);

    /* create some more points with attributes */
    VAcreate(CPointD3, &pt3, AXcoord, 0.2, AYcoord, 0.2, NULL_ARG);
    VAcreate(CPointD3, &pt4, AXcoord, 0.2, AYcoord, -1.0, NULL_ARG);

    /* use these points later ... */
    /* e.g. create a Point Marker Entity with pt3 as its center */
    Create(CPointMarkerEnt, &pm, AMarker, "+", ACenter, pt3, NULL_ARG);
    /* etc... */
}
```

Figure 2: Example of Using the C HLI

HLI_C.h

The header file **HLI_C.h** includes:

- *Type definitions and prototypes:* these define the object type ("class") used in creation (Class), the object handle type (Object), attribute types (Attr), the error status (Status), and the function prototypes for the HLI.

- *Attribute definitions:* these define some useful utilities for defining uniquely attribute types and manipulating them. For example,
    extern Attr AXcoord; // X coordinate

- *Object class definitions:* these define the types of objects that can be created through the C Binding and the attribute types that can be manipulated through the HLI. For example,
    extern Class CPointD2;

Note that all the types above are opaque handles from the point of view of the client (user). We provide useful utilities that allow the client to retrieve type/class "names" and other useful information from these opaque handles.

HLI_C.c

Most of the actual support for implementing the C HLI is provided by CSS objects. The file **HLI_C.c** implements the interface described in **HLI_C.h** above; in most of the cases, this is done by calling appropriate virtual functions on the Root CSS object, which then dispatch to the appropriate functions on the actual object.

Creation: The object-type ("class") specification passed as an argument to creation routines is initialized as a pointer to a static member function for creating that type of object. For example, the object-type specification CPointD2 above for the PointD2 object points to a static member function PointD2::Create( ), which implements the actual creation of PointD2 objects.[7] Thus, Create( ) just deferences the pointer and calls the corresponding creation function. VACreate( ) calls the basic creation routine followed by the varargs VASetAttribs member function on the newly created object.[8] FACreate( ) calls the basic creation routine followed by the fixed-arg FASetAttribs member function on the newly created object. Similarly, Duplicate( ) calls the creation routine for the *from* object to get the appropriate object handle that becomes the *to* object, and then invokes *copy* with the two object handles.

Deletion involves casting the object handle to a pointer to root object type (Root *) and invoking the C++ **delete** operator on it; this in turn calls the appropriate virtual destructor on the object. Similarly, *copying* involves casting the object handles to a pointer to the root object type (Root *) and invoking the corresponding virtual method on it.

Attribute Manipulation involves casting the object handles to a pointer to the root object type (Root *) and invoking the corresponding virtual method on it. As an example, obj→VASetAttr( ) invokes ((Root*)obj)→VASetAttribs( ), while obj→FASetAttr( ) invokes ((Root*)obj)→FASetAttribs( ).

Attribute Types are used in the attribute manipulation routines, such as VASetAttr( ) and VAGetAttr( ). These routines have to parse through the attribute type/value lists that they are passed, as well as retrieve a printable name for the attribute type (e.g., to print "Invalid attribute" messages). Our approach to defining attribute types allows these requirements to be met efficiently: attribute types are defined as opaque types that are initialized to point to a structure containing the attribute's printable name, etc. This approach guarantees a unique value for each type of attribute, allows attribute names to be retrieved in a language-independent manner, and allows attribute manipulation routines to directly compare type "values" (instead of having to use strcmp( ), for example). This approach also allows the user (or us) to extend available attribute types easily and be guaranteed a unique value for the "type."

---

[7] An alternate approach would be to use an enum to assign integer values to various object types, such as in,

typedef enum {CPointD2, CPointD3, ...} Class;

Our approach has two advantages over using the enumeration approach: (1) We do not need to have a large switch statement in the creation routine, and, (2) it is very easy for users (and us) to extend the types of objects available, without having to modify the creation routines, or the enumeration list (our approach automatically guarantees a unique value for each type ("class") of object).

[8] In this paper, we refer mainly to the varargs-based routines for attribute manipulation (these routines have VA in their name). The treatment of the equivalent fixed-argument versions, e.g. FACreate( ), is very similar, and is only occasionally discussed.

As an example, corresponding to the AXcoord attribute declaration given earlier,

> extern Attr AXcoord; // X coordinate

HLI_C.c defines[9]

> Attr AXcoord = new Attr("Xcoord");

Now, an attribute manipulation routine, while parsing through the argument list, can use:

> if (attribute_type == AXcoord) ...

4.2 CSS Support

Within CSS, support for the C HLI is provided in two parts (Figure 3 gives an example of these and is discussed further in the examples below):

- Methods to *match* the C HLI. These include:

    - methods defined only on Root and inherited by all CSS objects.

    - methods defined on all CSS objects; these are static (class) methods.

- Methods to *support* the implementation of the C HLI. These include:

    - methods defined only on Root and inherited by all CSS objects.

    - methods defined on all CSS objects; these are virtual methods.

C-HLI Matching Methods

These methods allow CSS objects to be manipulated identically in C or in C++:

- All CSS objects provide creation routines to match the creation routines, such as Create, available in C, for example,

    > static Status PointD2::Create(Object *);[10]

    Thus, instead of the following in C:

    > Object pt; Create(CPointD2, &pt)

    one could, in C++, say:[11]

    > Object pt; PointD2::Create(&pt)

---

[9] These definitions need not all be made in the same file; for example, a developer extending our CSS by adding a new class and some new attributes could put these definitions in his or her source files, and still be guaranteed unique values for the types.

[10] This routine is declared static since it is needed by HLI_C.c to initialize the "object types" used in the C HLI, independently of the existence of any object of that type.

[11] Note that normally a C++ client (user) could just say

> PointD2 *pt = new PointD2;

However, the C++ interface that mimics the C interface is provided for users who wish to mix C and C++ (thereby interfacing with the HLI in essentially the same way through C and C++), and for users who might be converting code from C to C++ (Section 5.3 explains this further).

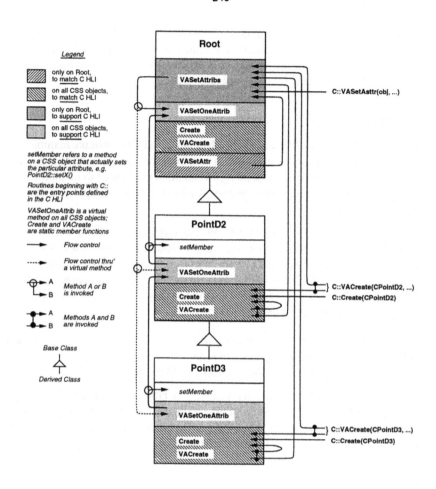

Figure 3: Portion of CSS Support for the C HLI Implementation

- Root provides methods, including error-handling and attribute manipulation routines, to match the corresponding routines available through C. These methods have the same names as the C HLI names, e.g. **Destroy()**, **VASetAttr()**, etc. Since these methods are inherited by all CSS objects, CSS objects can be manipulated identically in C or in C++. For example, instead of the following in C:

    VASetAttr(pt, AXCoord, 3.0, NULL_ARG)

one could, in C++, say:

    ((Root *)pt)→VASetAttr(AXCoord, 3.0, NULL_ARG)

The implementation of the above methods also follows that of the corresponding C HLI routine, both of which call appropriate virtual methods on Root.

Note that the design of the flow control shown in Figure 3 allows us to avoid duplicating code in corresponding C and C++ routines (despite the multiple entry points for manipulating attributes on an object), and to delegate the "real" work to specific methods (e.g. VASetOneAttr( ) on the CSS objects).

C-HLI Support Methods

- Root provides methods (these are called by both C and C++ attribute manipulation routines) that walk through the attribute list (in both, the varargs and fixed-argument cases) and then invoke a corresponding virtual method on Root to manipulate one attribute at a time. These virtual methods dispatch to the appropriate routines in the actual object.

  For example, both the C HLI routine VASetAttr( ) and the corresponding C++ method Root::VASetAttr( ) invoke the method Root::VASetAttribs( ), which uses the C++ varargs facility to pick one attribute type at a time from the argument list, then invokes Root::VASetOneAttrib( ) to do the "real work" for each type. Since Root::VASetOneAttrib( ) is a virtual method, it dispatches to the VASetOneAttrib( ) method on the actual object.

- All CSS Objects provide methods to do the "real work" when a C HLI routine is called to manipulate attributes. For example,
  virtual Status VASetOneAttrib(Attr, va_list);

  These routines, which are invoked repeatedly by Root::VASetAttribs( ), manipulate one attribute type/value pair at a time. The attribute type is compared to the attribute types that this object "knows about" in order to decide how to handle the attribute;[12] the value is taken from va_list based on the attribute type.

Examples

Figure 4 shows the calling sequences, based on Figure 3, for two cases (in the figures, routine names prefixed with C:: refer to C HLI entry points; routine names prefixed with C++ refer to C++ entry points (which match C HLI entry points of the same name[13])):

- *Creating a* PointD3 *object* (Figure 4a): Since the object "class" CPointD3 points to PointD3::Create( ), calling Create(CPointD3) through C invokes the corresponding C++ entry point PointD3::Create( ), which directly invokes the C++ new operator.

---

[12] As explained in Section 4.1 under *Attribute Types*, the type of the attribute can be decided by saying, for example,
  if (attribute_type == AXcoord) ...
Since only addresses are compared, attribute parsing does not in any way degrade system performance. Also, in our implementation, we provide a set of macros that simulate switch/case parsing of the attribute type, in order to avoid writing a long list of if-else-if statements.

[13] In the examples, the user can invoke only the C HLI routine or the C++ entry point; the rest of the methods are invoked by the CSS support routines. Footnote 11 and Section 5.3 explain the rationale behind having C++ entry points that match the C HLI.

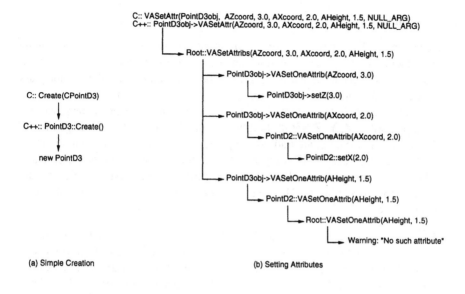

C:: VASetAttr(PointD3obj, AZcoord, 3.0, AXcoord, 2.0, AHeight, 1.5, NULL_ARG)
C++:: PointD3obj->VASetAttr(AZcoord, 3.0, AXcoord, 2.0, AHeight, 1.5, NULL_ARG)

Root::VASetAttribs(AZcoord, 3.0, AXcoord, 2.0, AHeight, 1.5)

PointD3obj->VASetOneAttrib(AZcoord, 3.0)

PointD3obj->setZ(3.0)

PointD3obj->VASetOneAttrib(AXcoord, 2.0)

PointD2::VASetOneAttrib(AXcoord, 2.0)

PointD2::setX(2.0)

PointD3obj->VASetOneAttrib(AHeight, 1.5)

PointD2::VASetOneAttrib(AHeight, 1.5)

Root::VASetOneAttrib(AHeight, 1.5)

Warning: "No such attribute"

C:: Create(CPointD3)

C++:: PointD3::Create()

new PointD3

(a) Simple Creation

(b) Setting Attributes

Figure 4: Calling Sequences based on Figure 3

- *Setting some attributes on a* PointD3 *object* (Figure 4b): both VASetAttr(...) (through C) and PointD3obj→VASetAttr(...) (through C++) invoke the method Root::VASetAttribs( ), which then invokes PointD3obj→VASetOneAttrib( )[14] three times. In the first instance, the setZ( ) method on the object can handle the attribute. In the second instance, the attribute is handled by the setX( ) method on the base class PointD2. Finally, in the third instance, the attribute is propagated all the way up to Root, at which point an "attribute invalid for PointD3" message is printed.

5 Analysis

The goal of the implementation strategy described above is to support the C HLI in an efficient manner that takes full advantage of C++'s object-oriented (inheritance, polymorphism, etc.) capabilities. This design also provides a simple and consistent mechanism for adding new object types and new attribute types. In this section, we compare our approach for the design and implementation of the C HLI to the traditional approach of providing a C routine for every public method.

---

[14] As Figure 3 shows, Root::VASetAttribs( ) actually invokes the virtual method Root::VASetOneAttrib( ), which, in this example, dispatches to the actual method PointD3obj::VASetOneAttrib( ).

5.1 Advantages

- *Name space:* The restricted set of C HLI routines in our approach has the advantage of reducing the number of function names that have to be used. To some extent, this is offset by the need to use a larger number of argument name and value pairs. However, often in a large CSS — especially in graphics toolkits (such as ours) and user-interface toolkits —, a lot of objects share the same attribute name space. For example, color, X, Y, Z, width, height, etc. may be applicable to a large number of objects. In this case, the traditional approach would have a function for setting color for each object—setRectangleColor, setPointColor, setLineColor, etc.— whereas our approach would only have one attribute name ("type")—Color—that would apply to all objects. Thus, we found that our approach has a smaller overall name space.

- *Ease of development:* The restricted set of routines eases the development and maintenance of the C HLI, while the CSS is being continuously developed in C++. Basically, instead of maintaining a large set of routines and their arguments (prototypes), as in the traditional approach, we need to maintain only a list of attribute types. Moreover, using the mechanisms described in the previous section, the approach for parsing attributes is all automated, except that each object only has to be able to handle its own attributes. Thus, a PointD2 has to only know about X and Y, while a PointD3 only needs to know about Z (since X and Y are already handled by its base object PointD2).

- *Attribute groupings:* In many applications, it is often important to be able to set groups of attributes together. For example, in a graphics CSS, this can help avoid visual flicker. Our approach makes it easier to support this capability.

  Suppose one has a PointD3 object, and one wishes to set its X, Y and Z attributes. In our approach, one could just say

  setAttr(pt, X, 50, Y, 55, Z, 70, NULL_ARG);

  Now, if the X, Y and Z attributes corresponded to the visible position of the point object on the screen, the user would just see the point move in one step. Also, often this approach provides a more "natural" style of programming. In the traditional approach, one would have to say:

  setPointD3X(pt, 50);
  setPointD3Y(pt, 55);
  setPointD3Z(pt, 70);

  Unfortunately, this might cause the visible display of the point to move in three steps.[15] Thus, there is no easy way to set groups of attributes together in one step in the traditional approach. One could, of course, provide a routine setPointD3XYZ(int x,int y,int z), but do we also need to provide setPointD3XY,

---

[15]Note that, similar to the example shown in Figure 4b, either of the two cases above would result in three internal calls inside the object. However, internal calls within the object are easy to control and batch in our system; thus, our approach still results in one visual change in the display from the user's viewpoint, whereas the traditional approach would result in three user-visible display changes.

setPointD3YZ, etc., to allow the user all possible combinations? In our approach, one setAttr routine allows us to choose any of the options, again contributing to a smaller name space.

- *Extensibility:* Our approach makes it easier to extend the CSS (e.g., by adding a new class and its attributes) and make available the extensions through the C HLI: once the class is implemented in C++, the implementer only has to define the attribute names (if they do not already exist) and add them to the routine that automatically parses the attribute list. Thus, the name space only grows if new attribute types are added. In the traditional approach, one has to define new C routines for each of the attributes and make them available to the global name space; thus, name space is guaranteed to grow by the total number of attributes in the class, not just new types.

- *Inheritance and Ease of use:* Consider the example that we used in this paper: the class PointD2 has attributes X and Y; a derived class, PointD3, adds the attribute Z. In our approach, the user of the C HLI can set X, Y and Z for a PointD3 object simply as:

      setAttr(pt, X, 50, Y, 55, Z, 70, NULL_ARG);

From the user's point of view, s/he doesn't care that X and Y were actually implemented by the PointD2 class. S/he just knows that a PointD3 has X, Y, Z; therefore, any of those can be manipulated. From the class implementer's point, all s/he has to do is be able to handle the Z attribute, and pass X and Y, to the base class. Thus, our approach uses the C++ inheritance mechanism very efficiently, and makes the inheritance transparently available to the user.

In the traditional approach, setting Z is easy:

      setPointD3Z(pt,70);

But how does one set X and Y? Do we say

      setPointD2X(pt, 50); setPointD2Y(pt, 55);

or, do we say

      setPointD3X(pt, 50); setPointD3Y(pt, 55);

In the first case, the user has to be very aware of the class structure and remember that PointD3 derives from PointD2. (Thus, if the class hierarchy changes somewhat, or an attribute is moved to a base/derived class, users have to change their code significantly.) In the second case, the name space for the C HLI routines would become really large: each derived class would have to provide a C HLI routine for *all* the attributes that it inherits; for example, PointD3 would have to provide a C HLI routine for manipulating X, Y and Z attributes, even though there already are C HLI routines for manipulating the X and Y attributes of PointD2 objects. Moreover, this would cause significant overhead for the implementers as well.

- *Performance:* Since C++ is a language that emphasizes efficiency, we would like to emphasize that the "generic" nature of the C HLI and the support required from the CSS *do not*, in any way, encumber the direct C++ portion of the CSS with performance penalties.

5.2 Restrictions

- *Type checking:* While the object-specific methods in our approach to the C binding can be type-safe, the common object-manipulation functions cannot be type checked except for the generic types (Object, Attribute, etc.) and the types of arguments allowed in ANSI-C as portable across variable argument functions. Note, however, that in any approach to a C binding that does not wish to expose internal C++ structures or objects to the C application, only limited type safety can be provided even in the traditional approach. Also interesting to note is that the X toolkit [Asen90] has become a widely used standard, even though the attribute manipulation routines (XtSetValues and XtGetValues) only offer limited type-checking, very similar to our approach.

- *CSS library design:* Our approach imposes two restrictions on the design of the CSS class hierarchy: all the classes that support the common-object manipulation routines need to derived from the Root class, and all such classes need to provide a default constructor.

  In any reasonably large class hierarchy that employs C++ polymorphism usefully (for example, the widely-used NIH class library [Gorl90]), the first restriction above is not significant: most of the class objects will already have a virtual table pointer; hence, deriving from Root, even if only to support our approach, should not impact the size of the objects or the performance. (In our graphics subsystem, the few classes that did not already employ polymorphism — and for which adding the extra pointer would have degraded system performance — were handled through object-specific methods in the C binding.)

  Similarly, we did not find it difficult to provide a default constructor for all the classes that supported the common-object manipulation routines (again, this also seems to be the case with many of the class libraries we have examined, including, for example, the NIH class library mentioned above).

5.3 Recommendations

As discussed above, our approach offers significant advantages over the traditional one for both the *users* and *implementers/extenders* of CSS, but with some restrictions as well. The actual choice of which approach to use would thus depend on the priorities of the application. However, in Section 2, we mentioned that one of our goals was to facilitate the transition of applications using our C HLI to move to using our C++ HLI. We feel that our approach is significantly better-suited to this problem. As a sample transition, we might consider:

- The application currently uses our C HLI and wishes to move over to the C++ HLI.

- As a first step, the C HLI is identically supported in the C++ HLI, so the application compiles and works without change.

- As resources become available, calls to the common object-manipulation routines can be changed over to calls to the appropriate C++ class-specific methods. For example,

```
Object pt;
Create(CPointD3, &pt)
setAttr(pt, X, 50, Y, 55, Z, 70, NULL_ARG);
```

(which works in both C and C++), can be changed to

```
PointD3 *pt = new PointD3;
pt→setX(50);
pt→setY(55);
pt→setZ(70);
```

Two important points should be noted: most of these changes can be done automatically, and it is not necessary to make the changes all at once. The latter is especially important for projects that have aggressive schedules in which intermediate releases are made fairly often.

In our organizaton, the primary motivation for providing the C HLI was that many applications that used our CSS would be written in C so as to meet product release deadlines and to allow developers to acquire C++ training; as resources became available and developers were trained in C++, the applications would move over to C++. Thus, our approach to the C HLI was designed with the explicit goal of supporting this type of transition.[16] We believe that, in contrast, the traditional approach to a C HLI — that of one C routine per C++ method — would be more useful (because of not having the restrictions mentioned above) in a CSS where the class structure (i.e., the class hierarchy and data members) is fairly fixed and where the applications intend to remain in C.

6 Summary and Conclusions

In this paper, we addressed the problem that many C++ libraries or subsystems under active development face: that of providing and maintaining a C HLI for the subsystem. The traditional approach to providing a C HLI is to have a C routine corresponding to each public method that the CSS wishes to expose to the users. However, this approach has many problems, as we discussed earlier.

To address this problem, we designed a C HLI that met the goals of maintainability and extensibility, and whose implementation strategy supports the C HLI in an efficient manner and takes full advantage of C++'s object-oriented (inheritance, polymorphism, etc.) capabilities. In addition, our strategy provides a simple and consistent mechanism for adding new object types and new attribute types, and facilitates the transition of applications from C to C++.

We expect that in actual applications, the majority of CSS's would be best served by a hybrid approach: most of the CSS would be exposed through our approach ("common

---

[16]We believe that the above scenario is currently quite common in many organizations. Of course, another scenario that occasionally occurs (less so now than a few years ago) is that of applications wishing to use a C binding to a C++ library because of reluctance to move to C++, based on *presumed* system-performance degradation and language-learning difficulty. In those scenarios, our approach offers the advantage that the CSS takes care of parsing the attributes and offers a much simpler interface to the C users, especially with respect to inherited attributes (see *inheritance* issues in Section 5.1 above).

object-manipulation"), with direct C bindings provided for only a few routines ("convenience routines"). As an example, the C HLI might provide attributes for X and Y position. However, if Move is an intrinsically important operation for the subsystem, it might also provide a Move(int dx, int dy) routine. In our object-oriented, graphics CSS, we found that less than 1 percent of the C++ methods required convenience routines; the rest were exposed in a natural manner through the common object-manipulation set.

Acknowledgments

I would like to thank all the CV R&D members who have contributed their suggestions to the work described in this paper, including John Weber, Radha Srinivasan, Paul Romagna, Tom Gross, Jim Hall, and Mark Villiard.

References

[Asen90] Asente, P. J. and Swick, R. R. 1990. *X Window System Toolkit*. Digital Press, Bedford, MA.

[Cunn92] Cunningham, S., Craighill, N. K., Fong, M. W., and Brown, J. R., editors. 1992. *Computer Graphics Using Object-Oriented Programming*. Wiley, New York.

[Gorl90] Gorlen, K. E., Orlow, S. M., and Plexico, P. S. 1990. *Data Abstraction and Object-Oriented Programming in C++*. Wiley, New York.

[Hans91] Hansen, T. 1991. "Moving a project from C into C++," *The C++ Journal*, **1(4)**:10–24.

[Koch92] Kochhar, S. and Hall, J. 1992. "An object-oriented CAD/CAM presentation system," *Proceedings of the Third Eurographics Workshop on Object-Oriented Graphics*, October 28-30, Champery, Switzerland.

[Koch94] Kochhar, S. 1994. "Object-oriented paradigms for graphical-object modeling in computer-aided design: A survey and analysis," in *Proceedings of Graphics Interface '94*, Banff, Canada, May 16-20.

[Stro91] Stroustrup, B. 1991. *The C++ Programming Language*. Addison-Wesley, New York.

[Wiss90] Wisskirchen, P. 1990. *Object-Oriented Graphics: From GKS and PHIGS to Object-Oriented Systems*. Springer-Verlag, New York.

Integrating Objects
with
Constraint-Programming Languages

Massimo PALTRINIERI

Ecole Normale Supérieure
Département de Mathématiques et d'Informatique
45 rue d'Ulm - Pavillion P1
75230 Paris - Cedex 05
France
palmas@dmi.ens.fr

Abstract. Constraint-programming languages represent an emerging paradigm for solving combinatorial problems, where programs define sets of variables and sets of constraints on these variables. The execution of a constraint program determines the values of the variables that satisfy the constraints. This paper enhances the notions of variable and constraint with characteristics of the object-oriented paradigm, such as abstraction and hierarchy. Variables become objects, semantically richer, that are instances of classes organized into a hierarchy, while constraints can be defined both on objects and classes. The semantics of the new model in terms of the traditional model is presented. This bears interesting consequences, such as the possibility to easily implement preprocessors that transform object-oriented constraint programs into traditional constraint programs. A design methodology to interactively define combinatorial problems is also presented. The models produced applying such a methodology are extremely compact and can be automatically executed. An example of application of the methodology to a real planning problem is presented. The number of constraints defined in the model is reduced of 21 times, compared to previous formulations.

1. Introduction

Constraint programming is a method of implementation in which programs are organized as constraints, i.e. invariant relationships, among variables ranging over domains. Constraint languages provide efficient consistency techniques to remove values from domains that are inconsistent with the constraints and to determine assignments of values to variables such that all the constraints are satisfied.

Object-oriented programming is a method of implementation in which programs are organized as cooperative collections of objects, each of which represents an instance of some class, and whose classes are all members of a hierarchy. Object-oriented languages provide facilities to support a programming style where: objects, not algorithms, are the fundamental logical building blocks; each object is an instance of a class; classes are organized into a hierarchy.

The constraint and object-oriented programming paradigms have distinguished elements, such as declarativeness and reasoning for the former, abstraction and hierarchy for the latter. On the other hand, both paradigms share common advantages: reduced development time; reduced source-code size; flexibility of programs which are easier to modify and extend; reusability.

The first part of this work proposes an object-oriented extension to constraint languages that introduces some of the elements of object orientation, namely abstraction and hierarchy, while retaining the advantages of constraint programming, namely declarativeness and reasoning. Rather than limiting to a specific constraint language, a general framework is developed that can be instantiated to specific constraint languages. This extension can be approached from two different perspectives: from the constraint programming viewpoint, abstraction and hierarchy are added to variables and constraints; from the object-oriented programming viewpoint, procedural methods are replaced with declarative relationships that are automatically enforced by the system. We position ourselves in the first streamline and view the framework as an object-oriented extension to constraint programming, rather than the introduction of constraints into object-oriented programming, because the framework is targeted to the solution of combinatorial problems, so the constraint satisfaction component is more characterizing.

The second part of the paper presents a design methodology for the framework. Its purpose is the object-oriented definition of models of combinatorial problems. We refer to it as a design methodology because the outcome is a model of the problem in exam and because its components are those of traditional design methodologies: notation and process. On the other hand, there is a main difference with traditional design methodologies: instead of providing a path from requirements to implementation, it provides a path from requirements to solutions. The model is not an input to a following implementation activity, but it is directly executed to generate solutions. For this reason, the model produced through design can also be viewed as a program expressed in a graphical formalism or an executable specification of the problem.

2. Constraint Programming

Several constraint-programming languages are today available both at the academic and industrial level (for a survey of commercially available constraint-programming languages see [Rot93]). Prolog III [Col90], CLP(R) [Jaf88] and Chip [Din88] are logic-programming languages replacing the pattern-matching mechanism of unification, as used in Prolog, by a more general operation called constraint satisfaction; Charme [Opl89] is the first industrial constraint-programming language and is based on a simple syntax similar to traditional third-generation languages; Bertrand [Lel88] is a rule-based language that implements constraint-satisfaction through an augmented term rewriting mechanism; in TK!Solver [KoJ84] and IDEAL [VaW82] the constraints are stated as equations; constraint-programming languages integrating some object-oriented components are Thinglab [Bor79], Socle [Har86], Equate [Wil91], Garnet [MGV92], Kaleidoscope [FBB92], Solver [Pug92], Cspoo [Kök93], Devi [ThS94] and Codm [SRR94]. These languages differ in the programming paradigm they adopt, the syntax they follow, the resolution strategy they implement, etc., but they are all made to solve, flexibly and efficiently, a large class of combinatorial problems, called constraint satisfaction problems, consisting of a set of variables, each associated to a domain of values, and of a set of constraints that limit the combination of values of the variables. Due to this common factor of all constraint systems, definitions of constraint program and constraint language can be stated that do not make any assumptions on paradigm, syntax, strategy, etc., and are in fact general enough to cover all the constraint systems.

A *constraint program* is a syntactical construct including a set of variable declarations, associating a domain of values to each variable, and a set of constraints, i.e., pieces of syntax constraining the values of variables occurring in them. A *constraint-programming language* defines the set of syntactically-correct constraint programs.

Semantically, to each constraint is associated a relation given by a set of tuples having one value for each variable occurring in the constraint. A *solution* to a constraint program is an assignment of values to the variables, such that for each constraint, the tuple determined by the solution is in the relation associated to the constraint. Executing a constraint program means determining a solution.

Starting from these few general notions (variable, domain and constraint), new structures (object, class, inheritance, etc.) are added to provide abstraction on and hierarchy of variables and constraints, and to define a framework where combinatorial problems are solved just through design, rather than design and programming.

3. Constraint Satisfaction Problems

A *constraint satisfaction problem* (CSP) is defined by a set $X_1,...,X_n$ of variables, each associated with a domain $D_1,...,D_n$ respectively, and a set $C_1,...,C_m$ of constraints, i.e., subsets of $D_1 x..x D_n$. Each CSP can be graphically represented as a *constraint graph* where nodes represent variables and edges represent constraints.

An example of CSP is the Canadian-Flag Problem, the problem of coloring the Canadian flag (Fig. 1) using only red and white in such a way that each region has a different color from its neighbors and the maple leaf is red. In this problem, the set of variables is V, Y, U, Z, the domains are $D_V = D_Y = D_U = D_Z = \{red, white\}$, and the constraints are $V != Y$, $Y != Z$, $U != Y$, $U = red$ ("!=" means different from). The first three constraints establish the difference of values for pairs of adjacent regions; the fourth constraint establishes that the color of the leaf region is red. The constraint graph of the Canadian-Flag Problem is shown in Fig. 2.

A constraint program for the Canadian-Flag Problem is a syntactical construct that first declares the domain of the variables and then states the constraints (other features can be added, such as search-strategy directives, but this is not of interest to our framework). Constraint programs of the Canadian-Flag Problem for the Chip and Charme systems are shown in Fig. 3 and Fig 4.

The solution (the only one existing) to the Canadian-Flag Problem obtained by executing the programs is $V = red, Y = white, U = red, Z = red$, assigning the value *red* to the left-hand region, *white* to the center region, *red* to the leaf region and *red* to the right-hand region. Such an assignment is a solution because the pairs <*red, white*> and <*white, red*> are in the != relation, and the pair <*red, red*> is in the = relation, so the four constraints are satisfied by the assignment.

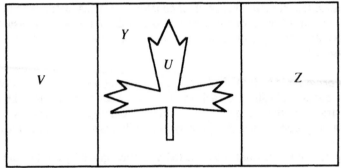

Fig. 1. The Canadian-Flag Problem.

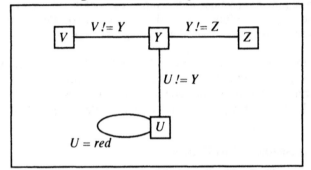

Fig. 2. The constraint graph of the Canadian-Flag Problem.

```
domain canadian-flag([red, white]).

canadian-flag([V, Y, U, Z]) :-
V != Y,
Y != Z,
U != Y,
U = red.
```

Fig. 3. Chip program for the Canadian-Flag Problem. The variable declaration is followedby the four constraints.

```
define main() {
V in [red, white];   Y in [red, white];
U in [red, white];   Z in [red, white];
    V != Y;
    Y != Z;
    U != Y;
    U = red; }
```

Fig. 4. Charme Program for the Canadian-Flag Problem. The variable declaration is followedby the four constraints.

4. Enhancing Constraint Satisfaction Problems

Several notions, such as attribute, object, class, inheritance, etc. are added to the model of CSP. Before the formal presentation of the next sections, the main concepts are informally introduced here.

An *attribute* is a feature of some *type*. Types are associated with domains. An *object* is a collection of attributes. Object attributes correspond to variables in CSP's. The set of attributes of an object defines the *structure* of the object. Objects sharing the same structure are grouped into *classes*. Classes are organized into a *hierarchy*. The structure of a lower class includes that of a higher class. Constraints can be defined both on objects and on classes. Constraints on objects have the same meaning as in CSP's, while constraints on classes induce constraints on objects.

Constraint programming systems may adopt different languages to formulate this richer version of CSP's. We abstract away from the syntactic details of such languages by taking a multi-sorted first-order logic in which the domain of interpretation for sorts has been fixed. The *well-formed formulae* of such a language are obtained by connecting, through logical connectives, predicate symbols whose arguments are terms, i.e., constants, objects, classes, object attributes and class attributes as well as functions on terms. Formulae on classes induce formulae on objects. An *object-oriented constraint satisfaction program* (OOCSP) consists of a declaration of objects and classes, and of a set of formulae expressed in this language. A *solution* is an assignment of domain values to object attributes such that all the formulae, including those induced, are satisfied in the classical sense.

The formulae on objects induced by a formula on classes are called *instances* of the given formula. They are obtained by replacing each class with its objects, or the objects of its derived classes, in all the possible combinations. The notion of instance defines the semantics of OOCSP's, where constraints are defined on objects and classes, in terms of CSP's, where constraints are defined on variables. Simple preprocessors, transforming OOCSP's into CSP's that traditional constraint-programming languages handle, can be obtained by implementing the notion of instance.

5. Object-Oriented Constraint Satisfaction Problems

The formal definition of OOCSP's is presented. An intuitive description of the semantics is also given.

5.1 Formal Definition

Types. A set $T=\Omega\cup\Sigma=\{\tau_1,...,\tau_{n_T}\}$, where $\Omega=\{\omega_1,...,\omega_{n_\Omega}\}$ and $\Sigma=\{\sigma\}$.

Alphabet. The set $\mathcal{A}=K\cup A\cup O\cup C\cup C'\cup F\cup P$ of symbols consists of
a finite set of constant symbols $K=\{k_1,...,k_{n_K}\}$
a finite set of attribute symbols $A=\{a_1,...,a_{n_A}\}$
a countable set of object symbols $O=\{O_1,O_2,...\}$
a finite set of class symbols $C=\{C_1,...,C_{n_C}\}$

a countable set of generic-object symbols $C'=\{C'_1,C''_1,...,C''_{n_C},C''_{n_C}...\}$
a finite set of function symbols $F=\{f_1,...,f_{n_F}\}$
a finite set of predicate symbols $P=\{P_1,...,P_{n_P}\}$.
Symbols are typed: constants and attributes have types in Ω; objects, classes and generic objects have type σ; functions have types of the form $\omega_1 x..x\omega_n \rightarrow \omega$; predicates have types of the form $\tau_1 x..x\tau_n$.

Term. A constant of type ω is a term of type ω.
An object is a term of type σ.
A class is a term of type σ.
A generic object is a term of type σ (think of a generic object C'_i as of a universally quantified variable ranging on the objects of the class C_i). If O is an object, C a class, C' a generic object and a an attribute of type ω, then $O.a$, $C.a$ and $C'.a$ are terms of type ω, called object attribute, class attribute and generic-object attribute, respectively. Attributes alone are not terms, unless associated to objects, classes or generic objects. If f is an n-ary function of type $\omega_1 x..x\omega_n \rightarrow \omega$ and t_i is a term of type ω_i, (i=1,..,n), then $f(t_1,..,t_n)$ is a term of type ω.

Atomic Formula. If P is an n-ary predicate symbol of type $\tau_1 x..x\tau_n$ and t_i is a term of type τ_i, (i=1,..,n), then $P(t_1,..,t_n)$ is an atomic formula.

Well-Formed Formula. Each atomic formula.
If φ and γ are wff's, then $\varphi \wedge \gamma$, $\varphi \vee \gamma$, $\varphi \rightarrow \gamma$ are wff's.

Language. The set L of all wwf's.
The following definitions are made with respect to some given language.

Declaration. The set D of the following functions ($\wp$ denotes the powerset)
  (1) *superclass:* $C \rightarrow \wp(C)$
  (2) *structure:* $C \rightarrow A^h$
  (3) *instance:* $C \rightarrow \wp(O)$
where
  (1) *superclass*$(C_i)=\{C_{i_1},..,C_{i_n}\}$ is a partial function meaning that class C_i is a subclass of classes $C_{i_1},..,C_{i_n}$ (this defines multiple inheritance; for simple inheritance *superclass* is a function)
  (2) *structure*$(C_i)=<a_{i_1},..,a_{i_n}>$ associates to each class C_i a tuple of attributes called the *structure* of C_i, where $a_{i_1} \in A,..,a_{i_n} \in A$; if $C_j \in superclass(C_i)$, then *structure*$(C_i) \supseteq structure(C_j)$.
  (3) *instance*$(C_i)=\{O_{i_1},..,O_{i_n}\}$ associates to each class C_i a set of objects $O_{i_1},..,O_{i_n}$.

Hierarchy. Let $<$ be the partial order on C defined by the transitive closure of *superclass*, i.e., $C_i<C_j$ (read C_i is *derived* from C_j) iff either $C_j \in superclass(C_i)$ or $\exists C_k$ such that $C_k \in superclass(C_i)$ and $C_k<C_j$. The partial order $<$ defines a hierarchy of classes.

Instance. Let $\varphi(C_1,..,C_n,C'_1,..,C'_n)$ be a formula over classes and generic objects. An *instance* of φ is a formula $\varphi'(O_1,..,O_n,O'_1,..,O'_n)$ such that $O_i,O'_i \in instance(C_{k_i})$, for some $C_{k_i} \leq C_i$ (i=1,..,n). In other words, φ' is obtained from φ by substituting each class and generic-object symbol with an object symbol of either that class or of a derived class. Since classes may contain several objects and several classes may be derived from a given one, wff's can be instantiated in several ways.

OOCSP. A pair $P=<D,\mathcal{F}>$, where D is a declaration and $\mathcal{F}$ a set of wff's.

5.2 Semantics

The semantics of OOCSP's, including notions as interpretation, satisfaction, etc., is not presented here for space reasons. Roughly speaking, an *assignment* maps object variables into elemts of their domains. An instance atomic formula is *satisfied* by an assignment if the tuple determined by the interpretation of the argument terms is in the relation associated by the interpretation to the predicate symbol of the atomic formula. Well-formed instance formulae follow the classical interpretation of logical connectives. A formula over classes is satisfied iff all its instances are satisfied. An assignment is a *solution* to an OOCSP iff all the formulae in the problem are satisfied by such an assignment.

6. Design of OOCSP's

Several object-oriented design methodologies have been proposed since more than a decade now (for a survey see [Fow93]). Rather than proposing yet another design methodology, we adopt the Booch methodology, rated as the "best" one in several comparison papers. Only a subset of the Booch methodology is retained for our purposes. Such a subset is common to all the object-oriented design methodologies, so the observations that follow apply to the other methodologies as well.

6.1 The Booch Methodology

Proposed in 1981, improved through use in hundreds of software projects, the Booch methodology is in the public domain and can be adapted as required by the needs of the application. It encompasses a *notation*, for capturing and reasoning about the problem's design decisions and a *process*, for breaking a problem into classes and objects and defining their interactions. The result of the process is a model represented in accordance with the notation.

Notation. The notation consists of the following diagrams:
- class
- object
- module
- process
- state transition
- interaction.

The class and object diagrams show the existence of classes and objects and their relationships in the logical design of a system. The module diagram shows the allocation of classes and objects to modules in the physical design. The process diagram shows the allocation of processes to processors in the physical design. The state transition diagram shows the state space of a given class, the events that cause the transition from one state to the next one, and the actions that result from a state change. The interaction diagram shows the time or event-ordering of events as they are evaluated.

Process. The process is split into *micro* and *macro development*; the former is conceived for the individual developer or the small team and aims at defining the entities and relationships participating to the problem at different levels of abstraction, while the latter serves as a controlling framework for the former.

The micro development process consists of the following activities:
- identify classes and objects
- identify the semantics of these classes and objects
- identify the relationships among these classes and objects
- specify the structure of these classes and objects.

The macro development process consists of the following activities:
- establish the core requirements (conceptualization)
- develop a model (analysis)
- create an architecture (design)
- evolve the implementation (evolution)
- manage post delivery evolution (maintenance).

6.2 Design, Specification and Development

The model proposed for developing OOCSP's is less extended in the horizontal dimension but more in the vertical dimension, compared to the Booch model; in other words, it covers less aspects but in greater detail: some components are dropped, but the remaining ones are enriched. For instance, the physical view and the dynamic semantics are eliminated from the notation, as explained in the next section. On the other hand, objects may be partially specified, and the logical formulae added to the specification of associations allow the system to automatically refine the initial information. These differences are due to the nature of the problems in exam: a general-purpose object-oriented design methodology is targeted to a large scope of different problems, so it must be equipped to represent several different aspects; OOCSP's confine their difficulty in the combinatorial explosion of their search space, but they are usually static and declaratively definable.

The purpose of an object-oriented design methodology is the creation of models of problems that bring discipline to the development of software systems that solve those problems. The purpose of our design methodology is the creation of models of problems that can be directly executed to determine solutions to those problems. This objective bears interesting implications both on the notation and process of the object-oriented design methodology proposed for OOCSP's.

An alternative viewpoint is to not consider the proposed methodology as a design methodology. In fact, a design phase is usually followed by a development phase. This is not the case for OOCSP's, where the model produced is directly interpreted. From this perspective, the model can be considered as a program represented through a graphical notation.

A third viewpoint is to see the process as a specification activity. A specification is the characterization of the relation between input and output. In this context, the input is a set of objects partially defined plus a set of associations among them, while the output is the determination of the missing information that respects the associations. The specification can be directly executed to compute the output.

Our choice is to continue to refer to it as an object-oriented design methodology, keeping in mind that the product of the activity can be viewed either as a model directly interpretable, or as a program expressed in a graphical formalism, or even as an executable specification.

6.3 Notation

The subset of the notation that Booch suggests to apply during analysis and early design, consisting basically of the class and object diagrams, is here adopted. This is also called the *logical view* of the system, since it describes the existence and meaning of the key abstractions and mechanisms that form the problem space, as opposed to the *physical view*, that describes the concrete software and hardware composition of the system's implementation. The physical view is not of interest in our framework because no software or hardware systems have to be developed.

Class, object, module and process diagrams define the *static* meaning of a problem. The *dynamic* semantics, such as object creation and destruction, messages, external events, etc., is defined by the state transition and the interaction diagrams. We are not concerned with dynamic aspects because in our approach objects evolve through constraints rather than through messages; also, objects are assumed static and no external events are (at least for now) considered.

Class and object diagrams are merged into a single diagram in which class icons include the icons of their object instances within them. This corresponds to the intuitive set-element notation in which the elements of a set are depicted inside it. The notation consists of graphical entities that are combined to generate *object-constraint graphs*, the graphical models of OOCSP's. The basic notation for the design of OOCSP's is shown in Fig. 5.

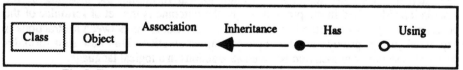

Fig. 5. The notation consists of graphical entities that are combined into object-constraint graphs, the graphical models of OOCSP's.

Dotted boxes denote *classes*; solid boxes denote *objects*; undirected edges denote *associations*; directed edges, with the arrow at the end of the base class, denote *inheritance*; edges with a close circle at the end of the containing class denote aggregation (*has*); edges with an open circle at the end of the using class denote the *using* relationship. Although class and object icons have the shape of clouds in the Booch notation, Booch himself observes that to facilitate drawing diagrams, rectangles are acceptable alternatives for representing classes and objects [Boo94] (this is also similar to the Rumbaugh notation).

Nodes are logically on two different levels: classes are at a higher level because they contain objects that can only be within classes. On the other hand, edges can join classes to classes, objects to objects and classes to objects. Association edges are labeled with names to which corresponds (in the specification) a formula defining the meaning of the associations.

In the examples of models presented in former stages of this research, classes and objects were graphically depicted on two different plans. It was pointed out by colleagues and reviewers that the readably of complex models was quite compromised by that choice. For this reason, we represent now objects within classes, rather than on a different plane.

6.4 Process

Being the macro development process a management concern, independent from the programming paradigm or language, it is no further discussed here: if desired, it can be adopted without major changes.

The micro development process that we propose for OOCSP's consists of the following four steps:
- identify classes and objects
- identify the semantics of these classes and objects
- identify the associations among these classes and objects
- identify the semantics of these associations.

The purpose of the first step is identifying classes and objects to establish the boundaries of the problem. The purpose of the second step is establishing the features of the abstractions identified at the previous step; the outcome is the program declaration. The purpose of the third step is identifying the dependencies among abstractions. The fourth step of the Booch methodology is not included in the process because there is no need to map abstractions on the physical model. It is replaced by a new step that formally identifies, through logical formulae, the meaning of the associations identified in the previous steps; the outcome is the set of formulae of the program. In the Booch methodology, the semantic association between abstractions is expressed just to provide a clear input to implementation. This new step formally defines the semantic association between abstractions in a logical language.

The process is incremental and iterative. It is incremental because when new classes, objects or associations are identified, existing classes, objects and associations can be refined and improved. It is iterative, because the definition of new classes, objects and associations often gives new insights on the problem that allow the user to simplify and generalize the design.

7. Example

The Bridge Problem [Van89] is a real-life project-planning problem consisting of minimizing the time to build a five-segment bridge (see Fig. 6). The project (see Fig. 7) includes 46 tasks (*A1*, *P1*, etc.) that process bridge components (*pillar1*, *abutment1*, etc.) and employ resources (excavator *Ex*, concrete-mixer *CM*, etc.). The constraints of the problem include 31 precedence constraints (execute task *T5* before task *V2*, execute task *M5* before task *T4*, etc.), 77 resource constraints (task *A1* and *A2* cannot overlap because they both employ the excavator, tasks *T2* and *T5* cannot overlap because they both employ the crane, etc.), 60 specific constraints (the time between the completion of task *S1* and the completion of task *B1* is at most 4 days, the time between the completion of task *A4* and the completion of task *S4* is at most 3 days, etc.), for a total of 168 constraints.

7.1 Traditional Solution

The solution to the Bridge Problem obtained with traditional constraint languages, such as Chip and Charme, is here outlined.

The Chip program [Van89] consists of 55 (Prolog-like) facts defining the data and of 20 (Prolog-like) procedures defining the process. The total size of the program (data and process) is about 140 lines. Data facts define tasks, durations, resources, components, relations and constraints. Process procedures basically iterate over data to set the appropriate constraints. No code concerns constraint propagation since it is taken into account by the language (and it is in fact what differentiates Chip from Prolog).

The Charme program [Bul91], consists of data (arrays and structures) declarations and of 10 (Pascal-like) procedures defining the process. The total size of the program (data and process) is also about 150 lines. As for the Chip program, the process procedures access data and set constraints. Again, no code concerns constraint propagation, as it is built into the language.

7.2 Proposed Solution

Our methodology is now employed to design the Bridge Problem.

Identify Classes and Objects. The basic class of the problem is *Task*. Tasks can be of 14 different types (*Excavation*, *Foundation*, etc.). Each concrete task is an object, instance of one of such classes. For example, *A1* is an instance of *Excavation*, *P1* is an instance of *Foundation*, etc. The resources (excavator, concrete-mixer, etc.) are also objects (*Ex*, *CM*, etc.), instances of the class *Resource*.

Identify the Semantics of These Classes and Objects. Each task is characterized by a *name*, *start time*, *duration*, *component* that it processes, *resource* that it employs and a set of tasks that come *before* it. All these features are attributes of the generic class *Task* (and of the 14 derived subclasses). The *start time* is the unknown to be determined, so it is a variable. The initial value is 0..200, meaning that the start time of each task is initially unknown, it will be automatically determined by the system, and it will be included between 0 and 200 days. Resources have no attributes, so their structure is empty.

Identify the Associations Among These Classes and Objects. The 31 precedence constraints, the 77 resource constraints and the minimality constraint can be expressed as three class constraints, referred to as *Precedence*, *Disjunction* and *Minimal*, respectively. The 60 specific constraints can also be expressed at the class level, with five class constraints referred to as *K1-K5*. Finally, the standard *Using* relation is defined between the classes *Excavation*, *Piles*, *Formwork*, *Foundation*, *Masonry*, *Delivery*, *Positioning* and *Filling*, and the objects *Ex*, *PD*, *Ca*, *CM*, *Bl*, *Cr*, *Cr* and *Cp*, respectively.

Identify the Semantics of These Associations. The semantics of these associations is specified through logical formulas on classes and objects:

Disjunction. $[Using(Task1, Resource) \land Using(Task2, Resource)] \rightarrow$
$[Task1.start + Task1.duration \leq Task2.start \quad \lor$
$Task2.start + Task2.duration \leq Task1.start]$

Precedence. $[Task1.name \in Task2.previous] \rightarrow$
$[Task1.start + Task1.duration < Task2.start]$

Minimal. $Minimal(Stop.start + Stop.duration)$

Using. $Using(Excavation, Ex), Using(Piles, PD), Using(Formwork, Ca),$
$Using(Foundation, CM), Using(Masonry, Bl), Using(Delivery, Cr),$
$Using(Positioning, Cr), Using(Removal, Cp).$

K1. $[Formwork.component = Foundation.component] \rightarrow$
$[Foundation.start + Foundation.duration - 4 \leq$
$Formwork.start + Formwork.duration]$

K2. $[Excavation.component = Formwork.component] \rightarrow$
$[Formwork.start - 3 \leq Excavation.start + Excavation.duration]$

K3. $Housing.start \leq Formwork.start - 6$

K4. $Masonry.start + Masonry.duration - 2 \leq Removal.start$

K5. $Delivery.start = Beginning.start + 30.$

The design of the Bridge Problem is complete. The model (see Fig. 8) is ready to be interpreted and executed by the system, that automatically solves the problem determining the start time of the tasks. The model consists of 1 base class, 14 derived classes, 46 objects, 1 class relation and 8 class constraints. The fact that there are no constraints on objects means that the model is well conceived, because abstraction has been fully exploited to factorize common information. As a result, the 168 constraints of the problem are expressed with just 8 class constraints, a gain of 21 times, compared to the traditional formulation [Van89].

The problem can be designed in other ways. For example, components could be defined as objects, rather than task attributes. It is just a matter of individual perception of the problem. What has to be kept in mind, is that expressing as much as possible at the class level, i.e., exploiting abstraction, is an important target to be pursued, because it reduces the number of constraints producing models that are more compact and clear.

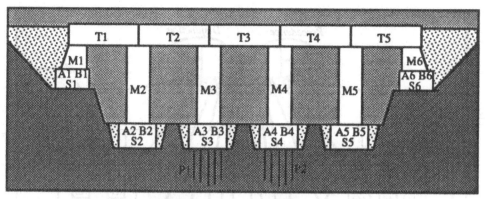

Fig. 6. The five-segment bridge.

N	Name	Description	Duration	Resource
1	PA	beginning of project	0	-
2	A1	excavation (abutment 1)	4	excavator
3	A2	excavation (pillar 1)	2	excavator
4	A3	excavation (pillar 2)	2	excavator
5	A4	excavation (pillar 3)	2	excavator
6	A5	excavation (pillar 4)	2	excavator
7	A6	excavation (pillar 5)	5	excavator
8	P1	foundation pile 2	20	pile-driver
9	P2	foundation pile 3	13	pile-driver
10	UE	erection of tmp. housing	10	-
11	S1	formwork (abutment 1)	8	carpentry
12	S2	formwork (pillar 1)	4	carpentry
13	S3	formwork (pillar 2)	4	carpentry
14	S4	formwork (pillar 3)	4	carpentry
15	S5	formwork (pillar 4)	4	carpentry
16	S6	formwork (abutment 2)	10	carpentry
17	B1	concrete found. (abutment 1)	1	concrete-mixer
18	B2	concrete found. (pillar 1)	1	concrete-mixer
19	B3	concrete found. (pillar 2)	1	concrete-mixer
20	B4	concrete found. (pillar 3)	1	concrete-mixer
21	B5	concrete found. (pillar 4)	1	concrete-mixer
22	B6	concrete found. (abutment 2)	1	concrete-mixer
23	C1	concrete setting (abutment 1)	1	-
24	C2	concrete setting (pillar 1)	1	-
25	C3	concrete setting (pillar 2)	1	-
26	C4	concrete setting (pillar 3)	1	-
27	C5	concrete setting (pillar 4)	1	-
28	C6	concrete setting (abutment 2)	1	-
29	M1	masonry work (abutment 1)	16	bricklaying
30	M2	masonry work (pillar 1)	8	bricklaying
31	M3	masonry work (pillar 2)	8	bricklaying
32	M4	masonry work (pillar 3)	8	bricklaying
33	M5	masonry work (pillar 4)	8	bricklaying
34	M6	masonry work (abutment 2)	20	bricklaying
35	L	delivery of bearers	2	crane
36	T1	positioning (bearer 1)	12	crane
37	T2	positioning (bearer 2)	12	crane
38	T3	positioning (bearer 3)	12	crane
39	T4	positioning (bearer 4)	12	crane
40	T5	positioning (bearer 5)	12	crane
41	UA	removal of tmp. housing	10	-
42	V1	filling 1	15	Caterpillar
43	V2	filling 2	10	Caterpillar
44	K1	costing point 1	0	-
45	K2	costing point 2	0	-
46	PE	end of project	0	-

Fig. 7. The 46 tasks are characterized by a name, an action they perform, a duration and a resource they employ.

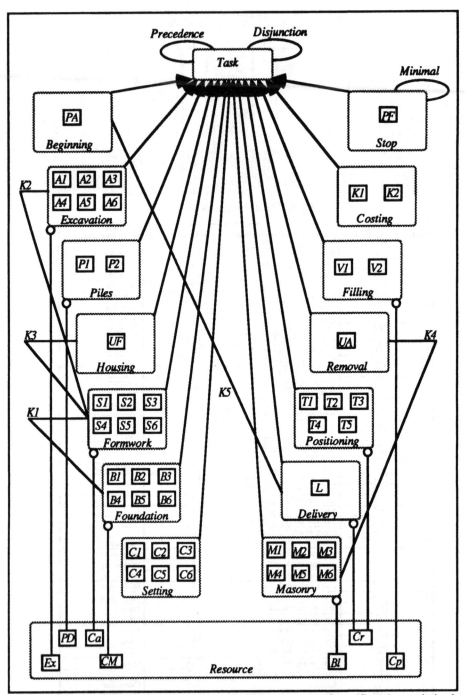

Fig. 8. The Bridge Problem formulated as an OOCSP; 14 classes of specific tasks are derived from the base class *Task*; 7 resources are used to accomplish the tasks as defined by the standard relation *Using*; the 8 class constraints are *Precedence*, *Disjunction*, *Minimal*, *K1*, *K2*, *K3*, *K4*, *K5*.

8. Related Works

Systems integrating some object-oriented component with constraint programming are Thinglab, Socle, Equate, Garnet, Kaleidoscope, Solver and Cspoo.

ThingLab [Bor79] is an augmented planned local propagation system based on virtual variables. Each virtual variable is linked to a real variable through a path. The planner uses the paths to avoid conflicts, cycles and various dataflow problems that are common to local propagation systems. However, because the planner has no information on the implementation of the constraints or the objects, it is unable to handle simultaneous constraints on an object, unless it is explicitly told that those constraints are applied to separate parts of the objects.

Garnet [MGV92] is used to create large-scale user interfaces combining pre-defined objects into collections, using constraints to define the relationship among them, and then attach pre-defined "interactor" objects to cause the objects to respond to input. The interface to objects is usually through direct accessing and setting of data values, rather than through methods. Constraints have to be programmed and can be any Lisp expression that defines the operations on objects.

Devi [ThS94] is a constraint-based 3D geometric editing environment that uses flexible user-interface techniques to simplify the task of editing 3D geometry. It infers constraints on geometric objects as they are created and manipulated. In order to help understand and debug the design in a graphical fashion, DEVI presents the network of constraints and geometry in a constraint-network browser.

Kaleidoscope [FBB92] mixes the declarative nature of constraints with the imperative nature of object-oriented languages. In this object-oriented constraint imperative programming framework, the left variable of an assignment can be connected, through constraints, to other variables, so the current and previous values of variables must be explicitly stored. To handle this possibility, all expressions are defined relative to a current time and a specific semantics of time is proposed.

Solver [Pug92] is a C++ library of classes defining variables, constraints and algorithms. Variables can be object attributes, possibly inherited through a class taxonomy. There are no restrictions on the type of variable values: for instance, it is possible to define variables whose values are objects. New algorithms can be defined by deriving specialized classes from existing algorithm classes.

Cspoo [Kök93] is an object-oriented extension of Lisp with pre-defined classes such as variable, constraint and solver. The class solver is parametrical, so specific strategies and heuristics can be selected for the given problem. Constraints are classes, organized in an extensible hierarchy, but cannot be defined over classes.

Equate [Wil91] is a constraint solving method that obeys the principle of encapsulation, in the sense that constraints do not refer directly to an object's implementation. Equate decomposes constraints in smaller constraints for which solutions are known, then combines those solutions into a solution that satisfies the original constraints. The only constraints taken into account by Equate are equations. Other features of object-orientation besides encapsulation, e.g. inheritance, are not considered.

Socle [Har86] is an hybrid system that contains a structured partitioning component and a constraint component. The former component is supported by a frame representation language, the latter by a constraint based language used to express dependencies. In Socle, frame nodes and constraint nodes are separated, so the advantage of structured decomposition are reflected into constraints.

Codm [SRR94] is an object-based data model to represent partially-specified information. A declarative language, Coql, can be used to reason with information representaed in the Codm. A Coql program infers new relationships between existing objects and monotonically refines objects, in response to additional information.

The objective of the framework proposed in this paper, the graphical design of models of CSP's that can be automatically executed, is original with respect to the mentioned works, but they relate to such an objective at some degree: ThingLab, Garnet and Devi implement "constraints-for-graphics" rather than "graphics-for-constraints" systems; Kaleidoscope, Solver and Cspoo integrate constraints with objects into imperative constraint languages, whereas we propose a graphical setting; Equate, Socle and Codm are closer to our approach because they are declarative languages, but such a feature is employed for purposes (equation solving for Equate, reasoning for Socle and Codm) different from the graphical design of CSP's.

9. Discussion

This work presents a model of combinatorial problems that is expressive enough to represent real-world applications while it is formal enough to be executable. Then it proposes a methodology to define such model interactively.

The motivation goes back to the author's professional experience at the Artificial Intelligence Department of Bull France where the first constraint-programming industrial environment, Charme, and a number of real-world applications [Cha93, Gos93, MaT89, PMT92, SGA91] based on it were developed. From this experience, it followed that a relevant cost in constraint-based applications is due to design. It was also observed the lack of a methodology to define the model of the problem, possibly in tight collaboration with the user.

Compared to the works mentioned in the previous section, the originality of this research consists of integrating in one framework

- an object-oriented constraint language that introduces abstraction and hierarchy on variables and constraints
- a grahical design methodology for the language that yields compact object-oriented models
- a preprocessor that translates such models into executable programs of traditional constraint-programming languages.

The priority of future research is applicative and concerns instantiating the framework to an existing constraint language. This consists of taking a constraint language that is not object-oriented and interfacing it with a preprocessor that automatically maps declarations defined in the proposed language into equivalent declarations of the target language and formulae defining associations into corresponding derived instance sets expressed in the target language.

Acknowledgments

Many thanks to François Fages for fruitful discussions on this topic and to the referees for their helpful comments. The author was partially supported by an assistantship of the French Government in collaboration with Ministero Italiano degli Affari Esteri.

References

[Bor79]   A. Borning: Thinglab: A Constraint-Oriented Simulation Laboratory, *Ph.D. Thesis*, Stanford University, CA, 1979.

[Boo94]   G. Booch: *Object-Oriented Analysis and Design with Applications*, Redwood City, CA: Benjamin/Cum., II Ed., 1994.

[Bul91]   Bull S.A. Ed.: *Manuel Charme First*, Bull Publication No. 95-F2-52GN-REV0, Annexe A, pages 29-49, Paris, France, 1991.

[Cha93]   P. Chan: Charme Technical Bulletin, *Bull BSP/CEDIAG Internal Report No.1-5*, Paris, France, 1993.

[Col90]   A. Colmerauer: An Introduction to Prolog III, *Communications of the ACM*, Vol. 33 (7), 1990.

[Din88]   M. Dincbas, P. Van Hentenryck, H. Simonis, A. Aggoun, T. Graf, F. Berthier: The Constraint Logic Programming Language CHIP, *Proc. of the Int. Conf. on Fifth Generation Computer Systems*, Tokyo, Japan, 1988.

[FBB92]   B. Freeman-Benson, A. Borning: Integrating Constraints with an Object-Oriented Language, *Proc. of the 1992 European Conference on Object-Oriented Programming*, June 1992.

[Fow93]   M. Fowler: A Comparison of Object-Oriented Analysis and Design Methods, in *Approaches to Object-Oriented Analysis and Design*, A. Carmichael Ed., Ashgate, 1993.

[Gos93]   V. Gosselin: Train Scheduling Using Constraint Programming Techniques, *Actes 13eme Journée International sur les Systèmes Expert et Leur Application*, Avignon, 1993.

[Har86]   D. R. Harris: A Hybrid Object and Constraint Representation Language, *AAAI-86*, pages 986-990, Philadelphia, Pennsylvania, 1986.

[Jaf88]   J. Jaffar, S. Michaylov, P.J. Stuckey: The CLP(R) Language System, *draft for Constraints & Languages W/S*, 1988.

[KoJ84]   M. Konopasek, S. Jayaraman: *The TK!Solver Book*, Osborne/McGraw-Hill, Berkeley, CA, 1984.

[Kök93]   T. Kökény: CSPOO: Un Système à Résolution de Contraintes Orienté Objet, *Réprésentation Par Objet*, La Grande Motte, pages 39-49, July 1993.

[Kum92]   V. Kumar: Algorithms for Constraint Satisfaction Problems: a Survey. *AI Magazine*, 13, 1992, 32-44.

[Lel88]   W. Leler: *Constraint Programming Languages*, Addison-Wesley Publishing Company, 1988.

[MaT89] J. Marcovich, Y. Tourbier: Une Application de la Programmation par Contraintes: Construction de Plans d'Experience Orthogonaux au Sens Strict avec Condor, *Actes des Journées Internationales d'Avignon*, 1989.

[MGV92] B. A. Myers, D. A. Giuse, B. Vander Zanden: Declarative Programming in a Prototype-Instance System: Object-Oriented Programming Without Writing Methods, *OOPSLA'92*, pages 184-200, 1992.

[Opl89] A. Oplobedu: Charme: Un Langage Industriel de Programmation par Contraintes, *Actes 9eme Journée International sur les Systèmes Expert et Leur Applications*, Vol. 1, 55-70, Avignon, 1989.

[PMT92] M. Paltrinieri, A. Momigliano, F. Torquati: Scheduling of an Aircraft Fleet, *AAAI Tech. Rep.* SS-92-01. Also available as *NASA Tech. Rep.* FIA-92-17, NASA Ames, Moffet Field, CA, USA, 1992.

[Pug92] J.-F. Puget: Programmation Par Contraintes Orientée Objet, *12th International Conference on Artificial Intelligence, Expert Systems and Natural Language*, pages 129-138, Avignon, France, 1992.

[Rot93] A. Roth: Constraint Programming: A Practical Solution to Complex Problems, *AI Expert*, pages 36-39 Sept. 1993.

[SGA91] D. Sciamma, V. Gosselin, D. Ang: Constraint Programming and Resource Scheduling: The Charme Approach, *Gintic Symposium on Scheduling*, Singapore, 1991.

[SRR94] D. Srivastava, R. Ramakrishnan, P. Z. Revesz: Constraint Objects, *Second International Workshop on Principles and Practice of Constraint Programming*, Orcas Island, WA, May 1994.

[ThS94] S. Thennarangam, G. Singh: Inferring 3-dimensional Constraints with DEVI, *Second International Workshop on Principles and Practice of Constraint Programming*, Orcas Island, WA, May 1994.

[Van89] P. Van Hentenryck: *Constraint Satisfaction in Logic Programming*, The MIT Press, Cambridge, Massachusetts, 1989.

[VaW82] C. J. Van Wyk: A High-Level Language for Specifying Pictures, *ACM Transactions on Graphics* 1(2), 163-182.

Object-Oriented Representation of Shape Information

G. Boccignone, A.Chianese[1], M. De Santo, A. Picariello[2]

DI[3]E - Dipartimento di Ingegneria dell'Informazione e Ingegneria Elettrica
Università di Salerno
84084 Fisciano (Salerno), Italy

[1]DIS - Dipartimento di Informatica e Sistemistica
Università di Napoli
v. Claudio, 21 - 80125 Napoli, Italy

[2]IRSIP-CNR - Istituto di Ricerca Sistemi Informatici Paralleli
v. Pietro Castellino, 111 - 80131 Napoli, Italy

> *Oscura e profonda era e nebulosa*
> *tanto che, per ficcar lo viso a fondo,*
> *io non vi discernea alcuna cosa...*
> (Dante Alighieri, *Divina Commedia*, Inferno, Canto IV)

Abstract. The Object Oriented paradigm is considered a natural and effective approach for Image Processing and Analysis purposes. Nevertheless, despite its intuitive convenience, the use of object orientation within this complex realm has not undergone to a rapid growth as happened in other fields, where such paradigm has been introduced. The most part of reported applications deals with system architecture problems or is tailored to specific case-studies. In this paper, with the aim of developing a more comprehensive framework, we outline an Object Oriented model for Image Processing And Analysis, and we discuss how to address the critical issue of representing shape information. A preliminary prototype of the model is presented, and results of experimental work summarized.

1 Introduction

With respect to images and, more generally, to spatial information, the Object-Oriented (O-O) approach has been mainly used for storage and retrieval purposes, in order to overcome typical drawbacks of the relational data model in handling 2-D data.

An object representation for pictorial information exploits the fact that any spatial entity having a defined shape can be figured as an individual object, thus capturing the structure of the image data in a hierarchical fashion. Objects can be created at various levels of spatial resolution and the information about the hierarchical links between objects can be stored along with the objects themselves. On this basis, the O-O models can be precisely used, and abstract formalisms for representing spatial knowledge can be supported [1].

Unfortunately, the extensive work reported in this field of application is of little help if images are approached from an analysis and recognition point of view. It is a matter of evidence that when dealing with the Image Analysis And Computer Vision domains, far other complex questions arise, than those posed within the database field.

On the one hand, as first pointed out by Rutovitz [2] there are peculiar processing requirements to meet. Several types of operations on images produce other images, or image related structures. An example is segmentation, which can give origin to an arbitrary number of new objects that may or may not be of the same class of the input object. Object creation is a frequent activity in Image Processing and Analysis (IP&A), stressing the need for object destruction, record keeping, link control. Composite objects are of great importance, as well as methods operating on several objects simultaneously like, for example, dilation by a structuring element, convolution by a matrix of numbers, finding the Voronoi polygon determined by a set of objects, etc.

On the other hand, moving toward the field of the analysis, description and recognition of images, the challenge turns to be even harder: the central purpose is to describe and to identify objects within a scene, analyzing one or more images of the scene itself. For such ends, shape (or equivalently, structure, form) certainly brings the most important information. The vision process starts with a spatial representation of a two-dimensional or a three dimensional scene. Raw images representing the scene may be computationally thought of as continuous functions of two variables defined on some bounded and usually rectangular region of a plane. These value maps usually are video images or stored digital images, where the physical meaning of the values depends on the type of sensors that have been used during detection. From this standpoint, any type of observation over the bare value map can be considered as a structuring activity which builds forms over form in a recursive fashion [3]: the resulting image is thus the primitive value map enriched and organized according to the set of structures induced over the initial image.

A suitable and operational definition of shape can be that proposed by Nagy [4]: a property of both a set of objects and a particular method of observation or measurement. Since the objective of image analysis is a quantitative treatment of shape, one should be able to formalize the concept in a suitable fashion. In the literature [3, 5, 6], it is largely agreed that a successive combination of intermediate shape hierarchies is a convenient representation.

Within the IP&A and Computer Vision fields the problem of building shape structures over a raw value map is related to the choice of the data structures for representing them. In the following discussion we shall use the term *shape structure* for representing perceptive structures induced on the image, and the term *data structure* for indicating the organization of data which characterize the shape structure. While a shape structure is generated according to the purposes of observation, a data structure may be chosen, beyond its data abstraction and representation capabilities, to save space and to allow for fast access to data. A variety of data structures have been used in picture processing [7, 8, 9].

Previous works devoted to the subject of this paper and reported in the literature, have addressed partial issues of this framework. An early and appealing discussion of how O-O techniques could be used as the basis for an IP&A system is reported by

Piper and Rutovitz in [2]. They introduce images as subtypes of the W-object class which is defined by a type member, a geometrical region (function domain), a function definition (grey table), and a property list. Image processing subroutines access W-objects by means of "workspace" objects created dynamically. In such way the authors generalize a variety of data structures based on interval coding representation, being their major concern, the transition from C to C++ language, of an existing image processing system [10].

Jagadish and O'Gorman [11] have presented an object model for image recognition, and their major interest was thus in concept modelling with respect to line-image analysis. Authors point out several advantages of using the O-O paradigm in image recognition but also refer some difficulties in strictly adhering to traditional notion of object orientation. They organize line images in two structural hierarchies, physical and logical, communicating one another. As the authors underline, as long as they constrain the image to a single image recognition paradigm, the notion of level within the hierarchy is unambiguous; but it is not, in the case different algorithms are adopted with respect to different parts of the image.

Line processing is also addressed by Taniguchi et al. [12], who have developed an image processing support system in which the image data type is modelled as an object implementing a frame structure; new image classes are derived by inheritance, and a detailed hierarchy of image classes is built. Formalization and representation of image concept is discussed by Yoshida and Hino [13] within a "pure" object-oriented framework; therein, object based model is proposed for representing both the image concept hierarchies and sensed stimuli organization; the work also discusses, how to find the concept which matches a sample, simulating the search in concept hierarchy by means of the agent/blackboard model. Other works have been mainly concerned with the goal of building specific architecture's for realizing image processing systems [14, 15, 16].

In our research we have followed a different approach, so as to look at the problem in a more general framework. The main goal of our work is to develop a comprehensive O-O approach to the definition and the use of data models in Image Processing and Analysis.

With respect to the definition of the O-O data model, the rationale behind this framework takes into account some critical issues. First of all, extensive research on data structures pursued in the Computer Vision field should be taken into account as a starting point. Secondly, a reformulation of shape structures in a O-O perspective must emphasize the critical aspects of coping with the use of different data structures.

It must be noted that, with respect to the use of the model, it is necessary to incorporate within the model itself, the definition of Processor objects together with processing protocols describing the dynamics of interactions among Image objects and Processor objects. In this paper we mainly concentrate on the definition of the data model, being the processing protocols matter of going on research. Nevertheless, we shall outline main features of this last issue for a better understanding of our work.

In Section 2 we introduce and discuss an O-O model of shape. In Section 3 we highlight relevant features of the model by means of some examples. In Section 4 we discuss results and introduce some current research guidelines we are at present pursuing.

2. Overview of the Model.

We shall introduce a model in which the general classes of images are represented by an abstract data type (ADT) *Image* which can be obtained from the aggregation of a set *V* of types *VMap*, representing the primitive raw value maps, observed and measured by an observer, and a set *S* with elements *SMap*, each grouping all the structural shapes built over a *VMap* in successive observations.

We can therefore see an *Image* as the pair *Image* = <*V, S*>.

The ADT *VMap*, can be modelled as the 3-tuple *VMap* = < *ImageMemory, Write, Read*>.

The signature *ImageMemory* stands for the total function *ImageMemory* : *ImDomain* → *Value* where *ImDomain* = $0,..., (HRes \times VRes - 1)$, and *HRes, VRes, Value* ∈ *N*, being *N* the set of naturals, *HRes* and *VRes* respectively the horizontal and vertical resolution, and *Value* the intensity value of an element (e.g., the grey value of a pixel). *ImageMemory* is thus the abstraction of any memory support of the value map, either virtual or physical.

Thus, given an element $p \in ImDomain$, the signature *Read* simply denotes the function which reads the value of *p*, while the signature *Write* indicates the operation of writing a new element in the *ImageMemory* and is obtained by overriding of the *ImageMemory* with a function that maps element *p* to the new value *Val*.

In defining the *Image* ADT, there are some constraints that we must introduce. When an object of the class *Image* is created, it can have one or more *VMap* objects and only one *SMap* object, i.e. $Card(V) \geq 1, Card(S) = 1$. Since we will in the following concentrate on *SMap* modelling, for the sake of simplicity, we assume a single *VMap* object in the Image.

We do not assume in principle that a *VMap* may only exist as included in an Image object. In fact a *VMap* can have an its own life until any observation starts on it for building the *Image*. Such degree of freedom expresses the fact that, when dealing with a real vision system, it is not implausible that a *VMap* object references a frame memory region of an image processing board, which is actually independent from images successively built on it. For the identical reason, the same *VMap* could be used in different *Images* by different observers.

On the contrary, for semantic convenience, we assume that each *SMap* uniquely refers to a *VMap* and to an *Image*.

The concept of shape structures is strictly connected to that of data structure. Among different data structure families, a powerful and general one is that of Spatial Data Structure (SDS) [17] which is a recursive structure that can be used to represent different types of objects and relationships. SDS generalizes hierarchical structural descriptions.

In order to extend in an O-O perspective such concepts, so as to tailor them as a building block of our image model, meanwhile overwhelming some drawbacks of realization and management of classical complex recursive data structures, we must cope with some problems. The *SMap* must be defined recursively as an aggregation of structural objects. More precisely, *SMap* is an aggregation neither fixed nor simply variable but it can be made up by components which are of the same class of the aggregate itself. Moreover, the twofold nature (node/relation) of such structural objects is stated dynamically by the level at which we consider them.

Let us characterize the *SMap* as a class including at least an object belonging to the class *SNode*, representing a family of structural node objects. Such structural node objects model the structural shape concept. Thus, we define as structural node a recursive object that might identify, at each level, either a node of a relation or a relation over other nodes.

At the most general level, the *SNode* class is an ADT defined as the 4-tuple $SNode = < NA, RA, FN, FR >$, being the sets of properties *NA* and *RA* respectively the node attributes and relationship attributes, and *FN* and *FR* respectively the sets of node operations and relation operations.

We can therefore think of such ADT as composed by two atomic ADTs: the *Node*, defined as the pair $Node = \langle NA, NF \rangle$; the structural relation *SRel* defined as the pair $SRel = \langle RA, RF \rangle$. Thus, $SNode = SRel \circ Node$. An *SRel* within its relational attributes will include a k-tuple $< l_1, ..., l_k >, k \in N$, being $l_i \in L$ a linking reference to an SNode, $L \subseteq SRel \times SNode \subseteq RA$. We define k, as the degree deg_S of the *SRel*, $k = deg_S$. According to the value of k, *SRel* will represent relational structures of different type: for $k=1$, linear lists; $k=2$, binary trees; $k=4$, quartic-trees; $k>4$, graphs.

Moving from the ADT notation into the O-O notation [18], classes and relations among them can be represented as in the following figure (Fig.1).

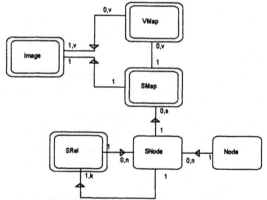

Figure 1. An Object Oriented representation of the Image model

The notation shows how the *Image* class is given by composing *VMap* and *SMap* classes, denoting composition with *part-of* relations indicated by arrows. By means of *part-of* relations we represent either a proper inclusion of a class within another or a relation $l_i \in L$. Range markings on lines show explicitly lower and upper bounds of mappings that may occur among objects. The ranges for mappings among *Image*, *VMap* and *SMap* classes quantify the constrains assumed at the beginning of this Section.

An *SMap* may have either a number *l* of *SNodes* or none when no observations on the *VMap* have been performed. The *SNode* class aggregates *SRel* and *Node* classes. Only a specific *SRel* can be part of an *SNode*. Meanwhile, *SRel* may refer to a different number *k* of *SNodes*. The graphical formalization visualizes straightforwardly the recursive definition of the *SNode* class by means of a closed loop on *part-of* relations between *SRel* and *SNode*.

By means of such compact representation, we can express basic structures needed in IP&A like lists, graphs, quadtree.

We have at this point defined the basic features of the O-O data model. Nevertheless, in order to satisfy the initial assumption that shape is a property of both a set of objects and a particular method of observation or measurement, it is necessary to incorporate within the model, definition of Processor objects together with processing protocols describing the dynamics of interactions among Image objects and Processor objects. This specific subject goes beyond the aims of the present paper, but we will anyway outline some guidelines, with the twofold aim of providing a clearer glance of the overall model, and of clarifying some of the example we will give.

The approach, we are at the moment experimenting, starts from the idea that a measurement/observation on an image can be represented as an interaction of an image processor object *P* (alternatively, a *probe*) with the image object *I*. We can consider such interaction, at the most general level, as the setting of a "point of view" on the image: such *action upon* the image is the induction on the image of a property. More precisely, in the case of a shape observation, the property is a structure S_i.

From a general standpoint, the action of *P* on an object (or a set of objects) of the class Image can be considered a transformation *Image* → *Image'* .

Since an image *I* is the pair *<V, S>*, we assume to distinguish between two classes of probes: the value-map processors *(VMP)*, that operate only on the value-map $V^* \in V$ of the image; the shape-map processors *(SMP)* which act on the shape-map $S^* \in S$ of *I*. For instance, some low level processing operations (e.g., a filtering) can be seen as *VMP* actions, while intermediate and high level processing operations (e.g., the description of an image) are *SMP* actions.

Note that the action scope is defined considering which object of the couple *(V*,S*)* changes at the end of the observation: a segmentation process is to be considered as *SMP*, since it starts from the value map but it induces a new structure $S^* = \{R_1, R_2, ..., R_n\}$, namely the ordered set of regions in which the image has been partitioned.

We may summarize the protocol of interaction of a shape probe SP_i with an image I_j as follows.

SP_i receives a message requesting a specific operation O_k to be performed on I_j: $SP_i.O_k(I_j, <p_1...p_n>)$, where $<p_1...p_n>$ is an *n-tuple* of parameters, some of which for asking SP_i to use a specific relational structure (*request level*). SP_i links to I_j and exchange preliminary information (*handshaking level*). For instance, if *VMap* is needed for computation, SP_i requests to I_j whether *VMap* is realized on some physical device: if so, it links also to a *DeviceManager* object for specific operations on physical devices. At a successive level SP_i serves the requested operation (*service level*). Then, it adds a new structural node object to the shape map. This means that new properties are given to the *SMap* object, and for composition these are attributed to the *Image*, changing therefore its state space. We call this last action of the probe on the image, the *marking*.

In the coming Section we present basic features of a preliminary implementation of the model and provide some examples.

3. Implementation and Examples

A preliminary prototype has been developed for experimental purposes and is working on the platform defined in [14]. Its main features will be pointed out by showing key parts of the code, written using C++ language.

According to the abstract types previously introduced, we provide the following classes: Image, SMap, VMap, SNode, SRel, Node.

When constructed by the operator Image(), the basic Image class always includes at least a void value map and a shape map, referencing them by pointers pvmap and psmap.

A second constructor Image(VMap *pOldVMap) gives the possibility of building a new image over an existing value map:

```
class Image{
//...
public:
        SMap *psmap;
        VMap *pvmap;
        //...
        Image();
        ~Image();
        Image( VMap *pOldVMap);
        //...
};
```

The class VMap allows the observer to manipulate the elements of the image. The manipulation must take into account the physical device on which the image data are stored.

For the sake of generality, in our implementation we defined a structure DATA in which data are allocated. We keep all the information about the format of image data (e.g., horizontal resolution, vertical resolution, colour planes, etc.) in a DATAINFO structure.

```
class VMap{
        HDevice *pdevice; //the pointer to the physical device
        DATA *pdata;
        DATAINFO *pdi;
//...
public:
        VMap( );
        VMap(Hdevice *pActualDevice, DATAINFO *padi);
        ~VMap();
        Value (*Read) (int, int);
        void (*Write)(int, int, Value);
        void setDevice(HDevice *);
        HDevice *getDevice();
//...
}.
```

Note that operators Read and Write are implemented as function pointers, since they depend on the way the structure DATA is chosen. The constructors of VMap must allocate memory for DATA, and define the physical device.

The SMap class is built assuming that it includes at least a reference to an object of the type SNode:

```
class SMap{
// ... list of features collected in SMap
public:
        SMap();
        ~SMap();
        SNode *psnode;
//....
}.
```

The SNode class realizes shape structures whose specific nature is characterized by means of a NodeType:

```
class SNode{
//...
        NodeType type;
        SRel *psrel;
        Node *pnode;
public:
        SNode();
        SNode(int , Node *);
        ~SNode();
        virtual void add(Node *);
        virtual NodeType IsKindOf();
}.
```

It is constructed by means of an object of the class Node, i.e. the class for storing information characterizing the structural nodes, and by means of the class SRel:

```
class SRel{
//...
        SNode **psnode;
        int numberOfRelations;
//...
public:
        SRel();
        SRel(int);
        ~SNode();
//...
}.
```

Objects of this class will have a list of SNodes as private references, and their constructor SRel(int) will provide the possibility of setting the degree of the relation, numberOfRelations.
The next example shows how the model can be used in a real application.

Given a value map obtained acquiring and digitizing a microscope photograph of a C-banded Y-chromosome, the following processing steps are performed:
- segmentation of the value map into regions
- contour extraction of each region.

These steps can be coded as beneath:

```
main(){
        //...
        Image *pImg;
        Contour *pContour, *pList;
        //Acquisition and creation of an Image
        //...
        //we start building the SMap as a list of structures
        pImg->psmap=(SNode *)pList;
        //...
        SegmenterProcessor *SP = new SegmenterProcessor(pImg);
        SP->Segment();
        ContourProcessor *CP = new ContourProcessor();
        CP->ContourFinder(pImg, pContour);
        //...
}.
```

Note the use of two different approaches to the interaction between processor objects and specific data structures. On the one hand, the object SP belonging to the class SegmenterProcessor will adopt its default structure (a quad tree) to perform the segmentation process and store the results. On the other hand, the ContourProcessor receives as a parameter the structure to utilize (in this case, a linear list):

```
void ContourProcessor::ContourFinder(Image *pImg, SNode *pSNode)
{
// ...this is a description of the method:
while( !Stop){
    while( !found){
            // ...detect contour extracting a point P of it
            pSNode->put(P); //adds point to structure
            // ...
    ...}
pImg->psmap->psnode->add( pSNnode);   //this is the marking of the SMap
}.
```

The results of computation are shown in Figure 2.a. The Segmenter has partitioned the value map in regions R1 (background), R2 (Y-chromosome), R3 (centromere). The ContourProcessor has detected the border of regions R2 and R3, respectively C2, C3. Figure 2.b shows the resulting organization of the structures obtained.

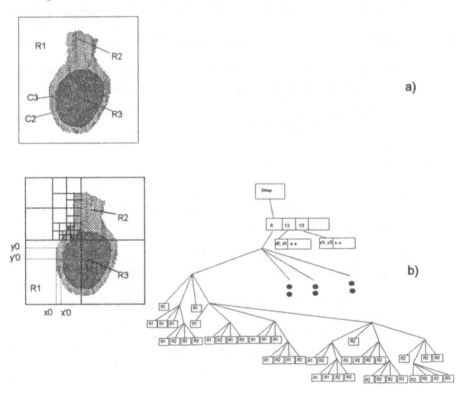

Figure 2. The Chromosome Image detected regions and contours (a) and its SMap representation (b)

4. Discussion and Conclusions

The most relevant result of the presented work is the definition and realization of *shape* as a structural class, which generalizes recursive data structures in the literature. Such generalization directly derives from our definition of *SMap* as a recursive structural class expressed in terms of other structural classes. Each of these classes represents an O-O mapping of a particular data structure together with the operations allowed on it.

In such way, as shown in the last example of previous Section, the definition of an *Image* object through the *SMap*, allows the homogeneous handling of heterogeneous types of data organization within the same Image. According to computational requirements, every *Processor* object can adopt the most suitable data-structure, linking the results of the computation to the *Image*, in spite of their organization.

Great deal of our experimental work is performed within biomedical image processing and cursive script segmentation. For such aims, the present authors have developed an O-O architecture and this has been used as the engineering context for testing the model [14]. In this environment, the possibility of considering the image value map either as a virtual memory device or as a frame memory of a real board has proved to be a reliable tool for exploiting several hardware devices that can be integrated in the context.

It has to be noted that both the decision of reducing the set V to a single *VMap*, and the work carried out by mainly using two dimensional images (as commonly generated in biomedical and document processing fields), lead to a lack of experimentation with respect to 3D scene analysis. However this is not an actual limitation to the model either at the conceptual level or at the design level.

From a conceptual standpoint, we can assume to represent a three dimensional object by a set of characteristic views or aspects, i.e. by a set of occurring two dimensional projections. From a design point of view, the problem can be solved at a twofold level. In a first step, relations with several *VMaps* are taken into account by the Image. In a second step, it is a task of the processors during the handshaking level to ask the image for the setting of the appropriate links.

A drawback of the present model, with respect to more classical data structures introduced in picture processing, is the difficulty of using the defined shape model for thoroughly comparing different shapes. Actually, a relevant point for image processing and analysis purposes, is that one of measuring similarity between two forms as a degree of similarity between two relational structures figuring the forms. For instance, in the case of the spatial data structure, it can be shown that it is possible to define a homomorphism from one structure to another [13]. In this respect, further investigation should be taken into account to work out plausible metrics for measuring distance between structures of heterogeneous objects.

References

1 L. Mohan, R.L. Kashyap: An Object - Oriented Knowledge Representation for Spatial Information. IEEE Trans. on Soft. Eng.,14, n.5, 1988, pp.675-681.

2 J. Piper, D. Rutovitz: An Investigation of Object-Oriented Programming as the Basis for an Image Processing and Analysis System. In: Proc. 9th ICPR, Roma, 1988, pp.1015-1019.

3 L. Uhr: Forms Structure Form at Ever "Higher" and "Lower" Levels. In: Visual Form, Plenum Press 1992, pp. 565-581

4 G. Nagy: The Dimensions of Shape and Form. In: Visual Form, Plenum Press 1992, pp. 409-420

5 M.A. Arbib: Schemas and Neural Networks for Sixth Generation Computing. Journ. of Paral. and Distr. Comp, vol.6,n.2, 1989, pp185-216

6 L. Shapiro: View-Class Representation and Matching of 3-D Objects. In: Visual Form, Plenum Press 1992, pp. 479-494

7 L. Shapiro: Data Structures for picture processing: A Survey. CGIP 11, 1979, pp. 162-184

8 H. Samet, R.E. Webber: Hierarchical Data and Algorithms for Computer Graphics. Part I: Fundamentals. IEEE Comp. Graph. and Appl., May 1988, pp. 48-68.

9 H. Samet, R.E. Webber: Hierarchical Data and Algorithms for Computer Graphics. Part II: Applications. IEEE Comp. Graph. and Appl., July 1988, pp. 59-75.

10 J. Piper, D. Rutovitz: Data Structures for Image Processing in a C Language and Unix Environment. Pattern Recognition Letters, vol. 3, 1985, pp. 119-129.

11 .V. Jagadish, L. O' Gorman: An Object Model for Image Recognition. IEEE Computer, vol. , n., 1989, pp. 33-41.

12 R. Taniguchi, M. Amamiya: Knowledge Based Image Processing System: IPSSENS-II. In: Proc. 3rd. IPA Warwick, UK ,1989, pp.462-466

13 N. Yoshida, K. Hino: An Object Oriented Framework of Pattern Recognition Systems. In: Proc. OOPSLA '88, pp. 259-266.

14 G. Boccignone, A. Chianese, M. De Santo, A. Picariello: Building an Object-Oriented Environment for Document Processing. In: Proc. ICDAR '93, Tokio, 1993, pp.

15 P. Gemmar, G. Hofele: An Object Oriented Approach for an Iconic Kernel System (IKS). In: Proc.10th Int.Conf. Patt. Rec., Atlantic City, 1990, pp 85-90.

16 H. Sato et al.: The VIEW-Station Environment: Tools and Architecture for a Platform Independent Image Processing Workstation. In: Proc. 10 th. Int.Conf. Patt. Rec., Atlantic City, 1990, pp 576-583.

17 L. G. Shapiro, R. M. Haralick: A General Spatial Data Structure. In: Proc. IEEE Conf. Pattern Recog. Image Process., Chicago, 1978, pp. 238-289.

18 P. Coad, E. Yourdon: Object-Oriented Analysis. Yourdon Press, Prentice Hall Inc, New Jersey, 1991.

The Development of an Object-Oriented Multimedia Information System

M. P. Papa, G. Ragucci, G. Corrente, M. Ferrise, S. Giurleo, D. Vitale

Bull HN Sud S.p.A. - Area R&D "Electronic Document Management"
Nucleo Industriale Pianodardine - 83030 Prata P.U. (Avellino) - ITALY
Tel. +39-825-764240 Fax +39-825-764230 Email m.papa@bsav.bull.it

Abstract. In this paper we focus on some implementation issues related to the development of an experimental Object-Oriented Multimedia Information System for an Office Environment which is going on in the R&D laboratories of Bull HN Sud. Multimedia objects in our system are created, structured, filed, retrieved and browsed. In this article we give a quick introduction of the whole system and a brief synthesis of the experience on using the OMT methodology. Than, we describe an Object-Oriented model of multimedia documents, based on the concept of Document Conceptual Structure, which is very useful in the process of efficient information retrieval. Moreover, we discuss in more details the architecture of the working prototype and two important implementation issues: the first one concerns with the development of an advanced browser of multimedia documents using the OLE (Object Linking & Embedding) technology, the second one has to do with our visual programming experience.

1.   Introduction

The OOCM (Object Oriented Content Management) project which we are going to talk about in this paper has the aim to improve and to add new advanced functionalities to ImageWorks, the multimedia platform of Bull. It has also the objective to deeply introduce developers of the "Electronic Document Management" area to the Object-Oriented techniques. In fact, the use of Object Orientation represents the only way to solve the software crisis question, strongly present in the industry world. That's why the development of this project embraces several aspects involving the Object-Oriented paradigm that go from the analysis and design to the implementation, from the choice of the C++ programming language to that of the Object Oriented Data Base Management System. It is very hard to synthesize in few pages the complete results of our experience, so we give a brief overview of the entire project and than we examine in more detail some implementation issues.

Multimedia documents in OOCM are collection of objects of different types such as text, images, voice, graphics and traditional formatted data. The multimedia document is the main information unit managed by our system. Electronic form of documents may be created in different ways. Multimedia documents may be interactively generated in a given station using an application that is external to our system. Alternatively, documents may be in a paper form. A scanner device and OCR capability are used for extracting information from the document. Moreover, they may be created by an application, which is proprietary of our system, specialized to deal with a certain kind of data. Finally, we might have a document which is a combination of portions arrived from all these different sources. In order to manage this hetereogeneous environment the system has to deal in a different way with each type of data.

The document model represents the unifying concept which gives the possibility to integrate different kinds of data and manage them in a homogeneous way. In the third chapter we synthesize the multimedia document model which we have designed and implemented; a complete description of this model is done in [12].

Document in our system exists in term of its *Content Portions* and of the following abstractions: *Profile, Conceptual Structure, Miniature and fasttalk*. Abstractions are known to the user and may assist him in many occasions, such as in the retrieval session to identify the appropriate document.

Profile is a set of attributes that characterizes the document and is used mainly for retrieval purposes. Examples of attributes are name, creation data, author, etc. They consist of formatted data as booleans, integers, reals and strings.

Conceptual Structure describes the document content in terms of its conceptual components. A conceptual component indicates a portion of a document having a particular meaning for the user and which can be used for some specific purpose. Examples are the address in a letter or the title, authors and abstract in a technical report. For many operations, such as query specification by content and document creation, it is important to see a document in terms of its conceptual components. In chapter 3 a clear description of the conceptual structure is done.

Miniatures are realistic visual abstractions of the document, which are displayed for the user during browsing. Miniature can be a reduced image of a meaningful page of the document.

Fasttalk is created manually by the user. It contains a short description othe document's content, or an excerpt of the document. Fasttalk, like miniatures, help the user during retrieval. On the basis of what the user sees and hears, he can decide if the document is one of the ones he wants retrieved. A similar idea was already experimented in a research prototype developed some years ago at University of Toronto ([3], [4])

Profile's attributes and text historically represent the only active components during the retrieval process of multimedia documents [1]. In fact, Data Base Management Systems and Information Retrieval technologies make available techniques for access methods definition and query processing aspects concerning attribute and text data respectively. A research activity has been done in the past years on document retrieval based on image content so that images contained in documents become active components in the formulation of queries and, therefore, in accessing documents ([5], [6], [13]).

In our system we assume to use document abstractions in order to improve the retrieval process and to provide the user with an help in query formulation and refining. However, we basically offer features of attributes and text searching; in addition, we give the possibility to formulate mixed queries on components of the documents conceptual structure; moreover, image (miniatures) data participate to the activity of user query refining.

The development of the system is based on a distributed architecture working on a client-server paradigm. Functionalities such as creation, modification and presentation of multimedia information are accessible to the user from the client workstation. Specific User Agents are provided in order to manipulate document structures. At the server station, an Object Oriented DBMS and an Information Retrieval Engine provide efficient filing and retrieval management. Hypermedia capabilities are provided as well, therefore user may also navigate links among documents. Documents are stored in large-capacity storage devices like optical disks and jukeboxes of optical disks residing at the server workstation.

In the fourth chapter we describe the system architecture which we have designed following the OMT guidelines [15]. Finally, we examine two implementation issues that we consider relevant in the O-O software development. They are related with the visual programming experience in the construction of the user interface.

2. The OMT Methodology

The whole development of the project has been guided by the OMT (Object Modelling Technique) methodology by which we were inspired in order to establish the steps of the software life cycle and to fix output products for each step. Figure 1 represents phases and activities that we followed during our work.

Dashed lines circumscribe the set of activities related to a specific phase of the methodology. Bold words specify phases and ellipses indicate activities. Arrows represent the iteration process among phases and among activities within phases.

One of the major advantages we have found in this approach is that everything moves around the concept of object, thus the object model provides a unifying element that is common to every phase of the life cycle. This uniformity provides a smooth transition from one phase to the next, so distinct boundaries between the phases of the O-O life cycle are eliminated.

A much more seamless interface between phases is provided also because objects and relationships, identified and documented in the analysis phase, serve as input to the design phase and as an initial layer in the design. Analysts, designers and programmers have worked with a common set of items, the object model of multimedia documents, upon which to build.

Moreover, we have found a real benefit in leaving the traditional *waterfall model* of software development because it does not support iteration and rapid prototyping. The object-oriented approach addresses each of these issues. It is clear from figure 1 that we have used a *fountin model*, so called by Henderson-Sellers and Edwards [8], where development reaches a high level only to fall back to a previous level to begin the climb once again. The blurring of the traditional design and implementation phases has been fueled by the development of encapsulation and abstraction mechanisms.

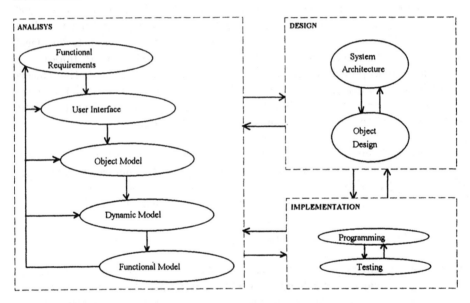

- Figure 1 - Software life cycle

An important advantage of the O-O approach was for us the emphasis on reuse, which we have taken into account primarily in the design of the system architecture. Finally, the methodology represented an excellent guideline for the production of a standardized documentation.

3.   The Object Model of Multimedia Documents

One of the important ideas adopted in our model is the description of the document in terms of its Conceptual Structure. This concept was firstly introduced in the document management field by the Multos project [14] [9]. Examples of conceptual components are sections, chapters, paragraphs of a book. The Conceptual Structure is basically a hierarchical structure composed of a root object, intermediate objects composed of one or more other objects, and leaf objects. The conceptual structure is important for query specification since conceptual components are more meaningful to the user than ODA[1] logical and layout components.

From what concerns operations such as creation, editing and presentation of multimedia content portions we leave these tasks to the applications that are able to handle them. This means that we have to deal with a complex environment of different formats (such as ODA [7], PDF [2], RTF [11]), external to the system, in order to control the addressing mechanism between the conceptual structure and the content portions. In figure 2 we describe this situation.

Basically, we assume to impose a conceptual structure on the content portions of the document, so the conceptual components have to address one or more blocks of data at the *Content Portion Level*. Because we have to do with different internal formats of Content Portions we need to introduce an intermediate level, called *Physical Structure Level*, which represents an indirect addressing mechanism from the *Conceptual Structure level* to the Content Portion level. This intermediate level acts as a filter of different formats, so that they are transparent to the higher level which works on the same way always, independently from the different kinds of data which is pointing to.

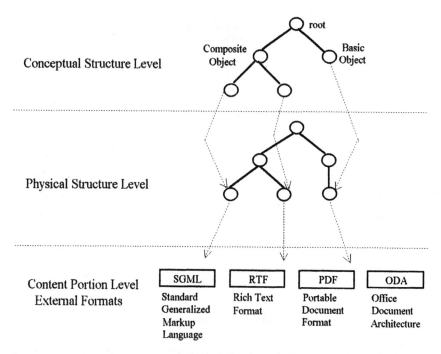

- Figure 2 - OOCM Document Model vs External World

---

[1]ODA is an international standard defined by ISO, ECMA and CCITT

Consequently, our system, on one hand, allows users to impose a Conceptual Structure on content portions created by different external applications and, on the other hand, it is able to interpret external formats, like ODA and SGML, that already contain information on the semantics of the content.

As it is easy to understand, the heart of our model is the *Document Conceptual Structure*, which we are going to define using an object-oriented data model.

The graph of figure 3 represents a typical document of our system with objects of the conceptual level, modeling the document conceptual structure, objects of the physical level, mapping the conceptual structure to the content portions, and objects of the hypertextual dimension, providing a linking mechanism among conceptual objects of the same or different documents.

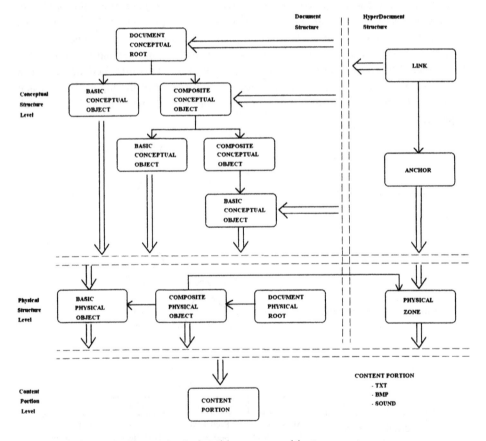

- Figure 3 - General relationships among objects

Objects have a unique identifier. Objects may have a set of attributes and methods associated with them. An object may be composed of other objects. For example a *Document Conceptual Root* object may be composed of more *Basic Conceptual*

Objects. The composition of more complex objects from more elementary ones forms an aggregation hierarchy.

Aggregation is a particular association with *is part-of* semantics. A generic example of association is represented by the hypertext link among conceptual objects of different documents (or of the same document). Hypertextual links are carried out in our system by autonomous objects (called *link*) which give more emphasis to the association itself. A link connects two objects of conceptual structure using the concept of hot area (or *anchor*) of the document content.

In figure 3 simple arrows represent the *is part of* association and double arrows represent other kind of associations.

A *Basic Conceptual Object (BCO)* may refer to a unique or more content portions. For example, if each Content Portion represents a physical page, a paragraph that starts in a physical page and ends in the middle of an other physical page, refers to at least two Content Portions (see figure 4). A *Basic Physical Object (BPO)* refers always to a unique Content Portion or to a part of a Content Portion. Consequently the Basic Conceptual Object may refer to one or more Basic Physical Objects. Viceversa, a BPO is always connected to one and only one BCO.

The set of BPO maps the whole document without intersections (each elementary part of the document content, that is to say a character of a text or a pixel of a bitmap or a frame of a sound, belongs to one and only one BPO).

As example, Figure 4 describes an instance of the Conceptual and Physical Structure at a certain moment of the document life.

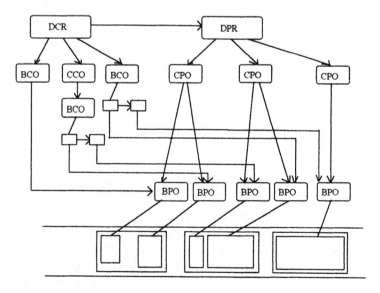

- Figure 4 - Document structure at a certain point of time

Physical Zones, instead, do not cover the entire document content. They are introduced in order to map anchors of the Hypertext Level on the Content Portion Level.

A *Composite Physical Object (CPO)* identifies a physical storage unit, such as a file, or a physical presentation unit, such as a page, which may be decomposed in directly addressable components. The Composite Physical Object may not contain other CPOs but it is composed of at least one BPO.

The *Content Portion objects* are in a one to one connection with the file of contents.

The physical structure serves the conceptual structure as a pointing mechanism towards the content. From the conceptual structure, only the BCOs (leaves) point to the BPOs. From the physical structure only the BPOs point to the actual content.

Objects we have talked about so far may be organized in classes through *instance-of* relationships. So, we consider the following classes:
Conceptual Structure Level: *Document Conceptual Root, Composite Conceptual Object and Basic Conceptual Object;*
Physical Structure Level: *Document Physical Root, Composite Physical Object, Basic Physical Object and Physical Zone;*
Hypertext Dimension: *Link and Anchor;*
Content Portion Level: *Content Portion.*

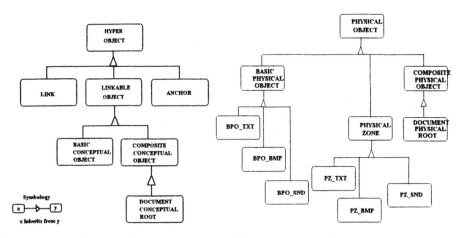

- Figure 5 - Inheritance hierarchies for objects of the document model

Classes may be organized into superclasses through an *is a* or generalization hierarchy. In figure 5 is represented the generalization hierarchy of Conceptual, Physical and Hypertext Levels. The *Linkable Object* class is superclass of *Basic Conceptual Object* and *Composite Conceptual Object* classes. A class may be subclass of more classes (for example the class *DCR* is subclass of the class *CCO* and of *Linkable Object*). A class has a set of common attributes for all instances of the class itself. All subclasses of such class inherit these attributes. Methods that are applicable to the objects of a certain class are also applicable to the objects that are instances of its subclasses. Figure 5 synthesizes the inheritance hierarchies existing among the specified classes.

Figure 5 shows two new superclasses for the Hypertext level: Hyper Object and Linkable Object. The Linkable Object is an abstract class; instances of its inherited subclasses may be source and/or destination point of a link. Hyper Object is an abstract class as well.

Hyper Object, Linkable Object, Link and *Anchor* classes allow to model the Hypermedia data base. Components of multimedia documents (*Document Conceptual Roots, Composite Conceptual Objects, Basic Conceptual Objects*) are *nodes* (*Linkable Objects*) of that data base; *links* specify two *anchors* located in two different linkable objects in order to allow navigation from *source node* to *destination node* of the data base itself.

Figure 6 introduces the following specialization classes: subclasses of Basic Physical Object: *BPO_TXT, BPO_BMP, BPO_SND;* subclasses of Physical Zone: *PZ_TXT, PZ_BMP, PZ_SND.*

In figure 6 are represented the aggregation hierarchies for objects of our model. Aggregation is the *part-of* relationship in which objects representing the components of something are associated with an object representing the entire assembly.

Arrows in figure 6 indicate the triggering operation. For triggering we intend the automatic propagation of an operation to a graph of objects when this operation is applied to an object of the graph.

Numbers at the ends of association lines in the object diagrams indicate multiplicity. They specify how many instances of one class may relate to a single instance of an associated class.

So far it is described the object model for the Conceptual Structure of the document; the focus was on conceptual objects, such as DCR, CCO and BCO, and on objects of the physical level, such as DPR, CPO and BPO, which realize the interface level between conceptual and content portion levels. We did not give yet a particular meaning to Conceptual Structure objects, we only said that a retrieval process based on conceptual objects, besides attributes and text, may be very effective. Authors of the current paper believe that an office filing and retrieval system providing the expressed feature is very useful to the end-user; on the other side, existing literature ([16] [9]) and research work currently going on [10] about related subjects encourage this belief.

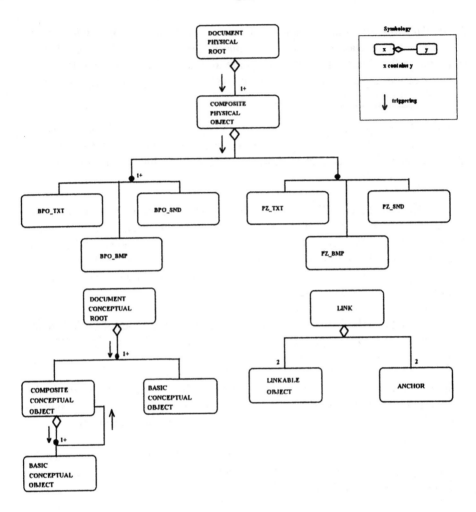

- Figure 6 - Aggregation hierarchies for objects of the document model

It is possible to introduce *component types* (such as the type address, date, abstract, chapter, etc.) and *document types* (such as letter, report, manual) within this model. Type is in our model a central concept, because it represents a structured approach to office documents. It is assumed that is necessary to focus on a regularity of office documents and this is expressed by the type concept. Whether such regularity exists always is subject to debate; not always there is a way of constraining knowledge to be formatted.

Types impose structure on documents in the same way that formatted data impose structure on knowledge. The user may not be left free to create documents with any structure he wants. The guidance to the use of predefined document types can be considered constraining by some people; in many cases it may result extremely convenient.

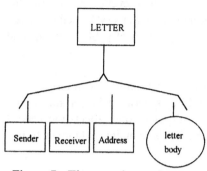

- Figure 7 - The generic type Letter

An example of a structure of a *component type* is Address which can be defined as the aggregation of the component types Street, City and Country; while an example of a structure of a *document type* is Letter which can be defined as the aggregation of the component shown in figure 7.

The fact that document and each component of it may be expressed in terms of its contained components and that order of components may be specified is a determinant factor for automatic generation of the document conceptual structure at capture time. The automatic extraction of conceptual structures is a key market requirement, because end-users do not want to be bored with a manual structuring process.

4.   Design and Implementation Issues

4.1   The System Architecture

A prototype of the system has been developed which implements the object model of multimedia documents presented in the last chapter. The Gemstone OODBMS provides the physical implementation of the object model including objects and methods in a unique physical representation. The prototype is based on a client-server architecture as shown in figure 8. Client stations are IBM PCs with DOS/Windows 3.1 O.S. and the server station is a DPX 20/RISC 6000 with AIX O.S.

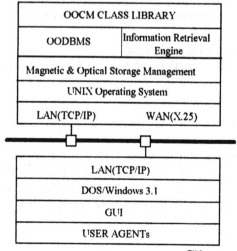

Server

Client

- Figure 8 - Architecture of OOCM

The system architecture was designed following the OMT guidelines. It is devided in subsystems. The decomposition of system in subsystems is organized as a sequence of horizontal levels and vertical partitions and the interaction between levels is of type client-server. Each subsystem is composed of a module or a set of modules, and each module is a set of classes. Thus, we provide a complete class library for each module of the system.

The representation in layers of the system architecture reduces system complexity emphasizing information hiding.

Each layer, in fact, has a well defined interface to the upper level of the system (this characteristic is of a closed architecture, suggested from the OMT methodology). Obviously the interface of one layer is represented by the set of public methods and variables of the class library of that layer.

The advantage of a closed architecture, where each layer is built only in terms of the immediate lower layer, is that it reduces dependencies between layers and allows changes to be made more easily because a layer's interface only affects the nearest upper layer. The drawback is that in some cases, levels contains redundant transit classes.

The decomposition in layers and partitions was not a very hard task to achieve, because the object-oriented paradigm provides natural support for decomposing a system into modules. So, classes of the object model, introduced during the analysis phase, represent a fine-grained approach which is input for system design.

We have used for our development an OODBMS. Object Oriented Data Base Management Systems technology currently represents a concrete way to better manage multimedia objects ([17], [18], [19], [20]). An OODBMS is defined as a DBMS that directly supports a model based on the Object-Oriented paradigm. OODBMSs support fundamental features required from multimedia documents management applications such as:
- filing of heterogeneous data in a unique database with uniform access methods and query process on different kinds of data;
- management of large repositories of unformatted data such as text data, images, voice which traditional DBMSs are not able to handle;
- management of composite objects (composite objects are objects defined as *parts of* other objects which means that there is an aggregation relation among objects);
- automation of large amounts of data with tight and complex interconnections and of data model that frequently changes over the time (such as Hypermedia, CAD and CASE systems);
- storing of reusable classes in order to increase productivity;
- integration in a unique data base of data description and methods implementing the object behaviour.

4.2   The Multimedia Document Browser

In this paragraph we describe a particular User Agent of our system, the Browser, which allows users to capture from different fonts Content Portions of different formats (text, images, graphics, spreadsheets, sounds, etc.), to aggregate them in a compound document, to present the obtained multimedia document, to manage the diverse Content Portions.

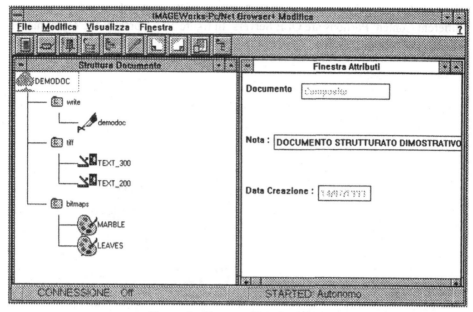

- Figure 9 - Browser User Interface

In figure 9 we show one moment of the Browser user interface. In the right window it is possible to see document attributes, in the left window the structured layout of the document is dsplayed. All different Content Portions composing the multimedia document are shown as diverse icons. These icons are active objects, in fact, by a double click on a particular icon, the object type handler is called (i.e. a double click on the "MARBLE" icon activates the PaintBrush application to handle the corresponding image portion).

The most important concept that we want to focus here is that we used a mechanism, called Object Linking and Embedding, in order to build this interface. OLE is a standard protocol based on a client/server paradigm. It allows to create a client application (called OLE Client) which may deal with different data formats; the OLE Client avails itself of the specific handlers (called OLE Servers) of each different data type. This approach allows data exchange among applications and supplies a way to present different data formats in the client application window. This is the case of the Word for Windows word processor, which is able to handle in an homogeneous environment texts and a lot of other objects types incorporated within the text itself. Thus Ole represent a very good mechanism to manage presentation and modification of multimedia documents. It emphasizes concepts typical of the O-O paradigm because it leaves the *application-centered* view of Windows programming and requires an higher specialization and modularization of applications which reduces code complexity. Moreover the support of Microsoft Foundation Classes for OLE helps developers reducing efforts in the construction of the application classes.

The window of our Browser is an OLE Client while applications able to manage different Content Portions are OLE Servers. In figure 10 we present the object model of this application.

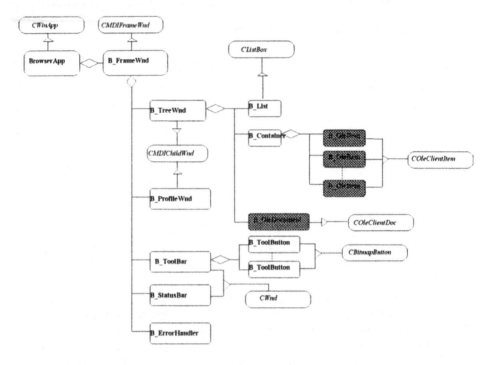

- Figure 10 - Multimedia Browser Object Model

Classes written in italics belong to the framework of classes offered by MFC; other classes belong to our application. Classes represented in green rectangles are classes inherited from MFC OLE classes. The general (containment and comunication) scheme of MFC OLE classes is illustrated in figure 11.

The relationships among objects in a client application are the followings:
- a client application can have 0 or more COleClientDocs, which means the possibility to open more than one document from the client application;
- each COleClientDoc can have 0 or more COleClientItems, which means the possibility to have in one document various different data formats (i. e. the icons of the Browser);
- each COleClientItem represents an OLE item. The Object_Oriented framework for the OLE protocol allowed us to implement in a sufficiently simple and elegant way a client application that is a very hard goal to achieve using C OLE API.

The following is a synthetic description of each class of our application:

- BrowserApp is a derived class to manage the Browser application,
- B_FrameWnd manages the main window,
- B_TreeWnd and B_ProfileWnd manage left and right windows, that are children windows of B_FrameWnd,
- B_ToolBar manages the tool bar at the top of the main window,
- B_StatusBar manages the status bar at the bottom of the main window,
- B_ToolButton manages a button of the tool bar.

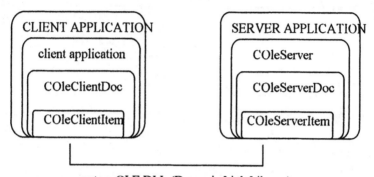

system OLE DLL (Dynamic Link Library)
- Figure 11 - Communication scheme among MFC OLE Objects

B_TreeWnd and B_ProfileWnd are derived from CMDIChildWnd which implement the concept of MDI (Multi Document Interface) child window. An MDI application may instantiate 0 or more children windows, one independent from each other. The Browser is an MDI application because two independent children windows, the attribute window and the structured layout window, are created.

The Browser was developed with a first release of MFC. In the next paragraph we will describe the Structure Builder user agent which we have developed using the last version of MFC coupled with the visual programming environment, Visual C++. The experience done in the last implementation gets us to consider that the development of the Browser with Visual C++ should have facilitated us in at least two situations: the MDI and the graphical objects handling.

4.2   The Structure Builder

The Structure Builder is another UA of the OOCM system. The goal of Structure Builder (SB) is to define conceptual objects on the content of each portion. For example a portion of type text representing a paper can be structured with a title, some authors, chapters, paragraphs, references and so on.

The user may see two views of the document, physical (Content Portions) and conceptual (Conceptual Components), by means of a *splitter window* devided in a Physical Viewer and in a Conceptual Viewer. Physical Viewer shows miniatures of the Content Portions and Conceptual Viewer shows objects of the Conceptual

Structure. User creates a new conceptual object by a drag operation on the content shown in the Physical Viewer (see figure 12).

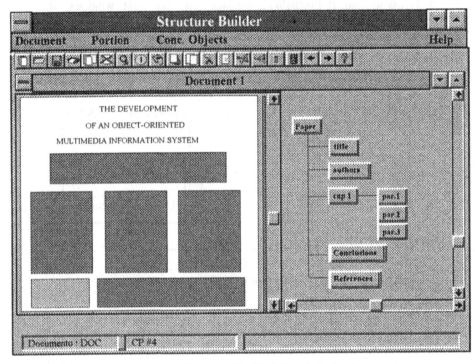

- Figure 12 - Structure Builder User Interface

In the Visual C++ programming environment, offered by Microsoft, the skeleton of an application is developed starting from a basic framework, the MFC 2.0 library. The fundamental elements of an MFC 2.0 application design are the following classes:

- *CDocument* which encapsulates and handles data related to a specific application; we derived from this class the class COocmDoc that represents our document data (see figure 13).
- *CView* which manages document data viewing and user-application interfacing. More than one view may be associated to an instance of a class CDocument; an example are physical and conceptual views of the OOCM document in the splitter window of the Structure Builder; classes of our application, derived from CView, are CConceptualView and CPhysicalView, that are specialized to show the OOCM document Conceptual Structure and the Content Portions respectively.
- *CFrameWnd* represents the main window and is able to manage it; particularly we used the CMDIFrameWnd, derived from CFrameWnd, because Structure Builder is an MDI application; we derived CMainFrame from this last class.
- *CDocumentTemplate* coordinates the creation of objects belonging to an application: objects of class CDocument, CView and CFrameWnd; processes

related to documents, views and framewindows creation are managed by the current class, actually by its derived classes: CSingleDocumentTemplate and CMultiDocumentTemplate, depending on the application type (SDI or MDI).

- *CWinApp* represents and manages the application; an instance of this class can manipulate one or more objects of the CDocumentTemplate class; we derived from the CWinApp class the COocmApp class that represents our application.

Visual C++ supplies the following set of tools that facilitates application development:

- *AppWizard* which automatically generates the minimal skeleton of the application,
- *AppStudio* that is a handler of user interface resources, a type of dialogue editor,
- *Class Wizard* which enables user to define a message handler and join it to a message_id for each object of the application. It creates the message map for each class and handles the correct routing of messages. Windows applications are, in fact, *message driven*: each user action generates messages that are dispatched to the windows of the application and managed by the corresponding *message handler*,
- *Browser* which allows direct accessing and consulting of the currently open project classes, because a repository of classes is supplied.

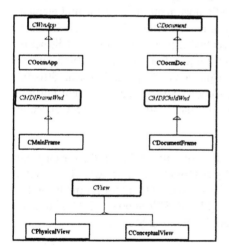
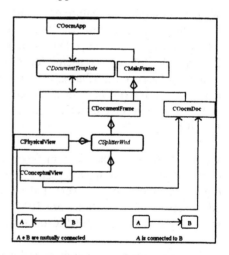

- Figure 13 - Simplified Inheritance Hierarchy of presentation classes and general containment and communication scheme of Structure Builder application

In summary, during our programming experience, we verified the following advantages:

- The clean separation between data/methods of a class and its interface to the external world, determined by the existence of classes CDocument and CView, is completely consistent with the Object-Oriented paradigm;
- Visual C++ supplies free features to user-interface management, such as the scrolling operation and the MDI Windows management;

- code is organized in a real object-oriented fashion: the environment transparently generates, for each class defined by ClassWizard, a header file and an implementation file (splitting between data and functions);
- ClassWizard and Browser help user in extending and refining code: ClassWizard allows automatic code generation of a new class offering an user-friendly interface for the specification of inheritance and aggregation associations respect to already existing classes; Browser, instead, enables user to directly access a specific portion of the class code in order to modify it.

The process development in such a type of environment results clearly improved in terms of increasing of productivity, reducing of code lines number and abatement of working time. Obviously, programmers discover all these advantages only after they have been achieved a good comprehension of the offered mechanisms and tools. A bad use of existing tools may cause trivial errors that are difficult to localize.

5.   Concluding Remarks

In this paper we have discussed issues related to the development of a multimedia information system for an office environment.

We have described the nature of the multimedia document, its fundamental elements (Content Portions, Attributes, Profile, Conceptual Structure, Miniatures) its object model, based on concepts of Document Conceptual Structure and Physical Structure. Conceptual Structure is useful for efficient information retrieval which, in our system, is based on attributes, content and Conceptual Objects. Physical Structure represents an intermediate level between Conceptual Structure and Content Portions, it allows to interpret different external file formats and to map the Conceptual Structure to the CP.

We have introduced the OMT methodology that we utilized during the development of our project and we have presented the Object-Oriented architecture of the system organized in horizontal layers and vertical partitions. The architecture is of type client/server: client stations are IBM PCs with DOS/Windows 3.1 O.S. and the server station is a DPX 20/RISC 6000 with AIX Operating System.

In the last chapter we have discussed some implementation results concerning with the use of the OLE technology and the visual programming experience.

Acknowledgements

We are grateful to Professor Elisa Bertino of the Departement of Computer Science of University of Milano for her precious suggestions, information and material on Object-Oriented Methodologies and O-O Data Base Management Systems. We really thanks her for the encouragements in writing this paper.

We thank other people that have partecipated to the activity of prototyping of this project: G. Molaro, P. Guarente, A. Forti, G. Rizzo, P. Russo, G. Amendola.

References

1. E. Bertino, S. Gibbs, F. Rabitti, C. Thanos-The design of a multimedia office filing system-Appeared in "Rivista d'informatica", n. 3, 1987

2. T.Bienz, R. Cohn-Portable Document Format Reference Manual-Edited by Adobe Systems Incorporated-Published by Addison Wesley, 1993

3. S. Christodoulakis, J. Vanderbroek, J. Li, T. Li, S. Wan, Y. Wang, M. P. Papa and E. Bertino-Development of a Multimedia Information System for an Office Environment-Proceedings of the tenth International Conference on "Very Large Data Bases", Singapore, August 1984

4. S. Christodoulakis, M. Theodoridou, F. Ho, M. P. Papa and A. Pathria-Multimedia Document Presentation, Information Extraction, and Document Formation in MINOS: A Model and a System-Appeared in "ACM Transactions on Office Information Systems", Vol. 4, No. 4, October 1986

5. P. Conti and F. Rabitti-Image Retrieval by Semantic Content-Appeared in "Multimedia Office Filing The Multos Approach" published by North-Holland Amsterdam- New York- Oxford-Tokyo 1990

6. P. Costantopoulos, Y. Drakopoulos and Y. Yeorgaroudakis-Multimedia Document Retrieval by Pictorial Content-Appeared in "Multimedia Office Filing The Multos Approach" edited by North-Holland Amsterdam- New York-Oxford-Tokyo 1990

7. Ecma Tc-29-Office Document Architecture-Standard Ecma-101, Sept. 1985

8. T. Korson, J. D. McGregor-Understanding Object-Oriented: A Unifying Paradigm-Appeared in Communications of the ACM, September 1990

9. C. Meghini, F. Rabitti, C. Thanos-Conceptual Modeling of Multimedia Documents-Appeared in "Computer" of IEEE Computer Society, October 1991

10. C. Meghini, F. Sebastiani, U. Straccia, C. Thanos-A Model of Information Retrieval based on a Terminological Logic-Proceedings of the Sixteenth Annual International ACM SIGIR Conference on Research and Development in Information Retrieval, Pittsburgh,PA USA, June 1993

11. GC0165: Rich Text Format (RTF) Specification Microsoft Product Support Services Application Note, June 1992

12. M. P. Papa, S. Giurleo, G. Rizzo, A. Forti, G. Corrente, G. Molaro-An Object-Oriented Approach to Manage Multimedia Documents-Proceedings of TOOLS EUROPE '94, Versailles, March 1994

13. F. Rabitti, P. Stanchev-Graphical Image Retrieval from Large Image Databases-Proceedings of AICA conference, Trento, settember 1987

14. F. Rabitti-The Multos Document Model-Appeared in "Multimedia Office Filing The Multos Approach" edited by North-Holland Amsterdam- New York-Oxford-Tokyo, 1990

15. J. Rumbaugh, M. Blaha, W. Premerlani, F. Eddy, W. Lorensen-Object-Oriented Modeling and Design-Published by Prentice Hall, 1991

16. Multimedia Office Filing The Multos Approach-Edited by C. Thanos-North-Holland-Amsterdam- New York-Oxford-Tokyo, 1990

17. MULTIMEDIA Tecnologia e applicazioni-edited by A. Waterworth-published by Muzzio Nuovo Millennio, 1991

18. E. Bertino-Sistemi di gestione di basi di dati orientate agli oggetti-Appeared in "Rivista di informatica", n.4, 1991

19. E. Bertino, L. D. Martino-Sistemi di basi di dati orientate agli oggetti Concetti e architetture-Published by Addison Wesley Masson, 1992

20. M. Atkinson, F. Bancilhon, D. DeWitt, K. Dittrich, D. Maier, S. Zdonik-The Object-Oriented Database System Manifesto-In Proceedings of the first International Conference on Deductive and Object-Oriented Databases, Kyoto, Japan, December 1989.

An Intelligent Information System for Heterogeneous Data Exploration

Maria Luisa Damiani

ELDA Milano S.r.L.
Via Pirelli 27, Milano, Italy
E-mail : maria@datamont.it

Abstract. The paper presents an industrial application of an object based knowledge representation system relying on description logics. The knowledge representation language is used as core component of a complex information system conceived to support data exploration. The system is called IDA and it has been developed within the Esprit project AIMS. In this paper we describe the motivations, the architecture of IDA and the methodological guidelines for building an exploration-oriented application in the IDA framework .

1 Introduction

An interesting application for intelligent information systems is to support the inspection and interpretation of large amounts of coarse data. Sample applications are: analysis of data generated by scientific experiments [16]; 'data mining' for knowledge discovery in large databases [4]; inspection of corporate business information [7]. A distinguishing feature of these applications is the high degree of indefiniteness of the search process. In fact in most cases the information which is actually "interesting" is not known in advance but results from a process of data *exploration*.

In the AIMS project[1] it has been developed an information management system called IDA to support the exploration of knowledge, database and multimedia information. The purpose of IDA is not to replace at any extent domain experts but rather to provide a very flexible environment for intelligently classifying and navigating related information even of different nature. The system results from the integration of different technologies: knowledge management, database, multimedia and visual programming. The core of the system is the so called Intelligent Repository.which is developed on top of an object oriented knowledge representation system. The other fundamental modules are: the IDA Desktop for the visualization and access of the Intelligent Repository, the Multimedia Object

---

[1]The work reported in the paper has been partially supported by the EEC under the ESPRIT Project 5210, AIMS. Partecipants are: Datamont (I), Quinary (I), Technische Universitat Berlin (D), Universidad Pais Vasco (S), Non Standard Logics (F), ONERA-CERT (F).

Manager (MOM) for the physical management of unstructured entities and the Database Linker for transparently accessing a preexisting relational database through the Intelligent Repository.

Glue of the system is the conceptual schema contained in the Repository. The primary role of the schema in IDA is to make the end user understand the content of the heterogeneous information base consisting of both structured and unstructured data. For responding to the demand of expressiveness and flexibility of the schema, a powerful knowledge representation system based on the novel paradigm of description logic has been used. This paradigm, though extensively studied from a theoretical point of view, is still little used in real applications. As a consequence, it lacks the practical experience which can help developers to decide which representation constructs are most suitable in which cases. In this paper we present some methodological hints for applying description logics to the development of exploration-oriented applications in the IDA context. For grounding the presentation on a concrete application, we refer to the case study developed in the course of the AIMS project, about the management of technical documentation.

The paper is structured as follows: first we describe some basic features of the exploration activity; next we introduce the baseline of the IDA approach and the general architecture; next we present some methodological guidelines; finally we describe how the exploration of multimedia information is supported in IDA.

2 The Exploration Activity

Throughout the paper we take the area of technical documentation management as sample application context for the IDA system. In organizations like engineering or manufacturing there is a great variety of documents and data such as drawings, technical specifications, measurement files. Documents are generated at different stages, by distinct departments and are generally accessed by professionals such as engineers or technicians. In this setting, information access is often performed by data exploration. In our case study, a sample activity based on data exploration is the diagnosis of critical faults in a plant for electric energy production. The critical step of the overall activity, which can take a few weeks, is indeed finding out the information which is relevant to detect the possible causes of the fault. In fact it does not exist any predefined path carrying to the useful information and the technician proceeds generally inspecting different data sets and reasoning on them.

Though quite simple, the example points out a number of features of the search process:

• search is content driven;

• search is a process not an atomic operation. It expands in time and has a context. The context is constituted by the relevant information progressively collected;

• the atomic operations of search are: querying and stepwise navigation;

• queries are ad hoc and not pre-packaged.

The goal of IDA is to support this abstraction in case information consists of both structured and unstructured data. For sake of simplicity, unstructured data is limited to images.

3 The IDA Approach

In our view the key issue for supporting exploration is to provide the user with an understandable representation of the heterogeneous information base structure and content, i.e. of the conceptual schema.

By definition, conceptual schemas capture the structure and constraints of the data that are recorded in a database so that only valid data is accepted for storage. In conventional DBMS the knowledge of the schema is generally not relevant for the end user. In fact schemas are either small and thus the user can easily memorize the database structure or the interaction is through pre-packaged queries. Conversely when data exploration is performed most user interactions are in the form of ad hoc queries. In combination with the size and complexity of the information bases this makes the knowledge of the schema much more valuable than in a conventional DBMS [16].

In IDA the conceptual schema is the central piece of information which provides a common foundation for all types of interaction between the users and the system. That introduces a number of requirements on the data model in which the schema has to be expressed:

• The data model must have high expressive power. The primitives of the data model are to be closely related to notions that users currently use.

• The schemas in the data model must have a succinct representation so that they are easily understood by users. Intuitive interaction metaphors supported by user-friendly interfaces are a prime requirement.

The approach proposed in IDA is to use an object-based knowledge representation language relying on description logics for representing the conceptual schema. These language, also known in literature as terminological languages all descend from the KL-ONE system [6] [14] and provide a sound and formal basis to the paradigm of semantic nets. The specific language we have used is called BACK [11][9].

3.1 The BACK Language

The BACK language and in general all description languages, distinguishes between *terminological* (TBOX) and *assertional* (ABOX) knowledge. Terminological knowledge captures the intensional aspects of a domain and consists of a set of *concepts* and *roles* organized in *subsumption taxonomies*. Concepts are used to collect relevant entities of a domain; roles are used to specify properties of concepts and thus model relationships between concepts. A distinguished feature of the language is the possibility of specifying definitional properties for both concepts and roles (i.e. properties necessary and sufficient for an individual/couple to be a concept/role instance). Concepts and roles which express definitional properties are called respectively *defined concepts* and *defined roles*. For example the declaration:

$$mother := woman \ and \ atleast(1, child)$$

specifies a necessary and sufficient condition for a woman being a mother. Conversely concept (roles) for which it is not possible to give a semantic characterization in terms of other concepts (roles) are called *primitive*. For example, the declaration:

$$person:<mammal$$

specifies that a person is necessarily a mammal, but it does not provide sufficient conditions to establish when an instance of the concept 'mammal' is also an instance of the concept 'person'.

The basic inference is called *classification*. It places automatically concepts in the net of concept descriptions depending on the specified properties, while instances are automatically completed with the most specific description. Both concepts and roles can be composed in complex terms by applying a number of composition operators: restrictions on values and cardinality of roles; conjunction of concepts and roles; transitive closure, inverse and composition of roles. Disjointeness of concepts can be stated as a constraint. It is possible to define simple rules on concepts (*I-links*). Finally in BACK it is possible to declare *functional roles*, that is roles in which the value of role fillers is computed by an external function. For an exhaustive description of both the syntax and semantics of the language - not included in this paper - refer to [9].

The aspects of BACK and in general of description languages which are relevant in the IDA framework are:

• the formalism is very expressive and the concepts are simple and intuitive;

• the inferential mechanisms can be exploited for performing intelligent information indexing and navigation;

• the language has a schema definition language, a data definition language and a powerful query language for retrieving information on both data and schema. The language is not thus only a notation like most semantic data models but rather an operational system.

3.2 Architecture

BACK is used for building the central component of IDA called *Intelligent Repository* which contains the conceptual descriptions of both the structured and unstructured entities in the domain. The architecture of the system is depicted in fig.1. A more extended description is given in [3]. Each entity in the domain is described by a BACK object. Actual entities can be stored in different places. Structured data can be stored in the repository itself, otherwise in an external and pre-existing database. In the latter case the integration strategy is based on the schema mapping approach. The idea is to abstract and represent in BACK the content of the database (or part of it) while maintaining in a "mapping" description the correspondence between the knowledge base structures and the database relations [13]. A Database Linker module is in charge of interpreting the queries, dispatching requests to the database and generating the answers in terms of instances which are entered into the knowledge base.

As concerns unstructured data, i.e. pictures the idea is to use BACK for modelling the conceptual and spatial description of images and to build a *Multimedia Object Manager (MOM)* for their physical management [1]. The MOM associates to each conceptual object a so called physical object which specifies low level attributes of pictures and the operations which can be called on them. The operations can also be performed by external applications interoperating with the MOM. In the latter case the approach used for coupling the system with the application tools is based on the

Operational Mapping [3].The idea of the strategy is to abstract a common protocol of operations for interacting homogenously with application tools. Therefore the integration protocol consists of a minimal set of messages to which each encapsulated application must respond.

The Intelligent Repository is accessed by the user through a visual interface consisting of a number of facilities for supporting explorative search and information updating. The interface constitute the *IDA Desktop* . A valuable feature of the IDA Desktop is that retrieval can be performed by interleaving querying and hypermedia-like navigation across the net of structured and unstructured objects. The basic facilities of the interface are: a query-by-form-like tool for querying the knowledge base augmented with images (Query-by-hyperform); a tool for navigating a collection of objects traversing in a stepwise manner the relationships which logically link objects (Navigator) ; a tool for creating and modifying links among objects (Creator).

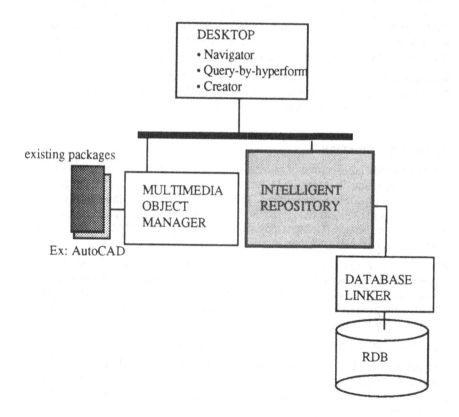

Fig. 1

4 The Intelligent Repository: Methodological Approach

Developing an application in IDA means essentially to build a repository which supports the exploration of a specific data set. A distinguishing feature of the process of knowledge base construction in IDA is that it exists a tight interconnection between the way information is structured and the way it is presented to the user. We remind that the user is supposed to be a domain expert thus someone who is not at all concerned with the deep technicalities of the system and strongly demand a simple to use system. For that reason, the effectiveness of presentation greatly depend on the conceptual clarity of the domain model. For example the user unlikely appreciates objects he/she is not familiar with, which have been possibly introduced only for representation convenience at knowledge base level. In that case it might be useful to distinguish in the specification what is domain dependent and what instead implementation dependent and have a different management of the entities at desktop level. The problem could be more elegantly approached by allowing the definition of some form of external schema for the knowledge base likewise in databases. In that case the external schema could be to some extent tailored on the user needs and the knowledge base could be developed almost independentely from presentation aspects. A proposal in that direction is described in [2]. However, even in the latter case it remains the problem of organizing the schema in a way understandable to the user. The issue is challenging. The methodology investigated does not solve the problem, nevertheless it offers some guidelines and suggests a few tricks which can clarify the way the knowledge representation language is used for exploration tasks.

In essence the idea is to exploit the representation and inferencial capabilities of the description language to provide a number of facilities called: *automatic indexing*, *object decomposition, automatic object linking*.

Automatic Indexing.

A fine grained classification of objects simplifies search but it can be too expensive if performed manually especially when there are many objects and many collections in which the objects can be entered. The so called automatic indexing is a facility which makes the system recognize the class/es an object belongs to on the basis of the object properties. Using a description language like BACK, the automatic indexing is given almost for grant.

However there are two cases to be distinguished which are to be differently represented in BACK: the first is when objects are described by properties which are *all* necessary and sufficient. In that case the automatic indexing onto a class is obtained simply representing the class as a BACK *defined concept*. As an example consider the following informal description:

A business_offer is a document sent by some supplier and whose subject is 'offer'

The properties of the business_offer are both necessary and sufficient. When a generic document is sent by someone which is known to be a supplier and the subject is an offer, the document is classified as a business_offer. In BACK it can be expressed as follows :

business_offer:= document and all(sender, supplier) and has_subject:'offer'

The second case is when only few (but not all) properties are sufficient. In that case the necessary properties are expressed introducing a primitive concept while the sufficient conditions are represented by rules (called I-links in BACK).

As an example consider a simplified typology of fault causes. Each cause can be described by a code and by a string. For example "Lack of maintenance" is given the internal code 2010 and a string "carenza manutenzione". The same string can be used to describe different faults. Conversely the code identifies univocaly the fault. In BACK it can be expressed as follows:

lack_of_maintenance:< cause and has_code: 2010 and has_label: "carenza manutenzione"

has_code: 2010 => lack_of maintenance [2]

Object Decomposition

Often an object can be identified through one or more of its parts. For instance a technical drawing is a composite picture made of significant parts which can be inspected during the search process. In general even for exploration purposes it seems important to represent the association commonly known as *part_of* which relates an object to its parts.

In BACK the part_of relation is not a native construct of the language. For sake of simplicity, instead of extending the language, we have preferred to represent the meaning of the relation directly in BACK [8]. We say that a relation is of part_of type when it represents a partial order over a set of objects, therefore it is antiriflexive, asymmetric and transitive. The object graph representing the partial order is thus directed and acyclic. The partial order has a *top element* which consists of the entire object. By definition, the top element cannot be part of any other object in the set. The set of objects on which the partial order is defined is called the *scope* of the relation. For example, the scope of the relation "part_of_engine" consists of the entire engine (top element) and of the elements composing it.

The above model of part_of can be expressed to a great extent in BACK. The *scope* of a part_of relation is represented by a BACK concept. Some *basic* roles are defined for the concept which are unique for each part_of relation: the role which relates a part to its immediate father and its inverse. The transitive property of the relation is expressed by two additional roles respectively for the ancestor and discendent parts which are defined as transitive closures of the basic roles. An example can clarify the approach. Consider the parts of an engine. The set of parts constitute the scope of the relation for which the basic roles are specified.

engine_part: < anything   ; scope

part_of_engine: <domain (engine_part) and range(engine_part)   ; basic role

consists_of_part: = INV(part_of_engine)   ; basic role

entire_engine:< engine_part and no (part_of_engine)   ; top element

ancestor_part:= TRANS (part_of_engine)   ; transitive closure

descendent_part:= TRANS (consist_of_part)   ; transitive closure

---

[2] BACK rule. Syntax : <concept_expression> => <concept_expression>

An important remark is that the property of asimmetricity of the part_of relation cannot be expressed in BACK because it is not possible to prevent cycles among objects.

A number of additional properties allow different types of part_of to be distinguished. We have made a classification of part_of which extends that proposed in [10]:

• *physical* or *logical* part_of (an object can be necessarely part of another object or not);
• *exclusive* or *shared* part_of (an object can be part of only one or more objects) ;
• *structured or unstructured part_of* (an object can consist of parts which can be homogeneous or not).

Unfortunately not all the forms of part_of can be fully represented in BACK. Note in particular that the physical part_of cannot be properly modelled in BACK. In fact an object which is defined to be necessarely part of another object is not invalidated when the object it belongs to is removed. That is due to fact that in description systems the delete operation is typically monotonic, that is the knowledge base remains consistent when an object is removed. In practice the consistency is preserved because the system replaces the given object with an "unknown" entity. As a consequence for representing the part_of relations which are not fully supported by BACK it is necessary to add a procedural part.

Derived Links

One of the atomic operations performed during exploration is the stepwise traversing of associations. In this respect the knowledge base provides a semantic foundation to the navigational facilities which have been developed at Desktop level. However in order to be really helpful, navigation must be very flexible:

• The user can desire to traverse in whatever direction the associations;

• The user can desire to move straightforward from an object to another object without need of traversing the intermediate path;

• More intricate is the net and more interdependent are the associations, more difficult is maintaining its consistency when something change.

To fulfill the navigation requirements, it has been introduced the notion of *Derived Links*. Derived Links are used for entering into the knowledge base inverse associations and path shortcut. Derived Links are simply represented in BACK by *defined roles*. By composing and inverting arcs, even arcs representing Derived Links, the graph can be tailored upon the navigational needs. The great benefit of using BACK is that the consistency of the net is preserved by the system when some change occurs, because of the addition or updating of instances. In fact the *defined role* is such that the system takes care of checking and propagating the effects of changes. An example of how a very simple net can be configured by the addition of a Derived Link is the following. Suppose you have entered this description into the knowledge base (for sake of simplicity the description is expressed in natural language instead of BACK):

• *dossiers contains documents*

- *documents refer necessarely to a plant*

- *documents can be about faults*

- *failures concerns necessarely a plant*

The graph representing the description is in fig.2. In this graphic notation circles stand for concepts and labelled arrows for roles. For a better comprehension of the picture concept forming operators are not represented.

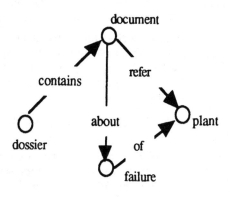

Fig. 2

The paths which can be traversed by the user at Desktop level are the paths of the directed graph. For example the user can take a dossier, then looks at the documents inside it and see the details of the plant a document refers to. The graph can be easily configured by adding arcs and thus introducing alternative paths. The sample arc connecting "failure" to "dossier" and expressing the relation between a failure and the dossier which contains documents about that failure can be expressed in BACK as follows:

SampleArc:= COMP (INV(contains) , INV (about))

5 The Exploration of Multimedia Information

We have presented so far some guidelines for building the IDA repositories to support the exploration task. We go now a step further and see how the strategy is applied for the exploration of multimedia information, consisting of knowledge and images. The key points of the approach to the management of images are:

- representation of images in the Repository

- management of the physical images

- navigation across knowledge and images

5.1 Representation of Images in the Repository

An image is assumed consisting of two dimensions, respectively conceptual and physical. At conceptual level, the image is described as an object representing some other object in the domain. In general, the meaning of an image is mostly domain dependent. The only aspect which can be generalized to a certain extent is the structural model. For that purpose, it has been defined a skeleton of the image structure which can be filled in and specialized for the different types of images. Accordingly pictures are represented by a specific concept called GrOb (Graphical Object). A GrOb expresses the following information:

• *represented entities* :a GrOb may represent some domain entity, that is some other conceptual object. This relationship may be modelled by the role *represent* between the concept GrOb and the concept standing for the domain entity ;

• *parts*: a picture consists of portions which in turn can contain other portions. The portions are Graphical entities too. A part_of relation relates the portions in a picture. This form of part_of has the following properties: physical (each portion is necessarely part of another one); exclusive (a portion is part of at most one other object); unstructured (the set of portions is homogeneous);

• *spatial relations:* simple spatial relations such as up, down, right, left can be defined between portions.

Because images are represented by BACK concepts, it makes sense to use automatic indexing to classify pictures on the basis of what they represent or contain. An example is the following. Suppose that *"DraftOfABB Turbine"* is defined as :

> *"a technical drawing which contains a portion which represent a turbine supplied by ABB"*

The system automatically sorts out the drawings which fulfill the descriptions. Similarly when a new technical drawing is entered and the relevant conceptual entities are determined, the system automatically checks the condition of containing the representation of a turbine supplied by ABB. If it is, the inference can be made that the technical drawing is of that type. Note that the reasoning process uses both textual and pictorial information. A more complex example in which this form of combined reasoning is performed is the following. Assume "dangerous plant" is defined as :

> *"a plant represented by a map which contains a portion representing a container of explosive near a portion representing a source of heat".*

Each time a new map is entered, the system checks whether the conceptual entities verify the spatial relationship of being near. In such a case the systems infers that a dangerous situation exist.

5.2 Desktop

The user perceives the knowledge base as a graph which can be traversed through the Desktop functionalities. As previously said the graph can be to a certain extent tailored on used needs and alternative paths can be added to the graph entering Derived Links into the knowledge base. The graph is used by the Desktop for guiding the user in an intuitive way within the knowledge base. Although the desktop provides three different ways for accessing the knowledge base, i.e. stepwise navigation, querying and creation/updating, the interaction style is rather homogeneous. Each object (i.e. BACK object) is displayed through a form . Forms can be linked through *link buttons* to other forms to graphically represent relationships among objects. The graph which is progressively traversed by the user while navigating the knowledge base or composing the query or the description is displayed by the so called *iconic browser* (Fig.3). In the browser window each object is represented by an icon, identical for all the elements of a concept. The user can position himself/herself on each node of the graph. Each navigation step is visualized by adding an arc to the iconic browser. Note that the user can move in two main directions, "horizontal" i.e. following the associations among objects, "vertical" when moving from the generic description to a more specific concept through the subsumption hierarchy. However the latter direction makes sense only when composing a query or a description .

During "navigation", images are accessed through a number of operations which are logically associated to the concept GrOb (Graphical Object) and actually provided by the Multimedia Object Manager. Each time the user is positioned onto an instance of GrOb, these operations are made available. The main operations: display, select (selection of a portion of an image), hide (hiding of the image). In Fig. 4, the operation of "display" is performed on an instance of "Drawing", which is a specialization of the GrOb concept. The image in this case is an AutoCAD draft. In spite of the different formats, images are modelled uniformly as consisting of portions which can be selected by a common operation "select". In Fig. 5 it is shown the result of a "select" performed on the previous drawing. A portion of the draft at Fig. 6 has been selected and the corresponding GrOb has been displayed and added to the iconic browser. The "display" of the corresponding draft is finally performed.

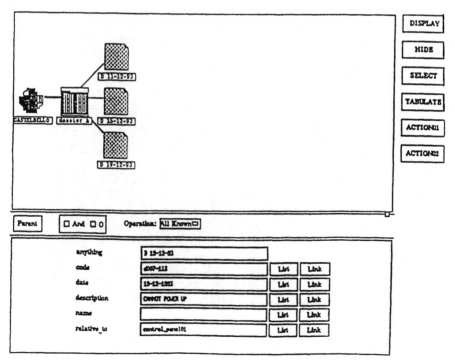

Fig. 3

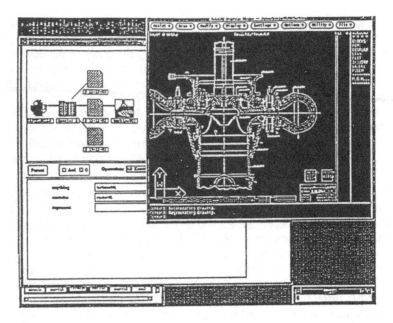

Fig. 4

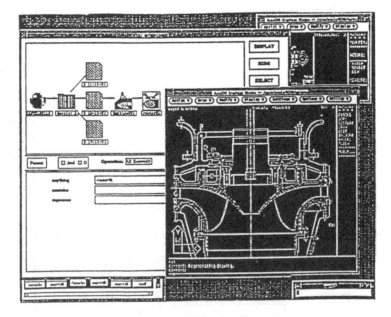

Fig. 5

6 Conclusion

In the AIMS project it has been defined an intelligent information management system for the development of exploration-oriented applications, that is applications entailing indexing and free consultation of complex structured information bases. A description language is used for building the conceptual model of the information base which is visualized to the user through the IDA Desktop.

One of the goals of AIMS was to assess the effectiveness of the BACK system (more in general of description logics) for the development of real application. The issue is challenging and widely debated in the research community as witnessed by the increasing number of application oriented papers. Nevertheless very often we cannot find in these papers a clear description of which representation constructs are actually useful for doing what. That would be important also from a didactic point of view because of the expensiveness of training on description logics. Description systems are very facinating for their formal base but difficult to use in practice. The questions which typically arise are: when is it convenient to use a defined concept or role instead of a primitive one? What is the usefulness of the classification inference?

We do not believe that univocal answers are to be searched for. The experiences of use can be very different. Nevertheless it is helpful trying to classify the way these systems are applied. From the IDA experience it turns out that, in essence, we have used description logics as an advanced and operational semantic data model equipped with inferential capabilities. The inferential capabilities are exploited for performing: automatic and content based indexing of instances, part_of modelling, flexible navigation of instances. The constructs which are mostly used are: defined concepts and rules for automatic indexing of instances; defined roles for the intelligent navigation of instances and part_of modelling; constraints. Note that in contrast with many current applications relying on description logics, we do not make an extended use of concept classification. We consider concept classification more as a facility for the application developer - because the system takes charge of making the necessary checks on the consistency of the taxonomy - rather than an inference benefiting the user. A final remark is about some challenging but very desirable - from an application point of view - extensions of the system. The first is on constraint management. Especially it would be very important to express constraints on the knowleability of objects. The second requirement is on a more efficient management of persistency.

We conclude with some notes about the status of implementation: a prototype of IDA comprehensive of all the modules previously described have been developed and the application for technical documentation management has been implemented for demonstration purposes.

References

[1]   E. Bertino, M. Damiani et al. Multimedia data handling in a knowledge representation system, Proc. Second Far-East Workshop on Future Database Systems, Kyoto (Japan), April 1992

[2]   E. Bertino, M. Damiani et al. A View Mechanism for a Knowledge Representation System, Proc. of the First International Conference on Information and Knowledge Management, Baltimora, November 1992

[3]   E. Bertino, M. Damiani et al. An Advanced Information Management System, Proc. Workshop on Interoperability among Multidatabase System IEEE Research Issues in Data Engineering, Wien, April 1993

[4]   R. Brachman, F. Halper, Knowledge Representation Support for Data Archeology, Proc. First International Conference on Information and Knowledge Management, Baltimora (Maryland - US), November 1992.

[5]   R. Brachman, D. McGuiness et al. Living with CLASSIC: When and How to Use a KL-ONE Like Language, May 1990

[6]   R. Brachman, J. Shmoltze, An overview of the KL-ONE knowledge representation system, Cognitive Science, April 1985,

[7]   M. Damiani, S. Bottarelli, A Terminological Approach to Business Domain Modelling, Proc. of the First International Conference on Database and Expert System Applications - DEXA 90, Wien, August 1990

[8]   M. Damiani, Representing the Part Of in Back: a Modelling Exercise, AIMS Final Deliverable, November 1993

[9]   T. Hoppe, C. Kindermann et al., BACK V5 - Tutorial and Manual,KIT Report, March 1993

[10]   V.Kim, E.Bertino, Composite Objects Revisited, Proceedings 1989, ACM Sigmod.

[11]   K. von Luck, B. Nebel et al., The anatomy of the BACK system, KIT Report 41, Department of Computer Science, Technical University Berlin , January 1987

[12]   J. Martin, J. Odell, Object Oriented Analysis and Design, Prentice Hall 1991

[13]   P. Menaglio, L. Spampinato et al. A Language to Manage Database Information with a Treminological System, AIMS Final Deliverable October 1993

[14]   P. Patel-Schneider et al., Term Subsumption languages in knowledge representation, The AI Magazine, 11(2), 1990

[15]   J.Rumbaugh, M.Blaha et al. Object Oriented Modelling and Design, Prenctice Hall International, 1991

[16]   Y. Ioannidis, M. Linvy, Conceptual Schemas: Multi-faceted Tools for Desktop Scientific Experiment Management, International Journal of Intelligent&Cooperative Information Systems, Dec 1992

Effective Optimistic Concurrency Control in Multiversion Object Bases*

Peter Graham and Ken Barker
Advanced Database Systems Laboratory
Department of Computer Science
University of Manitoba
Winnipeg, Manitoba
Canada R3T 2N2
{pgraham,barker}@cs.umanitoba.ca

June 28, 1994

Abstract

The use of versioned data has proven its value in many areas of Computer Science including concurrency control. In this paper we examine the use of versioned objects in object bases for the purpose of enhancing concurrency. We provide a framework for discussing multi-version objects which includes fundamental definitions, the abstraction of objects as automata and a model of object method executions as transactions. A practical optimistic concurrency control protocol for multiversion objects is then presented within the developed framework. This protocol avoids the high roll back costs associated with optimistic protocols in two ways. First, a less restrictive definition of conflict, compared to other definitions, is used to determine when concurrent executions are invalid. Fewer conflicts means fewer roll backs are necessary. Second, a *reconciliation* process is described which permits cost-effective recovery from invalid concurrent executions rather than roll back.

1 Introduction

Object base systems have been of particular interest to the research community recently with many interesting results being produced. One of the major motivations for developing object base systems is their suitability in supporting the advanced applications expected over the next decades. Anticipated future systems include cooperative work environments [8] and computer assisted design

---

*This research was partially supported by the Natural Science and Engineering Research Council (NSERC) of Canada under Operating Grants (OGP-0105566 and OGP-0121527).

systems [2], both of which support multiple users working toward some common goal, often on overlapping components. We argue that such applications require versioned objects to effectively provide the capabilities expected of them.

There are many reasons to support multi-version objects in an object base:

- Versioned objects permit increased concurrency in the execution of object method invocations.

- Design applications often require that multiple versions of objects be kept for history, software management, and recovery purposes.

- Systems having long-lived transactions may use multi-version objects to permit concurrent access to data by those transactions.

Little work has directly addressed the issues associated with supporting versioned objects in object base systems. The lack of interest is due to the absence of a carefully constructed model describing when versions are created, when versions may be deleted, and when *concurrent* object access is valid. It is also because of the drawbacks attributed to optimistic concurrency control protocols which are characteristic of multiversion concurrency control. This paper addresses both of these issues.

First, a simple model is proposed that describes the elements of an object base system that are of interest. These include *objects*, *transactions*, and *versions*. Then we formally define what constitutes a correct execution sequence in a way analogous to the definition of *serializability*.

Second, we address the fundamental deficiency of existing optimistic concurrency control schemes, namely, *roll back* cost. Optimistic schemes offer much reduced concurrency control overhead when conflicts are rare but require costly roll backs when conflicts occur. We reduce this cost in two ways; we provide a conflict definition which is less restrictive than that normally applied, and we *reconcile* rather than abort. We describe the basics of a reconciliation process which combines the effects of *conflicting* concurrent transactions on an object to produce a single, consistent object version. This is done at lower cost than aborting and re-executing one of the conflicting transactions.

This paper is organized as follows. Related work is described in Section 2. Section 3 presents our model. Section 4 discusses conflicts as they occur between transactions in an object base and defines a non-restrictive, fine-grained, conflict criterion. The reconciliation process is detailed in Section 5 while Section 6 presents a concurrency control algorithm that uses reconciliation in a multiversion object base. Finally, Section 7 makes some concluding remarks and proposes directions for future research.

2 Related Work

The seminal work on multiversion concurrency control in conventional databases is that of Bernstein and Goodman [3] which defines the model where *writes* to data items result in the creation of new versions of those items. This permits late *reads* to overlap with subsequent operations thereby enhancing concurrency. The basic work they describe has been extended and refined by numerous researchers including, Wu, *et al* [22] and Morzy [17].

Kelter [13] has addressed the problem of providing concurrency control for versioned objects in CAD databases and Kaifer has presented a "framework" for cooperative work based on versions [11]. Recently, Kaifer and Schöning suggest a mechanism for mapping existing version models to complex object models [12]. This work provides a concrete application of versioning in object systems.

Some existing object bases do support object versions, most notably ORION [15] and IRIS [21]. Object versions in these systems are, however, maintained explicitly by the user [14]. We exploit object versions exclusively for concurrency control purposes and thus the existence of multiple versions is transparent to the user.

To avoid rollback, multiple versions of an object which have been concurrently accessed must be reconciled to produce a single consistent version. Such reconciliation requires the capture of semantic information about the operations performed on object versions. Much work in the literature incorporating semantics into concurrency control is based on *commutativity* as described by Weihl [19]. A serious drawback to the use of commutativity is that the commutativity relations must be generated *manually*. This places an undue burden on the programmer. Other approaches refine concurrency control by using forms of semantic information about objects which are derived *automatically*. These include the work of Malta and Martinez [16], Graham, *et al* [7], and Hakimzadeh and Perrizo [10].

Reconciliation has been suggested for use in distributed systems to permit concurrent access to *all* file replicas despite network partitioning (e.g. the LOCUS distributed operating system [18]. Rather than limiting access to a single replica while the network is partitioned, reconciliation is used to "combine" the effects of any conflicting updates that occurr while the network is partitioned. Permitting optimistic access to replicas has also been suggested for use in distributed databases by Davidson [4]. Two fundamental differences between Davidson's work and ours are that she requires commitment delays (until recovery is performed) and requires complete transaction re-execution rather than reconciliation.

3   The Model

In our model, an object base consists of a set of uniquely identified objects each containing structural and behavioural components. The structural component is a set of uniquely identified data items referred to as *attributes* whose values define the object's state. The behavioural component is a set of procedures, usually called *methods*, that are the only means of accessing the structural components and thereby modifying the object's state. This paper denotes the jth attribute of object O_i as a_{ij}. Similarly, an object's method(s) are identified using the notation m_{ij}.

Object base users execute transactions on objects by invoking methods that manipulate their attributes. A transaction is a partial order of operations on objects in the object base. We denote an operation (i.e. *method invocation*) of a transaction T^i on object O_j by m^i_{jk} and the set of all operations of transaction T^i by OS^i. All transactions terminate by either committing or aborting. $N^i \in$ {commit, abort} is the termination condition for T^i.

Definition 1 A *transaction* T^i is a partial order $(\Sigma^i, \prec^i)$ where:

1. $\Sigma^i = OS^i \cup \{N^i\}$.

2. For any two conflicting operations $m^i_{jm}, m^i_{jn} \in OS^i$, then either $m^i_{jm} \prec^i m^i_{jn}$ or $m^i_{jn} \prec^i m^i_{jm}$.

3. $\forall m^i_{jk} \in OS^i, m^i_{jk} \prec^i N^i$. ∎

At any time, there exists a single committed version of each object in the object base called the *last committed version* (LCV). When a user accesses an object by issuing a transaction, an *active version* (AV) (which is a copy of the current LCV) is *derived*. Thus, there is an active version for each transaction accessing a given object. The LCV from which an AV is derived is called the *base version* of the object for the corresponding transaction. The version which is the *last* committed version changes as new versions are successfully committed. Committed versions are deleted once all active versions derived from them have either committed or aborted. All active versions which conflict with committed versions must be *reconciled* or aborted so that only "correct" effects are reflected in the object base.

Definition 2 An object version may be *committed* iff

1. it is an object in its initial state, or

2. the object has been moved from one consistent state to another consistent state by a committed transaction. ∎

3.1 Execution Model

Having defined the basic elements of a multiversion object base, it is now necessary to understand how these exist and interact. Multiversion object bases have multiple objects, several concurrently executing transactions, and possibly multiple versions of each object. This is viewed as a transaction system whose execution sequences may be captured by a *history*.

Intuitively, a history is a partial order of the executions of transaction operations where the ordering relation must include those pairs of operations that conflict.

Definition 3 A *history* H, of a set of transactions $T = \{T^1, T^2, \ldots, T^n\}$, is a partial order $(\Sigma_T, \prec_T)$ where:

1. $\Sigma_T = \bigcup_{i=1}^{n} \Sigma^i$.

2. $\prec_T \supseteq \bigcup_{i=1}^{n} \prec^i$.

3. For any two conflicting operations $m_{kr}^i, m_{ks}^j \in \Sigma_T$, either $m_{kr}^i \prec_T m_{ks}^j$, or $m_{kr}^j \prec_T m_{ks}^i$. ∎

This definition enables us to reason about histories as transaction operation execution sequences using the ordering relation $\prec_T$. For example, given that the initial state of an object O_k, prior to the execution of the transactions in T is S_k, then the three method invocations occurring in the order; $m_{kr}^i \prec m_{ks}^j \prec m_{kt}^l$ will move O_k into some state $S_{k'}$. This can be considered a sequence of state transition functions such that $S_{k'} = m_{kt}^l(m_{ks}^j(m_{kr}^i(S_k)))$.

Transaction models usually base correctness on a *serial* ordering where a single transaction executed alone on a consistent object base will produce a consistent object base. Multiversion object bases can use the same correctness criterion tailored to suit their unique characteristics. Since each transaction creates its own active object, it can freely modify the object without concern for other users. When a transaction commits it can replace the existing committed version of the object with the "new" active version and leave the object base in a consistent state.

Definition 4 A transaction T^i which accesses an object O_j will create an active object O_j^i, modify it to create $O_j^{i'}$ and then replace O_j with $O_j^{i'}$ when it commits. A *serial* history (H_s) is one which follows this sequence indivisibly for all transactions at all objects. ∎

In a serial execution (Definition 4) only one active version of any object will ever exist at a time (due to indivisibility). Thus, there can be no interleaving of operations from different transactions at an object.

Definition 5 A history H is serializable iff H is equivalent to some serial history H_S. ∎

Serializable histories and their corresponding transactions are, by definition, correct.

4 Conflicts

Using optimistic concurrency control *any* pair of concurrent method invocations on an object will result in a conflict requiring one method execution (and the corresponding transaction) to be aborted. One way to limit aborts, is through the use of a precise notion of conflict. The basis of our definition of conflict is traditional read/write and write/write conflicts but at a finer level of granularity than the entire object (as would be used, for instance in systems which apply object-level locking such as Orion [6, 15], O2 [5] and IRIS [21]). The attribute read/write behaviour of methods (i.e. the semantic information) needed to determine conflicts can be determined *automatically* when the methods are compiled.

Conflict *may* be occur when two method invocations occur concurrently on a single object O_i. In this case, O_i is initially in some state S_i and two method executions (say $f^s = m_{ix}^s$ and $g^t = m_{iy}^t$) perform state transforming functions on their local copies of the object. Since f^s and g^t are scheduled concurrently, we assume that they are unrelated[1] and their execution order is irrelevant as long as it is serializable. Thus to be correct, the new object state after the concurrent execution of f^s and g^t must be either $f(g(S_i))$ or $g(f(S_i))$. There is, however, no guarantee that an uncontrolled concurrent execution of f and g will produce a final object state equivalent to either. Transaction T^s which executes f will produce a version of O_i in state $f(S_i)$ while transaction T^t (executing g) will produce a version having state $g(S_i)$. These versions may not be "compatible" (i.e. $g(S_i) \neq f(S_i) \neq f(g(S_i)) \neq g(f(S_i))$). To know when concurrent executions will be incompatible we must know when the method executions conflict. We extend the common notion of conflict to object versions as follows:

Definition 6 Two *versions* of an object are said to *conflict* if they are produced by conflicting method executions on active versions of an object derived from the same base version. ∎

When two concurrent method invocations are made against some object O_i, two active versions (O_i' and O_i'') are created and these may be conflicting versions. Four possible "Reconciliation Cases" are possible depending on the kind of conflict which occurs (if any), each of which must be resolved to ensure object consistency.

Reconciliation Case 1 – If f^s and g^t are both read-only transactions with respect to the attributes of O_i, then no conflict occurred and no processing is required.

Reconciliation Case 2 – If f^s is read-only at O_i but g^t is not then the new object state must be set to $g^t(S_i)$. Similarly if g^t is read-only but f^s is not, the new object state must be set to $f^s(S_i)$. Additionally transaction T^s must be serialized before T^t in the first case and T^t must be serialized before T^s in the second.

Reconciliation Case 3 – If f^s and g^t conflict and f^s is a costly (as judged, perhaps, by a statically derived estimate of average number of instructions executed) operation then set the new object state to be $f^s(S_i)$ and re-execute g^t. Similarly if g^t is the costly operation but f^s is not then set the new object state to be $g^t(S_i)$ and re-execute f^s.

Reconciliation Case 4 – If f^s and g^t conflict and both f^s and g^t are costly then apply a reconciliation procedure to combine the effects of f^s and

---

[1] It is assumed that serial dependences in method executions are respected so concurrent method executions on an object arising from the same transaction do not occur.

Condition 1: $WS(f) \bigcap WS(g) = \phi$
Condition 2: $WS(f) \bigcap RS(g) = \phi$
Condition 3: $RS(f) \bigcap WS(g) = \phi$

Figure 1: Intersection Conditions

g^t to produce a new version having the consistent state $s' = f^s(g^t(S_i))$ or $g^t(f^s(S_i))$ whichever is cheaper to compute. The selection of reconciliation function determines the serialization order of transactions T^s and T^t.

To determine conflict in Reconciliation Cases 3 and 4 we define, for each method, m_{ik} in object O_i a read set ($RS(m_{ik})$) and a write set ($WS(m_{ik})$) of the object attributes. The contents of these sets are the *elemental* attributes of the object. Thus, if an object contains an array, each element in the array is considered to be a *separate* attribute which may appear in one, or both, of the read and write sets of each method in the object. Simple intersections between the read and write sets of method pairs is the basis for our determination of conflicts.

Consider two methods f and g on O_i and the three intersection conditions given in Figure 1. If all these intersection conditions hold then the updates made to the attributes of an object by method executions f^s and g^t are distinct and independent so the resulting object versions do not conflict. This means that both versions may be committed and the transactions may be serialized in either order. Unless both transactions are read-only "simple reconciliation" (discussed later) is required to ensure a final, consistent object state.

Intersection condition 1 tests to ensure that the updates are to distinct object attributes. The subsequent conditions test to ensure that no transaction reads a stale attribute value. If only the first condition and *one* of the last two holds then the Read-Write conflict may lead to an incorrect execution depending on the serialization order chosen. If the appropriate serialization order (having the writer follow the reader) is met, then no conflict occurs despite the intersection of the read and write sets. For example, if conditions 1 and 2 hold but 3 does not, then there is a conflict between transactions T^s and T^t at object O_i but provided that the transactions are serialized in the order $T^s \rightarrow T^t$ the execution is still correct. This is because an attribute read by f^s which is written by g^t is *not* stale. Since T^t serializes after T^s, f^s is expected to read the *old* value of the attribute.

5 Reconciliation

When intersection conditions 1,2,3 (or 1,2 or 1,3) hold and the required serialization order is followed (for 1,2 or 1,3), it is possible to combine the effects of the two transactions using "simple reconciliation".

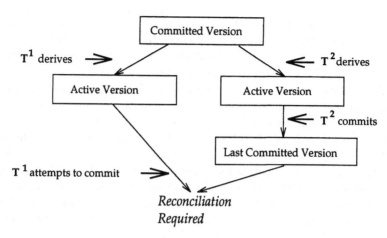

Figure 2: Reconciliation

Definition 7 *Simple reconciliation* is the process of reconciling f^s and g^t by setting the new object state on an attribute by attribute basis as follows: If S_i is the original object state and S_i' is the new, consistent object state, then for each attribute a_{ix}:

$$S_i'(a_{ix}) = \begin{cases} f^s(S_i)(a_{ix}) & \text{if } a_i \in WS(f^s) \\ g^t(S_i)(a_{ix}) & \text{if } a_i \in WS(g^t) \\ S_i(a_{ix}) & \text{otherwise} \end{cases}$$

where the notation $f^s(S_i)$ indicates the state of object O_i produced by executing method f from transaction T^s on the object state S_i. ∎

Complex reconciliation is required whenever two costly method executions produce *conflicting* versions based on violation of the intersection conditions of Figure 1. Figure 2 illustrates this situation (assuming T^1's accesses conflict with those of T^2). Although several method invocations may concurrently occur on the same object, in the interest of brevity, we deal only with the two invocation case. We argue that this approach illustrates the basic concept of reconciliation without exposing the unnecessary complexity of the more general problem[2].

We assume that nested objects are atomic. Thus an object attribute which is itself an object, is treated as a *single* entity. Any method invocation (i.e. operation) made on such a "sub-object" is conservatively assumed to conflict with any other such method invocation. This is not necessary but supporting non-atomic sub-objects is beyond the scope of this paper.

Reconciliation is most beneficial when the number of attributes involved in the conflict is small compared to the total number of attributes referenced. In this case only a small percentage of the accessed attributes have been incorrectly updated and rollback would result in a great deal of the method's work being unnecessarily lost. By reconciling rather than rolling back, this work is not

---

[2]Extension to general forms of sharing is the subject of a future paper.

lost[3] and a savings in execution overhead is achieved. Ideally, the reconciliation process will totally preserve the non-conflicting part of a method execution's work while re-executing only the conflicting part. In no case will reconciliation be more expensive than roll back and re-execution.

The results of the method execution which serializes (and commits) first are correct without modification but those of the other method execution must be changed so that they reflect the results which would have been produced had the initial state of the object used been that produced by the the first method's execution. Which object attributes must be recalculated to achieve this effect can be easily determined and we know that those attributes must be recalculated according to the execution semantics of the *second* method. Thus, if the operations m_{ij}^s and m_{ik}^t are to be serialized in the order $T^s \rightarrow T^t$ and the intersection condition $WS(m_{ij}^s) \cap RS(m_{ik}^t) = \phi$ is violated then any computation performed in m_{ik}^t which relies on an attribute value in $WS(m_{ij}^s)$ must be re-executed using the state $m_{ij}^s(S_i)$ as input. In effect, full reconciliation may thus be viewed as a *partial* re-execution of one of the methods involved.

The leading question is: "How to automatically generate the reconciliation procedures for each possible pair of object methods in each possible serialization order?" The reconciliation procedures suggested in this paper do not attempt to exploit *high level* semantics as in Weihl's work on commutativity. It is the need to understand high level program semantics that makes the automatic generation of commutativity tables and compensating transactions difficult. Each reconciliation procedure is a subset of one of the methods being reconciled and the determination of the subset is accomplished by exploiting well-understood data dependence [1] techniques.

Definition 8 Given two conflicting operations m_{ij}^s and m_{ik}^t to be serialized in the order $T^s \rightarrow T^t$, the *conflict set* for reconciliation specifies which attributes of O_i must be re-read from the state $m_{ij}^s(S_i)$ by the partial re-execution of m_{ik}^t and is defined as: $CS(m_{ij}^s, m_{ik}^t) = WS(m_{ij}^s) \cap RS(m_{ik}^t)$ ∎

Definition 9 Given two computation steps (i.e. operations acting on one or more attributes) s_i and s_j in a method, a *true dependence* (denoted $s_i \delta s_j$) occurs if s_j reads an attribute which was previously written (as judged by the execution semantics of the method specification language) by s_i. ∎

Definition 10 Given two computation steps s_i and s_j in a method, an *anti dependence* (denoted $s_i \bar{\delta} s_j$) occurs if s_j writes an attribute which was previously read (as judged by the execution semantics ...) by s_i. ∎

Definition 11 Given two computation steps s_i and s_j in a method, an *output dependence* (denoted $s_i \delta^o s_j$) occurs if s_j writes an attribute which was previously written (as judged by the execution semantics ...) by s_i. ∎

The attribute inducing the dependence is commonly specified as a subscript to the dependence symbol (e.g. $s_1 \delta_{a_{ix}} s_2$).

---

[3]Furthermore, the work of other method executions from the same transaction is not lost.

These definitions of dependence are easily extended to incorporate call statements to methods in sub-objects by considering such statements to read any attributes used as input parameters and to write any used as output parameters. This simple extension is sufficient because objects provide encapsulation. Dependence relations may also be extended to involve more than two computation steps by applying a form of transitive closure. For example, given the dependence relations; $s_1 \delta_{a_{ix}} s_2 \overline{\delta}_{a_{ix}} s_3$ there is also a transitive output dependence $s_1 \delta^o_{a_{ix}} s_3$ since s_1 writes a_{ix} and so does s_3 in a subsequent statement. Such transitive dependencies are indicated by suffixing a superscript asterisk to the dependence symbol (e.g. $s_1 \delta^{o*}_{a_{ix}} s_3$).

Existing techniques used in optimizing and parallelizing compilers can be used to partially order all the computation steps in a method according to their true data dependencies.

Definition 12 The dependencies between the computation steps in method m_{ij} ($OPS(m_{ij})$) induce a partial order ($OPS(m_{ij}), \prec_\delta$) which must be followed in any correct execution of that method or a reconciliation procedure which is a subset of it. ∎

Definition 13 A computation step $s_p \in m^t_{ik}$ reads a *critical input attribute* a_{ix} if it accesses it for reading, if $a_{ix} \in CS(m^s_{ij}, m^t_{ik})$, and if there is no output dependence $s_q \delta^{o*}_{a_{ix}} s_p$ for any $s_q \in m^t_{ik}$. ∎

Any computation step which directly reads a critical input attribute or which depends on a computation step that directly reads a critical input attribute, *depends* on that critical input attribute. All computation steps that depend on a critical input attribute must be re-executed to reconcile the method execution of which they are a part.

Computation steps may be simple assignments or complex, multi-instruction code blocks containing entire control structures. A simple assignment step accesses fewer attributes so it is less likely to depend on a critical input attribute and thereby require re-execution to effect reconciliation. Because it is impossible to know run-time values during compilation (when the reconciliation procedures are generated) and due to the inherent limitations on the computation of dependence information, it is not always possible to completely reduce each complex computation step to a collection of simple assignment operations. Thus, compile-time generation of reconciliation procedures is "conservative". Current dependence analysis techniques do provide sufficient information to make reconciliation practical in the domain of object-based systems.

Definition 14 The *dependence graph* of method m_{ij} is a graph $DG(m_{ij}) = (V, E)$ where V, the vertices in the graph, are the computation steps in m_{ij} and E, the edges connecting vertices in the graph, are determined by $\prec_\delta$ (the orderings determined by the *true* dependencies). ∎

The dependence graph of a method is a DAG[4] which effectively abstracts the computation performed by the method. Each reconciliation procedure may be similarly abstracted as a sub-graph of the dependence graph of the method.

For each pair of methods m_{ij} and m_{ik} in an object O_i two reconciliation procedures $reconcile(m_{ij}, m_{ik})$ and $reconcile(m_{ik}, m_{ij})$ must be generated, one for each possible serialization order.

Definition 15 A *reconciliation procedure* $reconcile(m_{ij}, m_{ik})$ is abstracted by the sub-graph of $DG(m_{ik})$ consisting of those vertices which are dependent on the critical input attributes in $\mathcal{CS}(m_{ij}, m_{ik})$ and the edges which connect those vertices. ∎

The automatic construction of an actual reconciliation procedure given its corresponding dependence sub-graph substitutes the appropriate computation steps from m_{ik} for each vertex in the sub-graph and emits the resulting code in an order given by a topological sort of the computation steps consistent with the partial order determined by the edges of the sub-graph (i.e. consistent with $\prec_\delta$).

6 Multi-Version Concurrency Control with Reconciliation

We have discussed both conflicts and the reconciliation process as if they were applicable to exactly two *active* transactions attempting to commit *simultaneously*. It is unacceptable to postpone the commitment of one transaction while waiting for another to complete. Thus, in the following algorithm we apply the basic techniques in a way which allows a single transaction to commit at a time.

The algorithm in Figure 3 describes the scheduling of multi-version object transactions with reconciliation. It accepts a transaction (T^i) as input and produces a response indicating success (commit) or failure (abort). When T^i is submitted the set of objects accessed $\mathcal{BS}^i$ is determined (line (2)). The algorithm assumes this is accomplished *á priori*. An active version is made of each object accessed and the operations on each object are mapped to references to that version (line (5)). The transaction then executes operations without restriction or further intervention from the scheduler until it either aborts or is prepared to commit. If T^i issues an abort operation, procedure **version_abort** (line (1)) is called from (line (7)) to discard all the active object versions created and the algorithm terminates and returns a failure indication.

Commit processing begins at line (12) where it is determined if another transaction has committed a new version of the object since the committing transaction began – this is the test for potential conflict. The various reconciliation cases are dealt with by (lines (13 – 21)). Note that read only access

---

[4]This assumes that loops are treated as single computation steps. This simplifying assumption does not affect the correctness of the computation only the granularity of the operations and hence the likelihood that they will need to be recomputed during reconciliation.

procedure Version Transaction Scheduler (T^i) : **returns** (result);
input: T^i : transaction to be executed;
output: result : boolean;

    procedure version_abort $(T^j, \mathcal{BS}^j)$;   (1)
    input: T^j : transaction to abort;
              $\mathcal{BS}^j$: Base Set of T^j;
    begin
        forall $O_k \in \mathcal{BS}^j$ **do** discard $O_k^{j'}$
    end /* version_abort */;

begin /* Transaction Scheduling */
    $\mathcal{BS}^i \leftarrow$ set of objects read/written by T^i;   (2)
    forall $O_k \in \mathcal{BS}^i$ (3)
        derive an *active* object $O_k^{i'}$ from the LCV of O_k;   (4)
    execute T^i: mapping each operation on O_l to an operation on $O_l^{i'}$ (5)
    if $(T^i$ aborts) **then begin**   (6)
        version_abort $(T^i, \mathcal{BS}^i)$;   (7)
        exit (FALSE);   (8)
    end;
    if $(T^i$ is prepared–to–commit) **then**   (9)
        forall $O_k \in \mathcal{BS}^i$ **do begin**   (10)
            lock (O_k);   (11)
            if $(O_k$'s LCV is not the base version of $O_k^{i'}$) **then begin** (12)
               /* A new LCV exists so ... */
               if (case 2 and $O_k^{i'} = LCV$) **then**   (13)
                   /* do reconciliation – we read stale data */
                   $complex\_reconcile(LCV(O_k), O_k^{i'})$;   (14)
               else if (case 3) **then**   (15)
                   /* reconciliation is cheap so do it */
                   $complex\_reconcile(LCV(O_k), O_k^{i'})$;   (16)
               else if (case 4) **then**   (17)
                 if (conditions in Figure 1 are met for the
                   order $T^{LCV} \to T^i$ at O_k) **then**   (18)
                   $simple\_reconcile(LCV(O_k), O_k^{i'})$;   (19)
                 else
                   $complex\_reconcile(LCV(O_k), O_k^{i'})$;   (20)
               else ; /* this version is OK */   (21)
            end;
        begin_atomic;   (22)
            forall $O_k \in \mathcal{BS}^i$ **do begin**   (23)
                commit $O_k^{i'}$ as O_k if $O_k^{i'}$ was updated;   (24)
                unlock (O_k);   (25)
            end
        end_atomic;   (26)
        exit (TRUE) ;   (27)
    end;
end /*Version Transaction Scheduler */

Figure 3: Transaction Scheduling with Reconciliation

occurring in Reconciliation Cases 1 and 2, are handled implicitly (lines (21) and (24)) because no new version is written if the active version is unchanged. Line (13) tests if T^i was read only at O_k and then determines if stale data was read (due to a previous committed transaction). If so, complex reconciliation (see Definition 15) is performed (line (14)). Similarly complex reconciliation is performed (line (16)) for Reconciliation Case 3. If T^i is the costly operation we must still reconcile it with the inexpensive one which created the current LCV since we have no ability to change the serialization order so that $T^i \rightarrow T^{LCV}$. If T^i is the inexpensive operation rather than re-executing it we also reconcile. This is reasonable since we know that reconciliation will never be more expensive than re-execution (the worst case is a reconciliation procedure which contains all the statements of the corresponding method). Reconciliation Case 4 is handled by performing either simple or complex reconciliation (lines (18 – 20)). Simple reconciliation (see Definition 7) is performed whenever the conditions in Figure 1 that correspond to the serialization order $T^{LCV} \rightarrow T^i$ are met. Complex reconciliation is performed otherwise.

The correctness of this algorithm is predicated upon the execution being equivalent to some serial execution. If no concurrent execution of methods occurs at any object, then the multi-version execution is equivalent to a non-multi-version serial execution and is therefore correct. This is easily seen because the commitment order is serial at every object. Since commitment involves generating a new LCV, which will be used by subsequent transactions, and because of the transactions' atomicity and durability properties, we are guaranteed that a subsequent method execution will see only correct, committed object state information when it derives its active version.

When two concurrent method executions occur at an object, one will finish and commit first. According to the algorithm presented, this determines the serialization order to be the commit order[5]. The committing transaction produces a new LCV. In any serial execution it is this version of the object which must be used as the base version for method invocations arising from any transaction serializing after the one which produced the new LCV. Since concurrency has occurred, the second method execution may have seen stale data from the previous LCV (its base version). For concurrent execution to be correct, the second method execution must execute as if it had read the new LCV and used it as its base version.

If the concurrent method executions do not conflict given the serialization order determined by their transaction's commitment order then the second method execution may commit freely without reconciliation and since it did not conflict with the first, it can safely generate a new LCV. If both method executions were read-only then no new LCV need be written by either committed transaction. If only the second method execution writes attributes, then it simply commits creating a single new LCV which is correct and consistent. If the first method execution writes attributes then, since we assume no conflict between the method executions, it must have written data that cannot affect the execution of the

---

[5]This need not be the case and is the subject of future research.

second method execution. This is the simple reconciliation case. We cannot allow the second transaction to commit and write its version back as the new LCV since this would not correctly reflect the updates made to object attributes by the first method execution (i.e. the lost update problem). We correct this by creating a new LCV which consists of the correctly updated attributes produced by *both* method executions.

Finally, if the method executions do conflict then complex reconciliation must be applied. To produce a correct execution, the result of complex reconciliation must be a version of the object in a state equivalent to that which would have resulted from the serial execution of the two method executions in the order of their transactions' serialization. This is exactly the effect provided by executing a reconciliation procedure constructed in the fashion described in the paper. Since any operation within the second method which depends on an attribute written by the first is re-executed as a part of the reconciliation procedure and since the execution order of statements within the reconciliation procedure adheres to the serial semantics (i.e. dependencies) of the original method, correctness is assured.

Correctness can also be illustrated in terms of transaction histories. Non-conflicting concurrent executions have histories which are serializable. Conflicting concurrent executions have non-serializable histories (since no concurrency control was enforced *a priori*). Reconciliation effectively re-orders the conflicting operations in a non-serializable history (re-executing operations as necessary) to make the history serializable.

7 Conclusions and Future Work

We have presented a formalism for describing multi-version object base systems and the transactions on them. We have also presented an algorithm (Figure 3) which offers both low-overhead concurrency control and negligible roll back costs. Further, the main cost associated with our approach (creating reconciliation procedures) is incurred at method compilation time and thus results in no runtime overhead.

Much work remains to be done. The stated limitations of the work presented in this paper can be improved upon. This includes the limitation of reconciling only *two* concurrent method executions on an object and the treating of sub-objects as atomic data. Our assumption that objects are not shared by multiple parents is too restrictive because sharing is a fundamental principle of object bases. Unfortunately, while this problem is simple to manage theoretically, a solution to it is quite difficult to implement efficiently.

As each transaction commits at a given object, the algorithm presented only attempts to commit the corresponding active version of the object *after* all other committed versions. This is restrictive since it means that the serialization order must follow the commit order. This too is unnecessary. Under certain conditions, it is possible to serialize a committing version *behind* other versions which have already committed. This may permit more transactions to actually commit without having to invoke a reconciliation procedure and is also the basis for allowing commitment of versions from different base versions.

The conditions under which "out-of-order" serialization may be done are straightforward, but the change in serialization order affects the serialization properties of the algorithm. No local atomicity [20] property is met so inter-object serializability must be *explicitly* ensured. The separation of intra- and inter-object serializability was suggested by Hadzilacos and Hadzilacos [9] and a model was proposed by Zapp and Barker [24, 23]. Efficiently ensuring inter-object serializability is another difficult problem.

Finally, it is difficult to judge the real costs inherent in maintaining the required multiversion object environment without having a prototype system. Similarly, speculation on the savings achieved by reconciling rather than re-executing is meaningless without a set of real applications and a system to test them with. Clearly, an important step in future research will be the construction of a testbed system to verify quantitatively the ideas proposed in this paper.

References

[1] U. Banerjee. *Dependence Analysis for Supercomputing*. Kluwer Academic, 1988.

[2] N.S. Barghouti and G.E. Kaiser. Concurrency Control in Advanced Database Applications. *ACM Computing Surveys*, 23(3):269–317, 1991.

[3] P.A. Bernstein and N. Goodman. Multiversion Concurrency Control – Theory and Algorithms. *ACM Transactions on Database Systems*, 8(4):465 – 483, 1983.

[4] S.B. Davidson. Optimism and Consistency in Partitioned Distributed Database Systems. *ACM Transactions on Database Systems*, 9(3):456 – 481, 1984.

[5] O. Deux *et al.* The Story of O_2. *IEEE Transactions on Knowledge and Data Engineering*, 2(1):91 – 108, 1990.

[6] J.F. Garza and W. Kim. Transaction Management in an Object-Oriented Database System. In *Proceedings of the ACM SIGMOD International Conference on the Management of Data*, pages 37 – 45. ACM, 1988.

[7] P.C.J. Graham, M.E. Zapp, and K. Barker. Applying Method Data Dependence to Transactions in Object Bases. Technical Report TR 92-7, University of Manitoba, Dept. of Computer Science, 1992.

[8] S. Greenberg, editor. *Computer-supported Cooperative Work and Groupware*. Academic Press, 1991.

[9] T. Hadzilacos and V. Hadzilacos. Transaction Synchronization in Object Bases. *Journal of Computer and System Sciences*, 43(1):2 – 24, 1991.

[10] H. Hakimzadeh and W. Perrizo. Instance Variable Access Locking for Object-Oriented Databases. *International Journal for Micro and Mini Computer Applications*, 1993. *in print*.

[11] W. Kaifer. A Framework for Version-based Cooperation Control. In *Proceedings of the 2nd International Symposium on Database Systems for Advanced Applications*, 1991.

[12] W. Kaifer and H. Schöning. Mapping a Version Model to a Complex-Object Data Model. Technical report, University Kaiserslautern, 1993.

[13] U. Kelter. Concurrency Control for Design Objects with Versions in CAD Databases. *Information Systems*, 12(2):137 – 143, 1987.

[14] W. Kim. *Introduction to Object-Oriented Databases*. MIT Press, 1990.

[15] W. Kim, J.F. Garza, N. Ballou, and D. Woelk. Architecture of the ORION Next-Generation Database System. *IEEE Transactions on Knowledge and Data Engineering*, 2(1):109 – 124, 1990.

[16] C. Malta and J. Martinez. Automating Fine Concurrency Control in Object-Oriented Databases. In *Proceedings of the International Conference on Data Engineering*, pages 253 – 260, 1993.

[17] T. Morzy. The Correctness of Concurrency Control for Multiversion Database Systems with Limited Number of Versions. *IEEE*, pages 595 – 604, 1993.

[18] B. Walker, G. Popek, R. English, C. Kline, and G. Thiel. The LOCUS Distributed Operating Systems. In *Proceedings of the Ninth ACM Symposium on the Operating Systems Principles*, pages 49 – 70, Bretton Woods, New Hampshire, 1983.

[19] W.E. Weihl. Commutativity-Based Concurrency Control for Abstract Data Types. *IEEE Transactions on Computers*, 37(12):1488 – 1505, 1988.

[20] W.E. Weihl. Local Atomicity Properties: Modular Concurrency Control for Abstract Data Types. *ACM Transactions of Programming Languages and Systems*, 11(2):249 – 282, 1989.

[21] K. Wilkinson, P. Lyngbaek, and W. Hasan. The Iris Architecture and Implemntation. *IEEE Transactions on Knowledge and Data Engineering*, 2(1):63 – 75, 1990.

[22] K-L. Wu, P.S. Yu, and M-S. Chen. Dynamic Finite Versioning: An Effective Versioning Approach to Concurrent Transaction and Query Processing. *IEEE*, pages 577 – 586, 1993.

[23] M.E. Zapp and K. Barker. Modular Concurrency Control Algorithms for Object Bases. In *International Symposium on Applied Computing: Research and Applications in Software Engineering, Databases, and Distributed Systems*, pages 28–36, Monterrey, Mexico, October 1993.

[24] M.E. Zapp and K. Barker. The Serializability of Transactions in Object Bases. In *Proceedings of the International Conference on Computers and Information*, pages 428–432, Sudbury, Canada, May 1993.

Reusing Object Oriented Design: An Algebraic Approach*

Francesco Parisi–Presicce[1] and Alfonso Pierantonio[2]

[1] Dip. Scienze dell'Informazione, Università di Roma La Sapienza, I–00198 Roma, Italy
[2] TFS, Fachbereich Informatik, Technische Universität Berlin, D–10587 Berlin, Germany

Abstract. Based on a model of class specification introduced in previous papers, an inheritance operator is defined which, applied to a class generates a new class which inherits by specialization from the old one. The correctness of the subclass is a consequence of the correctness of the superclass and the modification. Several properties of the operator, such as local confluence and compatibility with inheritance relation, are investigated. These properties form the basis of a reuse methodology for entire class hierarchies, focusing on design reuse instead of code reuse.

1 Introduction

The natural support to data abstraction, information hiding and other key techniques has conferred to the object oriented methodology a relevant role in the development of quality software. The object oriented paradigm is intended primarily as a technique for programming–in–the–large ([9, 17]). A system consists of an interconnection of software components, which realizes the hierarchical abstract data type and each component realizes the exported services in terms of those imported: the clientship relations so established are extended to the data type that the class defines.

System decomposition is an important tool to reduce the overall complexity in specifying and verifying large software systems. Each class is a capsule of behavior and a primary objective is to be able to design, implement and change modules independently, without affecting the clients of the component as long as such changes are semantically compatible.

It is important to distinguish between the task of defining a system interconnecting a number of modules possibly from a library and the design and implementation of a single component. These tasks deal with two kinds of knowledge: programming knowledge in the former case and application domain knowledge in the latter case [10].

The problem of defining a modular system interconnecting components from a library has been addresses in previous papers, e.g. [12]. The implementation of a self contained software component requires knowledge in a specific application domain; the outcome of the implementation phase is a hierarchy of refined classes where the knowledge is distributed monotonically from the topmost class via inheritance. Each

---

* This work has been partially supported by the European Community under ESPRIT Basic Research Working Group COMPASS and by the German DFG.

node of the hierarchy corresponds to a decision: new operations and/or new properties for old ones are added (non–monotonic derivations are shown to be reduced to monotonic ones [13, 18]). Each component is implemented through a step–by–step design phase realizing the vertical structure [2, 3, 11]. It is necessary to have compatibility between the horizontal and vertical structuring mechanisms.

Among the benefits of the object oriented paradigm there is the ease of making changes [19]: this is relevant since the main activities in maintaining software are devoted to enhancements due to adaptations rather than error correction. Another benefit is easier code reuse [9, 1]: brand new classes need not be developed from scratch, but can be constructed from the features of already existing classes. The correctness of a software artifact should be assured by the correctness of its components and of the interconnecting mechanisms. This leads to the notion of clean module operators [7].

In [13, 14] we have presented a formal model of classes based on algebraic specification techniques. A class specification consists of two export interfaces (one with the methods to manipulate objects and one –larger– to be used by other classes), a parameter part for modeling generics, a formal import interface, and an implementation part where the exported services are implemented in terms of those imported. In such a framework, different notions of inheritance have been defined as relations between class specifications. In particular, we have distinguished formally between reusing inheritance, which allows the reuse of the code of another class without any semantical constraint, and specialization inheritance, which allows the definition of new classes incrementally. Moreover, two clean operations among classes are provided, the combination and the actualization, both compatible with the inheritance relation. Such mechanisms are the basis for a class interconnection language. The formalism is based on algebraic techniques and methods since they have a well developped semantical framework. Many results are available and they offer enough generality and flexibility to analyze the mechanisms present in the object paradigm. For example, the use of signature morphisms between specifications bypasses the problem of name clashing.

In this paper, we present a specialization inheritance operator which allows one to reuse not only code but also its properties and verification. The correctness of the subclass is assured by the correctness of the superclass and that of the modification. In general, reuse of implementation is important but "reuse of interface design and functional factoring is more important because they constitute the key intellectual content of software and are far more difficult to create or re–create than code" [21]. The operator is shown to have very interesting compatibility properties which are necessary for the reuse of design. We view a hierarchy behind a software component as a skeleton implementation of an application subsystem in a particular problem domain. In essence, a hierarchy is viewed as a framework [21, 22, 5] although frameworks tend to be ever more integrated with tools which allow the definition of objects while we are concerned only with object types. The focus is on the riutilization of such schemas. The libraries are made of classes which are arranged according to the decisions taken by the software *architects* in their design stage.

After reviewing in section 2 some notation and in section 3 our model of class specification, we present in section 4 the inheritance operator and its main properties, used in section 5 to discuss how software design can be reused. The proofs of our results are omitted and can be found in [15]; here they are illustrated with examples.

2 Preliminary Notation

In this section, we briefly review some basic notions of algebraic specifications; details can be found in [6, 20].

- A *signature* Σ is a pair (S, OP) where S is a set of *sorts* and OP a set of *constants* and *function symbols*. A *pointed signature* is a signature $\Sigma = (S, OP)$ with a distinguished element $pt(\Sigma) \in S$.

- A Σ-*algebra* $A = (S_A, OP_A)$ on a signature $\Sigma = (S, OP)$ consists of a family $S_A = (A_s)_{s \in S}$ of sets and a set $OP_A = (N_A)_{N \in OP}$ of operations. The category of all Σ-algebras is denoted by $Alg(\Sigma)$.

- If $\Sigma_1 = (S_1, OP_1)$ and $\Sigma_2 = (S_2, OP_2)$ are signatures, a *signature morphism* $h : \Sigma_1 \longrightarrow \Sigma_2$ is a pair of functions $(h^S : S_1 \longrightarrow S_2, h^{OP} : OP_1 \longrightarrow OP_2)$ such that if $N : s_1 ... s_n \longrightarrow s \in OP_1$, then $h^{OP}(N) : h^S(s_1)...h^S(s_n) \longrightarrow h^S(s) \in OP_2$

- Every signature morphism $h : \Sigma_1 \longrightarrow \Sigma_2$ induces a *forgetful functor* denoted by $V_h : Alg(\Sigma_2) \longrightarrow Alg(\Sigma_1)$. Given a Σ_2-algebra A' with sets $S_{2A'}$ and operations $OP_{2A'}$, $V_h(A')$ is the Σ_1-algebra A where $S_{1A} = (A'_{h^S(s)})_{s \in S_1}$ and $OP_{1A} = (h^{OP}(N)_{A'})_{N \in OP_1}$. A *pointed signature morphism* is a signature morphism $h : \Sigma_1 \longrightarrow \Sigma_2$ such that $h^S(pt(\Sigma_1)) = pt(\Sigma_2)$.

- An *algebraic specification* $SPEC = (\Sigma, E)$ consists of a signature Σ and a set E of (positive conditional) equations.

- If $SPEC_1 = (\Sigma_1, E_1)$ and $SPEC_2 = (\Sigma_2, E_2)$ are two algebraic specifications, a *specification morphism* $f : SPEC_1 \longrightarrow SPEC_2$ is a signature morphism $f : \Sigma_1 \longrightarrow \Sigma_2$ such that the translation $f^\#(E_1)$ of the equations of $SPEC_1$ is contained in E_2. The notion of forgetful functor is the same as above.

- A *pointed algebraic specification* is an algebraic specification with a pointed signature. A *pointed specification morphism* between pointed specifications is a pointed signature morphism which is also a specification morphism. (For notational convenience, when $SPEC = (\Sigma, E)$ is a pointed specification the distinguished sort $pt(\Sigma)$ will be also denoted by $pt(SPEC)$).

- Given $f_1 : SPEC_0 \longrightarrow SPEC_1$ and $f_2 : SPEC_0 \longrightarrow SPEC_2$, $SPEC_1 +_{SPEC_0} SPEC_2$ denotes the pushout object of f_1 and f_2; intuitively, it is the disjoint union of $SPEC_1$ and $SPEC_2$ in which $f_1(x)$ and $f_2(x)$ are identified for all $x \in SPEC_0$. If f_1 and f_2 are inclusions and $SPEC_0$ is the intersection of $SPEC_1$ and $SPEC_2$, then $SPEC_1 +_{SPEC_0} SPEC_2$ is just the union.

3 The Class Model

In this section we review our model of a class specification which includes in generality the notion of class modelled in current object oriented programming languages. The main feature is encapsulation as a protection mechanism which draws a boundary between the implementation and the outside. The operations, over the instances of a class, which can be invoked are only those listed in the external interface of the class and any attempt at executing a private operation results in an error. There are two categories of clients of a class, those who need to manipulate objects (the clients of the instances) and those who want to reuse the class in order to specialize it or just reuse its code (the clients of the class) [16]. Thus, some languages have two external interfaces, one for each kind of client, and they are usually defined incrementally since the interface for the class clients has a greater view than the instance clients. We will call these interfaces *instance* and *class interface*.

Definition 1 Class Specification and Semantics. A class specification C_{spec} consists of five algebraic specifications PAR (parameter part), EXP_i (instance interface), EXP_c (class interface), IMP (import interface) and BOD (implementation part) and five specification morphisms as in the following commutative diagram.

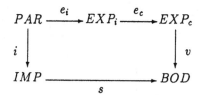

The specification EXP_i, EXP_c and BOD are pointed specifications, and e_c and v are pointed specification morphisms.

The semantics $SEM(C_{spec})$ of a class specification is the composition $V_v \circ Free_s$: $Alg(IMP) \to Alg(EXP_c)$. The class specification is *correct* if $V_s(Free_s(A)) = A$ for all $A \in Alg(IMP)$. The pointed sort $pt(EXP_i)$ is called class sort.

Interpretation Each of the five parts consists not only of signatures, but also of equations, which describe some of the properties of the operations. The interfaces EXP_i and EXP_c describe the external access functions and their behavior: the former describes the messages which can be sent to the objects that are instances of the class, while the latter contains the methods which can be used by other classes. The part of BOD not in EXP_c is hidden from other classes. The specification BOD describes an implementation of the exported methods using the ones provided by the IMP specification. The import specification IMP contains information about *what* is needed by BOD to implement EXP_c, but not *which* class can provide it: the latter task is provided by the interconnection mechanisms. The specification PAR models genericity, unconstrained if the specification consists of sorts only, constrained when the parameter is required to have operations satisfying certain properties. The semantics is a transformation from models of the import interface to models of the export interface; from the IMP–algebra, it constructs the BOD–algebra with all and only the features described in the body, and then, forgetting only all the hidden items, it returns an EXP_c–algebra. The correctness corresponds to requiring that operations, defined in the body, which return values of imported sorts are total and well defined.

Example 1. The morphisms in our examples of class specifications are just inclusions. In the notation, we use the keywords **Parameter, Instance Interface, Class Interface, Import Interface, Body** to declare the subspecification to be added to the parts already defined. For example, since $PAR \subseteq EXP_i$, after the keyword **Instance Interface** only $EXP_i - PAR$ is listed (if empty, the keyword is missing).

In the instance interface the distinguished sort $pt(EXP_i)$ is indicated by the keyword *class sort.*

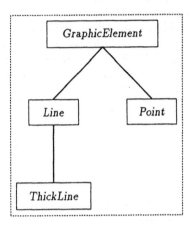

Fig. 1. A hierarchy of classes

The example of graphic elements is inspired by [2] with a number of modifications. The intention is to present the class hierarchy in fig. 1 and to show, in the next sections, how it is possible to reuse it in order to obtain that of fig. 4. Unfortunately, due to space limitation we present only part of the hierarchy, i.e. *GraphicElement* and *Point*. The rest of the example can be found in [15].

Both interfaces contain the standard specification of integers denoted by **int**. There is no body specification as this is an abstract class.

GraphicElement **is Class Specification**
Instance Interface
  int+
  <u>**class sort**</u> graphicelement
  <u>**sort**</u>   coord
  <u>**opns**</u>   BLC, TRC:graphicelement⟶coord
           MOVE:graphicelement int int⟶graphicelement
           $(\_,\_)$:int int⟶coord
           ADD:coord coord⟶coord
  <u>**eqns**</u> $BLC(MOVE(g,x,y)) = ADD(BLC(g),(x,y))$
           $TRC(MOVE(g,x,y)) = ADD(TRC(g),(x,y))$
           $ADD((p_1,q_1),(p_2,q_2)) = (p_1 + p_2,q_1 + q_2)$
Import Interface
  int+
  <u>**sort**</u>   coord
  <u>**opns**</u> $(\_,\_)$:int int⟶coord
           ADD:coord coord⟶coord

eqns $\mathrm{ADD}((p_1,q_1),(p_2,q_2)) = (p_1 + p_2, q_1 + q_2)$
End *GraphicElement*

This class model includes a large number of class structures as they are defined in current object oriented languages. We have focused on the importance of avoiding uncontrolled code reuse without any constraint, and therefore, in the proposed model, we provide an explicit import interface. None of the languages analyzed allows to specify some requirements for the import, although some allow the direct importing of other existing classes, incorporating (with the *use* clause) a combination mechanism. The set of all public operations of a class forms the external interface, called *instance interface*. To prevent another kind of client, the designer of a subclass, to access some variables, but to allow the visibility of more items than those contained in the instance interface, there is another interface, called *class interface*, which contains the instance one. In [14] we have indicated which of the components of our model of class are explicitly present in the notion of class in some of the analyzed languages along with a more adequate justification of the class model. The examples used here are intended to illustrate the novel ideas of design and reuse.

Inheritance is one of the main notions of the object oriented paradigm as it allows to reuse, extend and combine abstractions in order to define other abstractions. Unfortunately, in the space of languages, the notion of inheritance is not homogeneous since it ranges from functional specialization to the reuse of code without any constraint. Inheritance can be considered as a technique for the implementation of an abstract data type and its use is a private decision of the designer of the inheriting class (the omission and/or shadowing of features is permitted). Through this mechanism classes can be arranged in hierarchies which describe how programs are structured: this technique is called *reusing inheritance* (denoted Wreuse). Inheritance can also be considered as a technique for defining behavioral specialization and its use is a public declaration of the designer that the instances of the new class (the subclass) obey the semantics of the old class (the superclass). Thus each subclass instance is a special case of superclass instance: this kind of inheritance is called *specialization inheritance* (denoted Wspec).

We now formalize the notion of specialization inheritance which allows the enrichment of the functionalities of a class.

Definition 2 Specialization Inheritance. Let $C1$ and $C2$ be class specifications. Then $C2$ is a specialization of $C1$, notation $C2$ Wspec $C1$, if there exist pointed morphisms

$$f_i : EXP_{i1} \longrightarrow EXP_{i2}, \quad f_c : EXP_{c1} \longrightarrow EXP_{c2},$$

(called specialization morphisms) such that $e_{c2} \circ f_i = f_c \circ e_{c1}$, as in the commutative diagram in fig. 2;

Interpretation The morphisms f_i and f_c indicate that the exported part of $C2$ contains the exported part of $C1$ and possibly new auxiliary sorts, new operations and additional properties for both old and new methods.

Example 2. Here we introduce the *Point* class specification which is a specialization of the *GraphicElement* class already defined above.

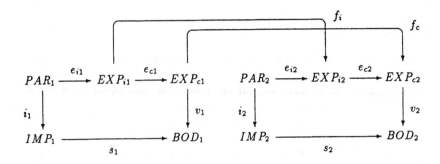

Fig. 2. Specialization Inheritance

Point **is Class Specification**
Instance Interface
  int+
  <u>class sort</u> point
  <u>sort</u>   graphicelement, coord
  <u>opns</u>   INIT:coord⟶point
           GETCOORD:point⟶coord
           SETCOORD:point coord⟶point
           BLC, TRC:point⟶coord
           MOVE:point int int⟶point
           BLC, TRC:graphicelement⟶coord
           MOVE:graphicelement int int⟶graphicelement
           $(\_,\_)$:int int⟶coord
           ADD:coord coord⟶coord
  <u>eqns</u> $BLC(p) = GETCORD(p)$
           $TRC(p) = GETCORD(p)$
           $GETCOORD(INIT(c)) = c$
           $SETCOORD(INIT(c_1),c_2) = INIT(c_2)$
           $MOVE(p,x,y) = SETCOORD(p,ADD(GETCOORD(p),(x,y)))$
           $BLC(MOVE(g,x,y)) = ADD(BLC(g),(x,y))$
           $TRC(MOVE(g,x,y)) = ADD(TRC(g),(x,y))$
           $ADD((p_1,q_1),(p_2,q_2)) = (p_1 + p_2, q_1 + q_2)$
Import Interface
  int+
  <u>sort</u>   coord
  <u>opns</u> $(\_,\_)$:int int⟶coord ADD:coord coord⟶coord
  <u>eqns</u> $ADD((p_1,q_1),(p_2,q_2)) = (p_1 + p_2, q_1 + q_2)$
Body
  <u>Structure</u>
           xy:coord
  <u>Behavior</u>
           $INIT(c) = <c>$
           $GETCOORD(self) = self.xy$
           $SETCOORD(self,c) = self.xy:= c$
           $MOVE(self,x,y) = self.xy:=ADD(self.xy,(x,y))$
End *Point*

The keywords *structure* and *behavior* in the body specification serve to describe the internal structure of the class and the effect of the methods. The structure definition corresponds canonically to the tuple constructor $<\_,...,\_> : s_1 \cdots s_n \longrightarrow s$ which is called representation record where $s_1,...,s_n$ are the sorts of the instance variables and s is the class sort. The name of the slots given in the structure declaration are projection functions. Accordingly are defined the access functions (those with the assignment symbol). In the behavior part, the self keyword formally is a logical variable as those used in the instance interface. Such name has been used in order to distinguish the controlling object from the argument objects: a method acts on the internal state of the controlling object, whereas the parameters are used as values. Apart from the abstract classes, all the classes have a class constructor (in the example the INIT function symbol) which is the only function described directly in terms of the representing record, while the other methods are specified as an internal transformation of state.

The other notion of inheritance, called reuse inheritance, can be formalized with the morphism from the class interface EXP_{c1} of $C1$ to the body BOD_2 of $C2$, indicating that everything in the class interface of $C1$ is available (possibly after the renaming determined by the morphism) in the body part of the class $C2$ and the part not in the codomain of v_2 is hidden and not re–exported by $C2$. Although both called inheritance, there is no confusion between the idea of code sharing and the notion of functional specialization. The two inheritance relations satisfy several properties formalized in [14]. Furthermore, we have shown in [13, 14] that it suffices to consider specialization inheritance as the only relation generating a hierarchy of classes.

4   Inheritance Operator

In the previous section we have seen inheritance as a binary relation between two existing class specifications. We now define an inheritance *operator* which takes two arguments, a base class C (arbitrary) and a *modification* Δ and returns a new class C' which inherits by specialization from C according to the modification Δ. The main advantage of such an operator is that if C and Δ are correct, then so is the resulting class C' and the semantics of C' can be defined explicitly in terms of the semantics of C and Δ. Before giving the formal definition, we illustrate it with the following example.

Point:GraphicElement is **Class Specification**
Instance Interface
  <u>class sort</u> point
  <u>opns</u>   INIT:coord⟶point
            GETCOORD:point⟶coord
            SETCOORD:point coord⟶point
            MOVE:point int int⟶point
  <u>eqns</u>   BLC(p) = GETCOORD(p)
            TRC(p) = GETCOORD(p)

$$GETCOORD(INIT(c)) = c$$
$$SETCOORD(INIT(c_1),c_2) = INIT(c_2)$$
$$MOVE(p,x,y) = SETCOORD(p,ADD(GETCOORD(p),(x,y)))$$

Body

Structure

xy:coord

Behavior

$$INIT(c) = <c>$$
$$GETCOORD(self) = self.xy$$
$$SETCOORD(self,c) = self.xy:=c$$
$$MOVE(self,x,y) = self.xy:=ADD(self.xy,(x,y))$$

End *Point*

The definition above is intended to modify the *GraphicElement* class. The modification Δ which the above definition implicitly describes is denoted explicitly by the following

$\delta(Point:GraphicElement)$ **is Class Specification**

Parameter

int+

sorts   graphicelement, coord

opns   BLC, TRC:graphicelement⟶coord

    MOVE:graphicelement int int⟶graphicelement

    (_,_):int int⟶coord

    ADD:coord coord⟶coord

eqns $BLC(MOVE(g,x,y)) = ADD(BLC(g),(x,y))$

    $TRC(MOVE(g,x,y)) = ADD(TRC(g),(x,y))$

    $ADD((p_1,q_1),(p_2,q_2)) = (p_1 + p_2,q_1 + q_2)$

Instance Interface

class sort point

opns   INIT:coord⟶point

    GETCOORD:point⟶coord

    SETCOORD:point coord⟶point

    MOVE:point int int⟶point

    BLC, TRC:point⟶coord

eqns $BLC(p) = GETCORD(p)$ $TRC(p) = GETCORD(p)$

    $GETCOORD(INIT(c)) = c$

    $SETCOORD(INIT(c_1),c_2) = INIT(c_2)$

    $MOVE(p,x,y) = SETCOORD(p,ADD(GETCOORD(p),(x,y)))$

Body

Structure

xy:coord

Behavior

$$INIT(c) = <c>$$
$$GETCOORD(self) = self.xy$$
$$SETCOORD(self,c) = self.xy:= c$$
$$MOVE(self,x,y) = self.xy:=ADD(self.xy,(x,y))$$

End $\delta(Point:GraphicElement)$

The result of the application of such modification Δ is the class *Point* already defined.

We can now formally define the inheritance operator $*$. The figure 3 illustrates the base class (lower class) and the modification (upper class) needed to apply the inheritance operator.

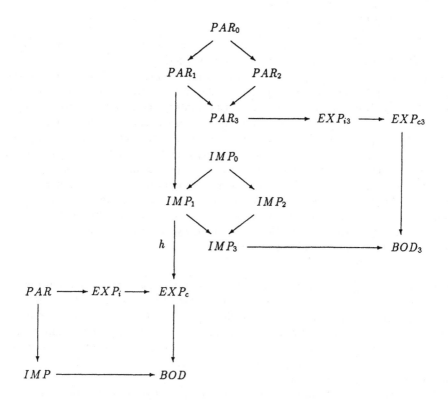

Fig. 3. The inheritance operator diagram

This operator needs

- a class $C = (PAR, IMP, EXP_i, EXP_c, BOD)$ from which the new class will be derived
- a modification Δ, itself a class, $(PAR_3, IMP_3, EXP_{3i}, EXP_{3c}, BOD_3)$ where $PAR_3 = PAR_1 +_{PAR_0} PAR_2$ and $IMP_3 = IMP_1 +_{IMP_0} IMP_2$
- a specification morphism $h : IMP_1 \rightarrow EXP_c$
- specification morphisms $PAR_0 \rightarrow PAR$ and $IMP_0 \rightarrow IMP$ such that $IMP_0 \rightarrow IMP \rightarrow BOD = IMP_0 \rightarrow IMP_1 \rightarrow EXP_c \rightarrow BOD$ and $PAR_0 \rightarrow PAR \rightarrow IMP = PAR_0 \rightarrow IMP_0 \rightarrow IMP$

The class $C^* = (PAR^*, IMP^*, EXP_i^*, EXP_c^*, BOD^*)$ resulting from applying the inheritance operator to C and Δ and denoted by $C *_h \Delta$ is defined by

- $PAR^* = PAR' +_{PAR_0} PAR_2$
  where PAR' is the intersection (pullback) of PAR and PAR_1 in EXP_c
- $IMP^* = IMP +_{IMP_0} IMP_2$
- $EXP_i^* = EXP_i +_{PAR'} EXP_{3i}$
- $EXP_c^* = EXP_c +_{PAR_1} EXP_{3c}$
- $BOD^* = BOD +_{IMP_1} BOD_3$

The five specification morphisms needed to complete the definition of C^* are induced (uniquely) by the universal property of the constructions.

Interpretation The morphism h indicates that the methods needed by Δ in the IMP_1 part of the import are provided by the class C from which the result will inherit. The IMP_2 part must be provided at a later time by another class using a clean interconnection [15]. The overlapping part IMP_0 cannot be chosen univocally by h since, as part of IMP_2 it could be determined later : hence it must be part of IMP, used but not defined in C. A similar argument also holds for the morphism $PAR_0 \rightarrow PAR$. The new class interface EXP_c^* consists of the old class methods EXP_c and of the new ones EXP_{3c} defined in the modification Δ, with the parametric ones in PAR_1 replaced by the corresponding ones in EXP_c. Similarly for EXP_i^*. Finally, the implementation (body) of the derived class is given by the two bodies BOD_3 and BOD where the methods of C used by Δ (via IMP_1 and EXP_c) are replaced by their implementations in BOD_3.

Remark. Notice that the definition has been given in full generality and that several parts of both C and Δ could be empty simplifying the constructions. If $IMP_0 = IMP_2$, then $IMP_1 = IMP$ and therefore the class (from which to inherit) C provides everything needed by Δ to realize in BOD the additional methods in EXP_c. In this case, there is no need to distinguish PAR_2 from the rest of the parameter part and thus $PAR_1 = PAR_3$. Then $IMP^* = IMP$, $PAR^* = PAR'$ (as in the definition of Combination [14]).

If IMP_0 (and hence PAR_0) is empty, then the part IMP_2 needed by Δ and not provided by C is disjoint from IMP_1. Hence IMP^* is the disjoint union of IMP and IMP_2, and PAR^* is the disjoint union of PAR' and PAR_2.

As mentioned, the correctness of the base class and of the modification are sufficient to guarantee the correctness of the derived class. Furthermore, it is possible to describe explicitly the semantics of the derived class (and thus predict its behavior based on that of the components C and Δ).

Theorem 3 Correctness. *If C, Δ and h are such that $C *_h \Delta$ is defined, then*

- *If C and Δ are correct, then so is $C *_h \Delta$*
- *The semantics SEM^* of $C *_h \Delta$ is given by*
  $SEM^*(A^*) = SEM_3(SEM(A) +_{A_0} A_2) +_{A'} SEM(A)$
  where $A^* = A +_{A_0} A_2 \in Alg(IMP^*)$ and $A' = V_{i_1}(SEM(A)) \in Alg(PAR_1)$.

The operator $*$ applied to the modification Δ has been called the *inheritance* operator: the next result justifies its name.

Theorem 4 Inheritance. *Let C, Δ and h be such that $C *_h \Delta$ is defined. Then $(C *_h \Delta)$ Wspec C.*

As expected, the result of applying the modification Δ to the class C via the inheritance operator is a class which inherits by specialization from C.

The inheritance operator satisfies several properties which make it a basic tool for hierarchy reuse. The first one is a "local confluence" result for which the order in which the modifications are applied does not affect the result. It is also possible to combine successive modifications into one in such a way that the inheritance operator applied to a base class and the composite modification yields the derived class obtained by the sequence of modifications. The base step of such a result is the second part of the following theorem.

Theorem 5 Local Confluence. *Let C be a class specification, Δ_1 and Δ_2 modifications, and h_1 and h_2 morphisms such that $C *_{h_1} \Delta_1$ and $C *_{h_2} \Delta_2$ are defined. Then there exist morphisms g_1 and g_2 such that $C^* = C_2 *_{g_1} \Delta_1 = C_1 *_{g_2} \Delta_2$. Furthermore, there exist a modification Δ and a morphism h such that $C^* = C *_h \Delta$.*

The result of this theorem is summarized in the following diagram.

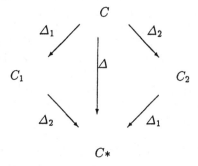

Note that the morphisms g_1 and g_2 along with the modification Δ and the morphism h can be constructed directly and explicitly from Δ_1 and Δ_2, and h_1 and h_2. For lack of space, we omit their construction.

In order to apply the inheritance operator to entire hierarchies, we first need to establish its compatibility with the relation of specialization inheritance.

Theorem 6 Compatibility. *Let C_1 and Δ be such that $C_1' = C_1 *_{h_1} \Delta$ is defined for some h_1 and let C_2 Wspec C_1 and Δ' Wspec Δ. Then the modification Δ' is applicable also to C_2 and, with $C_2' = C_2 *_{h_2} \Delta'$, we have C_2' Wspec C_1'.*

Again the morphism h_2 can be constructed from h_1, Δ and Δ'. The result of the theorem can be easily visualized in the following diagram.

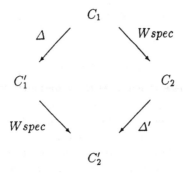

In the special case when $\Delta' = \Delta$, the inheritance operator commutes with the relation of specialization inheritance. The converse of this last theorem does not always hold: if C_2' Wspec C_1', then it may not be possible in general to find a specialization of Δ to use as modification to apply to C_2.

5 Reusing Software Design

Although the term *software reuse* was born many years ago, the reuse of software has failed to become standard practice for software development. Object oriented programming makes program components more easily reusable, but in the long run the reuse of design is probably more important than the reuse of code. Designing a self contained software artifact is regarded as an activity where the knowledge of a certain application domain is required. As a rule, classes are considered as incomplete specifications, which need to be monotonically refined via inheritance in further design stages. Non–monotonic modification can be reduced to monotonic ones via backtracking or generalization, already investigated in [13, 14]. Many approaches support this style (among these [4, 2, 3]), in which the inheritance is primarily a technique for refining sets of models. In general, the reuse of a single component is considered too fine–grained and inheritance allows only point–to–point derivations.

Since the hierarchies are considered the formalization of design processes, they can be viewed as frameworks, in the sense of [5, 21]. In general, such frameworks are software schemas made of abstract and concrete classes where the skeleton of a (sub)application is defined. This technique has already been used quite intensively in the development of (generic) user interface, allowing the interactive definition of a number of objects such as windows, buttons, etc. Therefore, frameworks consist of a very large library of classes and tools which allow the reuse of classes via instantiation and the addition of new subclasses. In our approach we do not discuss interactive definition of code fragment and system dynamics. Our specialization feature (in the sense of [9]) is based on the extension of a given hierarchy but also on standard subclass estension. In principle, the approach does not require specific design for the base hierarchy.

In the remaining of the section, we illustrate, through an example, how the formal properties of the inheritance operator allow the reuse of whole hierarchies. The methodology so defined shows how knowledge already represented can be reused when new software components are needed in application domains already investigated (e.g., to reuse a hierarchy which has been defined after a rapid prototyping stage of a system without modifying the source code).

Plain Graphic Element

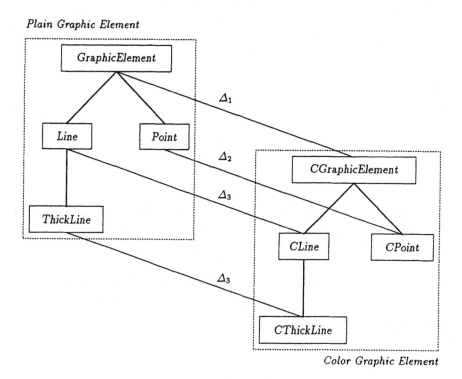

Fig. 4. A Reuse of Design

In the example, the graphical elements hierarchy (see fig. 1) is reused in order to define the colored graphical elements hierarchy. Fig. 4 illustrates how the latter hierarchy is designed extending the former one. The lines between classes within the dashed box containing the base hierarchy indicate the specialization inheritance, while the lines between the two dashed boxes indicate the relation implied by the use of the inheritance operator. The relations in the extended hierarchy are induced by the Local Confluence and Compatibility theorems. Although all the relations in this diagram are at the same level (in the sense that, for instance, *CLine* is a subclass of *Line* and *CGraphicalElement*), they have been developed separately in time and with different intentions.

Next are the modifications to the subhierarchy presented in the former section (the rest of the modifications are in [15]).

CGraphicElement:GraphicElement is **Class Specification**
Instance Interface
  <u>**class sort**</u> cgraphicelement
  <u>sort</u>   color
  <u>opns</u>   SETCOLOR:cgraphicelement color⟶cgraphicelement
           GETCOLOR:cgraphicelement⟶color
           WHITE, ..., BLACK:⟶color
  <u>eqns</u>   GETCOLOR(SETCOLOR(g,c)) = c
Import Interface
  <u>sort</u>   color
  <u>opns</u>   WHITE, ..., BLACK:⟶color
Body
  <u>**Structure**</u>
        c:color
  <u>**Behavior**</u>
        SETCOLOR(self,c) = self.c:=c
        GETCOLOR(self) = self.c
End *CGraphicElement*

The *CGraphicalElement* class is defined as a subclass of *GraphicalElement* with a new slot in the implementation in order to keep the current color of the figure and two access functions for manipulating the internal slot.

CPoint:Point(δ(CGraphicElement:GraphicElement)) is **Class Specification**
Instance Interface
  <u>**class sort**</u> cpoint
  <u>opns</u>   INIT:coord⟶cpoint
Body
  <u>**Behavior**</u>
        INIT(c) = <INIT(c),WHITE>
End *CPoint*

The class *CPoint* is obtained by applying to the class *Point* the modification from *GraphicalElement* to *CGraphicalElement*, the extra specification intended as an enrichment of the modification. The fact that *CPoint* turns out to be a subclass of *CGraphicalElement* is due to the Compatibility theorem. In this derivation it is not possible to rely on the Local Confluence theorem since the *Point* class has a constructor which is not present in the *GraphicalElement* class. This requires *more* modifications than from *GraphicalElement* to *CGraphicalElement*. The *more* underlies that the Δ_2 from *Point* to *CPoint* is a specialization of the one used from *GraphicalElement* to *CGraphicalElement*, although the augmentation is limited to a marginal part. This aspect characterizes the modifications, in the sense that they can be arranged in the specialization hierarchy as shown in fig. 5.

6   Concluding Remarks

In this paper, we focus on the problem of reusing design decisions by defining an inheritance operator which is shown to have properties of Local Confluence and

Delta hierarchy

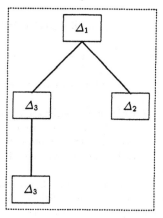

Fig. 5. Modification Specialization Hierarchy

Compatibility, very useful in defining a theory of software reuse. Regarding a hierarchy as the outcome of a design process, such an operator allows one to extend the hierarchy in a non–destructive way, preserving the relations among the classes in the base hierarchy. In a sense, this operator and its theory can be seen as a generalization of the object oriented paradigm since, as in the characterization given in [9], our approach presents all the features of a typical reuse context. The setting has

abstraction The main abstraction mechanism is the hierarchy specification, in the sense that we can regard not only classes but also whole hierarchies as specific entities.

selection The hierarchies can be easily located, being formally specified. Of course, if the knowledge base is very large, it is useful to have a tool for browsing and for automatically locating the components.

specialization The hierarchies can be specialized by means of the inheritance operator which is able to extend the base hierarchy, *augmenting* the design decisions taken in the base hierarchy.

integration The software components can be interconnected with the usual technique since these mechanisms are compatible with inheritance as shown in previous work.

In this respect, the object paradigm as a class reuse technique could be viewed as a special case of our theory, by considering a class as a trivial hierarchy.

In the near future, we intend to address the problem of locating hierarchies in a library by defining a suitable metric. This would allow us to give the specification of a goal hierarchy and locate the closest hierarchy in the system library, in order to reduce the amount of modification from the base hierarchy. Other important issues to consider are persistent objects and classes with extension and not just object types.

References

1. T.Biggerstaff, A.J.Perlis (Eds). Software Reusability. Volume I: Concepts and Models. ACM Press, 1989

2. R.Breu: Algebraic Specification Techniques in Object Oriented Programming Environments. Springer Lecture Notes in Computer Science 562, 1991

3. B.J.Cox: Object–Oriented Programming: An Evolutionary Approach. Addison–Wesley, 1986

4. S.Clerici, F.Orejas: GSBL: An Algebraic Specification Language Based on Inheritance. Proc. ECOOP 88, Springer Lecture Notes in Computer Science 322, 1988, 78–92.

5. L.P.Deutsch: Levels of reuse in the Smalltalk–80 programming system. In: T.Biggerstaff and A.J.Perlis (Eds). Software Reusability. Volume II: Applications and Expirience. ACM Press, 1989, 57–71

6. H.Ehrig, B.Mahr: Fundamentals of Algebraic Specification 1. Equations and Initial Semantics. EATCS Monograph in Computer Science, Vol.6, Springer Verlag, 1985

7. H.Ehrig, B.Mahr: Fundamentals of Algebraic Specification 2. Module Specifications and Constraints. EATCS Monograph in Computer Science, Vol.21, Springer Verlag, 1990

8. B.P.Lientz, B.Swanson: Software Maintenance Management. Addison–Wesley, 1980

9. C.Krueger: Software Reuse. ACM Computing Surveys, 24/2, Jun 92, 131–183

10. N.Iscoe, G.Williams, G.Arango: Domain Modeling for Software Engineering. Proc. ICSE–13, IEEE Press, 1991, 340–343

11. B.Meyer: Object–Oriented Software Construction. Prentice–Hall, 1988

12. F.Parisi–Presicce: A Rule–Based Approach to Modular Design. Proc. ICSE–12, IEEE Press, 1990

13. F.Parisi-Presicce, A.Pierantonio: An Algebraic Approach to Inheritance and Subtyping. Proc. ESEC91, Springer Lecture Notes in Computer Science 550, 1991, 364–379

14. F.Parisi-Presicce, A.Pierantonio: An Algebraic Theory of Class Specifications. Technical Report N.22/92, Dip. Matematica Pura ed Applicata, Univ. L'Aquila, 1992 (to appear in ACM TOSEM)

15. F.Parisi-Presicce, A.Pierantonio: Reusing Object Oriented Design: An Algebraich Approach. Technical Report N.35/93, Dip. Matematica Pura ed Applicata, Univ. L'Aquila, 1993

16. A.Snyder: Encapsulation and Inheritance in Object-Oriented Programming Languages. Proc. OOPSLA86, ACM Press, 1986, 38-45

17. W.F.Tichy: Programming–in–the–Large: Past, Present, and Future. Proc. ICSE–14, IEEE Press, 1992, 362–367

18. P.Wegner, S.Zdonik: Inheritance as an Incremental Modification Mechanism or What Like Is and Isn't Like. Proc. ECOOP 88, Springer Lecture Notes in Computer Science 322, 1988, 55–77

19. N.Wilde, P.Matthews: Maintaining Object–Oriented Software. IEEE Software, 10/1, Jan 93, 75–80

20. M.Wirsing: Algebraic Specification. In J. van Leeuwen, ed. Handbook of Theoretical Computer Science, Vol. B, North-Holland (1991) 677-788

21. R.J.Wirfs–Brock, R.Johnson: Surveying Current Research in Object–Oriented Design. Comm. ACM, 33/9, Sept 90, 105–124

22. R.J.Wirfs–Brock, B.Wilkerson, L.Wiener: Designing Object–Oriented Software. Prentice–hall, 1990

Reuse in Object-Oriented Information Systems Development

Silvana Castano (*) (°), Valeria De Antonellis (*)

(*) Politecnico di Milano
P.za Leonardo Da Vinci, 32 - 20133 MILANO - ITALY
e-mail: deantone@elet.polimi.it

(°) Università di Milano
via Comelico, 39 - 20135 MILANO - ITALY
e-mail: castano@ghost.dsi.unimi.it

Abstract. An approach for supporting reuse in object-oriented Information System conceptual design is presented. Reusable components are introduced as generic object classes with associated guidelines providing suggestions for their adaptation and tailoring in given contexts. Reusable components are derived from the analysis of similar object classes. Affinity criteria to classify object classes are presented, based on structural and contextual properties.

1 . Introduction

Modern methodological approaches suggest the adoption of the object-oriented paradigm in the information systems design process [4, 13]. In fact, object-oriented methodologies support modularity by providing a uniform conceptual framework for defining the information of interest in terms of objects at different levels of abstraction, and facilitate the design process by means of encapsulation and inheritance mechanisms. In particular, the inheritance mechanism allows the designer to specify new objects by addition of new properties besides the inherited ones, and, for this peculiarity, it constitutes a basic step for the "reuse" of existing components. Reuse is considered a fundamental aspect to facilitate both effective development of good quality applications - by exploiting already validated components - and easy re-development of applications - by encouraging a modular design approach [2]. As a consequence, it has become a crucial research issue and methodological approaches with reuse capabilities are being developed and experimented.

Several authors in software engineering literature have emphasized the importance of reuse models and techniques, considering the different life-cycle development phases and the corresponding different types of information (requirements, design specifications, code) [17, 22].

We investigate reuse in the area of information systems development to facilitate and shorten the design process, by tailoring and personalizing results of previous projects. In this paper, we describe an environment for building reusable components at the conceptual design level, in an object-oriented framework. Reusable components are defined as generic object classes and associated guidelines for reuse, and are properly organized in a reuse repository. Generic object classes are extracted from a set of candidate conceptual schemas, selected from previous projects [9, 14]. Guidelines associated with a reusable component provide a set of design suggestions about ways to incorporate that component in a new conceptual schema, by means of possible adaptations and transformations.

The paper is organized as follows. In Sect.2 the model for defining reusable components is presented. In Sect.3 basic concepts of the approach are introduced. In Sect.4, we illustrate the methodology for building reusable conceptual components. Concluding remarks point out open research issues in the area.

2. Reusable components

True reusability depends on the availability of a set of reusable components properly designed to capture generic concepts/objects in a domain, allowing the design-by-reuse activity be performed by adaptation/specialization of generic components, possibly enriching and modifying them according to given application requirements [19]. In the following, we propose a methodological approach to guide the reuse engineer in building generic components. The approach is based on the identification of common elements between classes in object-oriented conceptual schemas, to be abstracted and generalized into generic components.

Conceptual schemas are properly defined according to a selected model. Several object-oriented models have been proposed in literature for this purpose [4, 15]. To make the process of reusable components definition applicable to more than one model, we refer to a simple reference model that allows the definition of the constructs of the OO models. In the following we define the main constructs.

Class (C): it allows the definition of constructs used to describe objects of the real world within the schema (i.e., object class).

Structural Property (SP): it allows the definition of constructs used to describe a static feature of an object in a schema. SPs are expressed by means of attributes. A Structural Property sp_i is characterized by a name and a domain, that is:

$$sp_i = <pn_i, d_i>$$

specifying the type of values the property can assume at instance level. Domains can be predefined and complex [3].

Behavioral Property (BP): it allows the definition of constructs used to describe the behavior of an object in a schema. BPs correspond to the operations executable on an object, that can be requested by other objects through messages, according to the client/server viewpoint. A Behavioral Property bp_i is specified like a method signature [16], that is:

$$bp_i = <mn_i, [(<p_{1i}, d_{1i}>,...., <p_{ni}, d_{ni}>, d_{(n+1)i})] >$$

where mn_i indicates the name of the associated operation, $<p_{1i}, d_{1i}>,...., <p_{ni}, d_{ni}>$ is the list of parameters required to perform the operation, with the associated domains, and $d_{(n+1)i}$ indicates the domain of the produced result (the [] indicates that the contents are optional).

Dependency (D): it allows the definition of constructs used to describe relationships between two or more classes in a schema. Dependencies are expressed as implicit references, or objectified relationships in OO models [1].

Hierarchical Dependency (HD): it allows the definition of constructs used to describe specialization/generalization and aggregation relationships between two or more classes in a schema.

A reusable component is a *generic class* with associated *guidelines* providing suggestions about ways of adapting and tailoring the generic class in given application contexts, through conceptual design primitives [11]. A generic class is defined with a minimal number of properties (both structural and behavioral), sufficient to describe a set of similar objects in different applications. Moreover, for a generic class a set of linked classes can be specified. As an example, in the Transportation domain, from the classes Aircraft and Train shown in Fig.1, we abstract the generic class Transportation-Means, by properly generalizing the names and the domains of their common properties. For instance, the property 'Means_Code: integer' abstracts and generalizes the properties 'Train-Number: integer' of Train, and 'Aircraft-Number:integer' of Aircraft. Pilot and Location are an possible linked classes, since they are usually defined in association with a transportation means object in the Transportation domain.

To make easier the extraction of reusable components, we maintain, in the reuse repository, a library of selected conceptual schemas [5]. In the library, schemas belonging to one or more applications, in one or several domains, are properly classified and arranged in similarity cluster hierarchies, according to the domain they belong to [6, 7, 8]. Schemas to be stored are selected according to their quality and possibility of reuse [14].

3. Affinity criteria

The definition of reusable classes is based on the concept of similarity, here called *affinity*, which has been proved to be essential to extract common, and thus reusable, characteristics from a set of objects/systems in a given domain [19, 20], and to support view integration techniques [23].

Affinity exists between object classes in different schemas if they describe objects of the real-world that have common properties, behavior and context.

Let C be a class in a conceptual schema of an application, defined as follows:

Class C
Structural Properties
$sp_1 = <pn_1, d_1>$

...

$sp_n = <pn_n, d_n>$
Behavioral Properties
$bp_1 = <mn_1, [(<p_{11}, d_{11}>,...., <p_{n1}, d_{n1}>, d_{(n+1)1})] >$

...

$bp_q = <mn_q, [(<p_{1q}, d_{1q}>,...., <p_{mq}, d_{mq}>, d_{(m+1)q})] >$

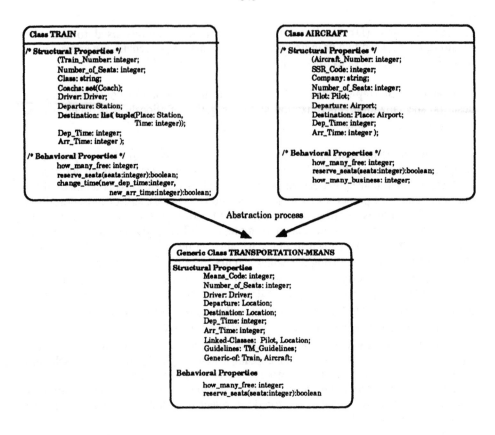

Fig.1 Example of extraction of generic component

A set of affinity criteria is defined to establish the level of affinity between two classes C_1 and C_2 belonging to different application schemas. Such criteria take into account both the structural features (Structural Affinity and Behavioral Affinity), and the contextual features, that is, is-a, part-of and relationships (Generalization Hierarchy Affinity and Adjacency Affinity respectively) of the classes within their respective schemas.

The affinity criteria are measured using the Dice's metric [18]:

$$\frac{2\,D}{A + B}$$

where D is the number of common elements of the considered classes, having a number A and B of elements, respectively. Each coefficient can assume values between 0 and 1. The value 0 represents a situation of absence of affinity (no commonalities exist between the examined classes for that coefficient), while the value 1 represents a situation of identity (examined classes are equally defined in both schemas, with respect to the coefficient). Intermediate values describe situations of more or less affinity, corresponding to more or less commonalities between the classes in their respective schemas.

Before illustrating in detail each affinity criterion, we introduce some definitions and conditions that will be used during the affinity coefficients computation.

Let SP be the set of Structural Properties of a class C. We define two sets, namely PRED, composed of the structural properties whose domain is a predefined domain, and REF, composed of the structural properties whose domain is a reference domain (i.e., a class name), such that $PRED \cup REF = SP$ and $PRED \cap REF = \emptyset$. For properties having a complex domain (that is, defined by using a constructor), we do not consider the used constructors, since they only impose a structure over the involved domains. The involved domains are included in the proper set, PRED or REF, depending on their nature.

Let is-a(C',C) be a predicate, that is true if C' is a subclass of C in a generalization hierarchy. We define for a class C two sets, $DirAnc(C) = \{ C_i \mid is\text{-}a(C,C_i)\}$, composed of the classes that are the direct ancestors of C in the generalization hierarchy, and $DirDesc(C) = \{ C_i \mid is\text{-}a(C_i,C)\}$, composed of the classes that are the direct descendants of C in the generalization hierarchy.

Affinity computation is mainly based on the comparison of property names and domains in different classes; so hereafter we give the affinity conditions that must hold for names and predefined domains.

The set Names of names and relevant relationships between names are maintained in a Thesaurus, which is an essential element of our approach. We suppose to have at disposal an initial Thesaurus for the domain we operate in, where the most significant and frequently used terms are listed, together with their synonyms, similar terms, generalization terms, and specialization terms. The Thesaurus is continuously enriched and updated with the knowledge derived from the affinity coefficients determined for the classes of schemas in the domain.

Name affinity condition
Given two names, n and n' $\in$ Names, they present affinity if:

(i) $\qquad n = n' \vee Syn(n,n') \vee Sim(n,n')$

that is, if they are equal, or if they are synonyms (e.g., 'Plain' and 'Aircraft'), or if they are similar (e.g., 'Aircraft' and 'Train'), according to the relationships stored in the Thesaurus.

Predefined domain affinity condition
Given two predefined domains, d and d', they present affinity if:

(ii) $\qquad d = d' \vee d \supset d' \vee d' \supset d$

that is, the domains coincide, or one is a subset of the other.

In the following, we describe in detail how each affinity criterion is computed.

Structural Affinity, $SA(C_1,C_2)$

To compute the Structural Affinity of a pair of classes, we examine their Structural Properties whose domain is a predefined/complex domain.

The Structural Affinity of two classes C_1 and C_2, $SA(C_1,C_2)$, is computed using the following function:

$$SA_{(C_1,C_2)} = \frac{2 * Card\left\{ sp_i \mid sp_i \in \left(C_1 \cap C_2 \right) \wedge sp_i \in PRED \right\}}{Card\left\{ sp_i \mid sp_i \in C_1 \wedge sp_i \in PRED \right\} + Card\left\{ sp_i \mid sp_i \in C_2 \wedge sp_i \in PRED \right\}}$$

Two structural properties sp_i and sp_j are considered common to both C_1 and C_2 (that is, they belong to the intersection of C_1 and C_2) if condition (i) is satisfied on property names, and condition (ii) is verified for domains.

Finally, it has to be noted that, in order to make the Structural Affinity coefficient more precise, properties that are not distinctive of a particular class (such as 'code', 'number', 'id' and so on) should be skipped. For this purpose, we propose to define and maintain a stop-list in the Thesaurus, listing the meaningless names for the domain.

Behavioral Affinity, $BA_{(C_1, C_2)}$

This coefficient is concerned with the behavior of the classes, and aims at defining the level of affinity of two classes with respect to the associated operations. At the requirement specification level, in order to evidence behavioral affinity between classes, we propose to focus only on the signature of the involved messages, without considering implementation details (related to method code), that can be dealt with in a subsequent phase of the requirements engineering process, specifically addressing the code reuse [17]. In this sense, our approach is similar to the approach proposed in [12], where signatures are introduced to abstract the semantics of a reusable component, in terms of domains and associated operations characterizing the component, following the algebraic specification paradigm.

The Behavioral Affinity is computed considering the signature of the messages that a class can send and receive (namely message names and the parameter list). Let 'bp_i $= <mn_j, [(<p_{1i}, d_{1i}>,...., <p_{ni}, d_{ni}>, d_{(n+1)i})] >$' a behavioral property of a class C. The Behavioral Affinity of two classes C_1 and C_2, $BA_{(C_1, C_2)}$, is computed using the following function:

$$BA_{(C_1, C_2)} = \frac{2 * Card\left\{bp_i \mid bp_i \in (C_1 \cap C_2)\right\}}{Card\left\{bp_i \mid bp_i \in C_1\right\} + Card\left\{bp_i \mid bp_i \in C_2\right\}}$$

Two behavioral properties '$bp_i = <mn_j, [(<p_{1i}, d_{1i}>,...., <p_{ni}, d_{ni}>, d_{(n+1)i})] >$' and '$bp_j = <mn_j, [(<p_{1j}, d_{1j}>,...., <p_{mj}, d_{mj}>, d_{(m+1)j})] >$' are considered common to C_1 and C_2 if they have the same arity, that is, if n=m, if condition (i) is verified on message and parameter names, and if condition (ii) is verified on parameter domains. For reference domains, they are considered common if the referenced class names verify condition (i).

Generalization Hierarchy Affinity, $GHA_{(C_1, C_2)}$

This coefficient computes the level of affinity of classes with respect to their contextual features in the generalization hierarchies the classes take part to.

If C_1 and C_2 belong to generalization hierarchies, ascendant and descendant classes of C_1 and C_2 are examined, to find out those common to both the hierarchies. Let C_i (C_j) be ascendant (descendant) of a class C.

The Generalization Hierarchy Affinity of C_1 and C_2, $GHA_{(C_1, C_2)}$, is computed using the following function:

$$GHA_{(c_1,c_2)} = \frac{2*\left(Card\{C_i|C_i \in DirAnc(C_1) \cap DirAnc(C_2)\} + Card\{C_j|C_j \in DirDesc(C_1) \cap DirDesc(C_2)\}\right)}{\left(Card\{C_i|C_i \in DirAnc(C_1)\} + Card\{C_i|C_i \in DirAnc(C_2)\}\right) + \left(Card\{C_j|C_j \in DirDesc(C_1)\} + Card\{C_j|C_j \in DirDesc(C_2)\}\right)}$$

Classes C_i and C_j are considered common to the generalization hierarchies of C_1 and C_2 if their names verify the affinity condition (i).

Adjacency Affinity, $AA(C_1,C_2)$

This coefficient computes the level of affinity of classes with respect to the classes with which they have a direct relationship, either an implicit reference or a part-of relationship. Classes having a direct relationship with a given class C are called the adjacent classes of C. The adjacency affinity of two classes C_1 and C_2, $AA(C_1,C_2)$, is computed using the following function:

$$AA_{(C_1,C_2)} = \frac{2*Card\{sp_i|sp_i \in (C_1 \cap C_2) \wedge sp_i \in REF\}}{Card\{sp_i|sp_i \in C_1 \wedge sp_i \in REF\} + Card\{sp_i|sp_i \in C_2 \wedge sp_i \in REF\}}$$

where only the structural properties that have reference domains are considered. Two adjacent classes C_i and C_j of C_1 and C_2 are considered common to C_1 and C_2 if the affinity condition (i) is verified on their names.

The whole level of affinity of C_1 and C_2 is given by the Global Affinity coefficient, $GA(C_1,C_2)$, which is the weighted sum of the affinity coefficients previously described, that is:

$$GA(C_1,C_2) = w_1 SA(C_1,C_2) + w_2 BA(C_1,C_2) + w_3 GHA(C_1,C_2) + w_4 AA(C_1,C_2)$$

Each w_i indicates a weight used to properly set the importance of the corresponding type of affinity. Through experimentation of the approach in case studies, we have noted that the greatest importance should be given to the structural and behavioral affinity coefficients, over the hierarchical and adjacency ones. This is because the level of affinity between different classes derives mostly from the structural and behavioral affinity coefficients, which express a strong class affinity, due to the intrinsic properties of the objects, independent of the context in which the classes are placed.

4. Engineering reusable components

To engineer reusable components we cluster object classes according to their affinity, by using Information Retrieval clustering techniques, and precisely the complete-link technique [21]. This technique has been chosen for its capability of precisely pointing out equalities and differences between similar classes belonging to different schemas, defining a large number of small clusters, called *affinity sets*, each one containing the most similar classes among those examined. To apply the complete-link technique, classes of the selected application schemas are submitted to pairwise affinity comparisons; a symmetric affinity matrix A is defined whose entry $A[i,j]$ indicates the global affinity coefficient between the class C_i and the class C_j, that is, $GA_{(C_i,C_j)}$. According to the contents of the affinity matrix, pairs of classes are sorted in decreasing order of affinity, and only those whose global affinity is greater than or equal to the established threshold are selected and proposed, in decreasing affinity order, for the complete-link technique.

For example, let us consider, in the Transportation domain, the object-oriented schema fragments Aircraft-Control-System and Train-Control-System shown in Fig.2a and 2b respectively, defined according to the O_2 model [15]. Such schemas describe object types, relationships, and operations characterizing the train and aircraft control. For instance, with reference to the schema shown in Fig.2a, the class Aircraft is characterized by the Flight-number, the SSR-code, the Company, the Number-of-Seats, the Pilot, and the information related to the departure and arrival locations and time (Departure, Destination, Arr_Time, Dep_Time). The Aircraft class has a relationship with the Airport and the Pilot classes, described by means of implicit references within the corresponding properties. For the Aircraft class are defined a set of methods, providing the services that can be requested on an aircraft object, such as the computation of the number of free places (How_many_free), the reservation of seats (Reserve_seats), and the computation of the total number of business class seats (How_many_business). The method signature specifies the type of the input and output parameters requested and produced by the method. In the same way, the classes Airport, Radar, Person, and Pilot are defined with their attributes and methods. In particular, the Airport is defined as a composite object, whose components are the Radar, the RPDC (Remote Data Processing Console), the Waiting_Room, and the Gate classes. Since there are several gates in an airport, the corresponding attribute in the Airport class has been defined as a complex type, using the constructor "set". In the same way, the classes constituting the Train-Control-System have been defined, namely the Train, Station, Driver, Person, and Master_Station classes, with their proper attributes and methods.

The reuse engineer examines, possibly with a help of the reuse tool [11], the mentioned classes and recognizes that affinity exists between classes of the examined schemas, using the affinity coefficients illustrated in Sect.3. According to such coefficients, the global affinity for Aircraft and Train is equal to:

$$GA_{(Aircraft,Train)} = w_1 (2*3/6+6) + w_2 (2*2/3+3) + w_3 0 + w_4 (2*3/3+4)$$

Setting $w_1=4$, and the remaining weights equal to 1, we have that $GA_{(Aircraft,Train)} = 3.52$. Note that the hierarchical affinity of the mentioned classes is equal to zero, since they do not participate in any generalization hierarchy. In the same way are computed the semantic affinity coefficients for all the pairs of classes of the considered schemas; setting the selection threshold equal to 3, the selected pairs of classes, listed in decreasing order are the following:

(Person, Person) = 4.09
(Aircraft, Train) = 3.52
(Pilot, Driver) = 3.5
(Airport, Station) = 3.1

Class AIRCRAFT

type tuple /* Structural Properties */
(Aircraft-Number: integer,
SSR_Code: integer,
Company: string,
Number_of_Seats: integer,
Pilot: Pilot,
Departure: Airport,
Destination: Airport,
Dep_Time: integer,
Arr_Time: integer)

method /* Behavioral Properties */
How_many_free: integer;
Reserve_seats(seats:integer):boolean;
How_many_business: integer;

Class PERSON

type tuple /* Structural Properties */
(Name: string,
Surname: string,
Address: tuple(City: string,
Street: string,
Number: integer))

Class AIRPORT

type tuple /* Structural Properties */
(Name: string,
Location: string,
Number_of_Gates: integer,
Composed_of: Radar,
Composed_of: RPDC,
Composed_of: Waiting_Room,
Composed_of: set(Gate))

method /* Behavioral Properties */
Open_Gate(gate:Gate):boolean;
Close_Gate(gate:Gate): boolean

Class RADAR

type tuple /* Structural Properties */
(Radar-Number: integer,
Position: tuple(coord1:integer,
coord2: integer,
coord3: integer),
Orientation: integer)

Class PILOT inherit PERSON

type tuple /* Structural Properties */
(Emp_Code: integer,
Flight_Licence: string,
Number_Flight_Hours: integer,
Salary: integer,
Duties: list(tuple(Day: string,
Time: integer
FlightNumber: integer)))

method /* Behavioral Properties */
Update_Flight_Hours(amount:integer): integer

Fig.2a Aircraft-Control-System schema

```
Class TRAIN

type tuple   /* Structural Properties */
             (Train-Number: integer,
             Number_of_Seats: integer,
             Class: string,
             Coachs: set(Coach),
             Driver: Driver,
             Departure: Station,
             Destination: list(tuple(Place: Station,
                                     Time: integer)),
             Dep_Time: integer,
             Arr_Time: integer )

method    /* Behavioral Properties */
          How_many_free: integer;
          Reserve_seats(seats:integer):boolean;
          Change_time(new_dep_time:integer,
                      new_arr_time:integer):boolean;
```

```
Class STATION

type tuple   /* Structural Properties */
             (Name: string,
             Location: string,
             Number_of_Platform: integer,
             Governed_by: Station_Master,
             Composed_of: Control_Centre,
             Composed_of: Waiting_Room,
             Composed_of: set(Platform),
             Composed_of: Time_Table )

method    /* Behavioral Properties */
          Update_Time_Table (number:integer,
                             place: string);
```

```
Class DRIVER inherit PERSON

type tuple   /* Structural Properties */
             (Op-Code: integer,
             Qualification: string,
             Salary: integer,
             Duties: list(tuple(Day: string,
                                Time: integer))
```

```
Class PERSON

type tuple   /* Structural Properties */
             (Name: string,
             Surname: string,
             Birth_Date: Date,
             Address: tuple(City: string,
                            Street: string,
                            Number: integer ))

method    /* Behavioral Properties */
          Compute_Age(Today: Date): integer;
```

```
Class MASTER_STATION inherit PERSON

type tuple   /* Structural Properties */
             (Emp-Code: integer,
             PhoneNumber: integer,
             FaxNumber: integer )
```

```
Class COACH

type tuple   /* Structural Properties */
             (Class: string,
             Type: string,
             Smokers: boolean,
             Number_of_Seats: integer,)
```

Fig.2b   Train-Control-System schema

In general, several distinct affinity sets are generated, including the most tightly linked classes among those selected. In Fig.3 the affinity sets for the Transportation domain are presented, computed starting from the class pairs previously listed.

The affinity sets are examined by the reuse engineer who evaluates the opportunity of defining the corresponding generic classes, analyzing the meaning and the role of each class included in the affinity set in their respective schema. For each affinity set that has passed the semantic analysis, the corresponding generic class is defined factoring out the structural and behavioral properties common to all the classes belonging to the affinity set. With reference to Fig.3, the reuse engineer can decide, for example, that the affinity set AS1 is meaningless, since a generic class Person is too general and provides little information in the Transportation domain, while the remaining affinity sets really describe relevant classes of objects in this domain. Let us consider, for example, the affinity set AS2, with members Aircraft and Train. For AS2 the corresponding generic class Transportation-Means is defined (see Fig.1), factoring out the structural properties common to the AS2's classes into the corresponding generic properties Means_code, Number_of_seats, Driver, Departure and Destination, Dep_time, and Arr_time, and factoring out the behavioral properties of the AS2's classes into the generic properties How_many_free and Reserve_seats.

The process of abstraction of the common properties into the corresponding generic class is formalized by using *abstraction mappings*, that have the purpose of determining the minimal structural and behavioral properties sufficient for characterizing all the classes of the considered affinity sets [10].

In general, during the abstraction process, the reuse engineer has in charge the task of choosing a meaningful name for generic properties, messages and classes. These names are defined on the basis of the personal domain knowledge of the reuse engineer, the role of the classes belonging to the affinity set, and from the information stored in the Thesaurus, about synonym, similar, generalization, and specialization terms in the domain.

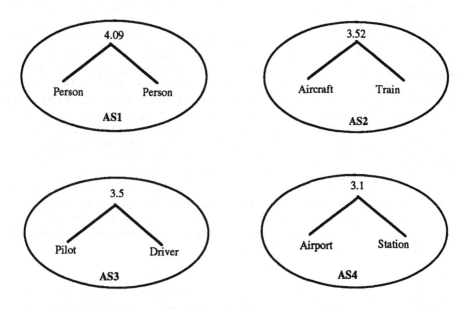

Fig.3 Affinity sets for the schemas in Fig.2 in the Transportation domain

Properties to be included within a generic class are selected using the affinity conditions illustrated in Sect.3, and the information stored in the Thesaurus, and are refined by the reuse engineer, according to his domain knowledge and schema contents. For instance, the reuse engineer decides to define for Transportation-Means the attribute Means_code, since both the Train and the Aircraft classes have an identification code in their respective schemas. As for behavioral commonalities, both the How_many_free, and the Reserve_seats methods are factored out in the Transportation-Means generic class, since they have the same arity, and compatible parameters in the Aircraft and Train classes. In the same way, are defined the generic classes Location, and Driver, considering the affinity sets AS3 and AS4 shown in Fig.3, composed of Airport and Station, Pilot and Driver, respectively.

To complete reusable component definition, guidelines are associated with newly created generic classes, describing how the generic class can be reused and tailored, using conceptual design primitives (e.g., modification of a class by adding new properties; specialization of the generic class; transformation of the generic class into a set of more specific classes). For example, with reference to the generic class Transportation-Means, possible suggestions can concern its specialization into a Military-Aircraft, by adding the properties "Missile-weapons, Missile", "Antimissile, Missile", and so on.

5. Concluding remarks

In this paper we presented a methodology for building object-oriented reusable conceptual components to be used during the Information System requirements specification phase. Reusable components are extracted and engineered from a set of application-dependent components, that present affinity. A set of affinity criteria and metrics have been presented to compute the level of affinity between object classes in different schemas.

Our research results are being experimented and validated within the ESPRIT Project n.6612 F^3 (From Fuzzy to Formal) whose purpose is the definition of an integrated environment aiming at improving the requirements engineering process. Specifically, in this project we have developed a reuse tool, called EXTRACT [11], which is an interactive tool capable of analyzing conceptual schemas and identifying similarities. In particular, EXTRACT automatically computes affinities, using the metrics illustrated in Sect.3, and automatically constructs affinity sets, using the complete-link algorithm. The reuse can finally decide reusable component definition, and interactively specify the reuse guidelines. A first prototype of tool is available on Sun 4, operating on Entity-Relationship conceptual schemas [6].

Future research work is needed to complete the approach. In particular, affinity criteria for complex domains will be refined, and the assimilation of new components in the reuse repository will be further investigated. Moreover, we are studying methods and techniques for organizing and clustering reusable components in the repository at different levels of genericity and abstraction.

Acknowledgements
Part of this work has been supported by the F^3 Esprit Project N.6612 and by the Italian National Research Council Project "Sistemi Informatici e Calcolo Parallelo", L.R.C. INFOKIT, and by MURST 40%.

References

1. ACM Issue on Next-Generation Database Systems, Communications of the ACM, Vol.34, N.10, October 1991
2. D.Batory, S.O'Malley, "The Design and Implementation of Hierarchical Software Systems with Reusable Components", *ACM Trans. On Software Engineering and Methodology*, Vol.14, No.4, 1992
3. E.Bertino, L.Martino, *Object-oriented Database Systems - Concepts and Architectures*, Addison Wesley, International Computer Sciences Series, 1993
4. G. Booch, *Object-Oriented Design*, Benjamin Cummings, 1991
5. J.Bubenko, C.Rolland, P.Loucopoulos, V.De Antonellis, "Facilitating "From Fuzzy to

Formal" Requirements Modelling", to appear in *Proc. of ICRE '94, IEEE Int. Conf. on Requirements Engineering*, Colorado Springs and Taipei, April 1994

6. S.Castano, V.De Antonellis, B.Zonta, "Classifying and Reusing Conceptual Schemas", in *Proc. of ER'92, Int. Conf. on the Entity-Relationship Approach*, Karlsruhe, LNCS, n.645, Springer Verlag, October 1992

7. S.Castano, V. De Antonellis, "Reuse of Conceptual Requirement Specifications", in *Proc. of RE '93, ACM/IEEE Int. Conf. on Requirements Engineering*, San Diego, CA, January 1993

8. S.Castano, V. De Antonellis, "A Constructive Approach to Reuse of Conceptual Components", in *Proc. of 2nd ACM/IEEE Int. Workshop on Software Reusability*, Lucca, Italy, March 1993

9. S.Castano, V. De Antonellis, "Reusing Process Specifications", in *Proc. IFIP Working Conference on Information System Development Process, IFIP WG 8.1*, Como, Italy, September 1993, North-Holland

10. S.Castano, V.De Antonellis, P.Sanpietro, "Reuse of Object-Oriented Requirements Specifications", in *Proc. ER '93, 12th Int. Conf. on The Entity Relationship Approach*, Dallas Arlinghton, TX, USA, December 1993

11. S.Castano, V.De Antonellis, C. Francalanci, M.G. Fugini, B. Pernici, R.Bellinzona, "Methodology for Reusable Requirements", F^3 Report, F^3.PdM.2-1-3-R2, Politecnico di Milano, December 1993

12. P.S.Chen, R.Hennicker, M.Jarke, "On the Retrieval of Reusable Software Components", in *Proc. of 2nd ACM/IEEE Int. Workshop on Software Reusability*, Lucca, Italy, March 1993

13. P.Coad, E.Yourdon, *Object-Oriented Design*, Yourdon Press Computing Series, 1991

14. V.DeAntonellis, S.Castano, L.Vandoni, "Building Reusable Components Through Project Evolution Analysis", Information Systems, Vol.19, No.4, Elsevier Science Ltd, 1994

15. O.Deux, "The Story of O_2", IEEE Trans. on Data and Knowledge Engineering, Vol.2, No.1, March 1990

16. W.Kim, "Object-Oriented Databases: Definition and Research Directions", invited paper, IEEE Trans. on Data and Konowledge Engineering, Vol.2, No.3, March 1990

17. C.W. Krueger, "Software Reuse", ACM Computing Surveys, Vol.24, No.2, June 1992, pp.131-183

18. Y.S.Maarek, D.M.Berry, G.E.Kaiser, "An Information Retrieval Approach For Automatically Constructing Software Libraries", IEEE TSE, Vol.17, No.8, August 1991, pp.800-813

19. N.A.Maiden, A.G.Sutcliffe, "Exploiting Reusable Specifications Through Analogy", Communications of the ACM, Vol.35, N.4, April 1992, pp.55-64

20. E.Ostertag, J. Hendler, R. Prieto-Diaz, C. Braun, "Computing Similarity in a Reuse Library System: An AI-Based Approach", ACM TOSEM, Proc. of COMPSAC '87, 1987, pp.23-2

21. G.Salton, *Automatic Text Processing - The Transformation, Analysis and Retrieval of Information by Computer* , Addison-Wesley, 1989

22. W. Schafer, R. Prieto-diaz, M.Matsumoto, *Software Reusability*, Ellis Horwood Workshops, 1993

23. W.W.Song, P.Johannesson, J.A.Bubenko, "Semantic Similarity Relations in Schema Integration", in *Proc. of ER'92, Int. Conf. on The Entity Relationship Approach*, Karlsruhe, Lecture Notes in Computer Science, n.645, Springer Verlag, October 1992

An Object-Oriented Approach to the Integration of Online Services into Office Automation Environments

P. Corbellini[1], P. Della Vigna[2], F. Mercalli[3], M. Pugliese[3]

1 - CedCamera - via Viserba 20, Milano - Italy
2 - Politecnico di Milano - p.za Leonardo Da Vinci 32, Milano - Italy
3 - Centro di Cultura Scientifica "Alessandro Volta" - Villa Olmo, 22100 Como - Italy
phone: +39 31 572213 - fax: +39 31 573395 - email: volta@imiclvx.bitnet

Abstract. In the Office Automation area, application environments and database technology evolve toward highly structured and object-oriented system models. Unfortunately a large quantity of valuable data is stored into old-fashioned online information services, in the form of poorly structured documents. The big difference in the data models and the diversity in the user interfaces, make it extremely difficult to integrate these data into modern application contexts. This paper presents a practical solution to this problem, based on an object-oriented approach studied in the frame of the ESPRIT Project 2109 TOOTSI. The approach is based on the definition of a uniform set of abstract operations, a common query language and a DDL for defining complex objects. Though targeted to online service integration, the approach presented here can be easily generalised to other cases.

1. Introduction

In the Office Automation area, application environments as well as database technology evolve toward more and more object-oriented models.

In modern windowing systems the attention is shifted from applications to documents. The concept of a document as a product of a single, closed application tends to disappear leaving the place to the document intended as a composite object, produced by the simultaneous cooperation of several applications.

For example, a business report is composed by text produced with a word processor, pictures produced with a draw application, interrelated figures produced with a spreadsheet, etc.

To fit in this new frame, data items should present themselves as autonomous entities, featuring a well defined and uniform behaviour, which depends on their meaning rather than on the application that manages them. In a word, they should present themselves as *objects*.

This leads to problems when integrating data produced in the past. A lot of valuable data is still managed by old-fashioned applications, representing closed worlds to which access is allowed only through a very specialised interface - different from application to application - hardly compatible with the object-oriented view mentioned above.

Due to the huge quantity of data involved, a migration toward a new DBMS is often impracticable for cost reasons.

These problems have been addressed in the frame of the ESPRIT Project 2109 TOOTSI (*Telematic Object-Oriented Tools for Services Interfaces*) - ended in 1992 - with particular concern to the integration of public online information services into office automation contexts [Mah90] [Bar91].

Online information services - such as yellow pages, business information, library services, data banks of all kinds, etc. - are a highly valuable, exhaustive, updated and reasonably priced source of information, which may be useful in a large number of professional fields, as for example engineering, marketing, patent managing, etc.

Unfortunately, they are exploited much less than expected because of the big difficulties encountered in integrating them in modern office automation environments, based on PCs and individual productivity tools.

These difficulties stem from two classes of problems.

First, online services feature old-fashioned, non-standardised interfaces - designed for dumb terminal access - that hide the real meaning of data stored behind them.

Second, the thousands of online services available, even with an extremely simple and inexpensive equipment - such as a PC connected to a telephone line through a modem - makes paradoxically worse the situation.

Users are faced with a mess of different services - featuring different interfaces, data models, tariffs schemes, etc. - that makes it virtually impossible for people without a specific and deep knowledge to profitably exploit this resource.

The TOOTSI approach to this problem is to exploit the local intelligence of the PC to provide a software system able to transparently manage the dialogue with online services, through their native interfaces, without requiring any modification on the service side, in order to extract information and construct *data objects* from it [Del92].

The data objects should feature methods allowing a uniform access to data, regardless of the underlying service idiosyncrasies and consistent with the semantics of the corresponding information, in order to facilitate the integration into popular productivity tools such as word processors, databases, spreadsheets and so on.

In this paper we present a possible implementation of the TOOTSI approach - called *Object Oriented Online Service* (OOOS) - currently under development by a cooperation of Centro di Cultura Scientifica "A. Volta" and the EDP Centre of the Chamber of Commerce of Milan (CedCamera).

Since long ago, the Chamber of Commerce of Milan is exploiting online services to satisfy the information needs of the associated Enterprises. At this purpose, it constituted the *Economical Information Centre*, where experts browse online services on behalf of enterprises' operators.

In order to try to "bring the expert on the end-user desktop", CedCamera and Centro "A. Volta" - former TOOTSI partner - are cooperating for the development of a software system able to provide end-users with a more friendly perception of online information services, described in the following sections.

In particular, section 2 illustrates a typical online service interface through an example, in order to better focus the problem. In section 3 the abstraction of the object-oriented online service provided by OOOS is shown. In section 4, the software architecture of OOOS is described in detail and in section 5 some concluding remarks are reported.

2. An online service interface example

In this section the typical interface of an online information service is illustrated by means of an example.

In particular, we consider here an online data bank containing bibliographical information regarding computer science.

Online services reside on remote host computers, easily accessible using a modem connected to a terminal (for example, a PC) and a communication network, such as a public circuit-switched telephone network or a public packet-switched data network. This is depicted in figure 1.

The first step to perform in order to access our example service is the *connection to the host computer*. This procedure may require a sequence of actions such as configuring a communication port on the terminal, dialing a phone number, calling a NUA, logging into the remote host computer, etc.

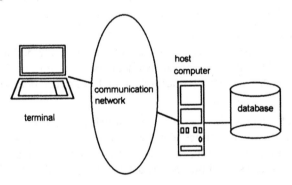

Figure 1. Connection to an online service.

When logged in the host computer, the second step to perform is the *connection to the service*. This means to choose the desired service among the many provided by the connected host. This is often done by means of a specific command, as for example

CONNECT BIBLIO

that connects to the service called *biblio*.

After completion of this two-steps procedure, the user has at her/his disposal a set of commands to examine the data bank content and retrieve data.

Online data banks are managed through information retrieval systems (IRS) based on inverted list technology.

Though the precise type, number and syntax of the available commands depend on the particular underlying IRS, it is nevertheless possible to identify some base functionalities provided by almost all services.

In particular, the service is perceived as a big repository of *documents* (the single bibliographical references, in the example at hand) consisting in some plain ASCII text, possibly organised into fields to which inverted lists, or *indexes*, are associated.

In figure 2, a couple of such documents is shown. Seven fields, named NO, TI, AU, AF, SO, AB and DE, can be identified.

```
=====================================================
NO: 90M180002
TI: STOP C.A.O.S.: A COMMON ACCESS TO ONLINE SERVICES;
AU: F. BARTOLOMUCCI, G. LELLA;
AF: SARITEL, POMEZIA;
SO: ANNUAL CONGRESS AICA 1991;
AB: THIS PAPER ADDRESSES THE PROBLEM OF OFFERING A COMMON QUERY
LANGUAGE TO ONLINE SERVICES FOR THEIR BETTER AND EASIER UTILISATION;
DE: ONLINE SERVICES, DYNAMIC PARSING, QUERY LANGUAGES;
=====================================================
NO: 90M000003
TI: ISSUES IN THE DESIGN OF OBJECT-ORIENTED DATABASE PROGRAMMING
LANGUAGES;
AU: T. BLOOM, S. B. ZDONIK;
AF: MIT LABORATORY FOR COMPUTER SCIENCE, BROWN UNIVERSITY;
SO: OOPSLA '87;
AB: THE PURPOSE OF THIS PAPER IS TO TRY TO UNCOVER SOME OF THE ACTUAL
PRESUPPOSITIONS THAT HAVE INHIBITED DEVELOPMENT OF A FULLY INTEGRATED
DATABASE PROGRAMMING LANGUAGE;
DE: OBJECT-ORIENTED, DATABASE, PROGRAMMING LANGUAGE;
=====================================================
```

Figure 2. Example of online data bank documents

A *search operation*, usually in the form of a **FIND** command, is used to select a subset of all documents contained in the data bank, on the basis of a predicate expressed in a query language specific to the considered service.

In the following, some examples of use of the **FIND** command are illustrated.

The command

FIND TOOTSI

retrieves all documents containing the term *tootsi* in any of their fields; the search is internally done by looking in a default index - the *basic index* - including most important terms from all fields;

FIND OBJECT-ORIENTED **AND** DATABASE

retrieves all documents containing both the terms *object-oriented* and *database* in any of their fields (again, the search is internally done by looking in the basic index);

FIND TI = DATABASE

retrieves all documents containing the term *database* in the TI field; the search is internally done by looking in the index associated with the TI field.

Once the query is issued, the IRS returns the cardinality of the selected subset. Based on this number the user can decide to enlarge or restrict the query, in order to obtain a correct number of documents.

When satisfied with his/her choice, he/she can *display the documents* in the subset. For example, the command

SHOW

instructs the system to show the first few documents that fit in the terminal screen, and

NEXT

instructs the system to go on, showing the next documents in the subset that fit in the terminal screen.

When the working session on the service is finished, the user has usually to *disconnect the service*, for example with the command

FIN

and then to *disconnect from the host computer*, by logging out and hanging up the communication line.

Many other functionalities are generally present in online services but what here explained is nevertheless enough to catch the key concepts involved.

3. The object-oriented online service

Based on the observations of the preceding section, we present here the online service abstraction provided by OOOS.

The OOOS abstraction aims mainly at providing the end-user with a uniform, object-oriented visibility of data contained in many different online services.

The effectiveness of the object-oriented approach in favouring the integration of independent, heterogeneous data repositories into applicative contexts has been recognised in several research studies and implementation works. See for example [Kim88] [Ber88].

In particular, the OOOS abstraction is built around three key concepts:

* a set of abstract operations;

- a query language for the search operation;
- a DDL for documents extracted from the online services.

They are separately detailed in the following.

Abstract operations

Abstract operations are the OOOS way to express the basic functionalities illustrated in section 2.

They are *abstract* in the sense that they are independent of the concrete details specific to any given service, thus guaranteeing uniformity.

OOOS is in charge of taking the suitable actions to translate each abstract operation into a sequence of commands to be issued through the native interface of the accessed service.

For sake of simplicity, we illustrate here only the very basic abstract operations defined in OOOS. Other operations can be easily added in the same way.

We make use of a C++ notation.

void **hconnect**(char *host_name)
  Performs a connection to the host computer *host_name*.

void **hdisconnect**()
  Disconnects from currently connected host computer.

void **connect**(char *service_name)
  Performs a connection to the service *service_name*.

void **disconnect**()
  Disconnects from the currently connected service.

long int **find**(char *query)
  Selects the subset of service's documents for which the predicate *query* evaluates to TRUE and returns the cardinality of this set.

document *first()
  Retrieves the first document of the last recently selected document subset.

document *next()
  Retrieves the next document of the last recently selected document subset.

It is important to note that the **find, first** and **next** operations provide the object-oriented view of data: **find** treats the online service as a repository of individual objects - the documents - that can be selected on the basis of queries, while **first** and **next** return these objects as complex structures belonging to class document rather than as simple ASCII text.

Query language

The **find** operation requires a query language for selecting documents.

At this purpose, OOOS defines TQL, a language that includes the most important features present in the majority of IRS query languages [Sal83].

In fact, TQL includes commonly found boolean operators, relational operators, proximity operators and truncation operators.

It is up to the OOOS system to translate a TQL query into the specific language of the accessed service.

It has to be noted that, in order not to limit the expressiveness of the language, the set of TQL functionalities is bigger than the intersection of the sets of functionalities found in the query languages of the majority of services, as illustrated in figure 3.

For this reason, it may happen that not all TQL features are supported by a particular service.

In figure 3, for example, functionality f_1 is supported by all services and also by TQL. On the other hand, functionality f_2, though still supported by TQL is not supported by service C.

This means that, before translating a TQL query, OOOS should check if the translation is defined for the particular service currently accessed.

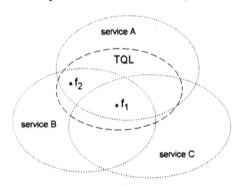

Figure 3. TQL functionalities.

Moreover, a formal way to describe to the end-user the TQL functionalities permitted for each service is needed.

Both problems are solved through the definition of a formal *permission definition language* that, substantially, lists for each service the boolean, relational, proximity and truncation operators allowed.

DDL for documents

Documents are displayed by online services as plain ASCII text.

The transformation of this text into distinct, structured objects representing single documents that can be easily integrated into modern object-oriented application contexts, is a central point for OOOS.

This goal is reached by requiring a document type declaration for each service integrated in OOOS. These declarations are called *document templates*.

The DDL for defining document templates is described in figure 4.

```
<document template> ::== <type>;

<type> ::==      RECORD {<label> : <type>} END |
                 LIST OF <type> |
                 TEXT

<label> ::==     identifier
```

Figure 4. DDL syntax

This DDL is based on concepts drawn from well-known object-oriented DBMSs, such as for example the O_2 system [Deu91].

In O_2 types are definable starting from six *atomic types* (*boolean, character, integer, real, string* and *bits*) recursively composed by means of three *type constructors* (*tuple, list* and *set*).

In OOOS the situation is simpler: there is only one atomic type - the *text* type, representing a string of characters - and two type constructors - the *record* constructor - corresponding to the O_2 tuple constructor - and the *list* constructor.

Since, at present, the main purpose of OOOS is to interface online information services providing textual information, this has been considered to be enough.

Abstract operations **first** and **next**, always return documents having a structure consistent with the document template declared for the currently accessed service.

4. Architecture of OOOS

In this section we illustrate the architecture on which the OOOS system is based.

The general architecture is depicted in picture 5. It can be observed that three main external interfaces are foreseen.

The first one is the interface toward the end-user - that is the application programmer that uses OOOS. It consist of a C++ object featuring a set of methods corresponding to the abstract operations illustrated in section 3.

The second interface is represented by the communication port used to connect to the communication equipment (generally a modem). In the system we are developing, this is a standard RS-232 interface.

The third interface is represented by the four dotted rectangles, outlined around the border of the OOOS system in figure 5. They represent files consulted run-time by the system, that in a sense describe the behaviour of the online services to be integrated.

These files should be prepared by an online service expert once and for all and then supplied to the system.

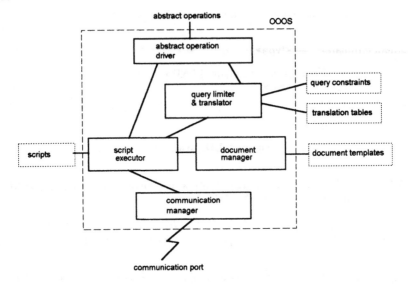

Figure 5. General OOOS architecture

The set of files related to a given service is said to constitute the *mapping* of that service to OOOS.

When a service is correctly mapped to OOOS, the end-user programmer can interact with it through the uniform, object-oriented interface made available at the abstract operations level, without worrying about lower level details.

Internally to the OOOS system, five main modules are present.

The *abstract operation driver* is the module that activates in the correct sequence the other modules in order to perform the actions needed to carry out a given abstract operation.

The *communication manager* is the part of the system that interacts with the RS-232 port in order to dialogue with the online services. The dialogue is carried out by means of a *communication session* object. A communication session object features four major methods:

- *Open*, to allocate resources and perform initialisation tasks;
- *Send*, to send data to the service;
- *Receive*, to receive and analyse data returned from the service;
- *Close*, to deallocate resources and perform final tasks.

The *query limiter and translator*, detailed in figure 6, is the system component in charge of checking the TQL query passed to the system with the **find** operation and to translate it into the specific query language of the current service.

The query limiter and translator reads two set of files containing the description of query constraints - that is TQL functionalities not supported by the query languages of integrated services - and translation tables - describing the translation from TQL to services access languages.

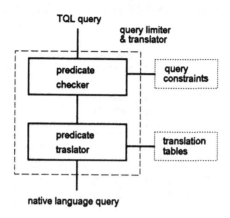

TQL query

query limiter
& translator

predicate
checker

query
constraints

predicate
traslator

translation
tables

native language query

Figure 6. The query limiter and translator

The *document manager*, detailed in figure 7, is the component in charge of managing document templates and creating document objects from them.

A *template compiler* transforms the textual template declaration, externally provided to OOOS, in a convenient internal form and stores it in the internal template database.

A *template manager* builds new document structures, based on the contents of the template database. The template manager can create whole documents or only part of them (for example to add new elements on lists).

The *document structures* are C++ classes representing the atomic types and type constructors illustrated in section 3. Record, list and text objects can thus be instantiated and passed to other modules of the system.

The *script executor*, illustrated in figure 8, is the real engine of the system.

A *script* in OOOS is a procedure written in a suitable language - called SL - which translates a given abstract operation in the sequence of steps needed to perform that abstract operation on the native interface of a specific service. Thus, the system must be provided with a script for each pair *(s,o)* - where *s* is a service integrated in OOOS and *o* is an abstract operation.

The SL language provides suitable statements to interact with the communication manager, the document manager and the query limiter and translator.

The script executor does not execute directly SL scripts. Instead it compiles them in a smaller intermediate language, for which an efficient interpreter is provided.

5. Concluding remarks

In the preceding sections the key concepts and the system architecture of the Object Oriented Online Service (OOOS) developed in cooperation by Centro "A. Volta" and CedCamera, on the basis of the ESPRIT Project TOOTSI research results, has been illustrated.

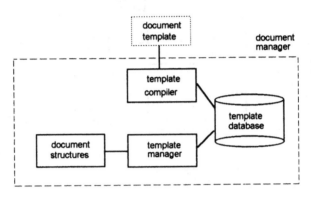

Figure 7. The document manager

The system provides a *uniform* and *object-oriented* view of data contained in many different online services.

The view is uniform since the system defines an unique set of abstract operations, that are transparently translated into specific actions on the native interfaces of the services to be accessed.

The view is object-oriented since data coming from the online services as plain ASCII text are analysed, broken into small components and then restructured into objects - called *documents* - defined by suitable document templates.

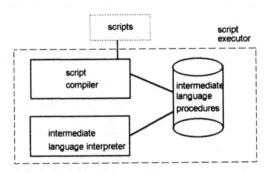

Figure 8. The script executor

The paper is concerned with the integration of online information services, but it is worth to note that the presented approach is quite general and can be applied to a large number of other data repositories by simply changing the set of abstract operations defined in section 3 and the communication manager described in section 4.

For example, to integrate plain file systems, the new set of abstract operations may include: check the existence of a file, read a file into an object described by a suitable document template, create a file, delete a file and so on.

The communication session object in the communication manager should perform open, send, receive and close operations by issuing file system commands rather that sending data to a communication line.

The prototype OOOS system will be ready for May 1994 and will be experimented by the Chamber of Commerce of Milan in its Economical Information Centre.

The most important future plan is concerned with making the DDL for document templates, described in section 3, fully object-oriented through the addition of the inheritance concept.

6. References

[Bar91] F. Bartolomucci, G. Lella, *Stop C.A.O.S.: a Common Access to Online Services*, Annual Congress AICA 1991;

[Ber88] E. Bertino et Al., *The COMANDOS Integration System: an Object-Oriented Approach to the Interconnection of Heterogeneous Applications*, 2nd Intl. Workshop on OO DB Systems Proc., Bad Munster am Stein-Ebernburg, 1988;

[Del92] P. Della Vigna, G. Lella, G. Lo Reto, D. Maino, F. Mercalli, *Issues in Mapping Online Service Interfaces to an Object-Oriented Data Model*, OpenForum '92, Utrecht, November 1992;

[Deu91] O. Deux et Al., *The O_2 System*, O_2 Technology, March 1991;

[Kim88] W. Kim, N. Ballou, H.T. Chou, J.F. Garza, D. Woelk, J. Banerjee, *Integrating an Object-Oriented Programming System with a Database System*, OOPSLA '88 Proc., 1988;

[Mah90] B. Mahon, F. Meinkhon, G. Lella, *TOOTSI: Creating a Toolkit for Building User Interfaces to Business Information Services*, Online Review, Vol 14, N.6, 1990;

[Sal83] G. Salton, M.J. McGill, *Introduction to modern Information Retrieval*, McGraw-Hill, Singapore 1983;

A Linguistic Approach to the Development of Object Oriented Systems using the NL System LOLITA

Luisa Mich

Dipartimento di Informatica e Studi Aziendali
University of Trento
Via Inama 5, 38100 Trento, Italy
Tel.: +39 461 882150; Telefax: +39 461 882124
e_mail: mich@cs.unitn.it

Roberto Garigliano

Laboratory for Natural Language Engineering
Department of Computer Science, University of Durham
Durham DH1 3LE, England
Tel.: +44 91 3742639; Telefax: +44 91 3743741
e_mail: Roberto.Garigliano@durham.ac.uk

Abstract. The problem tackled in this paper is that of using computer aided techniques to facilitate the building of Object Oriented models from natural language requirements. The authors believe that this could be achieved by the use of a Natural Language Processing System built according to the Natural Language Engineering principles such as LOLITA. The paper is devoted to explore this possibility and to show its potential using the Object Modeling Technique (OMT).

1 Introduction

The demands of large system development have driven in the last few years the extension of a relatively new approach — the object oriented (OO) paradigm — from the programming domain to the full development life cycle, including Analysis and Design. There has been a great deal of work in the area of object oriented methods (see, for example, [13]). Furthermore, new CASE tools have been developed to support those methods [12]. However, there are few tools which can offer an effective support, especially as far as the initial development phases are concerned. It is widely recognised that the main problems facing the analyst are the requirements elicitation and definition, and the validation phase [14].

Our goal is to implement a system capable of parsing the input requirements in natural language (NL) and extracting the objects and their association for use in creating an object oriented model. Fundamental points are that: (1) the document should be in their normal natural language form; (2) the user should not be pestered with continuous requests for clarification, and required to engage only in necessary and pleasant interaction; (3) the system should be able to deal in some measure with problems in the documents, be them linguistic, logic or due to clash of perspectives; (4) the system should be able, at least in principle, to work with any generally accepted OO methodology; (5) the final OO model output should not contain irrelevant information, or miss essential one, and it should indeed be a useful help to successive system analysis. In this paper we argue that these demands can be met with a general domain independent Natural Language Processing (NLP) System built according to the Natural Language Engineering principles such as LOLITA. The paper is devoted to explore this possibility and to show its potential using the Object Modeling Technique (OMT) [23], an OO methodology encompassing all the life-cycle phases, and sufficiently representative to not invalidate the generality of the argument.

The rest of the paper is organized as follows. Section 2 describes the role played by NL in the development of CASE tools devoted to the initial phases of system development and in OO modelling. Section 3 gives a short state-of-the-art on NLP-based CASE. In Section 4 a brief presentation of the LOLITA system and of the OMT is given, followed by some short examples of their possible combination. Finally, in section 5 conclusions are given.

2 The Problem

Whatever technique is used for the requirements elicitation (questionnaires and interviews, work observation, brainstorming, focus group, etc.), by far the largest and most important section of available information consists of natural language statements, often described in terms of what the system shall perform, what functionality the system shall support and what items should exist in the system. Moreover, many OO methodologies advice on the use of linguistic criteria for objects identification and for OO models construction.

The problem here is not to review all the advantages of a CASE tool based on a real NLPS: the point is that some of these features are a matter of peculiar interest in OO modelling. It is widely recognised that with an OO approach the semantic gap between reality and the model is reduced. All the more so because we build the world through the language [28], that is NL plays a predominant role in abstraction processes to develop OO models.

For this reason, the role of 'creativity' — understood as the ability to abstract suitable objects, and hence to interpret natural language descriptions coming from different fonts — is often considered crucial in the OO modelling process. However, without entering the debate on the final possibility of automatic production of 'creative' behaviour, it is clear from recent advances in Natural Language Engineering that major inroads are now possible in the interpretation of natural language descriptions.

This observation might explain the difficulties that are encountered in the development of non-NL-based CASE tools devoted to the initial phases of system development. The tools needed would have to guide the analyst in the gathering and interpretation of key messages, while keeping track of the interactions with a number of users\experts, during which the analyst's point of view contributes as much as anybody else's to determine the 'universe of discourse' of the problem under discussion.

It is important to underline here that this is not a problem of technological maturity, but one that is intrinsic to the deep nature of the process involved, and, as such, one that presents itself whatever the technology used.

It is thus our contention that, in order to develop a CASE prototype for generating object oriented requirements\models from textual requirements document, it is necessary to use a 'real' natural language system. Furthermore, it is necessary to account for ambiguities, contradictions, omissions, redundancies etc. and this can be done only if the inferential system is embedded in the natural language processing system. Most of these features correspond to LOLITA (Large-scale Object-based Linguistic Interactor, Translator and Analyser), a NLP system developed over the last eight years at the Laboratory for Natural Language Engineering, Computer Science Dept., at the University of Durham [11]. The proposed system should support the requirements analysis process by generating object oriented models using a module based on LOLITA. In a complementary fashion, the validation process is based on the automatic text generation from sections of the conceptual graph [25].

LOLITA can play a role from the very beginning of a system's development process; that is because the input texts can be corrected and normalised.

The output can then be used for a requirement validation if necessary, gearing it to the level of linguistic competence of the user or expert. Information is memorised in a logically correct form of semantic net known as 'conceptual graph' (CG), which can then be used to build the various models required by the particular OO methodology used.

3 The Others: from Abbot to the Case Grammar

In recent years a certain number of NLP-based CASE tools have been realised, in the areas of both SW and Information System development, and in the construction of conceptual schemas for Databases.

As far as the linguistic theories adopted are concerned, they range from the syntactic linguistic criteria proposed by Abbot [1] to works that attempt to realise a more sophisticated text analysis using variants of the Case Grammar by Fillmore [10]; however, even in the early work by Abbot the importance of a semantic analysis and of a real-world knowledge is recognised (under the general heading of 'understanding of the problem domain').

The basic approach by Abbot is developed further in a paper by Booch [4] which — together with the one by Abbot — is the most quoted with regard to the use of 'linguistic criteria' for the development of models of external world in terms of interconnected objects.

A process of incremental construction of SW modules starting from OO specifications obtained from informal NL specifications is described in [24], in which the transformation process takes place interactively and the analyst's role is very important, since the system is able to extract verbs and nouns from an informal specifications automatically, but not to determine which words are important for the construction of a formal specification. With respect to the approach by Abbot, the role of verbal patterns is underlined.

The NL specifications are analysed separately using two dictionaries, one for nouns and another for verbs, which are classified in way related to the OO model used for formal specifications. In this way, it is possible to supply to the lack of a real NLP system: this however is achieved at the cost of a considerable loss of information.

In order to limit this problem, Bailin [2] proposes a different solution, based on 'filtering' the requirements text to build a requirements Database, so as to simplify the search for nouns and noun-phrases. However, no details are given on how to achieve this simplification. As described later, LOLITA can indeed constitute a strong support tool in the initial phase thanks to its 'text normalisation' capabilities.

Another significant aspect in Bailin's work is the proposal to use Data Flow Diagrams (DFDs) in order to identify entities in the problem domain (although the author maintains that DFDs are not really part of OO specifications, and can only be used as an intermediate representation. It should however be noted that other OO methodologies, such as the Object Modeling Technique (OMT) [23] which we adopt in this paper, contemplate the use of DFDs as models for the functional aspects. We refer to the paper by Wieringa [27] for more information on the use of DFDs as part of OOA.

A well-known method for the construction of conceptual schemas for relational Database development is NIAM [8]. In order to obtain a domain-independent system, NIAM uses the result of the context-based NLP disambiguation. The analyst interacts with the system on a particular Universe of Discourse, utilising a subset of the NL which is similar to that produced by the LOLITA normaliser: just like other similar NLP approaches, this one lacks in generality, as it was built with that particular application in mind.

Among the systems devoted to the early stages development support for systems based on AI-style knowledge acquisition, the Requirements Apprentice (RA) [21] should be mentioned. To avoid the problems related to the complexity of the free language which the user is likely to employ, RA imposes a more restricted command language: this is an approach that may help the analyst, but not the requirement provider. On the other hand, this approach is instrumental in allowing RA to make a significant use of domain knowledge (expressed, e.g., in the 'Clichè Library').

The expert system ALECSI-OICSI [5] allows the user to express the requirements both in NL (French) and in graphic form, and the system builds conceptual structures. ALECSI, just like LOLITA, uses a semantic network to represent the domain knowledge [22]. The NL interpretation is based on the case semantics approach [10], according to which the meaning of a sentence can be extracted from the meaning of the verb and the recognition of the connected cases.

By applying the 'case' concept to the sentence level too, it is possible to obtain a top-down approach to the interpretation of complex phrases. Furthermore, since the linguistic patterns are independent from any particular mode building technique, they can be used with any development methodology.

OICSI is based upon the REMORA methodology, which identifies four basic concepts: objects actions, events and constraints, and four corresponding types of nodes in the semantic net used to implement the conceptual schema needed. There are five types of arcs, representing respectively: a relationship between two objects, an action modifying an object, an event triggering an action, an object changing state, and a constraint on a node.

Validation phase support is also present: starting from the semantic net, NL sentences are built using a Chomskian approach, which provide for the user a description of the application domain as close as possible to the one initially given to the system.

For a different validation support tool approach, in which the NL generator is built from a subset of Hobbs coherence relationships, see [6].

An extension of the case grammar is used also in the requirement analysis support system described in [3]. The prototype automatically performs a 'semantic case analysis' on sentence based on a subset of English (Analyst Constrained Language: ACL). It uses a form of Predicate Calculus, rather than a semantic net formalism. Its system architecture is based on four modules, three of which constitute the NLP system, while the fourth is the OO Analysis System (OOAS). The OOAS takes as an input from the NLP modules an annotated tree and case frames. From these two structures, roles, relationships and inheritance rules are derived, which are represented in relational tables. These tables are then used for requirement elicitation. In order to identify which noun-phrases from the input text represent candidate objects, heuristics are proposed for the analyst to apply. It is also claimed that, as a by-product, the prototype allows the automatic identification of ambiguities, inconsistencies etc.

Compared with the ALECSI-OICSI system, this is a less sophisticated system: rather than use a robust NLP system, it restricts the range of possible input texts, and takes advantage of the fact that the style in technical documents is simpler.

Among others support tools for the reorganisation and normalisation of NL input, we refer to the Fact Gathering and Analysis Tool [20], which aims to assist the analyst in collecting and digesting facts from end-users. This is, however, only a tool for the orderly classification of documents for automatic controls (such as aliases, homonymies etc.).

4 Our Own Project

An adequate CASE tool for OO system development should:

- deal with all the life cycle phases, including the very early requirement elicitation ones, and the validation phase;

- allow information handling using both text and graphics without requiring the user to learn new languages;

- support different methodologies.

As it was argued above, these demands can be met with a general domain independent NLP system which will not place restrictions on the language used.

This paper focuses on the potential of LOLITA for supporting object oriented analysis and specifically the very early phase of NL requirements acquisition and analysis and the construction of OO conceptual models.

In the rest of this paper a brief presentation of the LOLITA system and of the OMT is given, followed by some short examples of their possible combination.

4.1 LOLITA

LOLITA is a large scale natural language processing system, built according to the principles of Natural Language Engineering (NLE), an engineering endeavour, which is to combine scientific and technological knowledge in a number of relevant domains (descriptive and computational linguistics, lexicology and terminology, formal languages, computer science, software engineering techniques, etc.) NLE [17] is a new approach, with respect to the traditional Computational Linguistics one, and it is a pragmatic approach characterised by a readiness to use any means in order to build serious NLP programs: this means taking advantage of existing linguistic and logic theories where they exist and are suitable, and then develop localised theories, use knowledge-bases, statistical and adaptive mechanisms, and even ad-hoc solutions where everything else has failed. The goal is to produce systems which are large in scale, allow easy integration and expansion, are feasible both in terms of speed and of memory, are maintainable, robust and such that the intended users are able and willing to use them.

LOLITA meets most of these criteria (with the noticeable exception of the robustness one):

Size LOLITA is a program written in the pure functional programming language Haskell, and it comprises 140 separate modules and approx. 32,000 lines of code (corresponding to about 320,000 lines of an imperative language such as, e.g., C). Its semantic net contains 35,000 connected nodes, able to generate more than 100,000 inflected words in English. The network is in the process of being merged with WordNet from Princeton University, which will bring its size to about 100,000 nodes. The system is able to analyse serious text (such as newspaper articles); it has been under development for 8 years; at present a team of more than 20 researchers work on it.

Integration and maintainability Because of the modular nature of the program, and the features of Haskell, such as absence of side-effects, lazy evaluation, higher order function, polymorphic type structure, automatic type inference, type classes, mathematical notation and great conciseness, it has been possible to achieve high levels of both integration and maintenability; this is demonstrated by the fact that so many different applications are supported by the core system with little additional effort (e.g. the template module is only 0.5% of the whole code, and the translation one is even smaller), and that so many programmers are able to work simultaneously in a prototyping mode.

Feasibility LOLITA runs on a Sparcstation with 64 MB of memory, and all the algorithms used are checked for low complexity; the full template analysis of a newspaper article on a Sparc 10 takes approx. 20 sec.

Usability Although a graphical interface is provided, in general the interface look need to improve, when moved to a product stage.

Functionality LOLITA can analyse text morphologically (correcting misspelling and guessing new words), syntactically (both structure and feature analysis and normalisation, with the ability to repair text with missing or redundant parts, or broken), semantically, pragmatically and by discourse (the last two aspects are still rather naive). It has a powerful inference engine, based on an original form of conceptual graph [26], which can performs (beyond standard inferences) multiple and frame inheritance, epistemic reasoning, causal reasoning and various forms of plausible reasoning (such as reasoning by analogy and by closed personal world assumption). There is also a powerful NL generator, able to express pieces of graph in English in a style controlled by various parameters (such as length, register, rhythm, etc). Uncertainty is managed mainly through a Source Control System. Prototype applications at present include: query, template building, story rewriting, Chinese tutor, translation (from Italian to English, still at early stage), dialogue.

4.2 The Application of LOLITA to OO Modelling

LOLITA can intervene in the initial phases by analysing input texts at several levels in order to correct, select and normalise them, so as to generate a problem statement which in turn would be the starting point for the conceptual analysis. As described above, there are functionalities in LOLITA which allows text correction and completion, style difference elimination (eventually even differences in the actual language used), ambiguity resolution (at the grammatical, semantical, pragmatical, discourse and dialogue levels): all these are phenomena which occur very frequently in real and serious text. They are also features that require a real general purpose base NL system, which is way so many other problem specific systems use a pseudo-natural language.

Real NL text also brings problems of redundancy, inconsistency and omission management: as already pointed out, these are not problems connected to the automation of the process: they are intimately connected to the user-analyst relationship, in the requirement elicitation process itself, and have to be faced no matter what method, tool or system is used. There is an element of uncertainty (and thus of risk) in operating choices (e.g. between different viewpoints

[18]): in LOLITA this problem is managed through the use of the Source Control System, a method which allows for the evaluation of both information and sources together [19]. As a matter of fact, there is a school of thought in Information Systems Theory that underline the naivety of assuming competence or objectivity for each source of system requirements. Furthermore, the possibility of interacting with the user through a 'query' and a 'dialogue' modules, and of generating pieces of text allows the requirement elicitation process to be run interactively via a NL interface.

Finally, it is also possible to interact with the system with a graphical interface (developed by Siemens Plessey), which allows exploration and manipulation of the semantic net (see figure 1).

The second part of this approach starts from the semantic net, in which redundancies and inconsistencies have already been solved or flagged for user's attention, and involves the construction of an OO model.

Although there is no agreed formalism defining an OO approach, there are a certain number of basic concepts, common to most OO models, which can be defined as 'core model' [9]. In this work we use the Object Modeling Technique (OMT) [23], an OO methodology encompassing all the life-cycle phases, and sufficiently representative of those 'core model' as to not invalidate the generality of the argument.

The three aspects of an Information System: data, behaviour and functions are described in OMT by three models: Object Model, Dynamic Model and Functional Model. The most important one is the Object Model, which represents the static system structure in terms of classes and associations. The Functional Model shows how the output values depends on the input ones, without any reference to the internal computation needed. The Dynamic Model provides a state diagram for each Class with a relevant dynamic behaviour, and a global events diagram.

To summarise, the OMT analysis phase produces an Analysis Document comprising:

- a problem statement

- an Object Model

- a Dynamic Model

- a Functional Model

- a Data dictionary for Classes, Attributes and Associations.

With regard to the Object Model, here follows a brief reminder of the stages needed in OMT for its development:

(i) Identify objects and classes

(ii) Prepare a data dictionary

(iii) Identify associations (including aggregations) between objects

(iv) Identify attributes of objects and links

 (v) Organize and simplify object classes using inheritance

(vi) Verify that access paths exist for likely queries

(vii) Iterate and refine the model

(viii) Group classes into modules.

It is now shown how each of these steps can be achieved using LOLITA: it is worth underlining that, while some additional functionality is clearly required, the remarkable thing is how much of the task can be achieved with the existing set-up: this is further evidence of the good properties of integration and maintenability present in the LOLITA design. Each step will be taken in turn.

(i) Identify objects and classes
  Let's follow an example:
Roberto (proper noun) can be seen as the instance of a class. Starting from the application type and from the information expressed in the net it is possible to suggest a set of candidate classes.
  From the net (see figure 1) it is known that 'Roberto' is (among other things):

- owner

- bachelor

- lecturer

Let's assume that the Information System is to be developed for one of the following organisations:

- Custom and Excise

- Marketing Department, Statistics Department

- Local Council

- University.

'owner', 'lecturer' etc. are 'classes' in LOLITA. The problem, thus, is not so much that of defining the classes, or specifying the connections, but rather that of selecting only those needed in the application context.
  This is really the CENTRAL problem in using a real NLS such as LOLITA for OO modelling. The difficulty is that the objects model should provide a class-based representation at the right level of description: neither too generic, nor too detailed.
  In the example, 'lecturer' might not be a suitable class for a tax-related application, while it would be essential for a system to assign timetable slots to courses and lecturers.

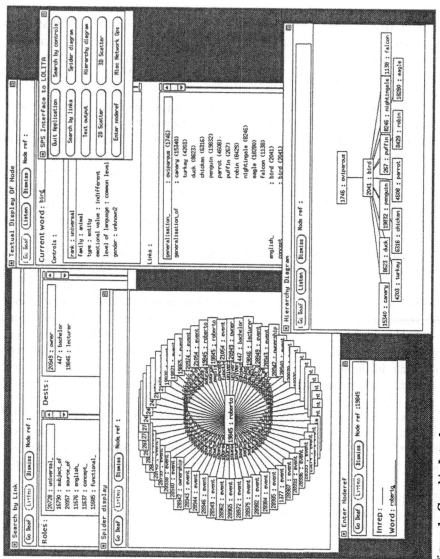

Figure 1: Graphic Interface

Its solution requires the definition of an application 'locality': a similar problem is treated in [16], but is made more complex here by the fact that some subclasses, even if they are richer in information under a logical point of view, are less relevant in the application context. It would seem that what is required is a semantic model of the application, to be used as a filter for the selection of classes, objects and attributes.

There is a problem of circularity in assuming a complete semantic model. However, if the user specifies the general application type in an header (e.g.: 'system for the control and allocation of tax returns, to be used in the local Excise office'), since these basic concepts are already defined in LOLITA, the header can be used as 'interest focus', from which to compute the 'semantic distance' of the various classes.

An other approach (which could be used in conjunction with that above) is analysing the whole text looking for 'semantic clusters', and then use that information to define the interest focus.

This filtering work is needed before any user intervention, because LOLITA produces too many nodes (representing classes, instances, events etc.) from a text of reasonable length for an user to grasp their relative importance.

The 'semantic distance' is a measure that is obtained from the semantic net: the simpler version (developed to support reasoning by analogy, see Long et. al. [16] works on the inclusion hierarchy only, and the events immediately connected to it; works is in progress on a more general version. The distance on the graph, in the sense of the number of arcs crossed, does not matter by itself; what matters is the quality and quantity of the shared information between two nodes. There are at present three fundamental parameters: the locality (the net area on which to compute), the minimum acceptable and maximum needed strength levels of the links, and the goal of the measure (e.g., a book is more similar to a brick than to a compact disc if it has to be thrown at someone, or used to block a door, but vice versa if it is needed to obtain information from).

(ii) Prepare a data dictionary
This is a trivial task, once the relevant classes have been identified.

(iii) Identify associations (including aggregations) between objects
What should be modelled as object or as association during the analysis depends on the information detail level that the system must capture for the functionality and the usage required by the temporal granularity on which the system must be modelled. Given a level of granularity it is possible to give a clear definition of what constitutes essential associations, states, functions, and the way they should be correlated in terms of consistency and cross-checking. D'Souza [7] recommends the use of use-cases [15], intended as stylised definitions for complete system interaction units: such units are the result of a conscious modelling choice. The concept of use-case is somehow equivalent to the components that the OMT uses in the Dynamic Model scenario construction. E.g., for an automatic room booking system, at a certain level the events are 'create a booking', 'change booking', 'cancel booking' etc.; at a more detailed level, there are events

such as 'insert card', 'insert password' etc. It seems that scenario might be obtained by transcribing the normalised form of all the facts related to a certain class.

(iv) Identify attributes of objects and links
Again, once the relevant classes have been selected, this issue is much simplified. There may still be the need to filter out some attributes, and to reorganise others (in LOLITA, attributes are divided into three subclasses: the extensional ones, such as 'red', which are treated as classes; the operational ones, such as 'potential', that are normalised out at the semantic stage, and replaced by a piece of graph; and the relational ones, such as 'rich' or 'pretty', which are represented as values in events which must indicate the terms of reference.

(v) Organize and simplify object classes using inheritance
This is done automatically in LOLITA and does not require any extra functionality.

(vi) Verify that access paths exist for likely queries
The query module is highly sophisticated (it is able, e.g., to deal with queries such as "tell me if it is true that you believe that I do not dislike you") and, as such, is highly unlikely that any access path for queries would be missing: if this were the case, however, this would not be treated as a special problem of this application, but as a signal of something missing in the core inference or analysis modules.

(vii) Iterate and refine the model
This process is made particularly easy in LOLITA by the facts that information is continuously added to the semantic net, that the user has control on what to save, and that the interaction takes place in NL itself (through either the query or the dialogue modules).

(viii) Group classes into modules
This is an application dependent functionality which can be added at little extra cost.

Examples:

Using some NL requirements of an hotel Information System, with the following otputs of LOLITA we may define an object class hotel and two instances.

meanings:
    0 Hotels. :
    inrep: 18254
    rank: universal
    family: inanimate manmade
    type: entity
    emotional value: indifferent

level of language: common level

instances:

1 The hotel that is near a station and that have two restaurants.:
    inrep: 29081
    rank: individual
    family: inanimate manmade
    type: entity
    emotional value: indifferent

2 The hotel that have a disco and that have twenty rooms. It is by a sea.:
    inrep: 29069
    rank: individual
    family: inanimate manmade
    type: entity
    emotional value: indifferent

At a different level, we could check a customer's reservation as follows:

command: q
information: did Roberto make a reservation in Hotel Bolzano?

    * event: 29107 *
subject_:
    yes_answer - 21165 -
action_:
    answer_of - 21166 -
object_:
    event - 29106 - rank: individual - question_
source_:
    lolita - 19874 - rank: named individual
time_:
    present_ - 20989 -
date:
    28 June 1994
cause_:
    event - 29093 - rank: individual

****
Yes, Roberto made a reservation for nine days.

As for the use of some commands of the NLP system, we conclude with the following observations.

To create a definition: a 'booking' is both an event (the act of booking) and an object (the result of that act). If the concept does not exist yet in LOLITA, it can either be input directly using the command 'ew' (enter word), or it can be used as part of a sentence, relying on LOLITA to guess its meaning from the context. If the event 'booking' exists, but it is not properly defined, the definition can be added by using the command 'def' and providing a natural language description such as "By issuing a booking, some clients declare their intention to visit an hotel for some days." Note that by this description, the object 'booking' is considered the instrument of the 'booking' event; if it is rather considered the result, or goal, the appropriate form should be used (e.g. 'to issue a booking,...'). A different approach would be to create a new command (say 'mkO') that requires the explicit filling (in NL) of slots such as: Definition, Association, Creation, Destruction, etc (according to the OM used). This is an easier approach, because of the structure imposed, but it would cause a loss of generality, since the input text should be divided in the corresponding parts, and is more suitable for an interactive system. A system relying heavily on interaction allows a more substantial user involvement; the static approach allows the use of requirement documents as they are, but there is less opportunity to adjust the process to the user's desires as it proceeds. A third approach would be to use a 'template' technique: in this case the system needs specialised inference rules in order to determine what belongs to which slot.

5 Conclusions

In this paper the case has been argued for real NLP systems as a tool for OO model extraction from requirements documents. Various previous related approaches have been discussed, and the fundamental common drawback pointed out: these may manifest themselves as need for a pseudo-language, or heavy domain dependency, or excessive reliance on user interaction, but can all the reconducted to the lack of proper NL facilities (at the analysis, reasoning and generation stages). The Natural Language Engineering paradigm has then been briefly presented, and a claim made that this is the way forward for real NLP. The LOLITA system has been presented, in relation to this paradigm, and shown to have the range of functionality needed for the OO Model construction. This claim has been further substantiated by the close pairing of LOLITA structures and operations with the OMT in its OM phase. It is clear that this is a fruitful direction of research to explore further: the next stage will be to implement the missing functionality and experiment with real life requirement documents.

References

[1] R.J. Abbot. Program design by informal english descriptions. *IEEE Transactions on Software Engineering*, 26(11):882–894, 1983.

[2] S.C. Bailin. An object oriented requirements specification method. *Communications of the ACM*, 32(5):608–623, 1989.

[3] B. Belkhouche and J. Kozma. Semantic case analysis of informal requirements. In S. Brinkkemper and F. Harmsen, editors, *4th Workshop on the*

Next Generation of CASE Tools (NGCT'93), Memoranda Informatica 93-32, pages 163–182, The Netherlands, May 1993. Universiteit of Twente.

[4] G. Booch. Object-oriented development. *IEEE Transactions on Software Engineering*, 12(2):211–221, 1986.

[5] C. Cauvet, C. Proix, and C. Rolland. ALECSI: An expert system for requirements engineering. In Andersen, Bubenko, and Solvberg, editors, *3rd International Conference on Advanced Information Systems Engineering (CAiSE'91)*, LNCS 498, pages 31–49, Trondheim, Norway, May 1991. Springer Verlag.

[6] H. Dalianis. A method for validating a conceptual model by natural language discourse generation. In P. Loucopoulos, editor, *4th International Conference on Advanced Information Systems Engineering (CAiSE'92)*, LNCS 593, pages 425–444, Manchester, UK, May (12-15) 1992. Springer Verlag.

[7] D. D'souza. Working with OMT. *Journal of Object Oriented Programming*, pages 63–68, october 1993.

[8] L. Dunn and M. Orlowska. A natural language interpreter for construction of conceptual schemas. In B. Steinholtz, A. Solvberg, and L. Bergman, editors, *2nd Nordic Conference on Advanced Information Systems Engineering (CAiSE'90)*, LNCS 436, pages –, Stockholm, Sweden, May (8-20) 1990. Springer Verlag.

[9] B. Elisa and L.D. Martino. *Sistemi di basi di dati orientati agli oggetti. Concetti e architetture.* Addison-Wesley Masson, Milano, 1992.

[10] C. Fillmore. The case for case. In E. Bach and R. Harms, editors, *Universal Linguistics*, pages 1–90. Rinehart and Winston, Chicago, 1968.

[11] R. Garigliano, R.G. Morgan, and LOLITA Group. *The LOLITA Project: the First Eight Years.* under negotiations with Lawrence Earlbaun, UK, 1994.

[12] van den G. Goor, S. Brinkkemper, and S. Hong. CASE tools for the support of object-oriented analysis and design methods. In A. Sutcliffe and N. Maiden, editors, *3rd Workshop on the Next Generation of CASE Tools (NGCT'92)*, Manchester, May 1992.

[13] I. Grahm. *Object Oriented Methods.* Addison-Wesley, Wokingham, UK, 1991.

[14] K. Huff and J. Mylopoulos. Developing intelligent information systems: A workshop summary. *Int. Journal of Intelligent and Cooperative Information Systems*, 1(2):233–237, 1992.

[15] I. Jacobson, M. Christerson, P. Jonsson, and G. Oevergaard. *Object-Oriented Software Engineering. A case driven Approach.* Addison-Wesley, Reading, MA, 1992.

[16] D. Long and R. Garigliano. *Reasoning by Analogy and Causality: Model and Applications.* Ellis Horwood, UK, 1994.

[17] LRE. Background document of the Linguistic Research and Engineering (LRE) European Programme. Technical report, EEC, 1992.

[18] M. Messaudi. *An Approach to Viewpoints Analysis through Source Control.* Phd thesis in Computer Science, University of Durham, UK, 1994.

[19] L. Mich, M. Fedrizzi, and R. Garigliano. Negotiation and conflict resolution in production engineering. accepted to IPMU'94 - Paris, 1994.

[20] H.B. Rego and J.R. Lima. A tool for automating facts analysis. In K. Spurr and P. Layzell, editors, *CASE on Trial*, pages 57–80, England, 1990. John Wiley.

[21] H.B. Reubenstein and R.C. Waters. The requirements apprentice: Automated assistance for requirements acquisition. *IEEE Transactions on Software Engineering*, 17(3):226–240, 1991.

[22] C. Rolland and C. Proix. A natural language approch for requirements engineering. In P. Loucopoulos, editor, *4th International Conference on Advanced Information Systems Engineering (CAiSE'92)*, LNCS 593, pages 257–277, Manchester, UK, May (12-15) 1992. Springer Verlag.

[23] J. Rumbaugh, M. Blaha, W. Premerlani, F. Eddy, and W. Lorensen. *Object-Oriented Modeling and Design.* Prentice-Hall, Englewood Cliffs, NJ, 1991.

[24] M. Saeki, H. Horai, and H. Enomoto. Software development process from natural language specification. In *International Conference on Software Engineering (ICSI'89)*, pages 64–73, Pittsburgh, 1989. ACM.

[25] M. Smith, R. Garigliano, and R.G. Morgan. Natural language generation in LOLITA: an engineering approach. accepted to 2nd International Workshop on Natural Language Generation - Maine, USA, 1994.

[26] Sowa. *Conceptual Structures.* Addison Wesley, 1983.

[27] R.J. Wieringa. Object-oriented analysis, structured analysis and Jackson system development. In F.J.M. Van Assche, B. Moulin, and C. Rolland, editors, *IFIP TC2/WG8.1 Working Conference on the Object-Oriented Approach in Information Systems*, pages 28–31, Quebec City, Canada, Oct (1-18) 1991. Elsevier Science (North-Holland).

[28] T. Winograd and F. Flores. *Understanding computers and cognition: a new fundation for design.* Ablex, Norwood, NJ, 1986. Trad. it. Calcolatori e conoscenza.

Springer-Verlag
and the Environment

We at Springer-Verlag firmly believe that an international science publisher has a special obligation to the environment, and our corporate policies consistently reflect this conviction.

We also expect our business partners – paper mills, printers, packaging manufacturers, etc. – to commit themselves to using environmentally friendly materials and production processes.

The paper in this book is made from low- or no-chlorine pulp and is acid free, in conformance with international standards for paper permanency.

Lecture Notes in Computer Science

For information about Vols. 1–786
please contact your bookseller or Springer-Verlag

Vol. 824: E. M. Schmidt, S. Skyum (Eds.), Algorithm Theory – SWAT '94. Proceedings. IX, 383 pages. 1994.

Vol. 825: J. L. Mundy, A. Zisserman, D. Forsyth (Eds.), Applications of Invariance in Computer Vision. Proceedings, 1993. IX, 510 pages. 1994.

Vol. 826: D. S. Bowers (Ed.), Directions in Databases. Proceedings, 1994. X, 234 pages. 1994.

Vol. 827: D. M. Gabbay, H. J. Ohlbach (Eds.), Temporal Logic. Proceedings, 1994. XI, 546 pages. 1994. (Subseries LNAI).

Vol. 828: L. C. Paulson, Isabelle. XVII, 321 pages. 1994.

Vol. 829: A. Chmora, S. B. Wicker (Eds.), Error Control, Cryptology, and Speech Compression. Proceedings, 1993. VIII, 121 pages. 1994.

Vol. 830: C. Castelfranchi, E. Werner (Eds.), Artificial Social Systems. Proceedings, 1992. XVIII, 337 pages. 1994. (Subseries LNAI).

Vol. 831: V. Bouchitté, M. Morvan (Eds.), Orders, Algorithms, and Applications. Proceedings, 1994. IX, 204 pages. 1994.

Vol. 832: E. Börger, Y. Gurevich, K. Meinke (Eds.), Computer Science Logic. Proceedings, 1993. VIII, 336 pages. 1994.

Vol. 833: D. Driankov, P. W. Eklund, A. Ralescu (Eds.), Fuzzy Logic and Fuzzy Control. Proceedings, 1991. XII, 157 pages. 1994. (Subseries LNAI).

Vol. 834: D.-Z. Du, X.-S. Zhang (Eds.), Algorithms and Computation. Proceedings, 1994. XIII, 687 pages. 1994.

Vol. 835: W. M. Tepfenhart, J. P. Dick, J. F. Sowa (Eds.), Conceptual Structures: Current Practices. Proceedings, 1994. VIII, 331 pages. 1994. (Subseries LNAI).

Vol. 836: B. Jonsson, J. Parrow (Eds.), CONCUR '94: Concurrency Theory. Proceedings, 1994. IX, 529 pages. 1994.

Vol. 837: S. Wess, K.-D. Althoff, M. M. Richter (Eds.), Topics in Case-Based Reasoning. Proceedings, 1993. IX, 471 pages. 1994. (Subseries LNAI).

Vol. 838: C. MacNish, D. Pearce, L. Moniz Pereira (Eds.), Logics in Artificial Intelligence. Proceedings, 1994. IX, 413 pages. 1994. (Subseries LNAI).

Vol. 839: Y. G. Desmedt (Ed.), Advances in Cryptology - CRYPTO '94. Proceedings, 1994. XII, 439 pages. 1994.

Vol. 840: G. Reinelt, The Traveling Salesman. VIII, 223 pages. 1994.

Vol. 841: I. Prívara, B. Rovan, P. Ružička (Eds.), Mathematical Foundations of Computer Science 1994. Proceedings, 1994. X, 628 pages. 1994.

Vol. 842: T. Kloks, Treewidth. IX, 209 pages. 1994.

Vol. 843: A. Szepietowski, Turing Machines with Sublogarithmic Space. VIII, 115 pages. 1994.

Vol. 844: M. Hermenegildo, J. Penjam (Eds.), Programming Language Implementation and Logic Programming. Proceedings, 1994. XII, 469 pages. 1994.

Vol. 845: J.-P. Jouannaud (Ed.), Constraints in Computational Logics. Proceedings, 1994. VIII, 367 pages. 1994.

Vol. 846: D. Shepherd, G. Blair, G. Coulson, N. Davies, F. Garcia (Eds.), Network and Operating System Support for Digital Audio and Video. Proceedings, 1993. VIII, 269 pages. 1994.

Vol. 847: A. L. Ralescu (Ed.) Fuzzy Logic in Artificial Intelligence. Proceedings, 1993. VII, 128 pages. 1994. (Subseries LNAI).

Vol. 848: A. R. Krommer, C. W. Ueberhuber, Numerical Integration on Advanced Computer Systems. XIII, 341 pages. 1994.

Vol. 849: R. W. Hartenstein, M. Z. Servít (Eds.), Field-Programmable Logic. Proceedings, 1994. XI, 434 pages. 1994.

Vol. 850: G. Levi, M. Rodríguez-Artalejo (Eds.), Algebraic and Logic Programming. Proceedings, 1994. VIII, 304 pages. 1994.

Vol. 851: H.-J. Kugler, A. Mullery, N. Niebert (Eds.), Towards a Pan-European Telecommunication Service Infrastructure. Proceedings, 1994. XIII, 582 pages. 1994.

Vol. 852: K. Echtle, D. Hammer, D. Powell (Eds.), Dependable Computing – EDCC-1. Proceedings, 1994. XVII, 618 pages. 1994.

Vol. 853: K. Bolding, L. Snyder (Eds.), Parallel Computer Routing and Communication. Proceedings, 1994. IX, 317 pages. 1994.

Vol. 854: B. Buchberger, J. Volkert (Eds.), Parallel Processing: CONPAR 94 – VAPP VI. Proceedings, 1994. XVI, 893 pages. 1994.

Vol. 855: J. van Leeuwen (Ed.), Algorithms – ESA '94. Proceedings, 1994. X, 510 pages.1994.

Vol. 856: D. Karagiannis (Ed.), Database and Expert Systems Applications. Proceedings, 1994. XVII, 807 pages. 1994.

Vol. 857: G. Tel, P. Vitányi (Eds.), Distributed Algorithms. Proceedings, 1994. X, 370 pages. 1994.

Vol. 858: E. Bertino, S. Urban (Eds.), Object-Oriented Methodologies and Systems. Proceedings, 1994. X, 386 pages. 1994.

Vol. 859: T. F. Melham, J. Camilleri (Eds.), Higher Order Logic Theorem Proving and Its Applications. Proceedings, 1994. IX, 470 pages. 1994.

Vol. 860: W. L. Zagler, G. Busby, R. R. Wagner (Eds.), Computers for Handicapped Persons. Proceedings, 1994. XX, 625 pages. 1994.

Vol: 861: B. Nebel, L. Dreschler-Fischer (Eds.), KI-94: Advances in Artificial Intelligence. Proceedings, 1994. IX, 401 pages. 1994. (Subseries LNAI).

Vol. 862: R. C. Carrasco, J. Oncina (Eds.), Grammatical Inference and Applications. Proceedings, 1994. VIII, 290 pages. 1994. (Subseries LNAI).

Vol. 863: H. Langmaack, W.-P. de Roever, J. Vytopil (Eds.), Formal Techniques in Real-Time and Fault-Tolerant Systems. Proceedings, 1994. XIV, 787 pages. 1994.

Vol. 864: B. Le Charlier (Ed.), Static Analysis. Proceedings, 1994. XII, 465 pages. 1994.

Vol. 865: T. C. Fogarty (Ed.), Evolutionary Computing. Proceedings, 1994. XII, 332 pages. 1994.

Vol 867: L. Steels, G. Schreiber, W. Van de Velde (Eds.), A Future for Knowledge Acquisition. Proceedings, 1994. XII, 414 pages. 1994. (Subseries LNAI).